The social life of things

The social life of things

Commodities in cultural perspective

Edited by
ARJUN APPADURAI
University of Pennsylvania

CAMBRIDGE
UNIVERSITY PRESS

PUBLISHED BY THE PRESS SYNDICATE OF THE UNIVERSITY OF CAMBRIDGE
The Pitt Building, Trumpington Street, Cambridge, United Kingdom

CAMBRIDGE UNIVERSITY PRESS
The Edinburgh Building, Cambridge CB2 2RU, UK
40 West 20th Street, New York, NY 10011–4211, USA
477 Williamstown Road, Port Melbourne, VIC 3207, Australia
Ruiz de Alarcón 13, 28014 Madrid, Spain
Dock House, The Waterfront, Cape Town 8001, South Africa

http://www.cambridge.org

First published 1986
First paperback edition 1988
Tenth printing 2003

Printed in the United Kingdom at the University Press, Cambridge

Library of Congress Cataloguing in Publication data
Main entry under title:
The social life of things.
Includes index.
1. Commerce – Social aspects – Addresses, essays,
lectures.   2. Economic anthropology – Addresses, essays,
lectures.   3. Commerce – History – Addresses, essays,
lectures.   I. Appadurai, Arjun.   1949–
GN450.S63   1986   360'.3   86–19529

British Library Cataloguing in Publication data
The social life of things: commodities in
cultural perspective.
1. Economic anthropology   2. Raw materials
I. Appadurai, Arjun
306'.3   GN450

ISBN 0 521 32351 7 hardback
ISBN 0 521 35726 8 paperback

Contents

Contributors

ARJUN APPADURAI is Associate Professor of Anthropology and South Asian Studies at the University of Pennsylvania. He is the author of *Worship and Conflict Under Colonial Rule* (1981).

C. A. BAYLY is Fellow of St. Catharine's College, University of Cambridge, and Smuts Reader in Commonwealth Studies. He has published *The Local Roots of Indian Politics: Allahabad, 1880–1920* (1975) and *Rulers, Townsmen and Bazaars: North Indian Society in the Age of British Expansion, 1770–1870* (1983).

LEE V. CASSANELLI teaches in the Department of History at the University of Pennsylvania. He is the author of *The Shaping of Somali Society: Reconstructing the History of a Pastoral People* (1982).

WILLIAM H. DAVENPORT teaches anthropology at the University of Pennsylvania, where he is also Curator for Oceania at the University Museum. He has done field research in Jamaica and the Solomon Islands and historical research on pre-European Hawaii, and has published extensively on all these areas.

PATRICK GEARY is Associate Professor of History at the University of Florida. He is the author of *Furta Sacra: Thefts of Relics in the Central Middle Ages* (1978) and *Aristocracy in Provence: The Rhone Basin at the Dawn of the Carolingian Age* (1985).

ALFRED GELL teaches social anthropology at the London School of Economics and Political Science. He is the author of *Metamorphosis of the Cassowaries: Umeda Society, Language and Ritual* (1975).

IGOR KOPYTOFF of the Department of Anthropology at the University of Pennsylvania is coeditor (with Suzanne Miers) of *Slavery in Africa: Historical and Anthropological Perspectives* (1977) and author of *Varieties of Witchcraft: The Social Economy of Secret Power* (forthcoming).

WILLIAM M. REDDY is Assistant Professor of History at Duke University and is the author of *The Rise of Market Culture: The Textile Trade and French Society, 1750–1900* (1984).

COLIN RENFREW is Disney Professor of Archaeology, University of Cambridge, and Fellow of St. John's College. He is the author of *Problems in European Prehistory* (1979) and *Approaches to Social Archaeology* (1984).

BRIAN SPOONER teaches in the Department of Anthropology at the University of Pennsylvania. He is the author of *Ecology in Development: A Rationale for Three-Dimensional Policy* (1984).

Foreword

The genealogy of any multidisciplinary volume is likely to be complex. The immediate antecedents of this one are clear: the vision and energy of the editor, Arjun Appadurai, have sustained the enterprise from beginning to end. But it is also a cooperative effort, and the symposium and workshop that produced the individual contributions are themselves the products of an ongoing dialogue that anthropologists and historians at the University of Pennsylvania began a decade ago under the aegis of the Ethnohistory Program. The original stimulus for the program came from a shared sense that the two disciplines had much to learn from each other. Just how much we had to learn became evident only as the dialogue progressed.

Exchange of a sort had already started. Social historians in recent years have been turning to anthropology for theoretical perspectives, as they expanded their interests to include peasants, ethnic minorities – the people without history – the family, and other topics thought to be the traditional domain of anthropologists. For those who wished to do history from the inside out as well as from the bottom up, anthropology offered the necessary dimension of culture, the systems of meaning that people invest in their social forms. Anthropologists' interest in history, although not entirely new, has become more intense and of a different kind. The past, once viewed as a more or less undifferentiated prelude to the ethnographic present, has increasingly come to represent a rich storehouse of information on sociocultural organization: empirical grist for anthropology's conceptual mill. If anthropologists were to tap this storehouse, they would have to master the sources and techniques of historical research.

Exchange at this rudimentary level is a form of mutual raiding, with history seen as merely a source of facts and anthropology a source of theories. The results can prove disappointing. Unlike most types of plunder, historical facts and anthropological models lose much of their value when removed from their original contexts. The Ethnohistory Program was founded with the idea that it would be profitable for both parties to try to understand the other's discipline, to get inside it and see how it works. Initially the attempt produced culture shock. The two disciplines do not always speak the same language; more unsettling, they sometimes use the same words to mean vastly different things. As in other forms of culture shock, the discovery of difference is the first step to enlightenment. Seen through anthropologists' eyes, myth, ritual, and symbol are no longer historical trivia, decorative elements that can be tacked onto the serious subjects of analysis when they do not obscure these altogether; they become vital clues, interwoven with and revealing the very issues considered the real stuff of history. Historians' perceptions of change are equally illuminating; change ceases to be a shift from one steady state to another and becomes instead a continuous process to which all systems are subject. And once change over time is accepted as a given, diachronic analysis based on chronology and causation has to be incorporated into the model-building scheme.

The next, more fruitful stage comes when the interests of anthropologists and historians converge to produce a set of common, as opposed to complementary, goals: the development of dynamic models that combine system with process in long-term patterns of sociocultural change. Along with common goals come common problems. Two in particular have loomed large in Ethnohistory Workshop discussions. The first relates to sources. How do you reconstruct past systems of meaning (let alone changes in them) when you can neither participate in nor directly observe the lives of the people? Partial answers lie in drawing on new types of evidence, such as visual imagery and oral traditions; in using a wider range of documentary sources; and in digging more deeply into those sources for information the authors did not consciously impart. Yet history is ultimately limited by what past "informants" chose to record and what accident has preserved.

The second problem relates to method. How exactly do you combine system with process? The one fits parts together in a synchronic relationship explained by function; the other links them sequentially through cause and effect. Clearly, the relationship has to be seen in motion, continually changing while remaining more or less integrated. This is more easily said than done. At some point or points the movement must be frozen to allow analysis of system qua system. Yet a succession of tableaux does not reveal process and can mask the often incremental and gradual nature of change. Although the two modes of analysis are not necessarily incompatible, they may resist synthesis on an equal footing. Some sense of motion may have to be sacrificed to the analysis of structure, or the order of priorities may need to be reversed.

The choice marks the boundary between the two disciplines. Along with other differences in emphasis, the choice comes, I suspect, from the basic difference in professional training, defined by either ethnographic fieldwork or documentary research. Historians and anthropologists may converge on the same ground, but they come from different places. They may understand and even engage in the other's mode of research, as well as use the data it generates. But they are most likely to use them as complements to their own, seeking either clues to the past from the present or clues to the present from the past.

The differences do not signify a failure of communication. The goal is to converse across disciplinary boundaries, not eliminate them; for there is little point in a dialogue if all speak with the same voice. Creative tension comes from the combination of two distinct perspectives, and from that creative tension new insights can continue to emerge.

This volume exemplifies the value to both anthropologists and historians of pooling their separate resources to focus on a single subject. Identities and approaches remain distinct despite varying degrees of overlap. Yet each contribution has gained from the dialogue, and the subject has been illuminated more brightly by the combined light. As the volume's editor so cogently argues in another context, exchange is the source of value.

NANCY FARRISS

Preface

Although anthropologists and historians increasingly talk about one another, they rarely talk to one another. This volume is the product of a year-long dialogue between historians and anthropologists on the topic of commodities. Three of the papers (by Cassanelli, Geary, and Spooner) were delivered to the Ethnohistory Workshop at the University of Pennsylvania during 1983–4. The others (with the exception of my own introductory essay) were delivered at a symposium on the relationship between commodities and culture hosted by the Ethnohistory Program, in Philadelphia, on May 23–5, 1984.

Lee Cassanelli, my colleague in the Department of History at the University of Pennsylvania, first proposed the theme of commodities and culture for the 1983–4 Ethnohistory Workshop. To him and to Nancy Farriss (also of the Department of History, and the guiding spirit of the workshop from its inception in 1975), I owe many years of stimulating interdisciplinary dialogue. Lee Cassanelli's proposal coincided fortuitously with a conversation I had with Igor Kopytoff and William Davenport (my colleagues in the Anthropology Department at Penn), in the course of which we agreed that the time was ripe for a revitalized anthropology of things.

The May 1984 symposium, which led directly to the planning of this volume, was made possible by grants to the Ethnohistory Program from the National Endowment for the Humanities and from the School of Arts and Sciences at the University of Pennsylvania. The success of that symposium owes much to the intellectual and logistical support of students and colleagues who attended it. In particular, I must thank Greta Borie, Peter Just, and Christine Hoepfner for all manner of assistance before and during the symposium.

I have also been the beneficiary of much generosity in the course of assembling this volume. Susan Allen-Mills, of Cambridge University Press, was a valuable source of intellectual and procedural guidance throughout. I owe a special debt to the staff at the Center for Advanced Study in the Behavioral Sciences, whose secretarial and administrative resources helped materially in the manuscript's speedy completion. In particular, it is a pleasure to thank Kay Holm, Virginia Heaton, and Muriel Bell.

Stanford, California   ARJUN APPADURAI

PART I

Toward an anthropology of things

CHAPTER 1

Introduction: commodities and the politics of value

ARJUN APPADURAI

This essay has two aims. The first is to preview and set the context for the essays that follow it in this volume. The second is to propose a new perspective on the circulation of commodities in social life. The gist of this perspective can be put in the following way. Economic exchange creates value. Value is embodied in commodities that are exchanged. Focusing on the things that are exchanged, rather than simply on the forms or functions of exchange, makes it possible to argue that what creates the link between exchange and value is *politics*, construed broadly. This argument, which is elaborated in the text of this essay, justifies the conceit that commodities, like persons, have social lives.[1]

Commodities can provisionally be defined as objects of economic value. As to what we ought to mean by economic value, the most useful (though not quite standard) guide is Georg Simmel. In the first chapter of *The Philosophy of Money* (1907; English translation, 1978), Simmel provides a systematic account of how economic value is best defined. Value, for Simmel, is never an inherent property of objects, but is a judgment made about them by subjects. Yet the key to the comprehension of value, according to Simmel, lies in a region where "that subjectivity is only provisional and actually not very essential" (Simmel 1978:73).

In exploring this difficult realm, which is neither wholly subjective nor quite objective, in which value emerges and functions, Simmel suggests that objects are not difficult to acquire because they are valuable, "but we call those objects valuable that resist our desire to possess them" (p. 67). What Simmel calls economic objects, in particular, exist in the space between pure desire and immediate enjoyment, with some distance between them and the person who desires them, which is a distance that can be overcome. This distance is overcome in and through economic exchange, in which the value of objects is determined reciprocally. That is, one's desire for an object is fulfilled by the sacrifice of some other object, which is the focus of the desire of another. Such exchange of sacrifices is what economic life is all

3

about and the economy as a particular social form "consists not only in exchanging *values* but in the *exchange* of values" (p. 80). Economic value, for Simmel, is generated by this sort of exchange of sacrifices.

Several arguments follow this analysis of economic value in Simmel's discussion. The first is that economic value is not just value in general, but a definite sum of value, which results from the commensuration of two intensities of demand. The form this commensuration takes is the exchange of sacrifice and gain. Thus, the economic object does not have an absolute value as a result of the demand for it, but the demand, as the basis of a real or imagined exchange, endows the object with value. It is exchange that sets the parameters of utility and scarcity, rather than the other way round, and exchange that is the source of value: "The difficulty of acquisition, the sacrifice offered in exchange, is the unique constitutive element of value, of which scarcity is only the external manifestation, its objectification in the form of quantity" (p. 100). In a word, exchange is not a by-product of the mutual valuation of objects, but its source.

These terse and brilliant observations set the stage for Simmel's analysis of what he regarded as the most complex instrument for the conduct of economic exchange – money – and its place in modern life. But Simmel's observations can be taken in quite another direction. This alternative direction, which is exemplified by the remainder of this essay, entails exploring the conditions under which economic objects circulate in different *regimes of value* in space and time. Many of the essays in this volume examine specific things (or groups of things) as they circulate in specific cultural and historical milieus. What these essays permit is a series of glimpses of the ways in which desire and demand, reciprocal sacrifice and power interact to create economic value in specific social situations.

Contemporary Western common sense, building on various historical traditions in philosophy, law, and natural science, has a strong tendency to oppose "words" and "things." Though this was not always the case even in the West, as Marcel Mauss noted in his famous work *The Gift*, the powerful contemporary tendency is to regard the world of things as inert and mute, set in motion and animated, indeed knowable, only by persons and their words (see also Dumont 1980:229–30). Yet, in many historical societies, things have not been so divorced from the capacity of persons to act and the power of words to communicate (see Chapter 2). That such a view of things had not disappeared even under the conditions of occidental industrial capitalism is one of the intuitions that underlay Marx's famous discussion, in *Capital*, of the "fetishism of commodities."

Even if our own approach to things is conditioned necessarily by the view that things have no meanings apart from those that human transactions, attributions, and motivations endow them with, the anthropological problem is that this formal truth does not illuminate the concrete, historical circulation of things. For that we have to follow the things themselves, for their meanings are inscribed in their forms, their uses, their trajectories. It is only through the analysis of these trajectories that we can interpret the human transactions and calculations that enliven things. Thus, even though from a *theoretical* point of view human actors encode things with significance, from a *methodological* point of view it is the things-in-motion that illuminate their human and social context. No social analysis of things (whether the analyst is an economist, an art historian, or an anthropologist) can avoid a minimum level of what might be called methodological fetishism. This methodological fetishism, returning our attention to the things themselves, is in part a corrective to the tendency to excessively sociologize transactions in things, a tendency we owe to Mauss, as Firth has recently noted (1983:89).[2]

Commodities, and things in general, are of independent interest to several kinds of anthropology. They constitute the first principles and the last resort of archeologists. They are the stuff of "material culture," which unites archeologists with several kinds of cultural anthropologists. As valuables, they are at the heart of economic anthropology and, not least, as the medium of gifting, they are at the heart of exchange theory and social anthropology generally. The commodity perspective on things represents a valuable point of entry to the revived, semiotically oriented interest in material culture, recently remarked and exemplified in a special section of *RAIN* (Miller 1983). But commodities are not of fundamental interest only to anthropologists. They also constitute a topic of lively interest to social and economic historians, to art historians, and, lest we forget, to economists, though each discipline might constitute the problem differently. Commodities thus represent a subject on which anthropology may have something to offer to its neighboring disciplines, as well as one about which it has a good deal to learn from them.

The essays in this volume cover much historical, ethnographic, and conceptual ground, but they do not by any means exhaust the relationship of culture to commodities. The contributors are five social anthropologists, an archeologist, and four social historians. No economists or art historians are represented here, though their views are by no means ignored. Several major world areas are not represented (notably China and Latin America), but the spatial coverage is nevertheless fairly wide. Though an interesting range of goods is discussed in these essays, the list of commodities *not* discussed would be quite long, and there is a tilt toward specialized or luxury goods rather than "primary" or "bulk" commodities. Finally, most of the contributors stick to *goods* rather than to *services*, though the latter are obviously important objects of commoditization as well. Though each of these omissions is serious, I shall suggest in the course of this essay that some of them are less important than they might seem.

The remaining five sections of this essay are devoted to the following tasks. The first, on the spirit of commodity, is a critical exercise in definition, whose argument is that commodities, properly understood, are not the monopoly of modern, industrial economies. The next, on paths and diversions, discusses the strategies (both individual and institutional) that make the creation of value a politically mediated process. The subsequent section, on desire and demand, links short- and long-term patterns in commodity circulation to show that consumption is subject to social control and political redefinition. The last substantive section, on the relationship between knowledge and commodities, is concerned with demonstrating that the politics of value is in many contexts a politics of knowledge. The concluding section brings the argument back to politics as the mediating level between exchange and value.

The spirit of the commodity

Few will deny that a commodity is a thoroughly socialized thing. The definitional question is: in what does its sociality consist? The purist answer, routinely attributed to Marx, is that a commodity is a product intended principally for exchange, and that such products emerge, by definition, in the institutional, psychological, and economic conditions of capitalism. Less purist definitions regard commodities as goods intended for exchange, regardless of the form of the exchange. The purist definition forecloses the question prematurely. The looser definitions threaten to equate commodity with gift and many other kinds of thing. In this section, through a critique of the Marxian understanding of the commodity, I shall suggest that commodities are things with a particular type of social potential, that they are distinguishable from "products," "objects," "goods," "artifacts," and other sorts of things – but only in certain respects and from a certain point of view. If my argument holds water, it will follow that it is definitionally useful to regard commodities as existing in a very wide variety of societies (though with a special intensity and salience in modern, capitalist societies), and that there is an unexpected convergence between Marx and Simmel on the topic of commodities.

The most elaborate and thought-provoking discussion of the idea of the commodity appears in Volume I, Part I, of Marx's *Capital*, though the idea was widespread in nineteenth-century discussions of political economy. Marx's own reanalysis of the concept of commodity was a central part of his critique of bourgeois political economy and a fulcrum for the transition from his own earlier thought (see especially Marx 1973) on capitalism to the full-fledged analysis of *Capital*. Today, the conceptual centrality of the idea of commodity has given way to the neoclassical, marginalist conception of "goods," and the word "commodity" is used in neoclassical economics only to refer to a special subclass of primary goods and no longer plays a central analytic role. This is, of course, not the case with Marxian approaches in economics and sociology, or with neo-Ricardian approaches (such as those of Piero Sraffa), where the analysis of the "commodity" still plays a central theoretical role (Sraffa 1961; Seddon 1978).

But in most modern analyses of economy (outside anthropology), the meaning of the term commodity has narrowed to reflect only one part of the heritage of Marx and the early political economists. That is, in most contemporary uses, commodities are special kinds of manufactured goods (or services), which are associated only with capitalist modes of production and are thus to be found only where capitalism has penetrated. Thus even in current debates about proto-industrialization (see, for example, Perlin 1982), the issue is not whether commodities are associated with capitalism, but whether certain organizational and technical forms associated with capitalism are solely of European origin. Commodities are generally seen as typical material representations of the capitalist mode of production, even if they are classified as petty and their capitalist context as incipient.

Yet it is clear that this is to draw on only one strand in Marx's own understanding of the nature of the commodity. The treatment of the commodity in the first hundred or so pages of *Capital* is arguably one of the most difficult, contradictory, and ambiguous parts of Marx's corpus. It begins with an extremely broad definition of commodity ("A commodity is, in the first place, an object outside us, a thing that by its properties satisfies human wants of some sort or another"). It then moves dialectically through a series of more parsimonious definitions, which permit the gradual elaboration of the basic Marxian approach to use value and exchange value, the problem of equivalence, the circulation and exchange of products, and the significance of money. It is the elaboration of this understanding of the relationship between the commodity form and the money form that allows Marx to make his famous distinction between two forms of circulation of commodities (Commodities-Money-Commodities and Money-Commodities-Money), the latter representing the general formula for capital. In the course of this analytic movement, commodities become intricately tied to *money*, an impersonal market, and exchange value. Even in the simple form of circulation (tied to use value), commodities are related through the commensuration capabilities of money. Today, in general, the link of commodities to postindustrial social, financial, and exchange forms is taken for granted, even by those who in other regards do not take Marx seriously.

Yet in Marx's own writings, there is the basis for a much broader, more cross-culturally and historically useful approach to commodities, whose spirit is attenuated as soon as he becomes embroiled in the details of his analysis of nineteenth-century industrial capitalism. By this earlier formulation, in order to produce not mere products but commodities, a man must produce use values for others, social use values (Marx 1971:48). This idea was glossed by Engels in a parenthesis he inserted into Marx's text in the following interesting way: "To become a commodity a product must be transferred to another, whom it will serve as a use-value, by means of an exchange" (Marx 1971:48). Though Engels was content with this elucidation, Marx proceeds to make a very complex (and ambiguous) series of distinctions between products and commodities, but for anthropological purposes, the key passage deserves quotation in full:

Every product of labour is, in all states of society, a use-value; but it is only at a definite historical epoch in a society's development that such a product becomes a commodity, viz. at the epoch when the labour spent on the production of a useful article becomes expressed as one of the objective qualities of that article, i.e., as its value. It therefore follows that the elementary value-form is also the primitive form under which a product of labour appears historically as a commodity, and that the gradual transformation of such products into commodities, proceeds *pari passu* with the development of the value-form. (Marx 1971:67).

The difficulty of distinguishing the logical aspect of this argument from its historical aspect has been noted by Anne Chapman (1980), whose argument I will return to shortly. In the above passage from *Capital*, the shift from product to commodity is discussed historically. But the resolution is still highly schematic, and it is difficult to specify or test it in any clear way.

The point is that Marx was still imprisoned in two aspects of the mid-nineteenth-century episteme: one could see the economy only in reference to the problematics of production (Baudrillard 1975); the other regarded the movement to commodity production as evolutionary, unidirectional, and historical. As a result commodities either exist or do not exist, and they are *products* of a particular sort. Each of these assumptions requires modification.

Despite these epistemic limitations, in his famous discussion of the fetishism of commodities, Marx does note, as he does elsewhere in *Capital*, that the commodity does not emerge whole-cloth from the product under bourgeois production, but makes its appearance "at an early date in history, though not in the same predominating and characteristic manner as nowadays." (Marx 1971:86). Though it is outside the scope of this essay to explore the difficulties of Marx's own thought on precapitalist, nonstate, nonmonetary economies, we might note that Marx left the door open for the existence of commodities, at least in a primitive form, in many sorts of society.

The definitional strategy I propose is a return to a version of Engels's emendation of Marx's broad definition involving the production of use value *for others*, which converges with Simmel's emphasis on exchange as the source of economic value. Let us start with the idea that a commodity is *any thing intended for exchange*. This gets us away from the exclusive preoccupation with the "product," "production," and the original or dominant intention of the "producer" and permits us to focus on the dynamics of exchange. For comparative purposes, then, the question becomes *not* "What is a commodity?" but rather "What sort of an exchange is commodity exchange?" Here, and as part of the effort to define commodities better, we need to deal with two kinds of exchange that are conventionally contrasted with commodity exchange. The first is barter (sometimes referred to as direct exchange), and the other is the exchange of gifts. Let us start with barter.

Barter as a form of exchange has recently been analyzed by Chapman (1980) in an essay that, among other things, takes issue with Marx's own analysis of the relationship between direct exchange and commodity exchange. Combining aspects of several current definitions of barter (including Chapman's), I would suggest that barter is the exchange of objects for one another *without* reference to money and *with* maximum feasible reduction of social, cultural, political, or personal transaction costs. The former criterion distinguishes barter from commodity exchange in the strict Marxist sense, and the latter from gift exchange by virtually any definition.

Chapman is right that, insofar as Marx's theory of value is taken seriously, his treatment of barter poses insoluble theoretical and conceptual problems (Chapman 1980:68–70), for Marx postulated that barter took the form of direct exchange of the product (x use value $A = y$ use value B), as well as direct exchange of the commodity (x commodity $A = y$ commodity B). But this Marxist view of barter, whatever problems it may pose for a Marxist theory of the origin of exchange value, has the virtue of fitting well with Chapman's most persuasive claim – that barter, as either a dominant or a subordinate form of exchange, exists in an extremely wide range of societies. Chapman criticizes Marx for inserting the commodity into barter and wishes to keep them quite separate, on the grounds that commodities assume the use of money objects (and thus congealed labor value), and not just money as a unit of account or measure of equivalence. Commodity exchange, for Chapman, occurs only when a money object intervenes in exchange. Since barter, in her model, excludes such intervention, commodity exchange and barter are formally completely distinct, though they may coexist in some societies (Chapman 1980:67–68).

In her critique of Marx, it seems to me, Chapman takes an unduly constricted view of the role of money in the circulation of commodities. Though Marx ran into difficulties in his own analysis of the relationship between barter and commodity exchange, he was right to see, as did Polanyi, that there was a *commonality of spirit* between barter and capitalist commodity exchange, a commonality tied (in this view) to the object-centered, relatively impersonal, asocial nature of each. In the various simple forms of barter, we see an effort to exchange things without the constraints of sociality on the one hand, and the complications of money on the other. Barter in the contemporary world is on the increase: one estimate has it that an estimated $12 billion a year in goods and services is bartered in the United States alone. International barter (Pepsico syrup for Russian vodka; Coca-Cola for Korean toothpicks and Bulgarian forklifts are examples) is also developing into a complex alternative economy. In these latter situations, barter is a response to the growing number of barriers to international trade and finance, and has a specific role to play in the larger economy. Barter, as a form of trade, thus links the exchange of commodities in widely different social, technological, and institutional circumstances. Barter may thus be regarded as a special form of commodity exchange, one in which, for any variety of reasons, money plays either no role or a very indirect role (as a mere unit of account). By this definition of barter, it would be difficult to locate any human society in which commodity exchange is completely irrelevant. Barter appears to be the form of commodity exchange in which the circulation of things is most divorced from social, political, or cultural norms. Yet wherever evidence is available, the determination of what may be bartered, where, when, and by whom, as well as of what drives the demand for the goods of the "other," is a social affair. There is a deep tendency to regard this social regulation as a largely negative matter, so that barter in small-scale societies and in earlier periods is frequently regarded as having been restricted to the relation *between* communities rather than *within* communities. Barter is, in this model, held to be in inverse proportion to sociality, and foreign trade, by extension, is seen to have 'preceded' internal trade (Sahlins 1972). But there are good empirical and methodological reasons to question this view.

The notion that trade in nonmonetized, preindustrial economies is generally regarded as antisocial from the point of view of face-to-face communities and thus was frequently restricted to dealings with strangers has as its close counterpart the view that the spirit of the gift and that of the commodity are deeply opposed. In this view, gift exchange and commodity exchange are fundamentally contrastive and mutually exclusive. Though there have been some important recent attempts to mute the exaggerated contrast between Marx and Mauss (Hart 1982; Tambiah 1984), the tendency to see these two modalities of exchange as fundamentally opposed remains a marked feature of anthropological discourse (Dumont 1980; Hyde 1979; Gregory 1982; Sahlins 1972; Taussig 1980).

The exaggeration and reification of the contrast between gift and commodity in anthropological writing has many sources. Among them are the tendency to romanticize small-scale societies; to conflate use value (in Marx's sense) with *gemeinchaft* (in Toennies's sense); the tendency to forget that capitalist societies, too, operate according to cultural designs; the proclivity to marginalize and underplay the calculative, impersonal and self-aggrandizing features of noncapitalist societies. These tendencies, in turn, are a product of an oversimplified view of the opposition between Mauss and Marx, which, as Keith Hart (1982) has suggested, misses important aspects of the commonalities between them.

Gifts, and the spirit of reciprocity, sociability, and spontaneity in which they are typically exchanged, usually are starkly opposed to the profit-oriented, self-centered, and calculated spirit that fires the circulation of commodities. Further, where gifts link things to persons and embed the flow of things in the flow of social relations, commodities are held to represent the drive – largely free of moral or cultural constraints – of goods for one another, a drive mediated by money and not by sociality. Many of the essays in this volume, as well as my own argument here, are designed to show that this is a simplified and overdrawn series of contrasts. For the present, though, let me propose one important quality that gift exchange and the circulation of commodities share.

My view of the spirit of gift exchange owes a good deal to Bourdieu (1977), who has extended a hitherto underplayed aspect of Mauss's analysis of the gift (Mauss 1976:70–3), which stresses certain strategic parallels between gift exchange and more ostensibly "economic" practices. Bourdieu's argument, which stresses the temporal dynamics of gifting, makes a shrewd analysis of the common spirit that underlies both gift and commodity circulation:

> If it is true that the lapse of time interposed is what enables the gift or counter-gift to be seen and experienced as an inaugural act of generosity, without any past or future, i.e., without *calculation*, then it is clear that in reducing the polythetic to the monothetic, objectivism destroys the specificity of all practices which, like gift exchange, tend or pretend to put the law of self-interest into abeyance. A rational contract would telescope into an instant a transaction which gift exchange disguises, by stretching it out in time; and because of this, gift exchange is, if not the only mode of commodity circulation practiced, at least the only mode to be fully recognized, in societies which, because they deny "the true soil of their life," as Lukács puts it, have an economy in itself and not for itself. (Bourdieu 1977:171.)

This treatment of gift exchange as a particular form of the circulation of commodities comes out of Bourdieu's critique not only of "objectivist" treatments of social action, but of the sort of ethnocentrism, itself a historical product of capitalism, that assumes a very restricted definition of economic interest.[3] Bourdieu suggests that "practice never ceases to conform to economic calculation even when it gives every appearance of disinterestedness by departing from the logic of interested calculation (in the narrow sense) and playing for stakes that are non-material and not easily quantified" (*ibid*:177).

I take this suggestion to converge, though from a slightly different angle, with the proposals of Tambiah (1984), Baudrillard (1968; 1975; 1981), Sahlins (1976), and Douglas and Isherwood (1981), all of which represent efforts to restore the cultural dimension to societies that are too often represented simply as economies writ large, and to restore the calculative dimension to societies that are too often simply portrayed as solidarity writ small. Part of the difficulty with a cross-cultural analysis of commodities is that, as with other matters in social life, anthropology is excessively dualistic: "us and them"; "materialist and religious"; "objectification of persons" versus "personification of things"; "market exchange" versus "reciprocity"; and so forth. These oppositions parody both poles and reduce human diversities artificially. One symptom of this problem has been an excessively positivist conception of the commodity, as being a certain *kind* of thing, thus restricting the debate to the matter of deciding *what kind* of thing it is. But, in trying to understand what is distinctive about commodity exchange, it does not make sense to distinguish it sharply either from barter on the one hand, or from the exchange of gifts on the other. As Simmel (1978:97–8), suggests, it is important to see the calculative dimension in all these forms of exchange, even if they vary in the form and intensity of sociality associated with them. It remains now to characterize commodity exchange in a comparative and processual manner.

Let us approach commodities as things in a certain situation, a situation that can characterize many different kinds of thing, at different points in their social lives. This means looking at the commodity potential of all things rather than searching fruitlessly for the magic distinction between commodities and other sorts of things. It also means breaking significantly with the production-dominated Marxian view of the commodity and focusing on its *total* trajectory from production, through exchange/distribution, to consumption.

But how are we to define the commodity situation? I propose that *the commodity situation in the social life of any "thing" be defined as the situation in which its exchangeability (past, present, or future) for some other thing is its socially relevant feature.* Further, the commodity situation, defined this way, can be disaggregated into: (1) the commodity phase of the social life of any thing; (2) the commodity candidacy of any thing; and (3) the commodity context in which any thing may be placed. Each of these aspects of "commodity-hood" needs some explication.

The idea of the commodity phase in the social life of a thing is a summary way to capture the central insight in Igor Kopytoff's important essay in this volume, where certain things are seen as moving in and out of the commodity state. I shall have more to say on this biographical approach to things in the next section, but let us note for the moment that things can move in *and* out of the commodity state, that such movements can be slow or fast, reversible or terminal, normative or deviant.[4] Though the biographical aspect of some things (such as heirlooms, postage stamps, and antiques) may be more noticeable than that of some others (such as steel bars, salt, or sugar), this component is never completely irrelevant.

The commodity *candidacy* of things is less a temporal than a conceptual feature, and it refers to the standards and criteria (symbolic, classificatory, and moral) that define the exchangeability of things in any particular social and historical context. At first glance, this feature would appear best glossed as the *cultural* framework within which things are classified, and it is a central preoccupation of Kopytoff's paper in this volume. Yet this gloss conceals a variety of complexities. It is true that in most stable societies, it would be possible to discover a taxonomic structure that defines the world of things, lumping some things together, discriminating between others, attaching meanings and values to these groupings, and providing a basis for rules and practices governing the circulation of these objects. In regard to the economy (that is, to exchange), Paul Bohannan's (1955) account of spheres of exchange among the Tiv is an obvious example of this type of framework for exchange. But there are two kinds of situations where the standards and criteria that govern exchange are so attentuated as to seem virtually absent. The first is the case of transactions across cultural boundaries, where all that is agreed upon is price (whether monetary or not) and a minimum set of conventions regarding the transaction itself.[5] The other is the case of those intracultural exchanges where, despite a vast universe of shared understandings, a specific exchange is based on deeply divergent perceptions of the value of the objects being exchanged. The best examples of such intracultural value divergence are to be found in situations of extreme hardship (such as famine or warfare), when exchanges are made whose logic has little to do with the commensuration of sacrifices. Thus a Bengali male who abandons his wife to prostitution in exchange for a meal, or a Turkana woman who sells critical pieces of her personal jewelry for a week's food, are engaging in transactions that may be seen as legitimate in extreme circumstances, but could hardly be regarded as operating under a rich shared framework of valuation between buyer and seller. Another way to characterize such situations is to say that in such contexts, value and price have come almost completely unyoked.

Also, as Simmel has pointed out, from the point of view of the individual and his subjectivity, *all* exchanges might contain this type of discrepancy between the sacrifices of buyer and seller, discrepancies normally brushed aside because of the host of conventions about exchange that *are* complied with by both parties (Simmel 1978:80). We may speak, thus, of the cultural framework that defines the commodity candidacy of things, but we must bear in mind that some exchange situations, both inter- and intracultural, are characterized by a shallower set of shared standards of value than others. I therefore prefer to use the term *regimes of value*, which does *not* imply that every act of commodity exchange presupposes a complete cultural sharing of assumptions, but rather that the degree of value coherence may be highly variable from situation to situation, and from commodity to commodity. A regime of value, in this sense, is consistent with both very high and very low sharing of standards by the parties to a particular commodity exchange. Such regimes of value account for the constant transcendence of cultural boundaries by the flow of commodities, where culture is understood as a bounded and localized system of meanings.

Finally, the commodity *context* refers to the variety of *social* arenas, within or between *cultural* units, that help link the commodity candidacy of a thing to the commodity phase of its career. Thus in many societies, marriage transactions might constitute the context in which women are most intensely, and most appropriately, regarded as exchange values. Dealings with strangers might provide contexts for the commoditization of things that are otherwise protected from commoditization. Auctions accentuate the commodity dimension of objects (such as paintings) in a manner that might well be regarded as deeply inappropriate in other contexts. Bazaar settings are likely to encourage commodity flows as domestic settings may not. The variety of such contexts, within and across societies, provides the link between the social environment of the commodity and its temporal and symbolic state. As I have already suggested, the commodity context, as a social matter, may bring together actors from quite different cultural systems who share only the most minimal understandings (from the conceptual point of view) about the objects in question and agree *only* about the terms of trade. The so-called silent trade phenomenon is the most obvious example of the minimal fit between the cultural and social dimensions of commodity exchange (Price 1980).

Thus, commoditization lies at the complex intersection of temporal, cultural, and social factors. To the degree that some things in a society are frequently to be found in the commodity phase, to fit the requirements of commodity candidacy, and to appear in a commodity context, they are its quintessential commodities. To the degree that many or most things in a society sometimes meet these criteria, the society may be said to be highly commoditized. In modern capitalist societies, it can safely be said that more things are likely to experience a commodity phase in their own careers, more contexts to become legitimate commodity contexts, and the standards of commodity candidacy to embrace a large part of the world of things than in noncapitalist societies. Though Marx was therefore right in seeing modern industrial capitalism as entailing the most intensely commoditized type of society, the comparison of societies in regard to the degree of "commoditization" would be a most complex affair given the definitional approach to commodities taken here. By this definition, the term "commodity" is used in the rest of this essay to refer to things that, at a certain *phase* in their careers and in a particular *context*, meet the requirements of commodity candidacy. Keith Hart's recent (1982) analysis of the importance of the growing hegemony of the commodity in the world would fit with the approach suggested here, except that commoditization is here regarded as a differentiated process (affecting matters of phase, context, and categorization, differentially) and the capitalist mode of commoditization is seen as interacting with myriad other indigenous social forms of commoditization.

Three additional sets of distinctions between commodities are worth making here (others appear later in this essay). The first, which is a modified application of a distinction originally made by Jacques Maquet in 1971 in regard to aesthetic productions,[6] divides commodities into the following four types: (1) commodities by *destination*, that is, objects intended by their producers principally for exchange; (2) commodities by *metamorphosis*, things intended for other uses that are placed into the commodity state; (3) a special, sharp case of commodities by metamorphosis are commodities by *diversion*, objects placed into a commodity state though originally specifically protected from it; (4) *ex-commodities*, things retrieved, either temporarily or permanently, from the commodity state and placed in some other state. It also seems worthwhile to distinguish "singular" from "homogeneous" commodities in order to discriminate between commodities whose candidacy for the commodity state is precisely a matter of their class characteristics (a perfectly standardized steel bar, indistinguishable in practical terms from any other steel bar) and those whose candidacy is precisely their uniqueness *within* some class (a Manet rather than a Picasso; one Manet rather than another). Closely related, though not identical, is the distinction between primary and secondary commodities; necessities and luxuries; and what I call mobile versus enclaved commodities. Nevertheless, all efforts at defining commodities are doomed to sterility unless they illuminate commodities in motion. This is the principal aim of the section that follows.

Paths and diversions

Commodities are frequently represented as mechanical products of production regimes governed by the laws of supply and demand. By drawing on certain ethnographic examples, I hope to show in this section that the flow of commodities in any given situation is a shifting compromise between socially regulated paths and competitively inspired diversions.

Commodities, as Igor Kopytoff points out, can usefully be regarded as having life histories. In this processual view, the commodity phase of the life history of an object does not exhaust its biography; it is culturally regulated; and its interpretation is open to individual manipulation to some degree. Further, as Kopytoff also points out, the question of what sorts of object may have what sorts of biography is more deeply a matter for social contest and individual taste in modern societies than in smaller-scale, nonmonetized, preindustrial ones. There is, in Kopytoff's model, a perennial and universal tug-of-war between the tendency of all economies to expand the jurisdiction of commoditization and of all cultures to restrict it. Individuals, in this view, can go with either tendency as it suits their interests or matches their sense of moral appropriateness, though in premodern societies the room for maneuver is usually not great. Of the many virtues of Kopytoff's model the most important, in my view, is that it proposes a general processual model of commoditization, in which objects may be moved both into and out of the commodity state. I am less comfortable with the opposition between singularization and commoditization, since some of the most interesting cases (in what Kopytoff agrees are in the middle zone of his ideal-typical contrast) involve the more or less permanent commoditizing of singularities.

Two questions can be raised about this aspect of Kopytoff's argument. One would be that the very definition of what constitutes singularities as opposed to classes is a cultural question, just as there can be unique examples of homogeneous classes (the perfect steel bar) and classes of culturally valued singularities (such as works of art and designer-label clothing). On the other hand, a Marxist critique of this contrast would suggest that it is commoditization as a worldwide historical process that determines in very important ways the shifting relationship between singular and homogeneous things at any given moment in the life of a society. But the important point is that the commodity is not one kind of thing rather than another, but one phase in the life of some things. Here, Kopytoff and I are in full agreement.

This view of commodities and commoditization has several important implications, some of which are touched upon in the course of Kopytoff's argument. Others are discussed later in this essay. But my immediate concern is with one important aspect of this temporal perspective on the commoditization of things, which concerns what I have called paths and diversions. I owe both these terms, and some measure of my understanding of the relationship between them, to Nancy Munn's contribution (Munn 1983) in an important collection of papers on a phenomenon that is of great importance to the topic of this volume, the celebrated kula system of the Western Pacific (Leach and Leach 1983).

The kula is the best-documented example of a non-Western, preindustrial, nonmonetized, translocal exchange system, and with the publication of this recent collection, it becomes, arguably, the most thoughtfully and fruitfully analyzed one. It now appears that Malinowski's classic account of this system (Malinowski 1922) was partial and problematic, though it has laid the foundation for even the most sophisticated recent analyses. The implications of this recent rethinking of the kula phenomenon for the general concerns of this volume are several. Although the essays I shall cite from this volume reflect different vantage points, both ethnographic and theoretical, they do permit some general observations.

The kula is an extremely complex regional system for the circulation of particular kinds of valuables, usually between men of substance, in the Massim group of islands off the eastern tip of New Guinea. The main objects exchanged for one another are of two types: decorated necklaces (which circulate in one direction) and armshells (which circulate in the other). These valuables acquire very specific biographies as they move from place to place and hand to hand, just as the men who exchange them gain and lose reputation as they acquire, hold, and part with these valuables. The term *keda* (road, route, path, or track) is used in some Massim communities to describe the journey of these valuables from island to island. But keda also has a more diffuse set of meanings, referring to the more or less stable social, political, and reciprocal links between men that constitute these paths. In the most abstract way, keda refers to the path (created through the exchange of these valuables) to wealth, power, and reputation for the men who handle these valuables (Campbell 1983a:203–4).

Keda is thus a polysemic concept, in which the circulation of objects, the making of memories and reputations, and the pursuit of social distinction through strategies of partnership all come together. The delicate and complex links between men and things that are central to the politics of the keda are captured in the following extract from the perspective of the island of Vakuta:

The successful keda consists of men who are able to maintain relatively stable keda partnerships through good oratorical and manipulative skills, and who operate as a team, interpreting one another's movements. Nevertheless, many keda collapse, regularly making it necessary for men to realign themselves. Some form completely different keda, while the remnants of a broken keda may want to form another keda by drawing in new men. Yet others may never kula again because of their inability to form another keda owing to a reputation for "bad" kula activity. In reality, the population of shell valuables in any one keda is migratory and the social composition of a keda transitory. A shell's accumulation of history is retarded by continual movement between keda, while men's claims to immortality vanish as shells lose association with these men after being successfully attracted into another keda, thus taking on the identity of its new owners. (Campbell 1983:218–19.)

The path taken by these valuables is thus both reflective and constitutive of social partnerships and struggles for preeminence. But a number of other things are worth noting about the circulation of these valuables. The first is that their exchange is not easily categorized as simple reciprocal exchange, far from the spirit of trade and commerce. Though monetary valuations are absent, both the nature of the objects and a variety of sources of flexibility in the system make it possible to have the sort of calculated exchange that I maintain is at the heart of the exchange of commodities. These complex nonmonetary modes of valuation allow partners to negotiate what Firth (following Cassady 1974) calls "exchange by private treaty," a situation in which something like price is arrived at by some negotiated process other than the impersonal forces of supply and demand (Firth 1983:91). Thus, despite the presence of broad conventional exchange rates, a complex qualitative calculus exists (Campbell 1983:245–6) which permits the competitive negotiation of personal estimates of value in the light of both short- and long-term individual interest (Firth 1983:101). What Firth here calls "indebtedness engineering" is a variety of the sort of calculated exchange that, by my definition, blurs the line between commodity exchange and other, more sentimental, varieties. The most important difference between the exchange of these commodities and the exchange of commodities in modern industrial economies is that the increment being sought in kula-type systems is in reputation, name, or fame, with the critical form of capital for producing this profit being people rather than other factors of production (Strathern 1983:80; Damon 1983:339–40). Pricelessness is a luxury few commodities can afford.

Perhaps even more important than the calculative aspect of kula exchanges is the fact that these recent studies make it very difficult to regard the exchange of kula valuables as occurring only at the boundaries between communities, with more giftlike exchanges occurring within these communities (Damon 1983:339). The concept of *kitoum* provides the conceptual and technical link between the large paths that the valuables take and the more intimate, regular, and problematic intra-island exchanges (Weiner 1983; Damon 1983; Campbell 1983; Munn 1983). Though the term kitoum is complex and in certain respects ambiguous, it seems clear that it represents the articulation between the kula and other exchange modalities in which men and women transact in their own communities. Kitoums are valuables that one can place into the kula system or legitimately withdraw from it in order to effect "conversions" (in Paul Bohannan's sense) between disparate levels of "conveyance" (Bohannan 1955). In the use of kitoum we see the critical conceptual and instrumental links between the smaller and bigger paths that constitute the total world of exchange in Massim. As Annette Weiner has shown, it is a mistake to isolate the grander interisland system of exchange from the more intimate, but (for men) more suffocating local transfers of objects that occur because of debt, death, and affinity (Weiner 1983:164–5).

The kula system gives a dynamic and processual quality to Mauss's ideas regarding the mingling or exchange of qualities between men and things, as Munn (1983:283) has noted with regard to kula exchange in Gawa: "Although men appear to be the agents in defining shell value, in fact, without shells, men cannot define their own value; in this respect, shells and men are reciprocally agents of each other's value definition." But, as Munn has observed, in the reciprocal construction of value, it is not only paths that play an important role, but diversions as well. The relations between paths and diversions is critical to the politics of value in the kula system, and proper orchestration of these relations is at the strategic heart of the system:

Actually, diversion is implicated in the path system, since it is one of the means of making new paths. Possession of more than one path also points to the probability of further diversions from one established path to another, as men become subject to the interests and persuasiveness of more than one set of partners. . . . In fact, men of substance in kula have to develop some capacity to balance operations: diversions from one path must later be replaced in order to assuage cheated partners and keep the path from disappearing, or to keep themselves from being dropped from the path. (Munn 1983:301.)

These large-scale exchanges represent psychological efforts to transcend more humble flows of things, but in the politics of reputation, gains in the larger arena have implications for the smaller ones, and the idea of the kitoum assures that both conveyances and conversions have to be carefully managed for the greatest gains overall (Damon

1983:317–23). The kula may be regarded as the paradigm of what I propose to call *tournaments of value.*[7]

Tournaments of value are complex periodic events that are removed in some culturally well-defined way from the routines of economic life. Participation in them is likely to be both a privilege of those in power and an instrument of status contests between them. The currency of such tournaments is also likely to be set apart through well understood cultural diacritics. Finally, what is at issue in such tournaments is not just status, rank, fame, or reputation of actors, but the disposition of the central tokens of value in the society in question.[8] Finally, though such tournaments of value occur in special times and places, their forms and outcomes are always consequential for the more mundane realities of power and value in ordinary life. As in the kula, so in such tournaments of value generally, strategic skill is culturally measured by the success with which actors attempt diversions or subversions of culturally conventionalized paths for the flow of things.

The idea of tournaments of value is an attempt to create a general category, following up a recent observation by Edmund Leach (1983:535) comparing the kula system to the art world in the modern West. Baudrillard's analysis of the art auction in the contemporary West allows one to widen and sharpen this analogy. Baudrillard notes that the art auction, with its ludic, ritual, and reciprocal aspects, stands apart from the ethos of conventional economic exchange, and that it "goes well beyond economic calculation and concerns all the processes of the transmutation of values, from one logic to another logic of value which may be noted in determinate places and institutions" (Baudrillard 1981:121). The following analysis by Baudrillard of the ethos of the art auction deserves quotation in full since it could so easily be an apt characterization of other examples of the tournament of value:

Contrary to commercial operations, which institute a relation of economic *rivalry* between individuals on the footing of formal *equality*, with each one guiding his own calculation of individual appropriation, the auction, like the fête or the game, institutes a concrete community of exchange among peers. Whoever the vanquisher in the challenge, the essential function of the auction is the institution of a community of the privileged who define themselves as such by agonistic speculation upon a restricted corpus of signs. Competition of the aristocratic sort seals their *parity* (which has nothing to do with the formal equality of economic competition), and thus their collective caste privilege with respect to all others, from whom they are no longer separated merely by their purchasing power, but by the sumptuary and collective act of the production and exchange of sign values. (1981:117.)

In making a comparative analysis of such tournaments of value, it may be advisable not to follow Baudrillard's tendency to isolate them analytically from more mundane economic exchange, though the articulation of such value arenas with other economic arenas is likely to be highly variable. I shall have more to say on tournaments of value in the discussion of the relationship between knowledge and commodities later in this essay.

The kula, at any rate, represents a very complex system for the intercalibration of the biographies of persons and things. It shows us the difficulty of separating gift and commodity exchange even in preindustrial, nonmonetary systems, and it reminds us of the dangers in correlating zones of social intimacy too rigidly with distinct forms of exchange. But perhaps most important, it is the most intricate example of the politics of tournaments of value, in which the actors manipulate the cultural definitions of path and the strategic potential of diversion, so that the movement of things enhances their own 'nding.

Diversions, however, are not to be found only as parts of individual strategies in competitive situations, but can be institutionalized in various ways that remove or protect objects from the relevant social commodity contexts. Royal monopolies are perhaps the best-known examples of such "enclaved commodities," as Kopytoff points out in Chapter 2. One of the most interesting and extensive discussions of this type of monopolistic restriction on the flow of commodities is that of Max Gluckman (1983) in the context of royal property among the Lozi of Northern Rhodesia. In his discussion of the categories "gift," "tribute," and "kingly things," Gluckman shows how even in a low-surplus agricultural kingdom, the flow of commodities had very diverse and important implications. In his analysis of "kingly things," it becomes clear that the main function of these royal monopolies was to maintain sumptuary exclusivity (as in the royal monopoly of eland fly whisks), commercial advantage (as with elephant tusks), and the display of rank. Such royal restrictions of things from more promiscuous spheres of exchange is part of the way in which, in premodern chieftainships and empires, royalty could assure the material basis of sumptuary exclusivity. This type of process might be called decommoditization from above.

But the more complex case concerns entire zones of activity and production that are devoted to producing objects of value that cannot be commoditized by anybody. The zone of art and ritual in small-scale societies is one such enclaved zone, where the spirit of the commodity enters only under conditions of massive cultural change. For an extended discussion of this phenomenon, we have William Davenport's essay on the production of objects for ritual use in the Eastern Solomons.

The phenomena discussed in Davenport's essay illuminate the commodity aspects of social life precisely because they illustrate one sort of moral and cosmological framework within which commoditization is restricted and hedged. In the funeral observances of this region, particularly the large-scale-*murina*, much energy and expenditure are invested in making objects that play a central role in the ritual but are scrupulously placed in the category of "terminal" commodities (Kopytoff, Chapter 2), that is, objects which, because of the context, purpose, and meaning of their production, make only *one* journey from production to consumption. After that, though they are sometimes used in casual domestic ways, they are never permitted to reenter the commodity state. What makes them thus decommoditized is a complex understanding of value (in which the aesthetic, the ritual, and the social come together), and a specific ritual biography. We may paraphrase Davenport's observations and note that what happens here, at the heart of a very complex and calculated set of investments, payments, and credits, is a special kind of transvaluation, in which objects are placed beyond the culturally demarcated zone of commoditization. This type of transvaluation can take different forms in different societies, but it is typical that objects which represent aesthetic elaboration and objects that serve as sacra are, in many societies, not permitted to occupy the commodity state (either temporally, socially, or definitionally) for very long. In the rigid commitment of traditional Solomon Islanders to placing their most aestheticized ritual products beyond the reach of commoditization, we see one variation of a widespread tendency.

A somewhat different example of the tension between sacra and commodity exchange is to be seen in Patrick Geary's analysis of the trade in relics in early medieval Europe. The relics he describes are, of course, "found" and not "made," and the circulation of these relics reflects a very important aspect of the construction of community identity, local prestige, and central ecclesiastical control in Latin Europe in the early medieval period.

These relics belong to a particular economy of exchange and demand in which the life history of the particular relic is essential, not incidental, to its value. The verification of this history is also central to its value. Given the general approach to the difference between gift and commodity that I have taken in this essay, I would suggest that Geary may draw too sharp a contrast between them; indeed, his own material shows that gift, theft, and commerce were all modes for the movement of sacra, in a larger context of ecclesiastical control, local competition, and community rivalry. From this perspective, medieval relics seem less carefully protected from the hazards of commoditization than Davenport's ritual objects. Yet the implication remains that commercial modes for the acquisition of relics were less desirable than either gift *or* theft, not so much because of a direct moral antipathy to trade in relics, but rather because the other two modes were more emblematic of the value and efficacy of the object.

Thus these relics, too, fall into the category of objects whose commodity phase is ideally brief, whose movement is restricted, and which apparently are not "priced" in the way other things might be. Yet the force of demand is such as to make them circulate with considerable velocity, and in much the same way, as their more mundane counterparts. Thus, even in the case of "transvalued" objects, which take on the characteristics of enclaved, rather than mobile, commodities, there is considerable variation in the reasons for, and the nature of, such enclaving. Gluckman's "kingly things," Geary's relics, and Davenport's ritual objects are different kinds of enclaved commodities, objects whose commodity potential is carefully hedged. It may also be appropriate to note that a very important institutional way to restrict the zone of commodity exchange itself is the "port-of-trade" associated with many premodern kingdoms (Geertz 1980), though such restrictions on trade in premodern politics may not have been as thoroughgoing as has sometimes been imagined (Curtin 1984:58). The reasons for such hedging are quite variable, but in each case, the moral bases of the restriction have clear implications for framing and facilitating political, social, and commercial exchanges of a more mundane sort. Such enclaved commodities bear a family resemblance to another class of thing, frequently discussed in the anthropological literature as "primitive valuables," whose specialness is directly linked to commodity exchange.

Though commodities, by virtue of their exchange destinies and mutual commensurability, tend to dissolve the links between persons and things, such a tendency is always balanced by a countertendency, in all societies, to restrict, control, and channel exchange. In many primitive economies, primitive valuables display these socially restricted qualities. We owe to Mary Douglas (1967) the insight that many such valuables resemble coupons and licenses in modern industrial economies. That is, although they resemble money, they are not generalized media of exchange but have the following characteristics: (1) the powers of acquisition that they represent are highly specific; (2) their distribution is controlled in various ways; (3) the conditions that govern their issue create a set of patron-client relationships; (4) their main function is to provide the necessary condition for entry to high-status positions, for maintaining rank, or for combining attacks on status; and (5) the social systems in which such coupons or licenses function is geared to eliminating or reducing competition in the interests of a fixed pattern of status (Douglas 1967:69). Raffia cloth in Central Africa, wampum among the Indians of the eastern United States, shell money among the Yurok and the shell currency of Rossell Island and other parts of Oceania are examples of such "commodity coupons" (in Douglas's phrase), whose restricted flow is at the service of the reproduction of social and political systems. Things, in such contexts, remain devices for reproducing relations between persons (see also Dumont 1980:231). Such commodity coupons represent a transformational midpoint between "pure" gifts and "pure" commerce. With the gift, they share a certain insensitivity to supply and demand, a high coding in terms of etiquette and appropriateness, and a tendency to follow socially set paths. With pure barter, their exchange shares the spirit of calculation, an openness to self-interest, and a preference for transactions with relative strangers.

In such restricted systems of commodity flow, where valuables play the role of coupons or licenses designed to protect status systems, we see the functional equivalent but the technical inversion of "fashion" in more complex societies. Where in the one case status systems are protected and reproduced by restricting equivalences and exchange in a *stable* universe of commodities, in a fashion system what is restricted and controlled is *taste* in an *ever-changing* universe of commodities, with the illusion of complete interchangeability and unrestricted access. Sumptuary laws constitute an intermediate consumption-regulating device, suited to societies devoted to stable status displays in exploding commodity contexts, such as India, China, and Europe in the premodern period. (These comparisons are pursued more precisely in the following section of this essay.)[9]

Such forms of restriction and the enclaved commodities they create sometimes provide the context and targets of strategies of diversions. Diversion, that is, may sometimes involve the calculated and "interested" removal of things from an enclaved zone to one where exchange is less confined and more profitable, in some short-term sense. Where enclaving is usually in the interests of groups, especially the politically and economically powerful groups in any society, diversion is frequently the recourse of the entrepreneurial individual. But whether it is groups or individuals who are involved in either kind of activity, the central contrast is that whereas enclaving seeks to protect certain things from commoditization, diversion frequently is aimed at drawing protected things into the zone of commoditization. Diversion, however, can also take the form of strategic shifts in path within a zone of commoditization.

In an extremely interesting discussion of British trade in Hawaii in the late eighteenth and early nineteenth centuries, Marshall Sahlins has shown how Hawaiian chiefs, in stretching traditional conceptions of *tabu* to cover new classes of trade goods (in keeping with their own cosmopolitical interests), succeeded in transforming the "divine finality" even of economic tabus into instruments of expedience (Sahlins 1981:44–5). Thus, what Sahlins calls "the pragmatics of trade" erodes and transforms the cultural bounds within which it is initially conceived. In a word, the politics of enclaving, far from being a guarantor of systemic stability, may constitute the Trojan horse of change.

The diversion of commodities from specified paths is always a sign of creativity or crisis, whether aesthetic or economic. Such crises may take a variety of forms: economic hardship, in all manner of societies, drives families to part with heirlooms, antiques, and memorabilia and to commoditize them. This is as true of kula valuables as of more modern valuables. The other form of crisis in which commodities are diverted from their proper paths, of course, is warfare and the plunder that historically has accompanied it. In such plunder, and the spoils that it generates, we see the inverse of trade. The transfer of commodities in warfare always has a special symbolic intensity, exemplified in the tendency to frame more mundane plunder in the transfer of special arms, insignia, or body parts belonging to the enemy. In the high-toned plunder that sets the frame for more mundane pillage, we see the hostile analogue to the dual layering of the mundane and more personalized circuits of exchange in other contexts (such as kula and gimwali in Melanesia). Theft, condemned in most human societies, is the humblest form of diversion of commodities from preordained paths.

But there are subtler examples of the diversion of commodities from their predestined paths. One whole area involves what has been dubbed tourist art, in which objects produced for aesthetic, ceremonial, or sumptuary use in small, face-to-face communities are transformed culturally, economically, and socially by the tastes, markets, and ideologies of larger economies (Graburn 1976). I shall have more to say on tourist art in the section of this essay on knowledge and commodities. Another, related area is that of the history and nature of the major art and archeology collections of the Western world, whose formation represents extremely complex blends of plunder, sale, and inheritance, combined with the Western taste for the things of the past and of the other.[10] In this traffic in artifacts, we can find today most of the critical cultural issues in the international flow of "authentic" (see Spooner, Chapter 7) and "singular" (see Kopytoff, Chapter 2) commodities. The current controversies between English and American museums and governments and various other countries raise all the moral and political delicacies that come into play when things get diverted, several times over, from their minimal, conventional paths and are transferred by a variety of modes that make their history of claims and counterclaims extremely difficult to adjudicate.

The diversion of commodities from their customary paths always carries a risky and morally ambiguous aura. Whenever what Bohannan (1955) called conveyances give way to what he called conversions, the spirit of entrepreneurship and that of moral taint enter the picture simultaneously. In the case of the kula exchanges of Melanesia, the movement of commodities across spheres, though somehow out of order, is also at the heart of the strategy of the skillful and successful kula player. Inappropriate conversions from one sphere of exchange to another are frequently fortified by recourse to the excuse of economic crisis, whether it be famine or bankruptcy. If such excuses are not available or credible, accusations of inappropriate and venal motives are likely to set in. Excellent examples of the political implications of diversion are to be found in the arena of illegal or quasilegal commodity exchanges, one case of which is discussed next.

Lee Cassanelli's intriguing paper in this volume discusses the shift, in the last fifty years in Northeastern Africa, in the political economy of a quasilegal commodity called *qat (catha edulis)*. Qat provides an excellent example of change in what may be referred to as a commodity ecumene,[11] that is, a transcultural network of relationships linking producers, distributors, and consumers of a particular commodity or set of commodities. What is particularly interesting, in this case, is the dramatic expansion of the scale of consumption (and of production) of qat which is clearly tied to changes in the technical infrastructure as well as the political economy of the region. Although the expansion of production appears consistent with conditions that fit with more universal patterns in the commercialization of agriculture, what is more intriguing is the expansion of demand and the response of the state – especially in Somalia – to the explosion in both the production and the consumption of qat.

The recent (1983) ban by the Somali government on the planting, importing, and chewing of qat clearly is the most recent move in a long tradition of state ambivalence toward a commodity whose consumption is perceived as tied to unproductive, and potentially subversive, forms of sociality. In the case of the current Somali ban, it appears that qat (like cloth in Gandhi's rhetoric) is seen as a multilevel problem, one that challenges not only state control over the economy, but state authority over the social organization of leisure among the newly rich and upwardly mobile citizens of urban Somalia. We are again reminded, with this example, that rapid changes in consumption, if not inspired and regulated by those in power, are likely to appear threatening to them. Also, in the case of Somalia, we have a very good example of the tension between a rapid shift in the political economy of a regional commodity ecumene and the authority of one state in this ecumene.

Of course, the best examples of the diversion of commodities from their original nexus is to be found in the domain of fashion, domestic display, and collecting in the modern West. In the high-tech look inspired by the Bauhaus, the functionality of factories, warehouses, and workplaces is diverted to household aesthetics. The uniforms of various occupations are turned into the vocabulary of costume. In the logic of found art, the everyday commodity is framed and aestheticized. These are all examples of what we might call commoditization by diversion, where value, in the art or fashion market, is accelerated or enhanced by placing objects and things in unlikely contexts. It is the aesthetics of decontextualization (itself driven by the quest for novelty) that is at the heart of the display, in highbrow Western homes, of the tools and artifacts of the "other": the Turkmen saddlebag, Masai spear, Dinka basket.[12] In these objects, we see not only the equation of the authentic with the exotic everyday object, but also the aesthetics of diversion. Such diversion is not only an instrument of decommoditization of the object, but also of the (potential) intensification of commoditization by the enhancement of value attendant upon its diversion. This enhancement of value through the diversion of commodities from their customary circuits underlies the plunder of enemy valuables in warfare, the purchase and display of "primitive" utilitarian objects, the framing of "found" objects, the making of collections of any sort.[13] In all these examples, diversions of things combine the aesthetic impulse, the entrepreneurial link, and the touch of the morally shocking.

Nevertheless, diversions are meaningful only in relation to the paths from which they stray. Indeed, in looking at the social life of commodities in any given society or period, part of the anthropological challenge is to define the relevant and customary paths, so that the logic of diversions can properly, and relationally, be understood. The relationship between paths and diversions is itself historical and dialectical, as Michael Thompson (1979) has skillfully shown in regard to art objects in the modern West. Diversions that become predictable are on their way to becoming new paths, paths that will in turn inspire new diversions or returns to old paths. These historical relationships are rapid and easy to see in our own society, but less visible in societies where such shifts are more gradual.

Change in the cultural construction of commodities is to be sought in the shifting relationship of paths to diversions in the lives of commodities. The diversion of commodities from their customary paths brings in the new. But diversion is frequently a function of irregular desires and novel demands, and we turn therefore to consider the problem of desire and demand.

Desire and demand

Part of the reason why demand remains by and large a mystery is that we assume it has something to do with desire, on the one hand (by its nature assumed to be infinite and transcultural) and need on the other (by its nature assumed to be fixed). Following Baudrillard (1981), I suggest that we treat demand, hence consumption, as an aspect of the overall political economy of societies. Demand, that is, emerges as a function of a variety of social practices and classifications, rather than a mysterious emanation of human needs, a mechanical response to social manipulation (as in one model of the effects of advertising in our own society), or the narrowing down of a universal and voracious desire for objects to whatever happens to be available.

Alfred Gell's marvelous picture in Chapter 4 of the dilemmas of consumption among the Muria Gonds of central India makes many interesting and important points about the cultural complexities of consumption and the dilemmas of desire in small-scale societies undergoing rapid change. After reading his paper, it would be difficult to see the desire for goods as being bottomless or culture free, and demand as being a natural and mechanical response to the availability of goods and the money with which to purchase them. Consumption among the Gonds is closely tied to collective displays, economic egalitarianism, and sociability. This poses a problem for those Muria who, as a consequence of shifts in the tribal economy over the last century or so, have acquired considerably more wealth than the rest of their communities. The result is a pattern of what, inverting Veblen, we might call "conspicuous parsimony," where simplicity in lifestyle and possessions is maintained against the growing pressures of increased income. When expenditures on commodities are made, they tend to revolve around traditionally acceptable commodity forms, such as brass pots, ceremonial finery, and houses, where collectively shared values are incarnated. This is not a world dominated by the ethos of limited good, as it might first appear, but one where there is no real interest in most of what the market has to offer. Group identity, sumptuary homogeneity, economic equality, and hedonistic sociality constitute a value framework within which most externally introduced goods are uninteresting or worrisome. The collective regulation of demand (and thus of consumption) is here part of a conscious strategy on the part of the wealthy to contain the potentially divisive implications of differentiation. The Muria example is a striking case of the social regulation of the desire for goods, even when the technical and logistical conditions for a consumer revolution have been met, as is the case with cloth in India, which is discussed next.

Christopher Bayly's contribution to this volume is an enormously subtle and suggestive analysis of the changing moral and political economy of cloth in India since 1700.[14] It demonstrates very clearly the links between politics, value, and demand in the social history of things. In Bayly's argument, the production, exchange, and consumption of cloth constitute the material of a "political discourse" (rather as qat does in Somalia) that ties together royal demand, local production structures and social solidarities, and the fabric of political legitimacy. It is the consumption side of this political discourse that accounts for the deep penetration of English textiles into Indian markets in the nineteenth century, and not just the brute logics of utility and price. Finally, in the nationalist movement of the late nineteenth and early twentieth centuries, especially in Gandhi's rhetoric, the many strands of the political discourse on cloth are reconstituted and redeployed in what might be called a language of commodity resistance, in which older as well as more recent meanings of cloth are turned against the British imperium. Bayly's paper (which is, among other things, an extraordinarily rich application of the ideas of Werner Sombart), by taking the long view of the social life of a particular significant commodity, affords us two insights that are of considerable comparative interest: first, that the customary consumption logics of small communities are intimately tied to larger regimes of value defined by large-scale polities; and that the link between processes of "singularization" and "commoditization" (to use Kopytoff's terms) in the social lives of things is itself dialectical and subject (in the hands of men like Gandhi) to what Clifford Geertz would call deep play.

Demand is thus the economic expression of the political logic of consumption and thus its basis must be sought in that logic. Taking my lead from Veblen, Douglas and Isherwood (1981), and Baudrillard (1968; 1975; 1981), I suggest that consumption is eminently social, relational, and active rather than private, atomic, or passive. Douglas has the advantage over Baudrillard of not restricting her views of consumption as communication to contemporary capitalist society but extending it to other societies as well. Baudrillard, for his part, places the logic of consumption under the dominion of the social logics of both production and exchange, equally. In addition, Baudrillard makes an immensely effective critique of Marx and his fellow political economists in regard to the twin concepts of "need" and "utility," both of which the latter saw as rooted in a primitive, universal, and natural substrate of basic human requirements.

My own inclination is to push Baudrillard's deconstruction of "need" and "utility" (and his relocation of them in the larger sphere of production and exchange) one step further and extend this idea to noncapitalist societies as well. What does this view of consumption entail? It means looking at consumption (and the demand that makes it possible) as a focus not only for *sending* social messages (as Douglas has proposed), but for *receiving* them as well. Demand thus conceals two *different* relationships between consumption and production: 1. On the one hand, demand is determined by social and economic forces; 2. on the other, it can manipulate, within limits, these social and economic forces. The important point is that from a historical point of view, these two aspects of demand can affect each other. Take *royal* demand, for example, as in Bayly's discussion of premodern India. Here royal *demand* is a message-sending or production-molding force, looked at from the internal point of view of eighteenth-century Indian society. That is, royal demand sets parameters for both taste and production within its relevant sphere of influence. But royal demand is also a message-receiving force, as is borne out in its relationship to contemporary European styles and products. Elite tastes, in general, have this "turnstile" function, selecting from exogenous possibilities and then providing models, as well as direct political controls, for internal tastes and production.

One mechanism that frequently translates political control into consumer demand is that of the "sumptuary laws" that characterize complex premodern societies, but also characterize small-scale, preindustrial, and preliterate societies. Wherever clothing, food, housing, body decoration, number of wives or slaves, or any other visible act of consumption is subject to external regulation, we can see that demand is subject to social definition and control. From this point of view, the plethora of "taboos" in primitive societies, which forbid particular kinds of marriage, food consumption, and interaction (as well as their cognate positive injunctions), can be seen as strict moral analogues to the more explicit, legalized sumptuary laws of more complex and literate societies. It is by virtue of this link that we can better understand the shrewd analogy that Douglas (1967) drew between "primitive" and "modern" rationing systems.

What modern money is to primitive media of exchange, fashion is to primitive sumptuary regulations. There are clear morphological similarities between the two, but the term fashion suggests high velocity, rapid turnover, the illusion of total access and high convertibility, the assumption of a democracy of consumers and of objects of consumption. Primitive media of exchange, like primitive sumptuary laws and taboos, on the other hand, seem rigid, slow to move, weak in their capacity to commensurate, tied to hierarchy, discrimination, and rank in social life. But, as Baudrillard (1981) and Bourdieu (1984) have shown so well, the establishments that control fashion and good taste in the contemporary West are no less effective in limiting social mobility, marking social rank and discrimination, and placing consumers in a game whose ever-shifting rules are determined by "taste makers" and their affiliated experts who dwell at the top of society.

Modern consumers are the victims of the velocity of fashion as surely as primitive consumers are the victims of the stability of sumptuary law. The demand for commodities is critically regulated by this variety of taste-making mechanisms, whose social origin is more clearly understood (both by consumers and by analysts) in our own society than in those distant from us. From the point of view of demand, the critical difference between modern, capitalist societies and those based on simpler forms of technology and labor is *not* that we have a thoroughly commoditized economy whereas theirs is one in which subsistence is dominant and commodity exchange has made only limited inroads, but rather that the consumption demands of persons in our own society are regulated by high-turnover criteria of "appropriateness" (fashion), in contrast to the less frequent shifts in more directly regulated sumptuary or customary systems. In both cases, however, demand is a socially regulated and generated impulse, not an artifact of individual whims or needs.

Even in modern, capitalist societies, of course, the media and the impulse to imitate (in Veblen's sense) are not the sole engines of consumer demand. Demand can be manipulated by direct political appeals, whether in the special form of appeals to boycott lettuce grown in bad labor conditions or in the generalized forms of protectionism, either "official" or "unofficial." Again, Bayly's treatment of Gandhi's manipulation of the meaning of indigenously produced cloth is an arch-example of the direct politicization of demand. Yet this large-scale manipulation of the demand for cloth in twentieth-century India was possible only because cloth had long been, at the local level, an instrument for the sending of finely tuned social messages. Thus we can state as a general rule that those commodities whose consumption is most intricately tied up with critical social messages are likely to be *least* responsive to crude shifts in supply or price, but most responsive to political manipulation at the societal level.

From the social point of view, and over the span of human history, the critical agents for the articulation of the supply and demand of commodities have been not only rulers but, of course, *traders*. Philip Curtin's monumental recent work on cross-cultural trade in the preindustrial world suggests that earlier models, such as Polanyi's, of administered trade may have overstated state control over complex premodern economies (Curtin 1984:58). What is clear is that the relations between rulers and states varied enormously over space and time. Though studies like Curtin's are beginning to show patterns underlying this diversity, the demand component in these trade dynamics remains obscure. The very close historical links between rulers and traders (whether of complicity or antagonism) might partly stem from both parties being claimants for the key role in the social regulation of demand. The politics of demand frequently lies at the root of the tension between merchants and political elites; whereas merchants tend to be the social representatives of unfettered equivalence, new commodities, and strange tastes, political elites tend to be the custodians of restricted exchange, fixed commodity systems, and established tastes and sumptuary customs. This antagonism between "foreign" goods and local sumptuary (and therefore political) structures is probably the fundamental reason for the often remarked tendency of primitive societies to restrict trade to a limited set of commodities and to dealings with strangers rather than with kinsmen or friends. The notion that trade violates the spirit of the gift may in complex societies be only a vaguely related by-product of this more fundamental antagonism. In premodern societies, therefore, the demand for commodities sometimes reflects state-level dynamics, *or*, as in the kula case, the hinge function of status competition between elite males in linking internal and external systems of exchange.

This may be an appropriate point at which to note that there are important differences between the *cultural biography* and the *social history* of things. The differences have to do with two kinds of temporality, two forms of class identity, and two levels of social scale. The cultural biography perspective, formulated by Kopytoff, is appropriate to *specific* things, as they move through different hands, contexts, and uses, thus accumulating a specific biography, or set of biographies. When we look at classes or types of thing, however, it is important to look at longer-term shifts (often in demand) and larger-scale dynamics that transcend the biographies of particular members of that class or type. Thus a particular relic may have a specific biography, but whole types of relic, and indeed the class of things called "relic" itself, may have a larger historical ebb and flow, in the course of which its meaning may shift significantly.

Colin Renfrew's paper on "Varna and the Emergence of Wealth in Europe" raises a series of important methodological as well as theoretical questions about commodities seen over the long run. His paper reminds us that commodities are central to some very early and fundamental shifts in human social life, specifically the shift from relatively undifferentiated hunter-gatherer societies to more complex early state societies. In the first place, to look at such processes over the very long run is necessarily to be involved in inferential models linking production with consumption. Second, to examine production processes in early human history entails looking at technological change. Here Renfrew shows us very persuasively that the decisive factors in technological innovation (which is critical to the development of new commodities) are often social and political rather than simply technical. Once this is seen, it follows, as Renfrew makes clear, that considerations of value and demand become central to the understanding of what look, at first glance, like strictly technical leaps.

Thus, in analyzing the role of gold and copper at Varna, and of similar objects of "prime value" in other prehistoric situations in Europe, Renfrew removes us from the temptations of the reflectionist view (where valuables simply reflect the high status of the people who use them) to a more dynamic constructionist view, in which it is the use of high technology objects that is critical to shifts in status structure. What is thus to be explained are changing notions of value, which in turn imply new uses of technological discoveries and new forms of political control of the products of such innovations. Renfrew's complex argument illustrates the point that changes in the social role of objects of display (themselves based on control over materials of prime value) illuminate long-term shifts in value and demand. At the same time, his paper reminds us that the cultural role of commodities (though the central theme of this volume) cannot ultimately be divorced from questions of technology, production, and trade. Yet, though the archeological problem serves to highlight the complexity and historical depth of the relationship between values, social differentiation, and technical change, the absence of more conventional written or oral documents does make the reconstruction of value change more difficult than the reconstruction of social or technical change. Renfrew's paper has the virtue of going against the grain of what his evidence most comfortably supports.

Long-term processes involving the social role of commodities have recently been studied in three major treatises, two by historians (Braudel 1982; Curtin 1984), one by an anthropologist (Wolf 1982). Each of these studies has some distinctive virtues, but there are also some significant overlaps between them. Curtin's book is a bold, comparative study of what he calls "trade diasporas," communities of traders that moved goods across cultural boundaries throughout recorded history and up to the age of European industrial expansion. It strives to maintain a non-Eurocentric view of world trade before the industrial age, and in this it has much in common with Eric Wolf's aims in his recent book. Yet, Wolf's study, partly because of the theoretical viewpoint of the author and partly because of its concern with a much more recent chapter in the history of Europe's link to the rest of the world, is oriented far more to Europe. Curtin's and Wolf's studies do a great deal to explode the idea of commodity flows as either recent or exclusively tied to metropolitan capitalism, and they serve as important reminders of the institutional, logistical, and political backdrops against which commerce has occurred across social and cultural boundaries. But, for different reasons in each case, Curtin and Wolf are less interested in the question of demand and the related problem of the cultural construction of value. The essays in the present volume, then, complement and enrich the largely institutional, technological and economic panorama of commodity flows contained in these two studies.

Braudel, the formidable doyen of the *Annales* school, is another matter. In the second volume of his magisterial study of capitalism and material life from about 1500 to 1800 A.D., Braudel is not content to give us a dense and dramatic picture of the making of the modern industrial world. In this volume, whose English title is *The Wheels of Commerce*, Braudel is concerned, as are Curtin and Wolf (along, of course, with many economic and social historians) with the nature, structure, and dynamics of commerce in the world after 1500. Indeed, taken together, these three studies present an astonishing picture of an extremely complex and interrelated set of what I have called "commodity ecumenes," which, starting around 1500 A.D., ties together many diverse parts of the world. Braudel does briefly discuss the demand side of this grand design. His argument concerning the relationship between supply and demand in the early capitalist world (Braudel 1982: 172–83), as always, sets things in a sweeping temporal perspective, but on the sources and consequences of changes in demand, he says little that was not anticipated by Werner Sombart, who is discussed below. Nevertheless, these three major recent treatments of the flow of commodities in the making of the world-system serve to highlight and provide context for what the essays in this volume seek to accomplish, and that is to illuminate the social and cultural dynamics of commodity flow. This tilt toward matters of value, career, and classification is, of course, intended to enrich our understanding of the idiosyncracies of things, a dimension to which previous scholarship has not paid much systematic attention.

The social history of things and their cultural biography are not entirely separate matters, for it is the social history of things, over large periods of time and at large social levels, that constrains the form, meaning, and structure of more short-term, specific, and intimate trajectories. It is also the case, though it is typically harder to document or predict, that many small shifts in the cultural biography of things may, over time, lead to shifts in the social history of things. Examples of these complex relations between small- and large-scale trajectories and short- and long-term patterns in the movement of things are not widespread in the literature, but we can begin to look at these relations with reference to the transformations of exchange systems under the impact of colonial rule (Dalton 1978:155–65; Strathern 1983), and to the transformations of Western society that have led to the emergence of the souvenir, the collectible, and the memento (Stewart 1984). In this volume, the essays by Bayly, Geary, Cassanelli, and Reddy are especially interesting discussions of the relationships between these two dimensions of the temporality of things. It is no coincidence that these scholars are all social historians, with an interest in long-term processes. The best general treatment of the relationship between demand, the circulation of valuables, and long-term shifts in commodity production appears in the work of Werner Sombart (Sombart 1967).

To Sombart we owe the major historical insight that in the period from approximately 1300 to 1800 in Europe, which he regards as the nexus of early capitalism, the principal cause of the expansion of trade, industry, and finance capital was the demand for luxury goods, principally on the part of the *nouveaux riches*, the courts, and the aristocracy. He locates the source of this increased demand, in turn, in the new understanding of the sale of "free" love, sensual refinement, and the political economy of courtship during this period. This new source of demand meant that fashion became a driving force for the upper classes, satiated only by ever-increasing quantities and ever-differentiated qualities of articles for consumption. This intensification of demand, sexual and political in its origins, signaled the end of a seigneurial lifestyle at the same time as it stimulated nascent capitalist manufacture and trade.

Although Sombart's general approach to the social history of capitalism was, during and after his lifetime, legitimately criticized for a variety of empirical deficiencies and methodological idiosyncracies, it remains a powerful (though subterranean) alternative to both the Marxian and the Weberian views of the origins of occidental capitalism. In its focus on consumption and demand, it belongs to an oppositional and minority tradition, as Sombart was well aware. In this sense, Sombart is an early critic of what Jean Baudrillard calls the "mirror of production," in which much dominant theory of the political economy of the modern West has seen itself. In his emphasis on demand, in his key observations about the politics of fashion, in his placement of economic drives in the context of transformations of sexuality, and in his dialectical view of the relationship between luxury and necessity, Sombart anticipates recent semiotic approaches to economic behavior, such as those of Baudrillard, Bourdieu, Kristeva, and others.

Sombart's approach has recently been revived in an extremely interesting study of the cultural background of early capitalism by Chandra Mukerji (1983). Mukerji's argument, which converges at several points with my own, is that far from being a *result* of the industrial/technological revolution of the nineteenth century, a materialist culture and a new consumption oriented to products and goods from all over the world was the *prerequisite* for the technological revolution of industrial capitalism. In this bold critique of the Weberian hypothesis about the role of Puritan asceticism in providing the cultural context for capitalist calculation, Mukerji follows Nef (1958) and others. Her argument is a sophisticated historical account of the cultural backdrop of early capitalism in Europe. It provides fresh evidence and arguments for placing taste, demand and fashion at the heart of a cultural account of the origins of occidental capitalism, and for the centrality of "things" to this ideology in Renaissance Europe (see also Goldthwaite 1983).

For our purposes, the importance of Sombart's model of the relationship between luxury and early capitalism lies less in the temporal and spatial specifics of his argument (which is a matter for historians of early modern Europe), than in the generalizability of the *logic* of his argument regarding the cultural basis of demand for at least some kinds of commodities, those that he calls luxuries.

I propose that we regard luxury goods not so much in contrast to necessities (a contrast filled with problems), but as goods whose principal use is *rhetorical* and *social*, goods that are simply *incarnated signs*. The necessity to which *they* respond is fundamentally political. Better still, since most luxury goods are used (though in special ways and at special cost), it might make more sense to regard luxury as a special "register" of consumption (by analogy to the linguistic model) than to regard them as a special class of thing. The signs of this register, in relation to commodities, are some or all of the following attributes: (1) restriction, either by price or by law, to elites; (2) complexity of acquisition, which may or may not be a function of real "scarcity"; (3) semiotic virtuosity, that is, the capacity to signal fairly complex social messages (as do pepper in cuisine, silk in dress, jewels in adornment, and relics in worship); (4) specialized knowledge as a prerequisite for their "appropriate" consumption, that is, regulation by fashion; and (5) a high degree of linkage of their consumption to body, person, and personality.

From the consumption point of view, aspects of this luxury register can accrue to any and all commodities to some extent, but some commodities, in certain contexts, come to exemplify the luxury register, and these can loosely be described as luxury goods. Looked at this way, all societies display some demand for luxury goods, and one could argue that it is only in Europe after 1800 (after the eclipse of the sumptuary laws), that this demand is freed from political regulation and left to the "free" play of the marketplace and of fashion. From this point of view, fashion and sumptuary regulation are opposite poles in the social regulation of demand, particularly for goods with high discriminatory value. In certain periods, the flow of luxury goods displays a powerful tension between these two pulls: the last centuries of the *ancien régime* in Europe, for example, show pulls in both directions. The first decades of colonial contact almost everywhere also display this tension between new fashions and existing sumptuary regulations. Fashion, in these contexts, is the urge to imitate the new powers, and this urge is often integrated, for better or worse, with traditional sumptuary imperatives. This tension, at the level of demand and consumption, is of course linked to the tensions between indigenous and introduced production systems and goods, and indigenous and introduced media of exchange. An extremely interesting case study of the complex links between trade, fashion, sumptuary law, and technology is Mukerji's discussion of the calico connection between England and India in the seventeenth century (Mukerji 1983:166–209).

The second important matter to which Sombart directs our attention is the complexity of the links between luxury goods and more mundane commodities. In the case with which he is concerned, the links principally involve the production process. Thus, in early modern Europe, what Sombart regards as primary luxury goods have as their prerequisites secondary and tertiary production processes: the manufacture of silk looms supports silk-weaving centers, which in turn support the creation of luxury furnishings and clothing; the sawmill produces wood that is critical to the production of fine cabinets; when timber is exhausted, coal comes to be in great demand for the glass industry and other luxury industries; iron foundries provide the pipes critical for the fountains of Versailles (Sombart 1967:145–66). To the degree that a growth in demand for primary luxury goods is critical to the expansion of production of second-order and third-order instruments, then the demand for luxuries has system-wide economic implications. Such is the case for complex early modern economies.

But in economies of different scale, structure, and industrial organization, the connection between luxury goods and goods from other registers of use may involve not the ripples of a complex set of production milieux and forms but, critically, the domains of exchange and consumption. Thus, to return to the kula systems of Oceania, recent analyses make it clear that the "trade" in kula valuables is related in a complex social and strategic dialectic with inputs from, and drains into, other exchange registers, which may involve marriage, death, and inheritance, purchase and sale, and so forth (see especially Weiner 1983).

Last, trade in luxuries may well provide an amicable, durable, and sentimental framework for the conduct of exchange in other goods and in other modes: here again the occurrence of *gimwali* or market-style exchange against the backdrop of kula is an apposite primitive example (Uberoi 1962). A very modern example of this type of relationship between trade in the luxury register and trade in less symbolically loaded registers is the commercial relationship between the

United States and the USSR. Here, the strategic arms limitations talks can be seen as a highly competitive species of luxury trade, where the luxury in question is the guaranteed nuclear restraint of the opposite side. The ups and downs of this trade are the prerequisite for the movement of other commodities, such as foodgrains and high technology. It is precisely this type of politically mediated relationship between different registers of commodity trade that is aggressively exploited in the recent U.S. policy of "linkage," whereby Soviet intractability in one sphere of exchange is punished in another. In simpler times and societies, the equivalent of the SALT talks was to be seen in the diplomacy of gift exchange between traders and chiefs or simply chiefs and other chiefs, disturbances in which could abort trade in less loaded registers.

In all these ways, we can see that the demand for the kinds of valuables we call luxuries and what I have called the luxury register of any particular flow of commodities is intimately connected with other, more everyday, high-turnover registers in the language of commodities in social life.

This may also be the appropriate juncture at which to make a general point about the commodities dealt with in this volume, many of which have a strong luxury dimension and thus appear to constitute a sample that is bound to favor a cultural approach in a way that humbler, more mass-produced commodities might not. The fact is that the line between luxury and everyday commodities is not only a historically shifting one, but even at any given point in time what looks like a homogeneous, bulk item of extremely limited semantic range can become very different in the course of distribution and consumption. Perhaps the best example of a humble commodity whose history is filled with cultural idiosyncracies is sugar, as is shown in very different ways by Sidney Mintz (1979) and Fernand Braudel (1982: 190–4). The distinction between humble commodities and more exotic ones is thus not a difference in kind, but most often a difference in demand over time or, sometimes, a difference between loci of production and those of consumption. From the point of view of scale, style, and economic significance, Mukerji has made an eloquent argument, at least in the case of early modern Europe, for *not* drawing rigid boundaries between elite and mass consumption, luxury goods and humbler ones, consumer and capital goods, or the aesthetics of display as against the designs of primary production settings (Mukerji 1983: Chapter 1).

Demand is thus neither a mechanical response to the structure and level of production nor a bottomless natural appetite. It is a complex social mechanism that mediates between short- and long-term patterns of commodity circulation. Short-term strategies of diversion (such as those discussed in the previous section) might entail small shifts in demand that can gradually transform commodity flows in the long run. Looked at from the point of view of the reproduction of patterns of commodity flow (rather than their alteration), however, long-established patterns of demand act as constraints on any given set of commodity paths. One reason such paths are inherently shaky, especially when they involve transcultural flows of commodities, is that they rest on unstable distributions of knowledge, a subject to which we now turn.

Knowledge and commodities

This section is concerned with the peculiarities of knowledge that accompany relatively complex, long-distance, intercultural flows of commodities, though even in more homogeneous, small-scale, and low-technology loci of commodity flow, there is always the potential for discrepancies in knowledge about commodities. But as distances increase, so the negotiation of the tension between knowledge and ignorance becomes itself a critical determinant of the flow of commodities.

Commodities represent very complex social forms and distributions of knowledge. In the first place, and crudely, such knowledge can be of two sorts: the knowledge (technical, social, aesthetic, and so forth) that goes into the production of the commodity; and the knowledge that goes into appropriately consuming the commodity. The production knowledge that is read into a commodity is quite different from the consumption knowledge that is read from the commodity. Of course, these two readings will diverge proportionately as the social, spatial, and temporal distance between producers and consumers increases. As we shall see, it may not be accurate to regard knowledge at the production locus of a commodity as exclusively technical or empirical and knowledge at the consumption end as exclusively evaluative or ideological. Knowledge at both poles has technical, mythological, and evaluative components, and the two poles are susceptible to mutual and dialectical interaction.

If we regard some commodities as having "life histories" or "careers" in a meaningful sense, then it becomes useful to look at the distribution of knowledge at various points in their careers. Such careers have the greatest uniformity at the production pole, for it is likely that at the moment of production, the commodity in question has had the least opportunity to accumulate an idiosyncratic biography or enjoy a peculiar career. Thus the production locus of commodities is likely to be dominated by culturally standardized recipes for fabrication. Thus factories, fields, forges, mines, workshops, and most other production loci are repositories, in the first place, of technical production knowledge of a highly standardized sort. Nevertheless, even here it is worth noting that the technical knowledge required for the production of primary commodities (grains, metals, fuels, oils) is much more likely to be standardized than the knowledge required for secondary or luxury commodities, where taste, judgment, and individual experience are likely to create sharp variations in production knowledge. Nevertheless, the thrust of commoditization at the production end is toward standardization of technical (how-to) knowledge. Of course, with all commodities, whether primary or not, technical knowledge is always deeply interpenetrated with cosmological, sociological, and ritual assumptions that are likely to be widely shared. Evans-Pritchard's Azande potters (Evans-Pritchard 1937), Taussig's Colombian peasant producers (Taussig 1980), Nancy Munn's Gawan canoe makers (Munn 1977), Stephen Gudeman's Panamanian sugarcane producers (Gudeman 1984), all combine technological and cosmological layers in their production discourse. In most societies, such production knowledge is subject to some discontinuity in its social distribution, either by simple criteria of age or gender, by more complex criteria distinguishing artisan households, castes, or villages from the rest of society, or by even more complex divisions of labor setting apart entrepreneurs and workers, in role terms, from householders and consumers, as in most modern societies.

But there is another dimension of production knowledge and that is knowledge of the market, the consumer, the destination of the commodity. In small-scale, traditional societies, such knowledge is relatively direct and complete as regards internal consumption, but more erratic and incomplete as regards external demand. In precapitalist contexts, of course, the translation of external demands to local producers is the province of the trader and his agents, who provide logistical and price bridges between worlds of knowledge that may have minimal direct contact. Thus it is reasonably certain that traditional Borneo forest dwellers had relatively little idea of the uses to which the birds' nests they sold to intermediaries have played in Chinese medical and culinary practice. This paradigm of merchant bridges across large gaps in knowledge between producer and consumer characterizes the movement of most commodities throughout history, up to the present. Today, these bridges persist either because of unclosable cultural gaps (as between opium producers in Asia and the Middle East and addicts and dealers in New York) or because of the infinitesimal specialization of commodity production or its inverse – the distance between a particular bulk commodity (such as, say, copper) and the hundreds of transformations it will undergo before reaching the consumer. We note that such large gaps in knowledge of the ultimate market by the producer are usually conducive to high profits in trade and to the relative deprivation of the producing country or class in relation to the consumers and the trader (see Spooner, Chapter 7).

Problems involving knowledge, information, and ignorance are not restricted to the production and consumption poles of the careers of commodities, but characterize the process of circulation and exchange itself. In a powerful cultural account of the Moroccan bazaar, Clifford Geertz has placed the search for reliable information at the heart of this institution and has shown how difficult it is for actors in this system to gain reliable information either about people or about things (Geertz 1979). Much of the institutional structure and cultural form of the bazaar is double-edged, making reliable knowledge hard to get and also facilitating the search for it. It is tempting to conclude that such complex and culturally organized information mazes are a special feature of bazaar-style economies, and are absent in nonmarket, simple economies, as well as in advanced industrial ones. Yet, as Geertz himself suggests (p. 224) the bazaar as an analytical category may well apply to the used-car market (though not the new-car market) in contemporary industrial economies. We can put this point in a more general form: bazaar-style information searches are likely to characterize any exchange setting where the quality and the appropriate valuation of goods are not standardized, though the reasons for the lack of standardization, for the volatility of prices, and for the unreliable quality of specific things of a certain type may vary enormously. Indeed, systems for the exchange of kula valuables, of used cars, and of oriental rugs, though they occur in very different institutional and cultural settings, may all involve bazaar-style information economies.

But the gaps in knowledge and the difficulties of communication between producer and consumer are not really obstacles to the vigorous flow of bulk commodities intended for multiple industrial transformations before they reach the consumer. In the case of such commodities (sometimes called primary commodities), an almost infinite series of small, overlapping circles of knowledge can link original producer and terminal consumer. But this is not the case with commodities by destination, which are largely "fabricated," in Nancy Munn's sense, early in their careers (Munn 1977). These require more direct mechanisms for the satisfactory negotiation of price and the matching of consumer taste to producer skill, knowledge, and tradition. Perhaps the best examples of this kind of more direct communication involve the international commerce in ready-made clothes (Swallow 1982) and the tourist art trade in what Nelson Graburn (1976) has called the fourth world.

Whenever there are discontinuities in the knowledge that accompanies the movement of commodities, problems involving authenticity and expertise enter the picture. Several of the papers in this volume deal with these two issues. The first is Brian Spooner's paper on oriental carpets, which is a provocative anthropological interpretation of a problem that brings together art history, economic history, and cultural analysis. Spooner's topic – the shifting terms of the relationship between producers and consumers of oriental carpets – brings into focus a particularly striking example of a commodity linking two largely isolated worlds of meaning and function. Traded originally through a series of Asian and European entrepôts, each of which imposed economic and taste filters, today oriental carpets involve a much more direct negotiation between Western upper-middle-class tastes and Central Asian weaving organizations. But this shift involves not simply changes in the context of the negotiation of price. What is being negotiated, as Spooner pithily puts it, is authenticity. That is, as the pace of mobility and the crowding at the top of Western society become more marked, and as technology permits the multiplication of prestige objects, there is an increasingly ironic dialogue between the need for ever-shifting criteria of authenticity in the West and the economic motives of the producers and dealers. The world of dealers, further, becomes itself tied up with the politics of connoisseurship and the formalization of rug lore in the West.

In a general way, we can suggest that with luxury commodities like oriental rugs, as the distance between consumers and producers is shrunk, so the issue of *exclusivity* gives way to the issue of *authenticity*. That is, under premodern conditions, the long-distance movement of precious commodities entailed costs that made the acquisition of them *in itself* a marker of exclusivity and an instrument of sumptuary distinction. Where the control of such objects was not directly subject to state regulation, it was indirectly regulated by the cost of acquisition, so that they stayed within the hands of the few. As technology changes, the reproduction of these objects on a mass basis becomes possible, the dialogue between consumers and the original source becomes more direct, and middle-class consumers become capable (legally and economically) of vying for these objects. The only way to preserve the function of these commodities in the prestige economies of the modern West is to complicate the criteria of authenticity. The very complicated competition and collaboration between "experts" from the art world, dealers, producers, scholars, and consumers is part of the political economy of taste in the contemporary West. This political economy has perhaps best been explored in France, by Baudrillard (1981) and Bourdieu (1984).

There is a particular set of issues concerning authenticity and expertise that plagues the modern West, and this set, which revolves around the issues of good taste, expert knowledge, "originality," and social distinction, is especially visible in the domain of art and art objects. In his famous essay on "The Work of Art in the Age of Mechanical Reproduction," Walter Benjamin (1968; original edition, 1936) recognized that the aura of an authentic work of art is tied up with its originality, and that this aura, which is the basis of its authenticity, is jeopardized by modern reproductive technologies. In this sense copies, forgeries, and fakes, which have a long history, do not threaten the aura of the original but seek to partake of it. In a footnote to this essay, Benjamin made the following shrewd observation: "To be sure, at the time of its origin a medieval picture of the Madonna could not yet be said to be 'authentic.' It became 'authentic' only during the succeeding centuries and perhaps most strikingly so during the last one." (Benjamin 1936:243.) In an essay on the concept of the "signature" in the modern art world, Baudrillard (1981:103) pushes this point further:

Until the nineteenth century, the copy of an original work had its own value, it was a legitimate practice. In our own time the copy is illegitimate, inauthentic: it is no longer "art." Similarly, the concept of forgery has changed – or rather, it suddenly appears with the advent of modernity. Formerly painters regularly used collaborators or "negros": one specialized in trees, another in animals. The act of painting, and so the signature as well, did not bear the same mythological insistence upon authenticity – that moral imperative to which modern art is dedicated and by which it becomes modern – which has been evident ever since the relation to illustration and hence the very meaning of the artistic object changed with the act of painting itself.

With this in mind, it is possible to place the consumption side of the processes that Spooner observes in the context of what Baudrillard sees as the emergence of the "object," that is, a thing that is no longer just a product or a commodity, but essentially a sign in a system of signs of status. Objects, in Baudrillard's view, emerge fully only in this century in the modern West, in the context of the theoretical formulations of the Bauhaus (Baudrillard 1981:185), though it has recently been shown that the emergence of the object in European culture can be traced back at least to the Renaissance (Mukerji 1983). Fashion is the cultural medium in which objects, in Baudrillard's sense, move.

Yet problems of authenticity, expertise, and the evaluation of commodities are obviously not only twentieth-century phenomena. We have already mentioned Patrick Geary's paper in this volume, on the trade in relics in Carolingian Europe. Here there is a crucial problem with regard to authentication, and here too it is tied to the fact that relics circulate over long periods of time, through many hands, and over large distances. Here too there is a concern with fakery, an obsession with origins. But the cultural regime for authentication is quite different from the modern one. Though there is a small body of technical procedures and clerical prerogatives involved in authentication, it is by and large a matter in which popular understandings about ritual efficacy and folk criteria of authenticity play a central role. Authenticity here is not the province of experts and esoteric criteria, but of popular and public kinds of verification and confirmation.

The problem of specialized knowledge and of authenticity takes yet another form in William Reddy's fascinating case study of the shifts in the organization of expert knowledge in the textile industry in France before and after the Revolution of 1789. Focusing on two commercial dictionaries published in France, in the 1720's and in 1839, Reddy argues that though the French Revolution appeared to destroy a whole way of life overnight, this was not in fact the case. The vast edifice of everyday knowledge and practice changed slowly, uncertainly, and reluctantly. One example of this extended crisis – a period, that is, when knowledge, practice, and policy were notably out of step – was to be seen in the codified world of knowledge regarding the trade in textiles. In complex early modern systems of commodity flow, Reddy shows us, the relationship between technical knowledge, taste, and political regulation are very complex and slow to change. Ways of knowing, judging, trading, and buying are harder to change than ideologies about guilds, prices, or production. It took a very complex series of piecemeal and asynchronous shifts in politics, technology, and culture, stretching over a century, before a new epistemological framework emerged for classifying commercial products. In this new scheme, we might say that *goods* were reconceived as *products*, and the "gaze" (in Foucault's sense) of the consumer and the trader had given way to the "gaze" of the producer. Textiles, in the first third of the nineteenth century, came to be seen in what Baudrillard calls the "mirror of production." Authenticity, in this early industrial framework, is no longer a matter of connoisseurship, but of objectively given production methods. The expertise of the dealer and the financier gives way to the expertise of industrialized production. Reddy's essay reminds us that the social history of things, even of humble things like cloth, reflects very complicated shifts in the organization of knowledge and modes of production. Such shifts have a cultural dimension that cannot be deduced from, or reduced to, changes in technology and economy.

One final example of the very complex relationship between authenticity, taste, and the politics of consumer – producer relations concerns what have been called ethnic or tourist arts. These have been subject to fairly close study by anthropologists, and there is one important collection of essays on the subject (Graburn 1976). Though the phenomena discussed under these labels include a bewildering range of objects, as Graburn notes in his introductory essay, they constitute perhaps the best example of the diversities in taste, understanding, and use between producers and consumers. At the producer end, one sees traditions of fabrication (again, following Munn), changing in response to commercial and aesthetic impositions or temptations from larger-scale, and sometimes far-away consumers. At the other end, one has souvenirs, mementos, curios, collections, exhibits, and the status contests, expertise, and commerce on which they rest. In between one has a series of commercial and aesthetic links, sometimes complex, multiple, and indirect and sometimes overt, few, and direct. In both cases, tourist art constitutes a special commodity traffic, in which the group identities of producers are tokens for the status politics of consumers.

Alfred Gell's paper in this volume contains some particularly astute observations on the kinds of complicated refractions in perception that can accompany the interaction of small traditional populations with larger-scale economies and cultural systems. Reflecting on the Muria interest in brassware produced from outside their region, Gell notes that "the Muria, a traditional people with no home-grown tradition of craft and prestige-good production, are actually much more similar to Westerners, seeking authenticity in the exotic, than they are to traditional craft-producer societies, the category to which they are erroneously believed to belong." Recent work on exhibitions and museums by anthropologists and historians (Benedict 1983; Breckenridge 1984), as well as by semioticians and literary theorists, extends and deepens our understanding of the role of objects of the "other" in creating the souvenir, the collection, the exhibit and the trophy in the modern West (Baudrillard 1968, 1981; Stewart 1984).[10] In a more general way, it might be said that as the institutional and spatial journeys of commodities grow more complex, and the alienation of producers, traders, and consumers from one another increases, culturally formed mythologies about commodity flow are likely to emerge.

Culturally constructed stories and ideologies about commodity flows are commonplace in all societies. But such stories acquire especially intense, new, and striking qualities when the spatial, cognitive, or institutional distances between production, distribution, and consumption are great. Such distancing either can be institutionalized within a single complex economy or can be a function of new kinds of links between hitherto separated societies and economies. The institutionalized divorce (in knowledge, interest, and role) between persons involved in various aspects of the flow of commodities generates specialized mythologies. I consider, in this section, three variations on such mythologies and the contexts in which they arise. (1) Mythologies produced by traders and speculators who are largely indifferent to both the production origins and the consumption destination of commodities, except insofar as they affect fluctuations in price. The best examples of this type are the commodity futures markets in complex capitalist economies, specifically the Chicago grain exchange in the early part of this century. (2) Mythologies produced by consumers (or potential consumers) alienated from the production and distribution process of key commodities. Here the best examples come from the cargo cults of Oceania. And (3) mythologies produced by workers in the production process who are completely divorced from the distribution and consumption logics of the commodities they produce. The modern tin miners of Bolivia described by Michael Taussig in *The Devil and Commodity Fetishism in South America*, are an excellent case in point. In the following paragraphs, I briefly discuss each of these variations, starting with the capitalist commodity markets.

The commodity sphere in the modern capitalist world-system appears at first glance to be a vast, impersonal machine, governed by large-scale movements of prices, complex institutional interests, and a totally demystified, bureaucratic, and self-regulating character. Nothing, it appears, could be further from the values, mechanisms, and ethics of commodity flows in small-scale societies. Yet this impression is false.

It should by now be clear that capitalism represents not simply a techno-economic design, but a complex cultural system with a very special history in the modern West. This view, which has always had distinguished adherents in economic and social history (Weber 1958; Sombart 1967; Nef 1958; Braudel 1982; Lopez 1971; Thirsk 1978), has received a new impetus from anthropologists and sociologists of Euro-American culture (Baudrillard 1981; Bourdieu 1984; Douglas and Isherwood 1981; Mukerji 1983; Sahlins 1976).

The study of the cultural design of capitalism in its American form has been undertaken with enormous vigor in the last decade, and historians, anthropologists, and sociologists are beginning to put together a rich picture of the culture of capitalism in the United States (Collins 1979; DiMaggio 1982; Lears 1984; Marcus (in press); Schudson 1984). Though this larger context lies outside the scope of this discussion, it is quite clear that capitalism is itself an extremely complex cultural and historical formation, and in this formation commodities and their meanings have played a critical role. One example of the peculiar and striking cultural expressions of modern capitalism is the market in commodity futures in the United States, which developed in the middle of the nineteenth century and whose paradigmatic example is the Chicago Grain Exchange.

Trade in bulk commodities remains today an extremely important part of world trade and the world economic system (see, for example, Adams and Behrman 1982), and this large-scale commodity trade remains perhaps the central arena where the contradictions of international capitalism can be observed. Central among these contradictions is the one between the free-trade ideology of classical capitalism and the various forms of protectionism, cartels, and regulatory agreements that have evolved to restrict this freedom in the interests of various coalitions of producers (Nappi 1979). Commodity futures markets represent the institutional arena where the risks that attend the national and international flows of these commodities are negotiated by hedging on the part of some and sheer speculation on the part of others.

Markets in commodity futures revolve around a large number of transactions involving contracts to buy and sell commodities, at future dates. This trade in contracts is a paper trade, which rarely involves actual exchanges of the commodities themselves between traders. Like the stock market, these markets are speculative tournaments, in which the play of price, risk, and exchange appears *totally* divorced, for the spectator, from the entire process of production, distribution, sale, and consumption. One might say that speculating in commodity futures makes a dramatic separation between price and value, with the latter of no concern at all. In this sense, the logic of trade in commodity futures is, following Marx, a kind of meta-fetishization, where not only does the commodity become a substitute for the social relations that lie behind it, but the movement of *prices* becomes an autonomous substitute for the flow of the commodities themselves.

Though this double degree of removal from the social relations of production and exchange makes commodity futures markets very different from other tournaments of value, such as these represented in the kula, there are some interesting and revealing parallels. In both cases, the tournament occurs in a special arena, insulated from practical economic life and subject to special rules. In both cases, what are exchanged are tokens of value that can be transformed into other media only by a complex set of steps and only in unusual circumstances. In both cases, there are specific ways in which the reproduction of the larger economy is articulated with the structure of the tournament economy.

But perhaps most important, in both cases, there is an agonistic, romantic, individualistic, and gamelike ethos that stands in contrast to the ethos of everyday economic behavior. The role of kula participation in the construction of fame and reputation for individuals in island Oceania is very clear. But the same is the case with commodity futures markets. In the second half of the nineteenth century, the "wheat pit" (the Grain Exchange) in Chicago was obviously the scene of the making and breaking of individual reputations, of intense and obsessive competitions between specific individuals, and of hubristic efforts on the part of particular men to corner the market (Dies 1925; 1975). This agonistic, obsessive, and romantic ethos has not disappeared from the commodity markets, as we are reminded by the case of the Hunt brothers in regard to silver (Marcus: in press), although the moral, institutional, and political framework that governs speculation in commodities has changed a good deal since the nineteenth century. Of course, there are many differences between the kula and the commodity futures market in scale, instrumentalities, context, and goals. But the similarities are real, and, as I suggested earlier, many societies create specialized arenas for tournaments of value in which specialized commodity tokens are traded, and such trade, through the economies of status, power, or wealth, affects more mundane commodity flows. The trade in relics, the market in commodity futures, the kula, the potlatch, and the Central Asian *buzkashi* (Azoy 1982) are all examples of such "tournaments of value." In each case, we need a fuller examination of the modes of articulation of these "tournament" economies with their more routine commodity contexts than is possible here.

The mythology of circulation generated in commodity markets (as well as, in other ways, in stock markets) is a mythology of rumor mixed with more reliable information: regarding commodity reserves, government regulations, seasonal shifts, consumer variables, intra-market developments (including the rumored intention or motives of other speculators), and so on. These constitute an endlessly shifting (and potentially infinite) scenario of variables that affect price. Though there have been consistent improvements in the technical basis for analyzing and successfully playing the commodities market, there remains the quasi-magical search for the formula (divinatory rather than efficacious) that will prove to be the fail-safe predictor of price shifts (Powers 1973:47). The structural basis of this mythology of circulation of commodities is the fact that it plays *indefinitely* with the fluctuation of prices; that it seeks to exhaust an inexhaustible series of variables that affect price; and that its concern with commodities is purely *informational* and *semiotic* and is divorced from consumption altogether. The irrational desire to corner the market in some commodity, the counterintuitive search for magical formulas to predict price changes, the controlled collective hysteria, all these are the product of this complete conversion of commodities to signs (Baudrillard 1981), which are themselves capable of yielding profit if manipulated properly. The primitive counterpart to this type of mythological and context-free construction of commodities is to be found in that anthropological staple, the cargo cults that multiplied in the stateless societies of the Pacific in this century.

Cargo cults are social movements of intense, millennial character centered on the symbolism of European goods. They have occurred mainly in the Pacific since early colonial contact, though they have precolonial antecedents and analogies in other societies. They have been subject to intensive analysis by anthropologists, who have looked at them as psychological, religious, economic, and political phenomena. Though there has been considerable variation in the anthropological interpretation of these movements, most observers agree that the emergence of cargo cults in early colonial Pacific societies has something to do with the transformation of production relations in this new context, the inability of natives to afford the new European goods they desired; the arrival of a new theological and cosmological system through the missionaries; and the resulting ambivalence toward indigenous ritual forms. The result was a series of movements, spread throughout Oceania (and later Melanesia) of uneven success, duration, and intensity, which both mimicked and protested European social and ritual forms and took either strongly oppositional or strongly revivalistic positions in regard to their own myths and rituals of prosperity and exchange. In the symbolism of many of these movements, an important role was played by the promise by the leader/prophet of the arrival of valued European goods by plane or by ship and their "showering" upon the true believers in the movement and in the prophet.

It is difficult to doubt the contention of Worsely (1957) and others that the symbolism of the mysterious arrival of European goods has a lot to do with the distortion of indigenous exchange relations under colonial rule, the perception by the natives of the apparent contradiction between the wealth of Europeans (despite their lack of effort) and their own poverty (despite their arduous labor). It is no surprise, given their sudden subjection to a complex international economical system of which they saw only few and mysterious aspects, that their response was occasionally to seek to replicate what they regarded as the magical mode of production of these goods.

When we look at the symbolism and ritual practice of these movements, it is possible to see that they constitute not just a myth about the origins of European commodities, but an attempt to ritually replicate what were perceived as the social modalities of European life. This is the significance of the use of European military forms, speech forms, titles, and so forth, in these movements. Though often ordered in indigenous patterns, the ritual practice of cargo cults was in many cases no less than a massive effort to mime those European social forms that seemed most conducive to the production of European goods. In a kind of reverse fetishism, what was replicated was what was seen as the most potent of European social and linguistic forms in an effort to increase the likelihood of the arrival of European commodities. But Glynn Cochrane (1970) has reminded us that these cults were, however distorted, pursuits not of *all* European commodities, but only of those commodities that were seen as particularly conducive to the maintenance of status discontinuities in local societies. Cargo cults also represent a particular mythology of production of European finished goods by natives embroiled in the production of primary commodities for the world trade and an associated imitative and revitalistic ritual. The commodities involved in cargo, as with kula valuables, and other indigenous forms of specialized exchange, are seen as metonymic of a whole system of power, prosperity, and status. Cargo beliefs are an extreme example of the theories that are likely to proliferate when consumers are kept completely ignorant of the conditions of production and distribution of commodities and are unable to gain access to them freely. Such deprivation creates the mythologies of the alienated consumer, just as the commodity markets of modern capitalism spawn the mythologies of the alienated trader. We turn, finally, to the third variation, the mythologies of producers at the service of demand and distribution forces outside their control and beyond their universe of knowledge.

For this type of mythology, the best account we have is Taussig's analysis of the changing symbolism of the Devil among Bolivian tin miners since the arrival of the Spaniards (Taussig 1980). Briefly, the story runs as follows. Before the arrival of the Spaniards, mining was a small-scale activity run as a state monopoly. With the arrival of the Spanish, mining became a voracious keystone of the colonial economy, the cause of massive dislocation and increased mortality among the Aymara Indian population of Bolivia. Mining always involved ritual and magic, but only after the Spanish conquest did this involve the spirit of evil, symbolized in a figure called Tio (uncle), understood in the new Christian idiom as the Devil, who was seen as the spirit owner of the mines. This devil figure came to represent all the alien forces of the new capitalist economy, which miners simultaneously feared, hated, and served, in contrast to their traditional forms of reciprocal economy. Caught between state control of production and the international commodity market, on the one hand, and the Devil on the other, they worked out a ritual that reflects the ambiguities and contradictions of an economic practice that straddles two incompatible worlds:

In effect the extended chain of exchanges in the Andes is this: peasants exchange gifts with the spirit owner; the spirit owner converts these gifts into precious metal; the miners excavate this metal, which they "find" so long as they perform rites of gift exchange with spirit; the miners' labor, which is embodied in the tin ore, is sold as a commodity to the legal owners and employers; these last sell the ore on the international commodity market. Thus, reciprocal gift exchanges end as commodity exchanges; standing between the devil and the state, the miners mediate this transformation. This circuit ensures barrenness and death instead of fertility and prosperity. It is based on the transformation of reciprocity into commodity exchange. (Taussig 1980:224).

The rites of production in the tin mines of Bolivia and their associated mythology are not a simple carryover of peasant rites of production. They reflect the tensions of a society in which commoditization has not yet become commonplace, where the fetishism of commodities, because of its incomplete hegemony, is regarded as evil and dangerous, and there is thus a paradoxical attempt to envelop the Devil in reciprocal rituals. This is not commodity fetishism in the classic Marxian sense (where products conceal and represent social relations), but a more literal fetishism, in which the commodity, itself iconicized as the Devil, is made the pivot of a set of ritual transactions designed to offset the cosmological and physical risks of mining. In this mythology of alienated producers/extractors, the impersonal and invisible sources of control (the state) and of demand (the world commodity market) are relocated in an icon of danger and greed, social metaphors for the commodity economy. Though Taussig's account tends, like Gregory's and many others, to overstate the contrast between gift and commodity economies, his is a persuasive account of the literal fetishism of commodities that seems to accompany primary commodity production for unknown and uncontrolled markets.

In each of the examples I have discussed, the commodity futures market, cargo cults, and mining mythology, mythological understandings of the circulation of commodities are generated because of the detachment, indifference, or ignorance of participants as regards all but a single aspect of the economic trajectory of the commodity. Enclaved in either the production, speculative trade, or consumption locus of the flow of commodities, technical knowledge tends to be quickly subordinated to more idiosyncratic subcultural theories about the origins and destinations of things. These are examples of the many forms that the fetishism of commodities can take when there are sharp discontinuities in the distribution of knowledge concerning their trajectories of circulation.

There is one final point to be made about the relationship between knowledge and commodities, and it is one which reminds us that the comparison of capitalistic societies with other kinds of societies is a complicated matter. In complex capitalistic societies, it is not only the case that knowledge is segmented (even fragmented) as between producers, distributors, speculators, and consumers (and different subcategories of each). The fact is that knowledge *about* commodities is itself increasingly commoditized. Such commoditization of knowledge regarding commodities is of course part of a larger problem of the political economy of culture itself (Collins 1979), in which expertise, credentialism, and high-brow aestheticism (Bourdieu 1984) all play different roles. Thus, though even in the simplest economies there is a complex traffic in things, it is only with increased social, technical, and conceptual differentiation that what we may call a *traffic in criteria* concerning things develops. That is, only in the latter situation does the buying and selling of expertise regarding the technical, social, or aesthetic appropriateness of commodities become widespread. Of course, such a traffic in commodity criteria is not confined to capitalist societies, but there seems to be considerable evidence that it is in such societies that such traffic is most dense.

In contemporary capitalist economies, further, it is difficult to separate the commoditization of goods from the commoditization of services. Indeed the routine pairing of goods and services is itself a heritage of neoclassical economics. This is not to say that services (sexual, occupational, ritual, or emotional) lie wholly outside the domain of commoditization in noncapitalist societies. But it is only in complex postindustrial economies that services are a dominant, even definitive, feature of the world of commodity exchange. A thorough comparative analysis of the service dimension of commoditization, however, is something that a collection such as this one can only hope to stimulate.

But perhaps the best example of the relationship between knowledge and the control of demand is provided by the role of advertising in contemporary capitalist societies. Much has been written about this important topic, and in the United States there are signs of a revived debate about the functional effectiveness of advertising. In a widely publicized recent study, Michael Schudson (1984) has questioned the neo-Marxist analyses of the manipulation of consumers by advertising in America. He proposes that the textual and graphic images produced by the advertising machine are better regarded as a species of "capitalist realism," a form of cultural representation of the virtues of the capitalist lifestyle, rather than as techniques for seduction into specific acts of consumption. The adulation with which this argument has been greeted by the advertising profession is a source of some circumstantial doubt about the argument itself. What is probably the case is that any decisive analysis of the effects of advertising would have to proceed to see the images of advertising in tandem with changing ideas about art, design, lifestyle, and distinction, in order to unravel the role of this kind of "capitalist realism" in the social mobilization of demand (Hebdige 1983; Bourdieu 1984).

But it does seem worthwhile to make one observation about advertising that is relevant to the present argument. Whatever the effectiveness of advertising in ensuring the success of any particular product, it does seem true that contemporary modes of representation in advertising (particularly on television) share a certain strategy. The strategy consists in taking what are often perfectly ordinary, mass-produced, cheap, even shoddy, products and making them seem somehow (in Simmel's sense) desirable-yet-reachable. Perfectly ordinary goods are placed in a sort of pseudoenclaved zone, *as if* they were not available to anyone who can pay the price. The largely social images that create this illusion of exclusivity might be glossed as the fetishism of the consumer rather than of the commodity. The images of sociality (belonging, sex appeal, power, distinction, health, togetherness, camaraderie) that underly much advertising focus on the transformation of the consumer to the point where the particular commodity being sold is almost an afterthought. This double inversion of the relationship between people and things might be regarded as the critical cultural move of advanced capitalism.

The relationship between knowledge and commodities has many dimensions that have not been discussed here. But the essential point for my purposes is this: as commodities travel greater distances (institutional, spatial, temporal), knowledge about them tends to become partial, contradictory, and differentiated. But such differentiation may itself (through the mechanisms of tournaments of value, authentication, or frustrated desire) lead to the intensification of demand. If we look at the world of commodities as a shifting series of local (culturally regulated) commodity paths, we can see that the politics of diversion as well as of enclaving often is tied to the possibility or fact of commodity exchanges with other, more distant, systems. At every level where a smaller system interacts with a larger one, the interplay of knowledge and ignorance serves as a turnstile, facilitating the flow of some things and hindering the movement of others. In this sense, even the largest commodity ecumenes are the product of complex interactions between local, politically mediated, systems of demand.

Conclusion: politics and value

Apart from learning some moderately unusual facts, and regarding them from a mildly unconventional point of view, is there any general benefit in looking at the social life of commodities in the manner proposed in this essay? What does this perspective tell us about value and exchange in social life that we did not know already, or that we could not have discovered in a less cumbersome way? Is there any point in taking the heuristic position that commodities exist everywhere and that the spirit of commodity exchange is not wholly divorced from the spirit of other forms of exchange?

In answering these questions, I shall not conduct a tedious review of the main observations made in the course of this essay, but shall go directly to the substance of my proposal. This essay took as its starting point Simmel's view that exchange is the source of value and not vice versa. The papers in this volume permit us to add a critical dimension to Simmel's rather abstract intuition about the social genesis of value.

Politics (in the broad sense of relations, assumptions, and contests pertaining to power) is what links value and exchange in the social life of commodities. In the mundane, day-to-day, small-scale exchanges of things in ordinary life, this fact is not visible, for exchange has the routine and conventionalized look of all customary behavior. But these many ordinary dealings would not be possible were it not for a broad set of agreements concerning what is desirable, what a reasonable "exchange of sacrifices" comprises, and who is permitted to exercise what kind of effective demand in what circumstances. What is political about this process is not just the fact that it signifies and constitutes relations of privilege and social control. What is political about it is the constant tension between the existing frameworks (of price, bargaining, and so forth) and the tendency of commodities to breach these frameworks. This tension itself has its source in the fact that not all parties share the same *interests* in any specific regime of value, nor are the interests of any two parties in a given exchange identical.

At the top of many societies, we have the politics of tournaments of value, and of calculated diversions that might lead to new paths of commodity flow. As expressions of the interests of elites in relation to commoners we have the politics of fashion, of sumptuary law, and of taboo, all of which regulate demand. Yet since commodities constantly spill beyond the boundaries of specific cultures (and thus of specific regimes of value), such political control of demand is always threatened with disturbance. In a surprisingly wide range of societies, it is possible to witness the following common paradox. It is in the interests of those in power to completely freeze the flow of commodities, by creating a closed universe of commodities and a rigid set of regulations about how they are to move. Yet the very nature of contests between those in power (or those who aspire to greater power) tends to invite a loosening of these rules and an expansion of the pool of commodities. This aspect of elite politics is generally the Trojan horse of value shifts. So far as commodities are concerned, the source of politics is the tension between these two tendencies.

We have seen that such politics can take many forms: the politics of diversion and of display; the politics of authenticity and of authentication; the politics of knowledge and of ignorance; the politics of expertise and of sumptuary control; the politics of connoisseurship and of deliberately mobilized demand. The ups and downs of the relations within and between these various dimensions of politics account for the vagaries of demand. It is in this sense that politics is the link between regimes of value and specific flows of commodities.

Ever since Marx and the early political economists, there has not been much mystery about the relationship between politics and production. We are now in a better position to demystify the demand side of economic life.

Notes

This essay was written while the author was a Fellow at the Center for Advanced Study in the Behavioral Sciences, Stanford, California, in 1984–85. For financial support during this period, I acknowledge National Science Foundation Grant No. BNS 8011494 to the Center and a sabbatical grant from the University of Pennsylvania.

In the course of planning and writing this essay, I have accumulated many debts, which it is a pleasure to acknowledge here. In addition to the contributors to this volume, the following persons gave papers on the topic of commodities during 1983–84 at the University of Pennsylvania, which provided me with much to reflect on: Marcello Carmagnani, Philip Curtin, Mary Douglas, Richard Goldthwaite, Stephen Gudeman, George Marcus, Jane Schneider, Anthony Wallace, and Annette Weiner. Participants and commentators at the various sessions of the Ethnohistory Workshop at the University of Pennsylvania during 1983–84 and at the Symposium on Commodities and Culture in May 1984 enriched my own thinking. Igor Kopytoff's paper in this volume is the most recent in a long series of contributions he has made to my ideas about commodities.

Earlier versions of this essay were presented at the Center for Advanced Study in the Behavioral Sciences and at the Department of Anthropology at Stanford University. In these contexts, the following persons made helpful criticisms and suggestions: Paul DiMaggio, Donald Donham, Michael Epelbaum, Ulf Hannerz, Virginia Held, David Hollinger, Mary Ryan, G. William Skinner, Burton Stein, Dennis Thompson, Pierre van den Berghe, and Aram Yengoyan. Finally, as always, Carol A. Breckenridge provided sanity, stimulation, and a sharp critical eye.

1. In starting with exchange, I am aware that I am bucking a trend in recent economic anthropology, which has tended to shift the focus of attention to *production* on the one hand, and *consumption* on the other. This trend was a justifiable response to what had previously been an excessive preoccupation with exchange and circulation. The commodity angle, however, promises to illuminate issues in the study of exchange that had begun to look either boring or incorrigibly mysterious.

2. See Alfred Schmidt (1971:69) for a similar critique of the "idealist" tendency in Marxist studies, which promotes the view that "since Marx reduces all economic categories to relationships between human beings, the world is composed of relations and processes and not of bodily material things." Obviously, careless subscription to *this* point of view can lead to exaggerations of the "vulgar" variety.

3. The use of terms such as "interest" and "calculation," I realize, raises important problems about the comparative study of valuation, exchange, trade, and gift. Although the danger of exporting utilitarian models and assumptions (as well as their close kin, economism and Euro-American

individualism) is serious, it is equally tendentious to reserve for Western man the right to be "interested" in the give and take of material life. What is called for, and does not now exist, except in embryo (see Medick and Sabean 1984), is a framework for the comparative study of economies, in which the cultural variability of "self," "person," and "individual" (following Geertz and Dumont) is allied to a comparative study of calculation (following Bourdieu) and of interest (following Sahlins). Only after such a framework is developed will we be able to study the motives, instruments, telos, and ethos of economic activity in a genuinely comparative way.

4. Simmel (1978:138), in a quite different context, anticipates the notion that things move in and out of the commodity state and notes its Aristotelian pedigree.

5. Gray (1984) is an excellent discussion, also influenced by Simmel, of the divergences of value that can shape the nature of exchange across cultural borders. His study of lamb auctions on the English-Scottish borderlands is also a rich ethnographic illustration of what I have called tournaments of value.

6. I am indebted to Graburn (1976), whose use of Maquet's original terminology, in his classification of ethnic and tourist arts, inspired my own adaptation.

7. In coining the term tournaments of value, I was stimulated by Marriott's use, in a very different context, of the conception of tournaments of rank (Marriott 1968).

8. In his recent discussion of world's fairs and expositions, Burton Benedict (1983:6) has noted the elements of contest, competitive display, and status politics associated with these events.

9. Simmel (1957) is a seminal discussion of the cultural logic of fashion. See also the reference to Bouglé's analysis of consumption patterns in village India in Christopher Bayly's paper in this volume, and Max Weber (1978 [1922]).

10. An excellent example of this process appears in Hencken (1981).

11. My use of the term ecumene is a rather idiosyncratic modification of Marshall Hodgson's use of it in *The Venture of Islam* (1974).

12. Also compare to Alsop's (1981) notion that art collecting invariably "pries loose" the things that are collected from their former context of use and deprives them of significant social purpose.

13. It is worth noting that despite a superficial opposition between them, there is a deep affinity between trade and art, at least from the point of view of the material life of simpler societies. Both involve what might be called the *intensification of objecthood*, though in very different ways. Tourist art builds on this inner affinity.

14. For a fascinating account of the role of cloth in an evolving colonial sociology of knowledge in India, see Cohn (forthcoming).

References

Adams, F. G., and J. R. Behrman. 1982. *Commodity exports and economic development.* Lexington, Mass.: Lexington Books.

Alsop, J. 1981. *The rare art traditions: A history of art collecting and its linked phenomena.* Princeton, N.J.: Princeton University Press.

Azoy, G. W. 1982. *Buzkashi: Game and power in Afghanistan.* Philadelphia: University of Pennsylvania Press.

Baudrillard, J. 1968. *Le système des objets.* Paris: Gallimard.

1975. *The mirror of production.* St. Louis, Mo.: Telos Press.

1981. *For a critique of the political economy of the sign.* St. Louis, Mo.: Telos Press.

Benedict, B. 1983. *The anthropology of world's fairs: San Francisco's Panama Pacific International Exposition of 1915.* London: Scolar Press.

Benjamin, Walter. 1968. The work of art in the age of mechanical reproduction. In *Illuminations,* ed. Arendt (trans. Zohn), 219–23. New York: Harcourt, Brace. (Original publication, 1936.)

Bohannan, P. 1955. Some principles of exchange and investment among the Tiv. *American Anthropologist,* 57:60–70.

Bourdieu, P. 1977. *Outline of a theory of practice.* Cambridge: Cambridge University Press.

1984. *Distinction: A social critique of the judgment of taste.* Cambridge, Mass.: Harvard University Press.

Braudel, F. 1982. *The wheels of commerce.* New York: Harper.

Breckenridge, C. 1984. The subject of objects: The making of a colonial high culture. Unpublished paper.

Campbell, S. F. 1983. Kula in Vakuta;: The mechanics of Keda. In J. W. Leach and E. Leach, eds., *The kula: New perspectives on Massim exchange,* 201–27. Cambridge: Cambridge University Press.

Cassady, Jr., R. 1974. *Exchange by private treaty.* Austin: University of Texas Bureau of Business Research.

Chapman, A. 1980. Barter as a universal mode of exchange. In *L'Homme,* 20(3):33–83, July – Sept.

Cochrane, G. 1970. *Big men and cargo cults.* Oxford: Clarendon Press.

Cohn, B. S. (Forthcoming). *Cloth, clothes, and colonialism: India in the nineteenth century.*

Collins, R. 1979. *The credential society: A historical sociology of education and stratification.* New York: Academic Press.

Curtin, P. 1984. *Cross-cultural trade in world history.* Cambridge: Cambridge University Press.

Dalton, G. 1978. The impact of colonization on aboriginal economics in stateless societies. In G. Dalton, ed., *Research in Economic Anthropology,* 1:131–84. Greenwood, Conn.: JAI Press.

Damon, F. H. 1983. What moves the kula: Opening and closing gifts on Woodlark Island. In J. W. Leach and E. Leach, eds., *The kula: New perspectives on Massim exchange,* 309–42. Cambridge: Cambridge University Press.

Dies, E. J. 1925. *The wheat pit.* Chicago: Argyle Press.

1975. *The plunger: A tale of the wheat pit.* New York: Arno Press. (Original publication, 1929).

DiMaggio, P. 1982. Cultural entrepreneurship in nineteenth-century Boston: The creation of an organizational base for high culture in America. In *Media, Culture and Society,* 4:33–50 and 303–22.

Douglas, M. 1967. Primitive rationing: A study in controlled exchange. In R. Firth, ed., *Themes in Economic Anthropology,* 119–47. London: Tavistock.

Douglas, M., and Baron Isherwood. 1981. *The world of goods.* New York: Basic Books.

Dumont, L. 1980. On value (Radcliffe-Brown Lecture). *Proceedings of the British Academy*, LXVI, 207–41. London: Oxford University Press.

Evans-Pritchard, E. E. 1937. *Witchcraft, oracles and magic among the Azande*. Oxford: Clarendon Press.

Firth, R. 1983. Magnitudes and values in Kula exchange. In J. W. Leach and E. Leach, eds., *The kula: New perspectives on Massim exchange*, 89–102. Cambridge: Cambridge University Press.

Geertz, C. 1979. Suq: The bazaar economy in Sefrou. In C. Geertz, H. Geertz, and L. Rosen, *Meaning and Order in Moroccan Society*, 123–310. Cambridge: Cambridge University Press.

  1980. Ports of trade in nineteenth-century Bali. In George Dalton, ed., *Research in Economic Anthropology*, 3:119–22. Greenwich, Conn.: JAI Press.

Gluckman, M. 1983 Essays on Lozi land and royal property. In George Dalton, ed., *Research in Economic Anthropology*, 5:1–94. Greenwich, Conn.: JAI Press. (Original publication, 1943.)

Goldthwaite, R. 1983. The empire of things: Consumer culture in Italy. Paper presented at the Ethnohistory Workshop, University of Pennsylvania, Nov. 10.

Graburn, N. H., ed. 1976. *Ethnic and tourist arts*. Berkeley: University of California Press.

Gray, J. N. 1984. Lamb auctions on the borders. *European Journal of Sociology*, 25(1), 59–82.

Gregory, C. A. 1982. *Gifts and commodities*. London: Academic Press.

Gudeman, S. 1983. Rice and sugar in Panama: Local models of change. Paper presented at the Ethnohistory Workshop, University of Pennsylvania, Oct. 6.

Hart, K. 1982. On commoditization. In Esther Goody, ed., *From craft to industry: The ethnography of proto-industrial cloth production*. Cambridge: Cambridge University Press.

Hebdige, D. 1983. Travelling light: One route into material culture. *RAIN (Royal Anthropological Institute News)*, 59, Dec., 11–13.

Hencken, H. 1981. How the Peabody Museum acquired the Mecklenburg Collection. In *Symbols*, 2–3. Peabody Museum, Harvard University, Fall.

Hodgson, M. 1974. *The venture of Islam: Conscience and history in world civilization*, 3 vols. Chicago: University of Chicago Press.

Hyde, L. 1979. *The gift: Imagination and the erotic life of property*. New York: Random House.

Leach, E. 1983. The kula: An alternative view. In J. W. Leach and E. Leach, eds., *The kula: New perspectives on Massim exchange*, 529–38. Cambridge: Cambridge University Press.

Leach, J. W. and E. Leach, eds. 1983. *The kula: New perspectives on Massim exchange*. Cambridge: Cambridge University Press.

Lears, T. J. 1981. *No place of grace: Anti-modernism and the transformation of American culture, 1880–1920*. New York: Pantheon.

Lopez, R. S. 1971. *The commercial revolution of the middle ages, 950–1350*. Englewood Cliffs, N.J.: Prentice-Hall.

Malinowski, B. 1922. *Argonauts of the western Pacific*. London: Routledge.

Marcus, G. In press. Spending: The Hunts, silver, and dynastic families in America. *European Journal of Sociology*.

Marriott, M. 1968. Caste-ranking and food transactions: A matrix analysis. In M. Singer and B. S. Cohn, eds., *Structure and change in Indian society*, 133–71. Chicago: Aldine.

Marx, K. 1971. *Capital: Vol. I. A Critical analysis of capitalist production.* Moscow: Progress Publishers. (Original publication, 1887.)

1973. *Grundrisse: Foundations of the critique of political economy.* New York: Vintage Books.

Mauss, M. 1976. *The gift.* New York: Norton.

Medick, H., and D. Sabean, eds. 1984. *Interest and emotion: Essays on the study of family and kinship.* Cambridge: Cambridge University Press; Paris: Editions de la Maison des Sciences de l'Homme.

Miller, D. ed., 1983. Things ain't what they used to be. Special section of *RAIN* (Royal Anthropological Institute News), 59 (Dec.), 5–7.

Mintz, Sidney W. 1980. Time, sugar, and sweetness. *Marxist perspectives*, 2, No. 4 (Winter), 56–73.

Mukerji, C. 1983. *From graven images: Patterns of modern materialism.* New York: Columbia University Press.

Munn, Nancy D. 1977. The spatiotemporal transformation of Gawa Canoes. In *Journal de la Société des Océanistes*, 33 (mars-juin), Nos. 54–55, 39–53.

1983. Gawan kula: Spatiotemporal control and the symbolism of influence. In J. W. Leach and E. Leach, eds., *The kula: New perspectives on Massim exchange*, 277–308. Cambridge: Cambridge University Press.

Nappi, C. 1979. *Commodity market controls: A historical review.* Lexington, Mass.: Lexington Books.

Nef, John. 1958. *Cultural foundations of industrial civilization.* New York: Harper.

Perlin, F. 1983. Proto-industrialization and pre-colonial South Asia. *Past and Present*, 98:30–94.

Powers, M. J. 1973. *Getting started in commodity futures trading.* Columbia, Md.: Investor Publications.

Price, J. A. 1980. The silent trade. In G. Dalton, ed., *Research in economic anthropology*, 3:75–96. Greenwich, Conn.: JAI Press.

Sahlins, M. 1972. *Stone age economics.* New York: Aldine.

1976. *Culture and practical reason.* Chicago: University of Chicago Press.

1981. *Historical metaphors and mythical realities: Structure in the early history of the Sandwich Islands Kingdom.* Ann Arbor: University of Michigan Press.

Schmidt, A. 1971. *The concept of nature in Marx.* London: NLB.

Schudson, M. 1984. *Advertising, the uneasy persuasion: Its dubious impact on American society.* New York: Basic Books.

Seddon, D., ed. 1978. *Relations of production: Marxist approaches to economic anthropology.* London: Frank Cass.

Simmel, G. 1957. Fashion. *American Journal of Sociology*, LXII/6:541–58.

1978. *The philosophy of money.* London: Routledge.

Sombart, W. 1967. *Luxury and capitalism.* Ann Arbor: University of Michigan Press.

Sraffa, P. 1960. *Production of commodities by means of commodities.* Cambridge: Cambridge University Press.

Stewart, S. 1984. *On longing: Narratives of the miniature, the gigantic, the souvenir, the collection.* Baltimore: Johns Hopkins University Press.

Strathern, A. J. 1983. The kula in comparative perspective. In J. W. Leach and E. Leach, eds., *The kula: New perspectives on Massim exchange*, 73–88. Cambridge: Cambridge University Press.

Swallow, D. 1982. Production and control in the Indian garment export industry. In E. Goody, ed., *From craft to industry: The ethnography of proto-industrial cloth production*, 133–65. Cambridge: Cambridge University Press.

Tambiah, S. J. 1984. *The Buddhist saints of the forest and the cult of amulets*. Cambridge: Cambridge University Press.

Taussig, M. T. 1980. *The devil and commodity fetishism in South America*. Chapel Hill: University of North Carolina Press.

Thirsk, J. 1978. *Economic policy and projects*. Oxford: Clarendon Press.

Thompson, M. 1976. *Rubbish theory*. Oxford: Oxford University Press.

Uberoi, J. P. S. 1962. *Politics of the Kula ring*. Manchester: Manchester University Press.

Weber, M. 1958. *The Protestant ethic and the spirit of capitalism*. New York: Scribner's. (Original publication, 1904–5.)

    1978. Classes, status groups and parties. In W. G. Runciman, ed., *Max Weber: Selections in translation*, 43–61. Cambridge: Cambridge University Press.

Weiner, A. B. 1983. A world of made is not a world of born: Doing kula on Kiriwana. In J. W. Leach and E. Leach, eds., *The kula: New perspectives on Massim exchange*, 147–70. Cambridge: Cambridge University Press.

Wolf, E. 1982. *Europe and the people without history*. Berkeley: University of California Press.

CHAPTER 2

The cultural biography of things: commoditization as process

IGOR KOPYTOFF

For the economist, commodities simply are. That is, certain things and rights to things are produced, exist, and can be seen to circulate through the economic system as they are being exchanged for other things, usually in exchange for money. This view, of course, frames the commonsensical definition of a commodity: an item with use value that also has exchange value. I shall, for the moment, accept this definition, which should suffice for raising certain preliminary issues, and I shall expand on it as the argument warrants.

From a cultural perspective, the production of commodities is also a cultural and cognitive process: commodities must be not only produced materially as things, but also culturally marked as being a certain kind of thing. Out of the total range of things available in a society, only some of them are considered appropriate for marking as commodities. Moreover, the same thing may be treated as a commodity at one time and not at another. And finally, the same thing may, at the same time, be seen as a commodity by one person and as something else by another. Such shifts and differences in whether and when a thing is a commodity reveal a moral economy that stands behind the objective economy of visible transactions.

Of persons and things

In contemporary Western thought, we take it more or less for granted that things – physical objects and rights to them – represent the natural universe of commodities. At the opposite pole we place people, who represent the natural universe of individuation and singularization. This conceptual polarity of individualized persons and commoditized things is recent and, culturally speaking, exceptional. People can be and have been commoditized again and again, in innumerable societies throughout history, by way of those widespread institutions known under the blanket term "slavery." Hence, it may be suggestive to approach the notion of commodity by first looking at it in the context of slavery.

Slavery has often been defined, in the past, as the treatment of persons as property or, in some kindred definitions, as objects. More recently, there has been a shift away from this all-or-none view toward a processual perspective, in which marginality and ambiguity of status are at the core of the slave's social identity (see Meillassoux 1975, Vaughan 1977, Kopytoff and Miers 1977, Kopytoff 1982, Patterson 1982). From this perspective slavery is seen not as a fixed and unitary status, but as a process of social transformation that involves a succession of phases and changes in status, some of which merge with other statuses (for example, that of adoptee) that we in the West consider far removed from slavery.

Slavery begins with capture or sale, when the individual is stripped of his previous social identity and becomes a non-person, indeed an object and an actual or potential commodity. But the process continues. The slave is acquired by a person or group and is reinserted into the host group, within which he is resocialized and rehumanized by being given a new social identity. The commodity-slave becomes in effect reindividualized by acquiring new statuses (by no means always lowly ones) and a unique configuration of personal relationships. In brief, the process has moved the slave away from the simple status of exchangeable commodity and toward that of a singular individual occupying a particular social and personal niche. But the slave usually remains a potential commodity: he or she continues to have a potential exchange value that may be realized by resale. In many societies, this was also true of the "free," who were subject to sale under certain defined circumstances. To the extent that in such societies all persons possessed an exchange value and were commoditizable, commoditization in them was clearly not culturally confined to the world of things.

What we see in the career of a slave is a process of initial withdrawal from a given original social setting, his or her commoditization, followed by increasing singularization (that is, decommoditization) in the new setting, with the possibility of later recommoditization. As in most processes, the successive phases merge one into another. Effectively, the slave was unambiguously a commodity only during the relatively short period between capture or first sale and the acquisition of the new social identity; and the slave becomes less of a commodity and more of a singular individual in the process of gradual incorporation into the host society. This biographical consideration of enslavement as a process suggests that the commoditization of other things may usefully be seen in a similar light, namely, as part of the cultural shaping of biographies.

The biographical approach

Biographies have been approached in various ways in anthropology (for a survey, see Langness 1965). One may present an actual biography, or one may construct a typical biographical model from randomly assembled biographical data, as one does in the standard Life Cycle chapter in a general ethnography. A more theoretically aware biographical model is rather more demanding. It is based on a reasonable number of actual life histories. It presents the range of biographical possibilities that the society in question offers and examines the manner in which these possibilities are realized in the life stories of various categories of people. And it examines idealized biographies that are considered to be desirable models in the society and the way real-life departures from the models are perceived. As Margaret Mead remarked, one way to understand a culture is to see what sort of biography it regards as embodying a successful social career. Clearly, what is seen as a well-lived life in an African society is different in outline from what would be pronounced as a well-lived life along the Ganges, or in Brittany, or among the Eskimos.

It seems to me that we can profitably ask the same range and kinds of cultural questions to arrive at biographies of things. Early in this century, in an article entitled "The genealogical method of anthropological inquiry" (1910), W. H. R. Rivers offered what has since become a standard tool in ethnographic fieldwork. The thrust of the article – the aspect for which it is now mainly remembered – is to show how kinship terminology and relationships may be superimposed on a genealogical diagram and traced through the social-structure-in-time that the diagram mirrors. But Rivers also suggested something else: that, for example, when the anthropologist is in search of inheritance rules, he may compare the ideal statement of the rules with the actual movement of a particular object, such as a plot of land, through the genealogical diagram, noting concretely how it passes from hand to hand. What Rivers proposed was a kind of biography of things in terms of ownership. But a biography may concentrate on innumerable other matters and events.

In doing the biography of a thing, one would ask questions similar to those one asks about people: What, sociologically, are the biographical possibilities inherent in its "status" and in the period and culture, and how are these possibilities realized? Where does the thing come from and who made it? What has been its career so far, and what do people consider to be an ideal career for such things? What are the recognized "ages" or periods in the thing's "life," and what are the cultural markers for them? How does the thing's use change with its age, and what happens to it when it reaches the end of its usefulness?

For example, among the Suku of Zaire, among whom I worked, the life expectancy of a hut is about ten years. The typical biography of a hut begins with its housing a couple or, in a polygynous household, a wife with her children. As the hut ages, it is successively turned into a guest house or a house for a widow, a teenagers' hangout, kitchen, and, finally, goat or chicken house – until at last the termites win and the structure collapses. The physical state of the hut at each given age corresponds to a particular use. For a hut to be out of phase in its use makes a Suku uncomfortable, and it conveys a message. Thus, to house a visitor in a hut that should be a kitchen says something about the visitor's status; and if there is no visitors' hut available in a compound, it says something about the compound-head's character – he must be lazy, inhospitable, or poor. We have similar biographical expectations of things. To us, a biography of a painting by Renoir that ends up in an incinerator is as tragic, in its way, as the biography of a person who ends up murdered. That is obvious. But there are other events in the biography of objects that convey more subtle meanings. What of a Renoir ending up in a private and inaccessible collection? Of one lying neglected in a museum basement? How should we feel about yet another Renoir leaving France for the United States? Or for Nigeria? The cultural responses to such biographical details reveal a tangled mass of aesthetic, historical, and even political judgments, and of convictions and values that shape our attitudes to objects labeled "art."

Biographies of things can make salient what might otherwise remain obscure. For example, in situations of culture contact, they can show what anthropologists have so often stressed: that what is significant about the adoption of alien objects – as of alien ideas – is not the fact that they are adopted, but the way they are culturally redefined and put to use. The biography of a car in Africa would reveal a wealth of cultural data: the way it was acquired, how and from whom the money was assembled to pay for it, the relationship of the seller to the buyer, the uses to which the car is regularly put, the identity of its most frequent passengers and of those who borrow it, the frequency of borrowing, the garages to which it is taken and the owner's relation to the mechanics, the movement of the car from hand to hand over the years, and in the end, when the car collapses, the final disposition of its remains. All of these details would reveal an entirely different biography from that of a middle-class American, or Navajo, or French peasant car.

One brings to every biography some prior conception of what is to be its focus. We accept that every person has many biographies – psychological, professional, political, familial, economic and so forth – each of which selects some aspects of the life history and discards others. Biographies of things cannot but be similarly partial. Obviously, the sheer physical biography of a car is quite different from its technical biography, known in the trade as its repair record. The car can also furnish an economic biography – its initial worth, its sale and resale price, the rate of decline in its value, its response to the recession, the patterning over several years of its maintenance costs. The car also offers several possible social biographies: one biography may concentrate on its place in the owner-family's economy, another may relate the history of its ownership to the society's class structure, and a third may focus on its role in the sociology of the family's kin relations, such as loosening family ties in America or strengthening them in Africa.

But all such biographies – economic, technical, social – may or may not be culturally informed. What would make a biography cultural is not what it deals with, but how and from what perspective. A culturally informed economic biography of an object would look at it as a culturally constructed entity, endowed with culturally specific meanings, and classified and reclassified into culturally constituted categories. It is from this point of view that I should like to propose a framework for looking at commodities – or rather, speaking processually, at commoditization. But first, what is a commodity?

The singular and the common

I assume commodities to be a universal cultural phenomenon. Their existence is a concomitant of the existence of transactions that involve the exchange of things (objects and services), exchange being a universal feature of human social life and, according to some theorists, at the very core of it (see, for example, Homans 1961; Ekeh 1974; and Kapferer 1976). Where societies differ is in the ways commoditization as a special expression of exchange is structured and related to the social system, in the factors that encourage or contain it, in the long-term tendencies for it to expand or stabilize, and in the cultural and ideological premises that suffuse its workings.

What, then, makes a thing a commodity? A commodity is a thing that has use value and that can be exchanged in a discrete transaction for a counterpart, the very fact of exchange indicating that the counterpart has, in the immediate context, an equivalent value. The counterpart is by the same token also a commodity at the time of exchange. The exchange can be direct or it can be achieved indirectly by way of money, one of whose functions is as a means of exchange. Hence, anything that can be bought for money is at that point a commodity, whatever the fate that is reserved for it after the transaction has been made (it may, thereafter, be decommoditized). Hence, in the West, as a matter of cultural shorthand, we usually take saleability to be the unmistakable indicator of commodity status, while non-saleability imparts to a thing a special aura of apartness from the mundane and the common. In fact, of course, saleability for money is not a necessary feature of commodity status, given the existence of commodity exchange in non-monetary economies.

I refer to the transaction involving commodities as discrete in order to stress that the primary and immediate purpose of the transaction is to obtain the counterpart value (and that, for the economist, is also its economic function). The purpose of the transaction is not, for example, to open the way for some other kind of transaction, as in the case of gifts given to initiate marriage negotiations or to secure patronage; each of these cases is a partial transaction that should be considered in the context of the entire transaction. While exchanges of things usually involve commodities, a notable exception is the exchanges that mark relations of reciprocity, as these have been classically defined in anthropology. Here, gifts are given in order to evoke an obligation to give back a gift, which in turn will evoke a similar obligation – a never-ending chain of gifts and obligations. The gifts themselves may be things that are normally used as commodities (food, feasts, luxury goods, services), but each transaction is not discrete and none, in principle, is terminal.

To be saleable for money or to be exchangeable for a wide array of other things is to have something in common with a large number of exchangeable things that, taken together, partake of a single universe of comparable values. To use an appropriately loaded even if archaic term, to be saleable or widely exchangeable is to be "common" – the opposite of being uncommon, incomparable, unique, singular, and therefore not exchangeable for anything else. The perfect commodity would be one that is exchangeable with anything and everything else, as the perfectly commoditized world would be one in which everything is exchangeable or for sale. By the same token, the perfectly decommoditized world would be one in which everything is singular, unique, and unexchangeable.

The two situations are ideal polar types, and no real economic system could conform to either. In no system is everything so singular as to preclude even the hint of exchange. And in no system, except in some extravagant Marxian image of an utterly commoditized capitalism, is everything a commodity and exchangeable for everything else within a unitary sphere of exchange. Such a construction of the world – in the first case as totally heterogeneous in terms of valuation and, in the second, as totally homogeneous – would be humanly and culturally impossible. But they are two extremes between which every real economy occupies its own peculiar place.

We can accept, with most philosophers, linguists, and psychologists, that the human mind has an inherent tendency to impose order upon the chaos of its environment by classifying its contents, and without this classification knowledge of the world and adjustment to it would not be possible. Culture serves the mind by imposing a collectively shared cognitive order upon the world which, objectively, is totally heterogeneous and presents an endless array of singular things. Culture achieves order by carving out, through discrimination and classification, distinct areas of homogeneity within the overall heterogeneity. Yet, if the homogenizing process is carried too far and the perceived world begins to approach too closely the other pole – in the case of goods, that of utter commoditization – culture's function of cognitive discrimination is undermined. Both individuals and cultural collectivities must navigate somewhere between the polar extremes by classifying things into categories that are simultaneously neither too many nor too embracing. In brief, what we usually refer to as "structure" lies between the heterogeneity of too much splitting and the homogeneity of too much lumping.

In the realm of exchange values, this means that the natural world of singular things must be arranged into several manageable value classes – that is, different things must be selected and made cognitively similar when put together within each category and dissimilar when put into different categories. This is the basis for a well-known economic phenomenon – that of several spheres of exchange values, which operate more or less independently of one another. The phenomenon is found in every society, though Westerners are most apt to perceive it in uncommercialized and unmonetized economies. The nature and structure of these spheres of exchange varies among societies because, as we can expect with Durkheim and Mauss (1963; original publication 1903), the cultural systems of classification reflect the structure and the cultural resources of the societies in question. And beyond that, as we may expect with Dumont (1972), there's also some tendency to impose a hierarchy upon the categories.

Spheres of exchange

A concrete example of an economy with clearly distinct spheres of exchange will help the discussion. In what is a classic analysis of a "multi-centric economy," Bohannan (1959) describes three such spheres of exchange as they operated before the colonial period among the Tiv of central Nigeria: (a) the sphere of subsistence items – yams, cereals, condiments, chickens, goats, utensils, tools, and the like; (b) the sphere of prestige items – mainly cattle, slaves, ritual offices, special cloth, medicines, and brass rods; and (c) the sphere of rights-in-people, which included rights in wives, wards, and offspring.

The three spheres represent three separate universes of exchange values, that is, three commodity spheres. Items within each were exchangeable, and each was ruled by its own kind of morality. Moreover, there was a moral hierarchy among the spheres: the subsistence sphere, with its untrammeled market morality, was the lowest, and the rights-in-people sphere, related to the world of kin and kin-group relations, was the highest. In the Tiv case (in contrast to that of many other similar systems), it was possible to move – even if in a rather cumbersome manner – between the spheres. Brass rods provided the link. In exceptional circumstances, people relinquished, unwillingly, rods for subsistence items; and, at the other end, one could also initiate with rods some transactions in the rights-in-people sphere. The Tiv considered it satisfying and morally appropriate to convert "upward," from subsistence to prestige and from prestige to rights-in-people, whereas converting "downward" was shameful and done only under extreme duress.

The problem of value and value equivalence has always been a philosophical conundrum in economics. It involves the mysterious process by which things that are patently unlike are somehow made to be alike with respect to value, making yams, for example, somehow comparable to and exchangeable with a mortar or a pot. In the terms we have been using here, this involves taking the patently singular and inserting it into a uniform category of value with other patently singular things. For all the difficulties that the labor theory of value presents, it at least suggests that while yams and pots can conceivably be compared by the labor required to produce them (even while allowing for the different investment in training that the labor represents in each case), no such common standard is available in comparing yams to ritual offices or pots to wives and offspring. Hence, the immense difficulty, indeed impossibility, of lumping all such disparate items into a single commodity sphere. This difficulty provides the natural basis for the cultural construction of separate spheres of exchange. The culture takes on the less sweeping task of making value-equivalence by creating several discrete commodity spheres – in the Tiv case, palpable items of subsistence created by physical labor, as opposed to the prestige items of social maneuvering, as opposed to the more intimate domain of the rights and obligations of kinship.

The drive to commoditization

From this perspective, a multi-centric economy such as that of the Tiv is not an exotically complicated rendering of a straightforward exchange system. It is rather the opposite – a feat of simplification of what is naturally an unmanageable mass of singular items. But why only three spheres and not, say, a dozen? The commoditization seems to be pushed to the limits permitted by the Tiv exchange technology, which lacked a common denominator of value more convenient than brass rods. One perceives in this a drive inherent in every exchange system toward optimum commoditization – the drive to extend the fundamentally seductive idea of exchange to as many items as the existing exchange technology will comfortably allow. Hence the universal acceptance of money whenever it has been introduced into non-monetized societies and its inexorable conquest of the internal economy of these societies, regardless of initial rejection and of individual unhappiness about it – an unhappiness well illustrated by the modern Tiv. Hence also the uniform results of the introduction of money in a wide range of otherwise different societies: more extensive commoditization and the merger of the separate spheres of exchange. It is as if the internal logic of exchange itself pre-adapts all economies to seize upon the new opportunities that wide commoditization so obviously brings with it.

One may interpret Braudel's recent work (1983) in this light – as showing how the development in early modern Europe of a range of new institutions shaped what might be called a new exchange technology and how this, in turn, led to the explosion of commoditization that was at the root of capitalism. The extensive commoditization we associate with capitalism is thus not a feature of capitalism per se, but of the exchange technology that, historically, was associated with it and that set dramatically wider limits to maximum feasible commoditization. Modern state-ordered, noncapitalist economies certainly show no signs of being systematically exempt from this tendency, even though they may try to control it by political means. Indeed, given their endemic shortages and ubiquitous black markets, commoditization in them expands into novel areas, in which the consumer, in order to purchase goods and services, must first purchase access to the transaction.

Commoditization, then, is best looked upon as a process of becoming rather than as an all-or-none state of being. Its expansion takes place in two ways: (a) with respect to each thing, by making it exchangeable for more and more other things, and (b) with respect to the system as a whole, by making more and more different things more widely exchangeable.

Singularization: cultural and individual

The counterdrive to this potential onrush of commoditization is culture. In the sense that commoditization homogenizes value, while the essence of culture is discrimination, excessive commoditization is anticultural — as indeed so many have perceived it or sensed it to be. And if, as Durkheim (1915; original publication 1912) saw it, societies need to set apart a certain portion of their environment, marking it as "sacred," singularization is one means to this end. Culture ensures that some things remain unambiguously singular, it resists the commoditization of others; and it sometimes resingularizes what has been commoditized.

In every society, there are things that are publicly precluded from being commoditized. Some of the prohibitions are cultural and upheld collectively. In state societies, many of these prohibitions are the handwork of the state, with the usual intertwining between what serves the society at large, what serves the state, and what serves the specific groups in control. This applies to much of what one thinks of as the symbolic inventory of a society: public lands, monuments, state art collections, the paraphernalia of political power, royal residences, chiefly insignia, ritual objects, and so on. Power often asserts itself symbolically precisely by insisting on its right to singularize an object, or a set or class of objects. African chiefs and kings reserve to themselves the right to certain animals and animal products, such as the skins and teeth of spotted wild cats. The kings of Siam monopolized albino elephants. And British monarchs have kept their right to dead whales washed ashore. There may be some practical side to these royal pretensions, which ecological and cultural materialists will no doubt diligently discover. What these monopolies clearly do, however, is to expand the visible reach of sacred power by projecting it onto additional sacralized objects.

Such singularization is sometimes extended to things that are normally commodities – in effect, commodities are singularized by being pulled out of their usual commodity sphere. Thus, in the ritual paraphernalia of the British monarchy, we find a Star of India that, contrary to what would normally have happened, was prevented from becoming a commodity and eventually singularized into a "crown jewel." Similarly, the ritual paraphernalia of the kings of the Suku of Zaire included standard trade items from the past, such as eighteenth-century European ceramic drinking mugs brought by the Portuguese, carried by the Suku to their present area, and sacralized in the process.

Another way to singularize objects is through restricted commoditization, in which some things are confined to a very narrow sphere of exchange. The Tiv system illustrates the principle. The few items in the prestige sphere (slaves, cattle, ritual offices, a special cloth, and brass rods), though commodities by virtue of being exchangeable one for the other, were less commoditized than the far more numerous items of the subsistence sphere, ranging widely from yams to pots. A sphere consisting of but two kinds of items – as in the classic model of the Trobriand kula exchange sphere of arm bands and bracelets – represents an even greater degree of singularization. The Tiv exchange sphere of rights-in-person achieved a singular integrity by a different though related principle, that of the homogeneity of its components. The two upper Tiv spheres, it may be noted, were more singular, more special, and hence more sacred than the lowest sphere, containing the many objects of mundane subsistence. Thus the moral hierarchy of the Tiv exchange spheres corresponded to a gradient of singularity.

If sacralization can be achieved by singularity, singularity does not guarantee sacralization. Being a non-commodity does not by itself assure high regard, and many singular things (that is, non-exchangeable things) may be worth very little. Among the Aghem of western Cameroon, with exchange spheres not unlike those of the Tiv, one could detect yet another and lower sphere, one below that of marketable subsistence items. Once, when trying to find out the precolonial exchange value of various items, I asked about the barter value of manioc. The response was indignant scoffing at the very idea that such a lowly thing as manioc should have been exchangeable for anything: "One eats it, that's all. Or one gives it away if one wants to. Women may help out one another with it and other such food. But one doesn't *trade* it." Lest the outburst be misunderstood and sentimentalized, let me stress that the indignation was not about a suggested commercial corruption of a symbolically supercharged staple, on the order, say, of bread among Eastern European peasants. The

Aghem are and were a commercially minded people, with no disdain for trade. The scoffing was rather like what an Aghem would get from a Westerner whom he asked about the exchange value of a match he proffers to light a stranger's cigarette. Manioc was part of a class of singular things of so little worth as to have no publicly recognized exchange value. To be a non-commodity is to be "priceless" in the full possible sense of the term, ranging from the uniquely valuable to the uniquely worthless.

In addition to things being classified as more or less singular, there is also what might be called terminal commoditization, in which further exchange is precluded by fiat. In many societies, medicines are so treated: the medicine man makes and sells a medicine that is utterly singular since it is efficacious only for the intended patient. Terminal commoditization also marked the sale of indulgences in the Roman Catholic Church of half a millennium ago: the sinner could buy them but not resell them. In modern Western medicine, such terminal commoditization is achieved legally; it rests on the prohibition against reselling a prescribed drug and against selling any medicine without proper licensing. There are other examples of legal attempts to restrict recommoditization: paperbound books published in Great Britain often carry a bewildering note forbidding the buyer to resell it in any but the original covers; and in America, an equally mystifying label is attached to mattresses and cushions, forbidding their resale.

Other factors besides legal or cultural fiat may create terminal commodities. Most consumer goods are, after all, destined to be terminal – or so, at least, it is hoped by the manufacturer. The expectation is easily enough fulfilled with such things as canned peas, though even here external circumstances can intrude; in times of war shortages, all sorts of normally consumable goods begin to serve as a store of wealth and, instead of being consumed, circulate endlessly in the market. With durable goods, a second-hand market normally develops, and the idea that it does may be fostered by the sellers. There is an area of our economy in which the selling strategy rests on stressing that the commoditization of goods bought for consumption need not be terminal: thus, the promise that oriental carpets, though bought for use, are a "good investment," or that certain expensive cars have a "high resale value."

The existence of terminal commoditization raises a point that is central to the analysis of slavery, where the fact that a person has been bought does not in itself tell us anything about the uses to which the person may then be put (Kopytoff 1982:223ff). Some purchased people ended up in the mines, on plantations, or on galleys; others became Grand Viziers or Imperial Roman Admirals. In the same way, the fact that an object is bought or exchanged says nothing about its subsequent status and whether it will remain a commodity or not. But unless formally decommoditized, commoditized things remain potential commodities – they continue to have an exchange value, even if they have been effectively withdrawn from their exchange sphere and deactivated, so to speak, as commodities. This deactivation leaves them open not only to the various kinds of singularization I have mentioned so far, but also to individual, as opposed to collective, redefinitions.

In the Bamenda area of western Cameroon, people prized large decorated calabashes that came over the border from Nigeria. The conduit for them was the Aku, a pastoral group whose women used them extensively and normally were willing to sell them. I had acquired several in this way. Yet one day I failed completely to convince an Aku woman to sell me a standard calabash to which she had added some minor decorations of her own. Her friends told her that she was being silly, arguing that for the money she could get a far better and prettier calabash. But she would not budge, no more than does that ever-newsworthy man in our society – part hero, part fool – who refuses to sell his house for a million dollars and forces the skyscraper to be built around it. And there is also the opposite phenomenon: the ideological commoditizer, advocating, say, the sale of public lands as a way of balancing the budget, or, as I have seen in Africa, calling for the sale of some piece of chiefly paraphernalia in order to provide a tin roof for the schoolhouse.

What these mundane examples show is that, in any society, the individual is often caught between the cultural structure of commoditization and his own personal attempts to bring a value order to the universe of things. Some of this clash between culture and individual is inevitable, at least at the cognitive level. The world of things lends itself to an endless number of classifications, rooted in natural features and cultural and idiosyncratic perceptions. The individual mind can play with them all, constructing innumerable classes, different universes of common value, and changing spheres of exchange. Culture, by contrast, cannot be so exuberant, least so in the economy, where its classifications must provide unambiguous guidance to pragmatic and coordinated action. But if the clash is inevitable, the social structures within which it takes place vary, giving it different intensities. In a society like the precolonial Tiv or Aghem, the culture and the economy were in relative harmony; the economy followed the cultural classifications, and these catered successfully to the individual cognitive need for discrimination. By contrast, in a commercialized, monetized, and highly commoditized society, the value-homogenizing drive of the exchange system has an enormous momentum, producing results that both culture and individual cognition often oppose, but in inconsistent and even contradictory ways.

Complex societies

I said above that the exchange spheres are, to us, more visible in non-commercial, non-monetized societies like the Tiv than in commercial, monetized ones like our own. Partly this is a matter of noticing the exotic and taking the familiar for granted. But it is more than that.

Certainly, in our society, some discrete spheres of exchange exist and are nearly unanimously accepted and approved. Thus, we are adamant about keeping separate the spheres of material objects and persons (a matter I shall elaborate on later). We also exchange dinners and keep that sphere discrete. We blandly accept the existence of an exchange sphere of political or academic favors, but would be as shocked at the idea of monetizing this sphere as the Tiv were at first at the idea of monetizing their marriage transactions. Like the Tiv, who carefully moved from the sphere of mundane pots to that of prestigeful titles by using the mediation of brass rods, so do our financiers cautiously navigate between exchange spheres in such matters as gift-giving to universities. A straight money donation in general funds, if it is of any size, is suspect because it looks too much like purchasing influence, and such donations, when made, are normally anonymous or posthumous. A money donation in installments would be particularly suspect, implying the donor's power to withhold the next check. But converting a large donation into a building moves the money into a nearly decommoditized sphere, freezes the gift into visible irrevocability, and shields the donor from suspicion of continuous undue influence on the university. Putting the donor's name on the building thus honors not simply the donor but also the university, which declares in doing so that it is free of any lingering obligations to the specific donor. The values underlying such transactions are, on the whole, societywide, or at least are held by the groups who wield cultural hegemony in our society and define much of what we are apt to call our public culture. "Everyone" is against commoditizing what has been publicly marked as singular and made sacred: public parks, national landmarks, the Lincoln Memorial, George Washington's false teeth at Mount Vernon.

Other singularizing values are held by more restricted groups. We have explicit exchange spheres recognized only by segments of society, such as professional and occupational groups, which subscribe to a common cultural code and a specially focused morality. Such groups constitute the networks of mechanical solidarity that tie together the parts of the organic structure of the wider society, the latter being ruled in most of its activities by commodity principles. Let me lead into my discussion by looking at an activity in one such group: the collection of African art among American Africanists.

In the simpler days of thirty or more years ago, African art picked up randomly in the course of fieldwork was placed entirely in a closed sphere with a sacred cast. The objects collected were greatly singularized; they were held to have for their collector a personal sentimental value, or a purely aesthetic one, or a scientific one, the last supported by the collector's supposed knowledge of the object's cultural context. It was not considered entirely proper to acquire an art object from African market traders or, worse, from European traders in Africa, or worse still, from dealers in Europe or America. Such an object, acquired at second hand, had little scientific value, and it was vaguely contaminated by having circulated in a monetized commodity-sphere – a contamination that was not entirely removed by keeping it thereafter in the same category as the objects "legitimately" acquired in the field. The exchange sphere to which African art objects belonged was extremely homogeneous in content. It was permissible to exchange them for other African (or other "primitive art") objects. One could also give them as gifts. Students returning from the field usually brought one or two as gifts to their supervisors, thus inserting them into another circumscribed sphere, that of academic patron-client relationships. The morality governing the sphere did not allow for them to be sold, except at cost to a museum. Nevertheless, as among the Tiv, for whom it was permissible though shameful to sell a brass rod for food, so here extreme need justified "liquidation" on the commercial art market, but it had to be done with appropriate discretion and it was certainly seen as converting "downward."

As Douglas and Isherwood (1980) show, the public culture in complex societies does provide broadly discriminating value markings of goods and services. That is, the public culture offers discriminating classifications here no less than it does in small-scale societies. But these must constantly compete with classifications by individuals and by small networks, whose members also belong to other networks expounding yet other value systems. The discriminating criteria that each individual or network can bring to the task of classification are extremely varied. Not only is every individual's or network's version of exchange spheres idiosyncratic and different from those of others, but it also shifts contextually and biographically as the originators' perspectives, affiliations and interests shift. The result is a debate not only between people and groups, but within each person as well. To be sure, the seeds for such debates also exist in societies like the precolonial Tiv, but there the culture and the economy joined hands to provide an approved model of classification. In a commercialized, heterogenous, and liberal society, the public culture defers most of the time to pluralism and relativism and provides no firm guidance, while the only lesson the economy can teach is that of the freedom and dynamism that ever-wider commoditization clearly brings with it.

The results can be partly glimpsed in what has happened to African art collecting over the past quarter century. The rules have been loosened in some of the same ways that monetization, according to Bohannan, loosened the rules among the Tiv − namely, by merging the previously distinct exchange spheres. There are, for example, no strictures now on buying an African art object at an auction in America, let alone from an African trader in Africa. Monetization in itself has become less contaminating as it has become more seductive, for no one can remain unaware that these objects are what every newspaper and magazine calls "collectibles." But the most noticeable change has been, quite simply, to make the rules less clear and more open to individual interpretations and to idiosyncratic systems of values. Where before the professional culture decreed that the value of these objects was sentimental when it was not scientific, now sentimental value is conferred as a matter of individual choice, perhaps more sincerely but also less widely. At the same time, puritans have arisen, thundering about the immorality of any kind of circulation of these objects and calling for their complete singularization and sacralization within the closed boundaries of the society that produced them. In brief, the rules of the professional culture have become less tight and the rules of propriety have become more idiosyncratic. The widespread rejection, since the 1960's, of the very idea of cultural restraints has, here as elsewhere, opened the door to a great variety of definitions by individuals and small groups.

What I am arguing here is that the crucial difference between complex and small-scale societies does not lie simply in the extensive commoditization in the former. There have been, we must not forget, small-scale societies in which commoditization (helped by indigenous money) was very extensive, such as the Yurok of northern California (Kroeber 1925) or the Kapauku of western New Guinea (Pospisil 1963). The peculiarity of complex societies is that their publicly recognized commoditization operates side by side with innumerable schemes of valuation and singularization devised by individuals, social categories, and groups, and these schemes stand in unresolvable conflict with public commoditization as well as with one another.

The dynamics of informal singularization in complex societies

There is clearly a yearning for singularization in complex societies. Much of it is satisfied individually, by private singularization, often on principles as mundane as the one that governs the fate of heirlooms and old slippers alike – the longevity of the relation assimilates them in some sense to the person and makes parting from them unthinkable.

Sometimes the yearning assumes the proportions of a collective hunger, apparent in the widespread response to ever-new kinds of singularizations. Old beer cans, matchbooks, and comic books suddenly become worthy of being collected, moved from the sphere of the singularly worthless to that of the expensive singular. And there is a continuing appeal in stamp collecting – where, one may note, the stamps are preferably cancelled ones so there is no doubt about their worthlessness in the circle of commodities for which they were originally intended. As among individuals, much of the collective singularization is achieved by reference to the passage of time. Cars as commodities lose value as they age, but at about the age of thirty they begin to move into the category of antiques and rise in value with every receding year. Old furniture, of course, does the same at a more sedate pace – the period that begins to usher in sacralization is approximately equal to the span of time separating one from one's grandparents' generation (in the past, with less mobility and more stylistic continuity, more time was required). There is also the modern and appropriately unhistorical adaptation of the antiquing process so perceptively analyzed by Thompson (1979) – the instant singularization of objects in the trash-pile-to-living-room decor of the upwardly mobile young professionals, bored with the homogeneous Scandinavian aridity preferred by the previous generation of their class.

As with African art, however, these are all processes within small groups and social networks. What to me is an heirloom is, of course, a commodity to the jeweler, and the fact that I am not divorced from the jeweler's culture is apparent in my willingness to price my priceless heirloom (and invariably overestimate its commodity value). To the jeweler, I am confusing two different systems of values: that of the marketplace and that of the closed sphere of personally singularized things, both of which happen to converge on the object at hand. Many of the new "collectibles" of the beer can variety are similarly caught in this paradox: as one makes them more singular and worthy of being collected, one makes them valuable; and if they are valuable, they acquire a price and become a commodity and their singularity is to that extent undermined. This interpenetration within the same object of commodity principles and singularization principles is played upon by firms specializing in manufacturing what might be called "future collectibles," such as leather-bound editions of Emerson, bas-relief renditions of Norman Rockwell's paintings on sculptured plates, or silver medals commemorating unmemorable events. The appeal to greed in their advertising is complex: buy this plate now while it is still a commodity, because later it will become a singular "collectible" whose very singularity will make it into a higher-priced commodity. I can think of no analogy to such possibilities among the Tiv exchange spheres.

Singularization of objects by groups within the society poses a special problem. Because it is done by groups, it bears the stamp of collective approval, channels the individual drive for singularization, and takes on the weight of cultural sacredness. Thus, a community of a few city blocks can suddenly be mobilized by a common outrage at the proposed removal and sale of scrap metal of the rusting Victorian fountain in the neighborhood. Such public conflicts are often more than mere matters of style. Behind the extraordinarily vehement assertions of aesthetic values may stand conflicts of culture, class, and ethnic identity, and the struggle over the power of what one might label the "public institutions of singularization."[1] In liberal societies, these institutions are higher nongovernmental agencies or only quasi–governmental ones – historical commissions, panels deciding on public monuments, neighborhood organizations concerned with "beautification," and so on; who controls them and how says much about who controls the society's presentation of itself to itself.

A few years ago, there was a public controversy in Philadelphia about a proposal to install a statue of the cinematic boxing hero Rocky on the Parkway in front of the Art Museum – an institution that happens simultaneously to serve as a public monument to the local social establishment and to satisfy the artistic needs of the professional intelligentsia. The statue came directly from the movie set of "Rocky," the success story of an Italian-American boxing champion from South Philadelphia. To the "ethnic" working-class sector of the Philadelphia population, the statue was a singular object of ethnic, class, and regional pride – in brief, a worthy public monument. To the groups whose social identities were vested in the museum, it was a piece of junk, deserving instant recommoditization as scrap metal. Here, the issues of singularization and commoditization were directly linked into disparate and morally charged systems. But the opponents of the statue were in a position to clothe their argument in the garb of public aesthetics, a field in which they held cultural hegemony. The statue was not installed at the Art Museum but in South Philadelphia, next to a stadium.

Most of the conflict, however, between commoditization and singularization in complex societies takes place within individuals, leading to what appear to be anomalies in cognition, inconsistencies in values, and uncertainties in action. People in these societies all maintain some private vision of a hierarchy of exchange spheres, but the justification for this hierarchy is not, as it was among the Tiv, integrally tied to the exchange structure itself; rather, the justification must be imported from outside the system of exchange, from such autonomous and usually parochial systems as that of aesthetics, or morality, or religion, or specialized professional concerns. When we feel that selling a Rembrandt or an heirloom is trading downward, the explanation for our attitude is that things called "art" or "historical objects" are superior to the world of commerce. This is the reason why the high value of the singular in complex societies becomes so easily embroiled in snobbery. The high value does not visibly reside in the exchange system itself – as it traditionally did among the Tiv, when, for example, the superiority in prestige (rather than mere exchange) of brass rods over pots was palpably confirmed by the ability of the brass rods to bring in ritual cloth or slaves. In a complex society, the absence of such visible confirmation of prestige, of what exactly is an "upward" conversion, makes it necessary to attribute high but non-monetary value to aesthetic, stylistic, ethnic, class, or genealogical esoterica.

When things participate simultaneously in cognitively distinct yet effectively intermeshed exchange spheres, one is constantly confronted with seeming paradoxes of value. A Picasso, though possessing a monetary value, is priceless in another, higher scheme. Hence, we feel uneasy, even offended, when a newspaper declares the Picasso to be worth $690,000, for one should not be pricing the priceless. But in a pluralistic society, the "objective" pricelessness of the Picasso can only be unambiguously confirmed to us by its immense market price. Yet, the pricelessness still makes the Picasso in some sense more valuable than the pile of dollars it can fetch – as will be duly pointed out by the newspapers if the Picasso is stolen. Singularity, in brief, is confirmed not by the object's structural position in an exchange system, but by intermittent forays into the commodity sphere, quickly followed by reentries into the closed sphere of singular "art." But the two worlds cannot be kept separate for very long; for one thing, museums must insure their holdings. So museums and art dealers will name prices, be accused of the sin of transforming art into a commodity, and, in response, defend themselves by blaming each other for creating and maintaining a commodity market. It would, however, be missing the point of this analysis to conclude that the talk about singular art is merely an ideological camouflage for an interest in merchandising. What is culturally significant here is precisely that there is an inner compulsion to defend oneself, to others and to oneself, against the charge of "merchandising" art.

The only time when the commodity status of a thing is beyond question is the moment of actual exchange. Most of the time, when the commodity is effectively out of the commodity sphere, its status is inevitably ambiguous and open to the push and pull of events and desires, as it is shuffled about in the flux of social life. This is the time when it is exposed to the well-nigh-infinite variety of attempts to singularize it. Thus, singularizations of various kinds, many of them fleeting, are a constant accompaniment of commoditization, all the more so when it becomes excessive. There is a kind of singularizing black market here that is the mirror-image of, and as inevitable as, the more familiar commoditizing black market that accompanies regulated singularizing economies. Thus, even things that unambiguously carry an exchange value – formally speaking, therefore, commodities – do absorb the other kind of worth, one that is non-monetary and goes beyond exchange worth. We may take this to be the missing non-economic side of what Marx called commodity fetishism. For Marx, the worth of commodities is determined by the social relations of their production; but the existence of the exchange system makes the production process remote and misperceived, and it "masks" the commodity's true worth (as, say, in the case of diamonds). This allows the commodity to be socially endowed with a fetishlike "power" that is unrelated to its true worth. Our analysis suggests, however, that some of that power is attributed to commodities after they are produced, and this by way of an autonomous cognitive and cultural process of singularization.

Two Western exchange spheres: people vs. objects

I have so far emphasized the sweeping nature of commoditization in Western society as representative of an ideal type of highly commercialized and monetized society. But the West is also a unique cultural entity, with a historically conditioned set of predispositions to see the world in certain ways.

One of these predispositions I have referred to before: that of conceptually separating people from things, and of seeing people as the natural preserve for individuation (that is singularization) and things as the natural preserve for commoditization. The separation, though intellectually rooted in classical antiquity and Christianity, becomes culturally salient with the onset of European modernity. Its most glaring denial lay, of course, in the practice of slavery. Yet its cultural significance can be gauged precisely by the fact that slavery did present an intellectual and moral problem in the West (see Davis 1966, 1975), but almost nowhere else. Whatever the complex reasons, the conceptual distinction between the universe of people and the universe of objects had become culturally axiomatic in the West by the mid-twentieth century. It is therefore not surprising that the cultural clash over abortion should be more fierce in the twentieth century than it ever was in the nineteenth, and that this clash should be phrased by both sides in terms of the precise location of the line that divides persons from things and the point at which "personhood" begins. For both anti-abortion and pro-abortion forces agree on one point: that "things" but not "persons" can be aborted. Hence the occasional court battles when pro-abortionists seek court injunctions against anti-abortionists' attempts to ritualize the disposal of aborted fetuses, since ritual disposal presumes personhood. In terms of underlying conceptions, both sides here stand together in striking cultural contrast to the Japanese. The latter have few misgivings about abortion but acknowledge the personhood of aborted children, giving them the special status of *misogo*, lost souls, and commemorating them by special shrines (see Miura 1984).

There is, therefore, a perennial moral concern in Western thought, whatever the ideological position of the thinker, about the commoditization of human attributes such as labor, intellect, or creativity, or, more recently, human organs, female reproductive capacity, and ova. The moral load in these matters comes partly from the long debates on slavery and the victory of abolition. Hence the tendency to resort to slavery as the readiest metaphor when commoditization threatens to invade the human sphere, slavery being the extreme case in which the totality of a person is seen as having been commoditized. The moral indictments of capitalism by both Marx and Pope Leo XIII derived their force from the notion that human labor should not be a mere commodity – hence the rhetorical power of such terms as "wage slavery." The conceptual unease of conjoining person and commodity renders, in most modern Western liberal societies, the adoption of a baby illegal if it involves monetary compensation to the natural parent – something that most societies have seen as satisfying the obvious demands of equity. In the modern West, however, adoption through compensation is viewed as child-selling and therefore akin to slavery because of the implicit commoditization of the child, regardless of how loving the adoptive parents may be. Thus, the law specifically punishes such compensation in Britain, in most Canadian provinces, and in almost all states in the United States.

The hallmark of commoditization is exchange. But exchange opens the way to trafficking, and trafficking in human attributes carries with it a special opprobrium. For example, we do not – we cannot at this point – object to the commoditization and sale of labor (by its nature, a terminal commodity). But we do object to the trafficking in labor that a complete commoditization of labor would imply. We have abolished indentured labor, and the courts have struck down the commoditization of the contracts of athletes and actors. The cultural argument against a team's or a film studio's "selling" a ballplayer or an actor to another employer is cast in the idiom of slavery. The transfer of a contract forces the worker to work for someone whom he had not chosen himself, hence forces him to work involuntarily. We see here a significant cultural detail in the Western commoditization of labor – the commoditization must be controlled by the laborer himself. By contrast, contractual obligations to pay, as in promissory notes or installment buying, and rent contracts are legally negotiable; they can be and are regularly sold and resold. By the same cultural logic, the idea of nearly confiscatory taxation is far less shocking to us than even a modest amount of corvée labor. As with trafficking in labor, we find the direct commoditization of sexual services (also a terminal commodity) by the immediate supplier less objectionable than the trafficking in them by pimps. And so also we find the imminent possibility of terminal sales of human ova somewhat more morally acceptable than the idea of a commercial traffic in them.

The question remains, however: how secure are the Western cultural ramparts that defend the human sphere against commoditization, especially in a secularized society that finds it increasingly difficult to appeal to any transcendental sanctions for cultural discrimination and classification? I have suggested that economies are inherently responsive to the pressures of commoditization and that they tend to commoditize as widely as the exchange technology allows. What then, we may ask, are the effects, on the divide between the human and the commodity spheres, of the developing technology of transfer of human attributes? I am speaking here of recent medical advances in the transfer of organs and ova and the development of surrogate motherhood. The realm of human reproduction is one in which the difference between persons and things is particularly difficult to define, defying all attempts at drawing a simple line where there is a natural continuum.

The idea of direct surrogate motherhood – in which a woman simply bears a child for the future legal mother – required, of course, a legal more than a technical innovation. The idea had taken hold at the same time that technical advances in coping with female infertility had begun to raise the hopes of childless couples but without, in fact, helping many of them. It also came in response to the shrinkage in the supply of babies for adoption that occurred in the 1960's with the pill and the 1970's with the wider legalization of abortions. More recently, the picture has been complicated by the development of technical means for the actual transplantation of ova, opening the possibility of trading in the physical means of reproduction. The popular objections to surrogate motherhood are usually phrased in the idiom of the impropriety of commoditization. In the words of a Canadian provincial minister of social services, expressing his opposition: "You can't buy a baby in Ontario." It is, however, more acceptable, at least to some, when the surrogate mother announces that she receives not "payment" but "compensation" of ten thousand dollars – "because of the inconvenience to my family and the risk involved." And the agency arranging for surrogate child production makes a point of declaring "We are not in the rent-a-womb business." In the meantime, while ethicists and theologians argue, the cost of securing a surrogate mother has now risen to around twenty-five thousand dollars (Scott 1984).

There is, of course, a precedent for the commoditization of physical human attributes: the supply of blood in American medical practice depends overwhelmingly on a straightforward commodity market in blood – in contrast, for example, to most European countries, which have deliberately rejected the commodity approach (Cooper and Culyer 1968). At present, advances in organ transplants and the inadequate supply of organs raises the same question of public policy that was confronted in the past in the case of blood: what are the best ways of ensuring an adequate supply? In the meantime, advertisements have begun to appear offering to buy kidneys for transplantation.

How to deal with ova is only beginning to be discussed. Culturally, the situation is perceived as being more complex than in the case of sperm, which has been commoditized for some time without a great deal of discussion. Is this because the ovum is seen as the basic core of the future human being? Or because women are expected to feel maternal toward the ova as potential babies and should not sell them, whereas men are not expected to have paternal feelings about their sperm?[2] (Many societies describe the generation of life as the union of two elements; Westerners, however, choose the scientific metaphor in which one speaks of the fertilization *of* the ovum *by* the sperm, so that the ovum becomes a homunculus being activated into life.) The inevitable development into routine procedures of the transplantation of ova and the freezing of ova for storage will represent an expansion of the possibilities of the exchange technology for human attributes, including the possibility of trafficking in them. The question is whether this will increase the permeability of the boundary between the world of things and that of people, or whether the boundary will be displaced by recourse to new definitions but itself remain as rigid as before.

Conclusion: kinds of biographies

Although the singular and the commodity are opposites, no thing ever quite reaches the ultimate commodity end of the continuum between them. There are no perfect commodities. On the other hand, the exchange function of every economy appears to have a built-in force that drives the exchange system toward the greatest degree of commoditization that the exchange technology permits. The counterforces are culture and the individual, with their drive to discriminate, classify, compare, and sacralize. This means a two-front battle for culture as for the individual – one against commoditization as a homogenizer of exchange values, the other against the utter singularization of things as they are in nature.

In small-scale uncommercialized societies, the drive to commoditization was usually contained by the inadequacies of the technology of exchange, notably, the absence of a well-developed monetary system. This left room for a cultural categorization of the exchange value of things, usually in the form of closed exchange spheres, and it satisfied individual cognitive needs for classification. The collective cultural classification thus constrained the innate exuberance to which purely idiosyncratic and private classifications are prone.

In large-scale, commercialized, and monetized societies, the existence of a sophisticated exchange technology fully opens the economy to swamping by commoditization. In all contemporary industrial societies, whatever their ideologies, commoditization and monetization tend to invade almost every aspect of existence, be it openly or by way of a black market. New technological advances (for example, in medicine) also open previously closed areas to the possibilities of exchange and these areas tend to become quickly commoditized. The flattening of values that follows commoditization and the inability of the collective culture of a modern society to cope with this flatness frustrate the individual on the one hand, and, on the other, leave ample room for a multitude of classifications by individuals and small groups. These classifications, however, remain private and, except in the case of culturally hegemonic groups, without public support.

Thus, the economies of complex and highly monetized societies exhibit a two-sided valuating system: on one side is the homogenous area of commodities, on the other, the extremely variegated area of private valuation. Further complications arise from the constant referring of private valuation to the only reliable public valuation that exists – which is in the commodity area. It is inevitable that if worth is given a price, the going market price will become the measure of worth. The result is a complex intertwining of the commodity exchange sphere with the plethora of private classifications, leading to anomalies and contradictions and to conflicts both in the cognition of individuals and in the interaction of individuals and groups. By contrast, the structure of the economies of small-scale societies in the past resulted in a relative consonance of economic, cultural, and private valuations. These differences lead to quite different biographical profiles of things.

A caveat is required at this point. While in this discussion I have dwelt on the gross contrast between two ideal and polar types of economies, the most interesting empirical cases to be studied, with ultimately the highest theoretical returns, are the cases in between. It is from these cases that we can learn how the forces of commoditization and singularization are intertwined in ways far more subtle than our ideal model can show, how one breaks the rules by moving between spheres that are supposed to be insulated from each other, how one converts what is formally unconvertible, how one masks these actions and with whose connivance, and, not least, how the spheres are reorganized and things reshuffled between them in the course of a society's history. Equally interesting would be the cases where the different systems of commoditization of different societies interact. For example, Curtin (1984) has shown the importance, for the history of world trade, of trade diasporas; in these, traders, constituting a distinct *quasi*-cultural group, provided the channels for the movement of goods between disparate societies. The usefulness of such trading groups in mediating between the different exchange systems is manifest. By cushioning the direct impact of world trade, this mediation spares the societies involved from seeing their particular ideas of commoditization challenged, sheltering their baroque exchange systems in the comfort of their cultural parochialism. This, perhaps, would explain the striking viability, historically, of parochial economic systems in the midst of worldwide networks of trade. And it might also explain what has long been a puzzle in economic anthropology – namely, the limited spread, until the twentieth century, of "all-purpose" currency, a spread far more limited than diffusion theory or commonsense utilitarianism would have suggested. Having said all this, let me nevertheless return to the gross contrast between the "complex, commercialized" and the "small-scale" societies, the implications of which I have pursued throughout this paper.

One can draw an analogy between the way societies construct individuals and the way they construct things. In small-scale societies, a person's social identities are relatively stable and changes in them are normally conditioned more by cultural rules than by biographical idiosyncrasies. The drama in an ordinary person's biography stems from what happens within the given status. It lies in the conflicts between the egoistic self and the unambiguous demands of given social identities, or in conflicts arising from interaction between actors with defined roles within a clearly structured social system. The excitement in the biographies is of the picaresque variety. At the same time, the individual who does not fit the given niches is either singularized into a special identity – which is sacred or dangerous, and often both – or is simply cast out. Things in these small-scale societies are similarly modeled. Their status in the clearly structured system of exchange values and exchange spheres is unambiguous. An eventful biography of a thing is for the most part one of events within the given sphere. Any thing that does not fit the categories is clearly anomalous and it is taken out of normal circulation, to be either sacralized or isolated or cast out. What one glimpses through the biographies of both people and things in these societies is, above all, the social system and the collective understandings on which it rests.

In complex societies, by contrast, a person's social identities are not only numerous but often conflicting, and there is no clear hierarchy of loyalties that makes one identity dominant over the others. Here, the drama of personal biographies has become more and more the drama of identities – of their clashes, of the impossibility of choosing between them, of the absence of signals from the culture and the society at large to help in the choice. The drama, in brief, lies in the uncertainty of identity – a theme increasingly dominant in modern Western literature where it is pushing aside dramas of social structure (even in the eminently structural cases dealt with in writings on women and "minorities"). The biography of things in complex societies reveals a similar pattern. In the homogenized world of commodities, an eventful biography of a thing becomes the story of the various singularizations of it, of classifications and reclassifications in an uncertain world of categories whose importance shifts with every minor change in context. As with persons, the drama here lies in the uncertainties of valuation and of identity.

All this suggests an emendation to the profound Durkheimian notion that a society orders the world of things on the pattern of the structure that prevails in the social world of its people. What also happens, I would suggest, is that societies constrain both these worlds simultaneously and in the same way, constructing objects as they construct people.

Notes

I owe thanks to Arjun Appadurai and Barbara Klamon Kopytoff for discussions that led to the writing of this paper, and to Jean Adelman, Sandra Barnes, Muriel Bell, Gyan Prakash, Colin Renfrew, and Barbara Herrnstein Smith for comments and suggestions that helped shape its final version.

1. I wish to thank Barbara Herrnstein Smith for drawing my attention to the importance of such institutions in the processes I am describing.

2. I am grateful to Muriel Bell for this suggestion.

References

Bohannan, Paul. 1959. The Impact of Money on an African Subsistence Economy. *Journal of Economic History* 19:491–503.

Braudel, Fernand. 1983. *The Roots of Modern Capitalism.* New York.

Cooper, Michael H., and Anthony J. Culyer. 1968. *The Price of Blood: An Economic Study of the Charitable and Commercial Principles.* London.

Curtin, Philip D. 1984. *Cross-Cultural Trade in World History.* Cambridge.

Davis, David Brion. 1966. *The Problem of Slavery in Western Culture.* Ithaca, N.Y.
    1975. *The Problem of Slavery in the Age of Revolution: 1770–1823.* Ithaca, N.Y.

Douglas, Mary, and Baron Isherwood. 1980. *The World of Goods: Towards an Anthropology of Consumption.* London.

Dumont, Louis. 1972. *Homo Hierarchicus.* London.

Durkheim, Emile and Marcel Mauss. 1963. *Primitive Classification.* Trans. Rodney Needham. London. (Orig. French ed., 1903).

Durkheim, Emile. 1915. *The Elementary Forms of Religious Life.* London. (Orig. French ed., 1912).

Ekeh, Peter P. 1974. *Social Exchange Theory.* London.

Homans, George. 1961. *Social Behavior: Its Elementary Forms*. New York.

Kapferer, Bruce, ed. 1976. *Transactions and Meaning*. Philadelphia.

Kopytoff, Igor, and Suzanne Miers. 1977. African "slavery" as an institution of marginality. In S. Miers and I. Kopytoff, eds., *Slavery in Africa: Historical and Anthropological Perspectives*, 3–81. Madison, Wis.

Kopytoff, Igor. 1982. Slavery. *Annual Review of Anthropology*, 11:207–30.

Kroeber, A. L. 1925. The Yurok. *Handbook of the Indians of California*. (Bureau of American Ethnology Bulletin 78).

Langness, L. L. 1965. *The Life History in Anthropological Science*. New York.

Meillasoux, C. 1975. Introduction. In Meillasoux, ed., *L'esclavage en Afrique précoloniale*. Paris.

Miura, Domyo. 1984. *The Forgotten Child*. Trans. Jim Cuthbert. Henley-on-Thames.

Patterson, Orlando. 1982. *Slavery and Social Death: A Comparative Study*. Cambridge, Mass.

Pospisil, Leopold. 1963. *Kapauku Papuan Economy*. (Yale Publications in Anthropology No. 61). New Haven, Conn.

Rivers, W. H. R. 1910. The Genealogical Method Anthropological Inquiry. *Sociological Review* 3:1–12.

Scott, Sarah. 1984. The Baby Business. *The Gazette*, B–1, 4. Montreal, April 24.

Thompson, Michael. 1979. *Rubbish Theory: The Creation and Destruction of Value*. New York.

Vaughan, James H. 1977. Mafakur: A limbic institution of the Marghi (Nigeria). In S. Miers and I. Kopytoff, eds., *Slavery in Africa: Historical and Anthropological Perspectives*, 85–102. Madison, Wis.

PART II

Exchange, consumption, and display

CHAPTER 3

Two kinds of value in the Eastern Solomon Islands

WILLIAM H. DAVENPORT

It has been many years since Malinowski made the useful distinction between ordinary commodities, which were exchanged in conventional markets, and valuables, which could be exchanged only for one another and in restricted, ritualized contexts. This distinction between general and restricted exchangeability has been one of the main topics (and source of contention) in the comparative study of economic systems. Here, I will describe how labor and materials are combined to produce durables that cannot be further exchanged. These are objects that are beyond the potential of exchangeability and therefore outside the category of commodities.

The geographic area I will be discussing is part of the Eastern Solomon Islands in the southwestern Pacific, comprising the eastern half of San Cristobal Island and the two small, off-lying islands of Santa Ana and Santa Catalina. All the communities in this area speak dialects of a language originally designated as Kahua;[1] all have local cultures that are quite similar and are different from cultures and languages of western San Cristobal and the Santa Cruz Islands to the east.[2] My focus will be the small island of Santa Catalina, or Aoriki, because that is where I did the most intensive fieldwork (1965–66) and where the precolonial culture was best preserved.

There are many occasions and events in these societies at which the exchange and consumption of key commodities are crucial to the maintenance and alteration of social relations, but those that command the greatest attention and that, at appropriate times, represent the ultimate social effort are the three commemorative celebrations, or -*murina*, for important deceased relatives. The three -*murina* are of increasing scale and, if celebrated, follow upon two initial funeral observances. Let me give a very brief outline of the sequence.[3]

Following the death of every man, woman, and child, there is a period of mourning over the corpse that lasts from a few hours for an infant to several days for an important adult. Burial, usually in a designated cemetery, follows this brief recognition of death. After burial everyone in the community observes some form of mourning,

95

and for important personages this may be very severe. For example, it may be decided, by consensus, to maintain total silence in the village; the effect is to immobilize close kin, while distant kin and nonrelatives move out of the residential area so they can carry on daily activities and provide for those who remain at home. However severe the mourning observances, in all cases when an adult dies, commerce in and out of the village is stopped. Canoe passages are closed, paths are barricaded.

After an interval of five or ten days, a small feast is given by close kin, as an expression of gratitude to the entire community. This is also regarded as a release of the community from its obligations to demonstrate grief, and it compensates everyone, in a small way, for the inconveniences mourning entailed. Still, some villagers choose to continue their mourning, and their observances range from mild to severe, depending on personal feelings and obligations toward the deceased.

Months later a second distribution is made to the entire community, with special presentations to those who have continued to show visible mourning. The special presentations must include pork, which raises its economic value above that of the first presentation, at which only feast-quality puddings, that is puddings made from fine-quality staples and canarium almonds (a highly valued tree crop), but no meat, were distributed. The total value of this second presentation can be increased by increasing the size of the pork presentations, by going outside the community to purchase a pig (which entails additional effort and expense), and by commissioning a craftsman to carve new wooden vessels for the main presentations. Commissioning a craftsman entails paying him in local currency for his work, as well as feeding him and his family while he is working (because he cannot carry out subsistence activities). The artisan can be brought in from another village, which indicates that those who are making the distribution are prepared to make an extra effort – that is, to go abroad – in order to get a notable carver.

These first two distributions constitute the funeral observances, and both are held for every adult death. The relative scale of the funeral observances are expected to be roughly commensurate with the social rank of the deceased. The spirit of the observances is, consciously, a show of gratitude on the part of the close kin of the deceased to the entire community for its expression of sorrow, especially to those few who observed prolonged bereavement. The persons who assume responsibility for the presentations are, of course, assisted by those who are closely associated with or obligated to them. Thus, it is a "kindred" of kith and kin standing behind one or several organizers that is the source of the wealth distributed. From the sponsors' point of view, organizing the funeral observances entails both calling in personal credits, which were established by assisting others with earlier observances, and creating new personal debts, which must be repaid in the future when the creditor calls for assistance in organizing a similar event.

Networks of personal credits and debits established in this way (among others) are the bases of social standing and rank. The more intricate the history of a person's credits and debits, the more important that person is to the community, the higher his or her social rank, and the greater his or her influence. All credits and debits of this kind are also part of a person's estate when he or she dies. Thus, when a person of great substance dies, there are usually credits that can be called in by the heirs to celebrate the funeral. Failure to repay debts incurred in the course of social transactions of this sort is a very serious legal offense. If the debtor, or in most cases one of his heirs, does not pay upon a public demand made by the creditor, the latter is entitled to seize garden land being used by the debtor. Garden lands are owned corporately by matrilineages, and thus a seizure is of concern to many people.

Comestible commodities, such as prepared foods and pork, are the foundations of social transactions. Between individuals all commodity transactions are economic contracts: what is given must be returned in exact amount on demand and within a "reasonable" period, but with no interest. However, when an individual distributes commodities to the public, so to speak, in the context of a social ritual, no economic debt is incurred. Instead, the giver is rewarded by the accrual of commensurate prestige. Since every social ritual that involves the distribution of commodities involves both repayments of debts established at earlier rituals and the formation of new debts that must be repaid at future rituals, each ritual is linked to ones that have gone before and to others that will be celebrated in the future.

For deceased adults of substantial social rank, further memorial observances may be initiated. However, the structure and organization of these memorials are different from those of the two funeral observances. The initiation of the first memorial of this kind (of a possible three) can be seen from two social points of view. Seen in one way, an individual, usually a man, who considers himself a successor to the deceased will decide to honor his predecessor (who may have been his father, his elder brother, his maternal uncle, or just a mentor), and he persuades other senior men of the community to do likewise for other persons they wish to honor in this way. Seen in another way, every few years a group of senior men and women decide to honor important persons who have died in the interval since the previous such celebration. On Aoriki this first special recognition following death is called *owota*, but other communities in the Eastern Solomons have different names for the event.

For the owota in each community is divided into moities (but the principles for this bifurcation vary from community to community) so that every mature person, but most importantly every man, is paired with someone of approximately the same social rank. All those who are honoring a deceased person make a presentation to their exchange partner. Later, at subsequent owota, the partners receiving presentations (or their successors) will reciprocate with equal or greater presentations.

The presentation consists of a large vessel, newly carved for the event, containing prepared food and a small cooked pig; the sizes of the vessel and of the pig vary, as may the effort and expense involved in commissioning the vessel, obtaining the pig, and securing the staples for the pudding. Each person invests in this effort the maximum he can afford, given the amount of support he can muster, his other obligations, and his long-term strategies for other presentations in the future. The size of each presentation should, however, be at least equal to one received in the past either by the giver or by a predecessor whose debt the giver has inherited or is assuming.

Some years later a second presentation of the same kind can be made by those who wish to honor the same deceased person again, and in so doing they improve their own social rank. On Aoriki the second memorial is called *rate mataufa*, loosely meaning "completing the grave." The scale of the rate mataufa is considerably greater, and the number of deceased so honored smaller, than with the owota.

The consequences of the two memorial exchanges are to establish and publicly validate the social hierarchy in the community, which is destabilized by the death of any important person or *arafa*. Seen another way, it is a collective rite of succession insofar as social rank is concerned. The occasions can be manipulated in various ways. One partner can challenge the other by aggressively making an unexpectedly large presentation, thus publicly shaming him. A receiving partner may claim to have received less than his due, thus insulting the giver; a giver can make an unexpectedly small presentation, claiming that is all his partner is worth. Potentially, then, these memorial exchanges can become competitions, and they can also be public forums for the airing of grievances and longstanding disputes, but this is not the rule. The ideal is that the exchanges should be harmonious and the community as a whole should feel satisfied by the transactions. In particular, the community should feel pride at having honored important deceased persons, and there should be general agreement about the hierarchy of social rank that is enacted among the principal participants.

The two kinds of memorial exchanges just described pertain only to the immediate community, that is, to a single village or a cluster of small, adjacent villages. The food that is amassed and given to an exchange partner is eventually redistributed, more or less evenly, and consumed locally. The carved vessels in which the presentations are made are not used again and serve only as material testimonials to the transactions. On balance, there is some loss of wealth from the community through the purchase of commodities and services, such as that of carvers, from other communities. Over time, however, these economic losses to other communities are made up by sales of commodities and specialized services to other communities that maintain the same kind of ceremonial observances, and that, as described earlier, enhance the value of some purchases by making the effort to go abroad for them.

One further note on the vessels that are carved solely for the food presentations: until a few years ago, they were never used in subsequent exchanges. As already mentioned, they were material evidence of an exchange, and they were often casually displayed outside a dwelling, but still utilized for mundane purposes. Babies were washed in them; children used them in the sea as miniature canoes; broken and decayed ones were used as feeding troughs for pigs. In other words, these special vessels, some of which were truly magnificent works of art, were used just once and then allowed to deteriorate.

There is one more kind of memorial, which is celebrated every decade or so, and is not only the largest of the series, but also the supreme social and economic effort that communities in the Eastern Solomons undertake. This is usually called -murina, commemoration.

A -murina is initiated by consensus of the important men and women of the community. The important considerations in coming to this agreement are a favorable assessment of the total resources of the community; a commitment of these resources to honoring important dead persons by undertaking any of several ambitious and costly tasks; and, at the same time, a commitment to celebrating the completion of these tasks by feasting and entertaining any and all persons who wish to participate. The entire undertaking takes several years to plan, prepare, and execute. The degree of success of the undertaking will be known to every community in the region and indicate the relative

economic and social strength of the organizing community. The
-murina also leaves a community temporarily exhausted, depleted of
energy and surplus wealth.

The main structural difference between the -murina and all the
other observances for the deceased is in the sociological units that
initiate the undertaking, support it, and receive gifts. At funerals it
is the bereaved close kin and friends who initiate the observances. In
the two memorials (owota and rate mataufa) for illustrious forebears,
the initiator is a collectivity of important persons (arafa). For the
-murina it is the community as a whole that takes the initiative. At
funerals the community closes itself off from others as it mourns, and
the concluding celebrations mark the gradual reinstitution of normal
social relations both within and without. With the memorials, the
community divides into mirror-image, stratified halves, which exchange evenly with each other. Little wealth leaves the community in
funerals and memorials. With the -murina the recipients are other
nearby communities. Reciprocal attendance is understood to be a
community obligation, with guests invited either in return for one it
hosted in the past at which the present hosts were guests, or with the
understanding that they are returning a social debt that must be
repaid, in kind, in the future. Although wealth flows out of the host
community in the -murina, most of it will be returned over the years
as other communities of the region celebrate equivalent rituals. The
reciprocal relations between communities that -murina establish are
significant sociological bonds that both define and unite a region in
the Eastern Solomon Islands.

The ambitious tasks that a community undertakes for a -murina
are constructions that remain as material testaments of the celebration
and also directly benefit the community. At a minimum, some kind
of elegant structure is built in which great vessels of food and pork
are displayed before being presented to the guests. For the structure,
gifted artisans from many communities are commissioned to carve
posts and design and execute other architectural details. Great presentation vessels (some as long as four-five meters) are also commissioned. And there is always the matter of planting extra crops, raising
and purchasing more pigs, planning and making trips to other communities, in order to purchase needed materials and foodstuffs.

The major tasks are usually the building of new canoes. One type
is the great trading or so-called war canoe, for which the Solomon
Islands are justly famous. These great plank-built canoes, which represent the greatest investment of capital for these communities, are
seen as lifelines on the small islands of Santa Ana and Santa Catalina,

which must import much of their food. The building of a new trading canoe does not occur only at a -murina – one can be built any time a man feels he can muster the resources; however, those built as a commemorative task are always constructed as elegantly as possible and hence are more expensive than the others. Trading canoes are not only essential to the economics of each community, they are also regarded as representations of the community abroad since they are used only to visit other communities.

Solomon Islanders may also build the special canoe used only to fish the seasonal schools of bonito and tuna. Even though bonito and tuna are much prized for food, the fishing of them is a sacred endeavor that is dedicated to major tutelary deities. Bonito canoes are considered the supreme expression of skill and artistry. In some instances experts are brought in to supervise the design and construction of these canoes, in other cases contracts are let to other communities for their construction. Each canoe constructed for a -murina, whether a trading canoe or a bonito canoe, is dedicated to an important deceased person. Once dedicated and launched, it becomes a sacred object that cannot be sold or traded.

Often, too, the skulls of the most important personages honored by the ceremony are disinterred and placed in special caskets for keeping in charnel houses and shrines. There is a great variety of reburial rites in the Eastern Solomons, which seems to be the result of innovations introduced in the context of -murina. One important goal of a -murina is to make a lasting impression on other communities, and one way to do this is to innovate in some way.

In a few of the Eastern Solomon communities, the supreme commemorative effort was to offer a price for the kidnapping of a child, who would be renamed after an honored deceased person and then treated as a sacred, living representation of that person. Those who did the kidnapping were usually from nearby communities, but they would travel afar, outside the range of communities that habitually interacted in the -murina celebrations, to obtain a victim. One community, probably the wealthiest in the area, is reported to have even offered prices for the delivery of adults who would be killed and consumed in honor of the deceased.

Human life might also be sacrificed for the dedication of a new trading canoe. This was accomplished by initiating the canoe with a raiding party on a distant community. Any available victim was selected. However, taking a human life was certain to cost a life in the canoe owner's community because direct retaliation was inevitable.

The construction of a new sacred bonito canoe entails a long-term commitment to maintaining a crew of vigorous young men during the annual bonito season to man it. All crews live apart from the village in the sacred canoe houses during the bonito season in order to keep themselves pure, free of the pollution of women and the domestic scene. Their food must be cooked separately. The cost of this special attention is considerable and must be borne by the owner of the canoe, the man who organized and paid for its construction. The owner wins personal renown if his canoe and crew succeed in catching the sacred fish. Moreover, a successful bonito canoe and crew is an indication that the tutelary deity and the spirit of the deceased to whom the canoe has been dedicated are favorably disposed toward the canoe owner and the entire community. The more successful bonito canoes a community can maintain, the greater its renown in the district.

Maintaining a trading canoe is a business venture for the person who sponsors and pays for its construction. It can be profitable or not. From the point of view of the entire community, however, many trading canoes, especially busy ones, signify prosperity to other communities.

The list of major efforts given here is not complete, and there seems always to have been a receptiveness to innovation. Ideally not only should the major commemorative effort of a -murina be difficult and expensive, but if possible, it should also be audacious. The same spirit applies to all the preparatory steps. Everything done, whether it is planting or harvesting for the celebration, going on trading trips, organizing ordinary work parties, is done with éclat. If there is a new way to do something, then it will be experimented with. Ideas are borrowed from celebrations observed elsewhere. Everyone who works is feasted and paid well by the sponsors of that activity. One such flourish is the importation of young women whose favors are awarded to young men as incentives for hard work.

Wherever possible, special attention is paid to aesthetics. Foodstuffs are not simply gathered together for preparation, they are carried from gardens or from the trading canoes by processions of young, singing women. Staples are not just heaped up before they are cooked; rather, much time is spent hanging and arranging them in attractive displays for everyone to admire. Prepared food, as mentioned, is ceremonially presented in vessels that are specially carved for the occasion, sometimes by gifted artisans from other communities. Moreover, after the vessels are filled with food, each is tastefully decorated with betel nuts, pepper leaves, and carefully sliced portions of pork.

Before the feast day the prepared food is displayed, for appraisal, in an elegant structure constructed for the purpose.

New songs are composed, dance teams spend long hours practicing, and arrangements are made to bring in groups of dancers and singers from far away to perform during the brief period of culmination, when the massive presentations to the guests are made. Even during the long preparation period, right up to the great giveaway, progress is marked with small feasts and celebrations in which the contribution of each and every adult is acknowledged with presentations of food. At the culminating event, at which all the results of planning, economic expenditure, and labor are on display, the festivities are infused with the spirit of an arts festival as well as an air of lavish expenditure.

Within the community not only the important men and women (arafa) make presentations in honor of deceased persons, but all other adults dedicate their labor to some deceased kin. Finally, at the culminating presentation, everyone makes a gift to a guest of roughly the same social rank, or to someone who made a gift to him in the past. In this way the entire community is involved in honoring the dead, and each individual is involved in a transaction with an outsider. There is a major difference, however, between the dedicatory efforts of arafa and those of ordinary persons: the spirits that are honored with a -murina, whether the material representations be a canoe, a house, a reburial casket, a kidnapped person, or a human sacrifice, become deified, whereas those deceased persons who are honored by only a presentation of food are merely being remembered and honored.

Harmony and the suppression of all animosity within the community is recognized as essential to the success of a -murina. It is partly for this reason that great care is taken to compensate everyone fully for every contribution of labor or commodities with social praise and material reward. There is the constant fear that if dissension develops, not only will work suffer, but on the culminating day, when hundreds of people from many communities are present to watch the formal presentations of food and pork, the exchanges may go awry. It could occur in this way: several principal participants are angry at another person who is not their exchange partner, so instead of making their presentations to their respective partners, they make them to the person against whom they have a grudge. This angers the expectant partners, who get nothing; it obligates the unsuspecting receiver to reciprocate, which he is unprepared to do. Such dissension turns the culminating event into a social disaster for the hosts.

A brief word about the theology, at least as it is on Aoriki. There are two separate orders of deities: one called the *ataro ni mwani*, "deities from humans," the other *ataro si fenua*, "deities of the land." The deification of spirits that occurs in the great -murina celebration involves the former, deities derived from human spirits. The deities of the land do not have personalities. They were present in and around the community before humans arrived; they made the environment usable, productive, and fertile. Thus, the deities of the land make it possible to amass material wealth, and they are separately honored annually by a lengthy ritual celebration that marks the new year. The deities derived from human spirits guide human destinies, give power, and protect people from alien spirits and enemies. They are honored and worshiped in several ways, by individuals and groups, in many different rites and rituals. The most important of these are periodic initiations of boys and the annual fishing quest for bonito and tuna.

The two classes of deities have no direct interaction. The only link between them is the humans who worship and depend upon both, but in different ways. My religious interpretation of the great memorial celebration, the -murina, is that it is a periodic test and demonstration of the strength and efficacy of the dual relationship between humans and the two orders of deities. But it also is a kind of final rite of passage for the spirits of a few men who during their lives were notable achievers. These select few are elevated to the company of those spirits who control the destinies of the living. The -murina does not mark internal social accommodations to the deaths of important people, as do the two preceding memorial celebrations. It does establish, however, the overall strength and well-being of the community in relation to other communities of the region.

The distributions just described, with their emphasis upon the production and distribution of a variety of commodities, can be viewed as compelling evidence for a strongly materialist and commodity-oriented value system in the subcultures of the Eastern Solomon Islands. Things are produced, manipulated, and consumed for personal, social, secular, and religious ends. We note, too, that the increased commitment of labor for production increases the value, that is, the economic value, of the total endeavor. Moreover, the increased value or scale of the collective efforts is positively correlated with the social and geographical scope of the celebrations.

It can be argued, too, that the material value of commodities is enhanced by the aesthetic embellishments, for these require additional effort and the utilization of rare skills. It would seem, too, that the ultimate value could be achieved only by the taking of human life, which as pointed out amounts to a forfeiture of life because one will certainly be taken in revenge. In this line of argument the human lives become commodities that are disposed of in the same manner as other material things.

However neat this materialist, commodity-oriented argument may appear, I do not propose it because I do not believe it. The reasons for this are to be found in the ways that aesthetic talents are regarded and in the fact that aesthetic embellishment and the sacrifice of human life involve the expression of the highest social values. I argue that by means of either or both, these societies transform commodities and commodity contexts into noneconomic goods and situations. Once the ritual transactions are completed, all objects associated with them are either consumed (for example, the food) or become sacra (such as the canoes). All things associated with the ritual are decommoditized.

On Aoriki at least, and I presume elsewhere in the Eastern Solomons as well, the talents of artisans, both men and women, are viewed as rare skills. The artist, however, as opposed to the artisan, is someone who is exceptional in all the skills that competent men and women should possess, plus a few others. For example, all adult men are expected to be proficient carpenters, to be able to build a house, to make an ordinary food bowl, to construct a serviceable fishing canoe, and so forth. Only a few men excel in all the masculine skills; fewer still are masters of those and also confident and competent enough to incise facial designs, which all islanders receive as children. Since all these skills – fine carpentry, sculpture, incision techniques, plus the ability to conceptualize complex designs and constructions – are required for the construction of bonito and trading canoes, possession of all the talents required to build one of these craft is the measure of a master craftsman, an artist, an exceptional person. The same evaluations pertain to women, but the skills are plaiting, basketry, tatooing, and other feminine arts.

An exceptional work is thought to be due to more than mere human talent. There must be inspiration and assistance that can come only from tutelary deities. Thus, in every truly great work of art there is a connection with the supernatural, an element of the spiritual.

The use of exceptional talent is confined to a limited set of objects for use only in ritualized or sacred contexts. For example, people eat every day out of simple but very well-carved wooden bowls, and any man minimally skillful should be able to make one. For sacred meals, however, food is served in bowls that are elegantly carved and inlaid – implements that not every man can make. The elegantly carved bowl sets the religious meals apart from everyday meals. The same difference applies to house posts for a dwelling and for a structure in which ritual presentations of food are displayed; to ordinary fishing canoes and the canoes used exclusively to catch sacred bonito and tuna; to canoes made expressly for trading by individuals and the larger canoes that make more ambitious trading voyages and were once used for raiding. No ordinary commodities are embellished or enhanced with exceptional aesthetic skills. In summary, the utilization of exceptional aesthetic skills is confined to objects used only in sacred and secular rituals.

Furthermore, all ritual objects are commissioned for particular events. No ritual object, no aesthetic object, is made for personal enjoyment. Each object made by a gifted artist is for use in a ritual, and afterward becomes a memento of the event for which it was created. Thus, art objects are not generalized types. Each object is unique for two reasons: it is an individualized creation, and it is a material record of the event for which it was made.

Still, it can be argued that the utilization of exceptional skills at a -murina is largely a show of wealth because the artists must be paid for their work, and the cost of their labor is another increment in the total economic value of the celebration. That argument is partly true, for the inclusion of the skills of exceptionally talented persons does, indeed, add substantially to costs. So, too, traveling long distances in order to procure something that could be had at home adds an investment of labor that increases the economic value of the commodity. But this is not the entire story. Once the object has been used in a ritual, either social or religious, it is never sold or exchanged again. Canoes for bonito fishing and trading are used repeatedly, but they are kept in the sacred precincts of a canoe house that is also the site of other religious observances. When these canoes become old and unserviceable, they must be allowed to rot away in the house with other cast-off sacra. The carved vessels in which food presentations are made are never used in a feast again, but are allowed to molder away. Special structures built for observances may be used as guest houses, but in the end they are not replaced but allowed to crumble in place.

My argument is that the utilization of exceptional skills, or what we think of as aesthetic expressions, sets certain objects apart from ordinary things and commodities and designates them for use on ritual occasions alone. It decommoditizes them. Put another way, aesthetically embellished objects signal ritual contexts and ritual utilization. It is as if a nonmaterial or spiritual, dimension is added to an object,[4] committing it to a domain in which social and religious values prevail over economic ones. Recall that the taking of human life can either be associated with the completion of a commemorative trading canoe or be a commemorative event in itself. Either taking a life or kidnapping a child amounts to forfeiting a life from one's own community because retaliation is assured. Such acts, then, become a sacrifice. When aesthetic expression is combined with the taking of human life, as it seems to be in these ritual contexts, it appears to be another kind of sacrifice. An embellished object is separated from the economic domain of purchase and exchange. Once it has been utilized in a social or religious ritual, the object is sacralized, and even further removed from the realm of secular and economic things.

There is no ritual for desacralizing sacred objects. The normal practice for dispensing with sacred objects, which includes even leftover foods, trash, and garbage from sacred meals, is to isolate them and allow them slowly to disintegrate. In each sacred canoe house there is a small enclosure for just this purpose. If the object is too large to dispose of in this way, it is merely allowed to disintegrate where it is, but it is always treated with deference.

Traditionally, sacred objects were never traded or sold. There was a market for the skilled labor to fabricate them, but not for the objects themselves. In point of fact, there was a fear of sacred objects that were associated with another person and with a tutelary deity other than one's own. Even after the islanders were converted to Christianity, the sale of sacred objects, greatly desired as exotic art by Europeans, was not condoned by community leaders. In 1964 I obtained a collection of ritual communion bowls from Natagera, Santa Ana (which had recently accepted Christianity), on the understanding that it was going into museum collections and would never be sold to or owned by individuals again.[5] Even so, the ritual bowl that belonged to the leader of the congregation and was dedicated to his tutelary deity was not turned over. Instead, an inferior copy was made of it, so that the set belonging to a single congregation would be complete in a material sense, but the most sacred piece could be allowed to disintegrate in the village.[6]

With the abandonment of the traditional religion, carving and other aesthetic expressions were no longer confined to the religious domain. However, despite the urgings of liberal clergy, there was strong resistance to a reassociation of them with Christian beliefs. On the other hand, with Christianity and an ever-increasing involvement with Europeans and their demands for exotic art, a new market for traditional aesthetic skills developed. The truly gifted artists, however, were not all drawn into the growing market for curios. The few that were attracted to it found difficulty in adjusting to the different demands this new market made on their skills. A different kind of craftsman has developed, the most successful of whom are responding, innovatively to be sure, to an entirely different realm of tastes.

Thus, I juxtapose two kinds of value in traditional Eastern Solomon Island cultures: one material and economic, the other mystical and spiritual. Economic value is derived from most kinds of labor and materials and is represented by commodities that are bought, sold, or traded. Spiritual value is associated with the supernatural, represented by inspired aesthetic accomplishment, and with human life itself. Representations of spiritual value are not marketable, that is, they are never commodities. However, representations of spiritual values are not manifested alone, that is, separately from the activities and materials that by themselves represent economic values. The objects and activities that express and communicate spiritual values are transformations of commodities. The means of making this transformation are the application of aesthetic skills and the taking of human life. Only when this transformation is made can the object or activity become a representation of the sacred and spiritual. And once this had been done, the object is forever removed from the economic realm of commodities.

Looking at Eastern Solomon Island rituals as events that express social values, they can be scaled from lesser to greater. The sequence, just described, that commences with every death and culminates every decade or so with the -murina represents such a gradient of cultural importance. It follows, too, that the greater the social value represented by the event, the greater the social span represented by the participants and the greater the economic expenditure. All commemorative events are set apart from others by the lavish display of rare aesthetic skills, and the greatest of them by the sacrifice of human life. These ritual events are occasions on which two kinds of values, economic and spiritual, are fused. Economic value is directly related to the size and scope of the celebration, that is to say, the number of participants and the number of communities they come from. The economic dimension of the celebrations finds expression in the tangible realm of commodities that are distributed and consumed. The spiritual value, as represented by the use of aesthetic skills and culminating in the sacrifice of human life, is an expression of the intangible realm of supernatural forces that influence all aspects of social life. Only by combining the two kinds of value, the material and the spiritual, are traditional social values fully expressed.

Notes

1. C. E. Fox, *The Threshold of the Pacific*, (New York: Knopf, 1925), pp. 4–6.
2. The major ethnographic descriptions of Santa Ana and Santa Catalina Islands are: Fox, *Threshold of the Pacific*; Hugo A. Bernatizik, *Owa Raha* (Vienna: Bernini Verlag, 1936); William Davenport, "Sculpture from the Eastern Solomon Islands," *Expedition* 10:(2)4–25, University Museum, Philadelphia, 1967; and "Male Initiation in Aoriki," *Expedition* 23:(2)4–19, University Museum, Philadelphia, 1980. None of these descriptions deals with the funeral and commemorative rituals described here.
3. Although I am writing in the ethnographic present, the period that I am referring to ended in the mid-1920's, when pacification was imposed by the British Government. At that time killings and kidnappings ceased, but the full cycle of funeral events continued until about 1950. In 1966 the only community in the Eastern Solomon Islands that still observed a full complement of rituals of all kinds was Aoriki, or Santa Catalina. In December 1971 Santa Catalina was devastated by a severe hurricane. All the sacred canoe houses, bonito canoes, and trading canoes were destroyed. The community did not rebuild them or reestablish all of the religious observances.
4. I do not use the concept of "spiritual" in the same way as W. Kandinsky does in his essay *Concerning the Spiritual in Art, and Painting in Particular* (New York: Wittenborn, 1972).
5. Half this collection is at the University Museum, Philadelphia, Pennsylvania, and half at the Solomon Islands Museum, Honiara.
6. The copy is of a bowl that was a replacement for the one published in Bernatizik, *Owa Raha*, Abb. 100. The remnants of bowl photographed by Bernatizik were still kept in a sacred place and recognizable in 1966.

CHAPTER 4

Newcomers to the world of goods: consumption among the Muria Gonds

ALFRED GELL

The theme of this paper is consumption as a form of symbolic action. Consumption goods are more than mere packets of neutral "utility." They are objects made more or less desirable by the role they play in a symbolic system. I will develop this entirely uncontroversial proposition on the basis of my observations of consumption behavior among the Muria of the north-central part of Bastar district, Madhya Pradesh, India.

The Muria belong to the "tribal" (*adivasi*) category established by the constitution of India, and according to the official stereotype of such groups they ought to be mired in poverty and exploitation. The official stereotype is not wide of the mark so far as most of the adivasi population are concerned (Fürer-Haimendorf 1982), but conditions in north-central Bastar are exceptional, for here the Muria enjoy considerable material advantages by comparison with small peasants elsewhere in the subcontinent (see Hill 1983). I will try to explain how this has come about in due course.

Amid the modest prosperity, or at least security, now enjoyed by most of the Muria population in north-central Bastar, one or two families in each village have enriched themselves to a greater degree than most, and it is on the consumption behavior of such rich Muria families that I wish to focus particular attention. I believe that "rich" Muria are a relatively new phenomenon, dating back no more than fifty years or so, and that this may help explain why their consumption behavior, which is marked by an exaggerated conservatism, assumes the rather peculiar form it does.

From an ethnohistorical point of view, then, I am dealing with a case in which a traditional consumption ethos and mode of assigning goods to symbolic categories lags behind objective changes in production techniques, which has resulted in enhanced economic productivity. Among the Muria production adheres to the premises of one kind of economy, whereas consumption continues to be based on the premise of a quite different economy. The net effect of this lag is that rich Muria accumulate wealth they dare not spend and would have no real idea how to spend had they the inclination.

To be possessed of conspicuous wealth, in this society, is to be in an unnatural condition, one that renders more problematic, not less, any contemplated act of consumption. The response of the rich Muria is to behave with what looks like excessive parsimony, but which is not really true miserliness of the Scrooge-Volpone variety. The true miser admits both the possibility and the desirability of self-indulgent consumption, thereby enhancing in his own eyes the virtue of his own restraint. Such behavior is egotistical and anti-social. Muria accumulation arises in a completely different way. The Muria consumption bottleneck reflects an intense sensitivity to social pressures, within the family, the village, and the wider society. Acts of conspicuous consumption not falling within the framework of traditionally sanctioned public feasting and display are seen as socially threatening, hubristic, and disruptive.

Consequently, the rich are obliged to consume as if they were poor, and as a result become still richer. The unintended consequence of a pattern of restraints on consumption geared to the maintenance of egalitarian norms has been the undermining of the economic basis for the traditional egalitarian ethos of Muria society. In the long run this may result in the emergence of clear economic stratification in what has been, historically, a homogeneous, clan-based society. A new category of rich peasants and quasi-entrepreneurs has come into existence in Muria villages, but this category has yet to define itself socially vis-à-vis the rest of Muria society, or to find an idiom for expressing its social and economic distinctiveness in the language of symbolic consumption. For these families the material symbols of wealth displayed by the better-off Bastar Hindus, and the middle-class officials in the towns, that is, non-adivasis of comparable income, are not acceptable symbols of status precisely because they are associated with non-Muria identity. I will provide detailed descriptions of two families facing this kind of consumption dilemma below.

Consumer goods and personal identity

Before turning to particular cases I would like to offer some remarks on the subject of consumption as a symbolic act. Douglas and Isherwood (1980) have devoted an interesting monograph to this subject, stressing the central importance of "consumption rituals" in the mediation of social life. This approach rests squarely on the accumulated wisdom of traditional structural-functional anthropology, particularly the branch of it that is summed up in the tag "the right hindquarters of the ox. . . . " Countless ethnographies bear witness to the way social relations are expressed, or more precisely produced, in the form of highly structured occasions of commensality, drinking bouts, sharing the pipe, and so on.

These are very recognizable forms of consumption, ones that perhaps may mislead us into making the false equation "consumption equals destruction" because on these occasions meat, liquor, and other valued substances are made to vanish. But consumption as a general phenomenon really has nothing to do with the destruction of goods and wealth, but with their reincorporation into the social system that produced them in some other guise. All goods, from the standpoint of sociological analysis, are as indestructible as kula valuables – the valuables that circulate in the kula exchange system described by Malinowski (1922) for the Trobriands. What they mostly lack is the impartibility and permanent identifiability as historically remembered objects that kula valuables possess (Leach and Leach 1984). But even quite ephemeral items, such as the comestibles served at a feast, live on in the form of the social relations they produce, and which are in turn responsible for reproducing the comestibles.

What constitutes the consumption of food at a feast is the transformation it effects – which may be minuscule or intensely significant, depending on the nature of the occasion – in the relative social identities of the parties to the host/guest, feeder/fed, transaction involved. This is analytically quite distinct from any contingent metabolic processes the food may undergo at the same time. In many feasts in New Guinea the food is not actually eaten by the participants, but the feasts remain consumption rituals in Douglas and Isherwood's sense (Brown 1978). What distinguishes consumption from exchange is not that consumption has a physiological dimension that exchange lacks, but that consumption involves the incorporation of the consumed item into the personal and social identity of the consumer.

For instance, Lord Rothschild has a Cézanne hanging on the wall of his sitting room. That makes him a member of the elite group of consumers of works by Cézanne, a category from which I am permanently excluded even though I have had the pleasure of looking at this painting in the past. I think of consumption as the appropriation of objects as part of one's *personalia* – food eaten at a feast, clothes worn, houses lived in. The incorporation of consumer goods into the definition of the social self arises out of a framework of social obligations and also perpetuates this framework. Consumption is part of a process that includes production and exchange, all three being distinct only as phases of the cyclical process of social reproduction, in which consumption is never terminal. Consumption is the phase of the cycle in which goods become attached to personal referents, when they cease to be neutral "goods," which could be owned by anybody and identified with anybody, and become attributes of some individual personality, badges of identity, and signifiers of specific interpersonal relationships and obligations.

Seen in this light, true misers of the Volpone-Scrooge variety are consumers too, consumers of money as a supremely valued attribute of personality, in defiance of transactional norms. But it is noticeable that we call misers greedy, the same word we employ to describe out-and-out consumers such as Falstaff, suggesting that we recognize the resemblance of all forms of excessive incorporation of value, whether they be a distended purse like Volpone's or a distended belly like Falstaff's. In the cases to be discussed below, we also encounter what appears to resemble classic miserly behavior, but which in reality is something else. It is not love of money (self-love disguised as pseudorational accumulation) that motivates the consumption patterns I will describe, but the impossibility of converting purchasing power into a socially coherent definition of the self, in accord with the "habitus" handed down by tradition and inculcated during the socialization process (Bourdieu 1977). Not the love of money but the unloveliness of goods lies at the roots of the consumption dilemmas of rich Muria, since outside a narrow range of socially legitimized consumption possibilities, the goods commercially available in Bastar markets either have no meaning for Muria or are fraught with magical dangers.

I was led to reflect on this subject by the extraordinary contrast that can exist between different groups experiencing improved economic conditions. Some societies take to consumerism without hesitation, and experience no difficulties elaborating a previously given set of status symbols and personality-marking possessions with goods previously unavailable or unknown. Others, including the Muria, are highly conservative in this respect.

The particular example that aroused my curiosity was provided by Jock Stirratt, who in the course of a seminar on the anthropology of money at the London School of Economics and Political Science (Stirratt n.d.) graphically outlined the uses to which certain Sri Lankan fishermen who have prospered in recent times put their new-found wealth. These fishermen's incomes, having been very low, have much increased since the local availability of ice has made it possible for their fish to reach inland markets, where they fetch high prices, in good condition. The fishermen's villages are still very remote, however, and at the time of the study, boasted no electricity, roads, or piped water supply. Despite these apparent disincentives, the richer fishermen were spending their excess earnings to purchase unusable television sets, to build "garages" onto houses to which no automobiles had access, and to install rooftop cisterns into which water never flows. All this, according to Stirratt, comes about in enthusiastic imitation of urban Sri Lanka's upper-middle class.

It is easy to laugh at such crass conspicuous expenditure, which by its apparent lack of utilitarian purpose makes at least some of our own consumption seem comparatively rational. Because the objects these fishermen acquire seem functionless in their environment, we cannot see why they should want them. On the other hand, if they collected pieces of antique Chinese porcelain and buried them in the earth as the Iban do (Freeman 1970), they would be considered sane but enchanted, like normal anthropological subjects. I would not wish to deny the obvious explanations for this kind of behavior – that is, status-seeking, keeping up with the Joneses, and so on. But I think one should also recognize the presence of a certain cultural vitality in these bold forays into new and untried fields of consumption: the ability to transcend the merely utilitarian aspect of consumption goods, so that they become something more like works of art, charged with personal expression.

Take these television sets, for instance. In purchasing such an item, to form the centerpiece of a personal collection of wealth-signifiers, the fisherman is *totalizing* his biography, his labor, his social milieu, in the form of an object whose technological associations dialectically negate the conditions under which the fisherman's wealth was actually obtained. By totalizing I mean, following Sartre (1968), bringing together disparate elements and reconciling their contradictions. In this instance, totalization applies to the elements of a biographical and social experience that are projected onto a collection of personal possessions that signify those experiences. The fisherman, to acquire wealth, has spent his days in a creaking, battered old boat, pursuing an all-too-familiar routine, and facing the all-too-familiar uncertainties of weather, movements of shoals of fish, and price fluctuations at the market. But he can turn all this labor, all this familiar messiness and uncertainty, into a smooth, dark cabinet of unidentifiable grainless wood, geometrically pure lines, an inscrutable gray glass face, and within, just visible through the rows of little holes and slots at the back, an intricate jungle of wire, plastic, and shining metal. He presumably knows that given the necessary electricity and transmissions, the set can be made to give forth more or less exciting pictures and voices. But that is not the point; what matters is the leap of imagination required for such a man to acquire and identify with such an object, adopting it as the emblem not of his middle-class aspirations, but of his actual achievements as a fisherman.

The television set, in this context, serves to objectify the fisherman's productive career, but it also transforms that career by invoking a technical and aesthetic universe (straight lines, smooth textures, plastic, aluminum, glass), that dialectically negate the objective conditions, technical processes, and sensory qualities of the labor process that, through the market, produced this same television set. In other words, the television set is a work of art, functioning like all genuine works of art to negate/transcend the real world. It is, in Jaspers's sense, a "cypher of the transcendent" (Jaspers 1971). One can call this commodity fetishism if one wishes, and consider it vulgar, but I believe that there is a valid distinction between dull, unimaginative consumerism, which only reiterates the class habitus, and adventurous consumerism like this, which struggles against the limits of the known world. I prefer to see here a creative process, one not at all deserving of the contempt that most of the participants at the aforementioned seminar seemed to think appropriate.

And I was struck by the stark contrast between the daring purchases made by erstwhile poverty-stricken Catholic fishermen in Sri Lanka, and the obsessive conservatism displayed by the newly rich in my own field area. I have no explanation to offer for the Sri Lankan fishermen, though I suspect that it has something to do with the relatively atomistic nature of their social and religious organization, compared to the Muria's, and the presence of some degree of class awareness (as opposed to traditional hierarchy, which is all the Muria recognize). But I hope I can fare a little better in explaining the Muria response to economic betterment, which is the topic I must now take up in earnest.

The traditional consumption ethos of the Muria

Bastar district, still the richest in forests of all the districts of peninsular India, has been one of the last land frontiers of the subcontinent. Not much more than a century ago, the earliest travelers described its inhabitants as lacking even cloth (they wore leaves), and the market system, which has expanded rapidly in the last fifty years, was then not even vestigially present. Only isolated enclaves of Hindu settlement existed, especially in south Bastar, near the royal capital or

Jagdalpur and along the valley of the Indrawati, and also along the north-south communication axis linking Jagdalpur to Raipur and Kanker to the north, and Warangal and Hyderabad to the south. Only in these areas were permanent fields in use; the bulk of the tribal population relied on slash-and-burn techniques. The tribal population consists of the Muria, the Maria, and the Bison-horn Maria, speakers of Gondi dialects and members of the congeries of "Gond" peoples found in a broad belt stretching between northern Andhra and southern Bihar.

Today only pockets of Maria subsist by means of techniques that appear to have been in general use when the country was first opened up to outside infiltration, following the imposition of political control by the British in the last quarter of the nineteenth century. Large areas have been acquired by Hindu cultivating castes (though landlords are few and small in the area I know). But much greater areas still remain in the hands of the Muria, who now cultivate their extensive lands using techniques they have borrowed from their Hindu neighbors. Except where the forest is preserved for commercial exploitation, the land has been cleared, and has been divided into leveled fields with water-retaining dikes wherever the topography permits. Only in the mountainous northwest of Bastar, where the Maria live, is shifting agriculture still practiced. In other words, in the past one hundred years, Bastar district has joined India, has acquired an Indian appearance, and (to some extent) enjoys an Indian economy.

The inhabitants of the north-central plains of Bastar most affected by these changes are the Muria. The Muria are, by degrees, becoming a straightforward "dominant caste" of land-owning peasant cultivators. But this has not quite happened yet: the Muria still eat beef, marry late, and maintain their traditional institutions such as the mixed-sex *ghotul* dormitory (Elwin 1947) and the cult of village and clan deities outside the Hindu pantheon. Around the old centers of power to the south, however, one finds "Raj" Gonds among whom the process of transformation from tribe to caste is more or less complete. The Raj Gonds have become Hinduized, and have been settled cultivators for many generations. In other areas, as land came under Hindu occupation, the local Gond inhabitants typically sought new land elsewhere, which was easily done since land was plentiful in north Bastar and labor in short supply.

The Muria can perhaps best be understood not as a tribe with an immemorial culture and way of life, but as a phase in the historical process that has been converting people with a culture roughly like that of the Maria into people like the Raj Gonds – and thence into straightforward cultivator castes, possibly even claimants to Rajput descent, like the Bhumia (Sinha 1962). In their locality the Muria have been the agents responsible for turning forest into India; and in so doing they are gradually turning themselves from a tribe into a caste. As I understand it, during the period of Hindu expansion in north Bastar during the last century, Muria moved into the forest, pushing out from the Hindu enclaves, felling trees and clearing fields, which then proved attractive to the incoming Hindus. The Hindus took over the land, expanding their enclaves, and the displaced Muria moved on, to repeat the process elsewhere. The Muria did not simply give way to *force majeure*; the land was ceded amicably against payment in animals, grain, liquor, and small quantities of gold and silver that would quickly be reconverted into food or, more likely, drink. Hindus we spoke to claimed that in the good old days it was possible to obtain large areas of land from Muria in exchange for a single gold earring or some other token payment. These Hindus attributed the Muria's fecklessness about land to their uncontrollable desire for intoxicating liquor.

I do not think such stories merely reflect ethnic stereotyping because they are consistent with the present-day distribution of land in north Bastar, and also with the current amicable relationships between Hindu and Muria cultivators in the countryside. The Muria are acknowledged to be the true owners of the land, and Hindus participate in the Muria ritual system because it is the Muria gods who ensure its fertility. This suggests that during the formative period, Muria-Hindu relationships assumed a stable configuration whereby Muria opened up new areas, cultivated them until they were exhausted, and when it was necessary for them to move on for eco-technological reasons of their own, turned them over to incoming Hindus for what seemed to the latter trifling sums and to the Muria pure profit. The Hindus could subsequently exploit the land using plows and animal fertilizers, techniques the Muria had not at that time adopted.

If this supposition is correct, as the virtual nonexistence of a landless category of Muria in the localities affected by Hindu immigration suggests it may be, then it may help explain the distinctive consumption ethos found in present-day Muria society. The stereotype of tribal innocence and hedonism, the eat, drink, and be merry for tomorrow we die attitude, has a basis in fact. The Muria really do eat, drink, and enjoy themselves to a far greater degree than Indian peasants are commonly described as doing. This is particularly noticeable among poorer Muria, who think nothing of drinking away their last rupee in the world, and treating you in the bargain. There is a basic assumption that there is more where that came from. This reflects the essentially unlimited resource base on which traditional Muria society rested (the forest), and the fact that prior to the transformation of Muria agricultural techniques in this century, wealth was not accumulated for lack of suitable stores of value (currency or cattle).

Muria hedonism is associated with collective (village and clan) institutions, all of which can be shown to be in some way associated with the Hindu/Muria interaction. The most famous of these institutions is the ghotul, the mixed-sex village dormitory described in detail by Elwin (though not entirely accurately; see S. Gell 1984). It is notable that the Muria ghotul, the very academy of hedonistic attitudes, assumes its most elaborated form only in the parts of north Bastar where Hindus are present; outside the range of Hindu influence, in Maria country, the ghotul exists in the very much duller form of a males-only dormitory, with none of the cultural elaboration the Muria ghotul has received. Similarly, betrothals and marriages are celebrated with much greater ceremony and expense among the Muria than among the Maria, as are collective feasts for clan and village deities. One only has to compare Elwin's splendid photographs of Muria and Maria taken in the 1930's and 1940's (Elwin 1947, 1943; Grigson 1937) to perceive that the material wealth of the Muria, as measured by such indicators as the amount of cloth, beads, jewelry, and metal tools evidently in circulation at that time, far exceeded that of the Maria. If we can assume that only a small proportion of this wealth came from the sale of cash crops – regional markets being little developed at that time – the only logical explanation for the relative wealth of the Muria is their relationship with the Hindus. Elwin does not describe the Muria of his time as rich in any except a cultural sense, and it is clear that their wealth consisted mainly of finery worn on festive occasions, and stores of food and liquor, also for public consumption at village rituals, or semi-public hospitality at other times. I would argue, though I am aware that the point is far from proven, that the Muria have elaborated "feckless" consumption into a cultural theme because they have been accustomed to having a high-consumption lifestyle subsidized by periodic injections of Hindu wealth.

The Muria associate liquidity with the selling off of capital assets (now held as livestock, since the Muria, for reasons to be discussed, nowadays rarely deal in land) in order to finance immediate consumption on a grandiose scale, usually in public contexts of some kind. These losses, traditionally, could always be recouped by pioneering new land, and although that is no longer possible, the labor market is such that the disappearance of land as a source of income is more than offset by the easy availability of relatively remunerative forms of employment.

The social and religious life of the Muria is conducted as a series of large-scale eating and drinking occasions (festivals of the gods, marriages, settlements of disputes, etc.), in which the village as a whole must participate. There are also obligations to extend hospitality to visiting affines and other kin, to religious specialists, shamans, local officials, and the like. Outside these formal occasions, it is customary for men and middle-aged women to drink deeply in one another's company as frequently as possible, and the ghotul boys and girls also conduct feasts and drinking parties. The important point to note, however, is that this social feasting and drinking is not undertaken in a competitive spirit, in order to demonstrate superiority along the lines of Melanesian ceremonial exchange, but is intended to demonstrate commitment to the village and to Muria values. The Muria do not reveal any paranoia about getting the worst of an exchange, as do members of societies in which the *mentalité échangiste* holds sway; their fears always lie in the direction of suffering social ostracism, of which the most extreme form is outright expulsion from the village. In village feasts, contributions are standardized, and accounts are kept to ensure that each household has given an identical amount, regardless of wealth. When marriages are celebrated, the groom's family has to feast not only the bride's kin (who reciprocate), but the whole of their own village; the villagers are responsible, however, for amassing plenty of liquor, so that a good time is had by all. When disputes are settled, the pattern is the same: the party found guilty is fined a cow, a goat, or a quantity of rice, and a feast is arranged. The most onerous financial obligations are incurred in connection with consumption rituals that bring the whole village together as a single commensual unit. Day-to-day expenditure is also largely devoted to acquiring the means, mainly in the form of liquor, to extend casual hospitality as freely as possible.

The need to finance public consumption establishes the major economic goals of a Muria household, and sets the standards whereby the Muria evaluate the world of goods. Objects are desirable if they have meaning within the context of public feasting; otherwise, they have no value. The main items the Muria buy at market are cloth, decorative trinkets, and jewelry. The Muria are addicted to finery, particularly the ghotul boys and girls, whose display and dancing during village ritual is a matter of deep concern to them and to the village as a whole. Each young dancer is responsible for purchasing his or her own finery, but it is always worn in the context of collective display and is selected with this in mind. In 1977, for instance, the ghotul girls of Manjapur all obtained new saris with identical border for the annual "Play of the Gods" (*pen karsana*), the highlight of the ritual calendar. The ghotul boys had uniform black singlets, voluminous white skirts, white turbans, and feather headdresses, for wear at all-night dances. The Muria propensity for contriving uniforms is not restricted to the young. The senior men of Manjapur all wear the same kind of blue shirt on public occasions, a village uniform that distinguishes them from men of other villages. This code of dress and adornment is not enforced by sanctions; the Muria themselves are not even particularly conscious of it. The stated criterion for making purchases of this kind is that such-and-such items are beautiful (*sobta*), not that they have overt symbolic meanings.

In fact, Muria dress is anachronistic rather than traditional, since in truly traditional times cloth and jewelry were unavailable. We can see this by studying Elwin's photographs of the Muria of forty-fifty years ago. These pictures show the grandparents of the present-day ghotul boys and girls to have been just as dressy as their descendants, but wearing fashions that have been abandoned long since in the areas in which they originated. One plate (Elwin 1947, p. 420) shows a group of boys wearing remarkable short-sleeved, collarless buttoned shirts and strange flattened turbans of a style now never seen, but which appear to be distant echoes of courtly styles of the nineteenth century, or even earlier, filtered to the Muria via the Hindus. The present-day Muria male hairstyle, the hair on the forehead shaved to the crown of the head, with the hair in back left long and tied into a bun, is the classical Hindu *bodi*, a style seen only in attenuated forms now among Hindus themselves but jealously preserved by the beef-eating, hard-drinking Muria. The "tribal" sari is a shorter, narrower version of the standard sari worn by neighboring Hindu women, tied the same way but worn without a bodice, which until very recently most Muria women considered an immodest item of clothing, liable to attract attention to the breasts rather than divert it. Tribal saris are now almost all manufactured in Bombay of flimsy cotton cloth, dyed in bright colors, especially for sale in the tribal areas: the much more durable local *ganda* cloth is now worn only by old ladies and conservative village elders. The Bombay saris, regarded by outsiders as signs of authentic tribal identity, mainly because they are scanty and reveal the legs and upper body, are considered by the Muria themselves not only exotic (because they come from outside Bastar) but also respectable and modest; wearing the 4.5-meter standard sari is regarded as ostentatious.

In fact, none of the vestimentary signs that betoken tribal identity to outsiders are produced by the Muria themselves or originated indigenously. Tribal finery, turbans, loincloths, short saris, and "tribal" jewelry (heavy silver torques, gold, silver, and brass earrings, gold necklaces, massive silver and brass bracelets,) – all these arrived in the area with the Hindus, and were adopted by the Muria in imitation of their betters. These items are obtained from Hindu traders in the markets, never from other Muria, and are associated with superior status.

A case in point is silver jewelry, which is made in Rajasthan and has been traded in Bastar by Marwari merchants during this century. The design of the jewelry is traditional to Rajasthan, though I do not know if it is worn there any more. The silver ornaments for sale in Bastar markets are mostly old, but are cleaned and repaired by the Marwari silversmiths so that to all appearances they are brand new. This is a source of perplexity to Western visitors in search of old and authentic-looking tribal jewelry (see Spooner's remarks in Chapter 7, on the authenticity of Turkmen carpets.) It is old, it is authentic, but it is none of it tribal. According to a Marwari informant, silver jewelry circulates among both Hindus and Muria, but is little worn by the Hindus, who keep it as a store of value and as a component of dowry payments. The Muria do not have dowries, and the silver with which Muria girls adorn themselves has been purchased by them, using their own money, obtained by selling produce at market and by wage labor. Among the Hindus jewelry is essentially family property, significant as a store of capital; among the Muria it is personal property, primarily significant as personal adornment.

One can summarize the traditional Muria attitude toward prestige consumption goods available in the markets as follows: the items sought – cloth, finery, jewelry – are all associated with non-Muria groups considered by the Muria to be higher on the social scale. The definition of prestige goods has been imposed on the Muria by outsiders, and is perpetuated by a marketing system that is in entirely non-Muria hands. But in taking over elements of a set of non-Muria prestige goods for internal consumption, the Muria have imposed their own set of social evaluations on them, which are quite distinct from the ones operative among the groups with whom these goods originated. Prestige consumption items are sought not because of an intravillage competition to be the most fashionably dressed, most bejeweled individual around, but because all villagers alike are attempting to live up to a particular collective image. The ghotul boys and girls are obliged to spend heavily on clothes and finery so as not to let the side down at festivals with dancers from other ghotuls. The older men are obliged to obtain the standard blue shirt so as to make a good show at market, sitting with their fellow villagers at their accustomed place (Gell 1982). Jewelry is worn so as to look respectable, rather than to dazzle. In other words, it is in order to express conformity, not originality or individuality, that such purchases are made. This has in turn had an effect on the selection of goods offered by traders to Muria at rural markets. One can now distinguish between a range of goods aimed specifically at tribal consumers, particularly saris, turbans, loincloths, decorations, and heavy silver jewelry, and a range of modern items that are not usually offered at the more rural markets, namely, shoes, trousers, jackets, woolens, 4.5-meter saris, printed cloth (Muria prefer plain colors and woven borders), intricate as opposed to massive jewelry, sunglasses, umbrellas, stationery, crockery, furniture, medicines, etc. These items are available from shops in the towns, which are very accessible to the Muria by local bus, but are not attractive to them.

Besides clothes and finery, the Muria also spend money on food and drink. In normal times, subsistence grains and pulses (dāl, chickpeas, lentils) are not obtained at market; most families are self-sufficient in food. But rice and vegetables such as radishes, eggplant, chilis, tomatoes, beans, and various greens are bought for important occasions, such as marriages. The luxury foods preferred by the Muria are all traditional – parched rice, dried fish, *pakhoras* (a deep-fried snack), leaf-tobacco – rather than modern delicacies such as sweets, cookies, tea, sugar, manufactured cigarettes, etc., which are popular with Hindus. The largest expenditure in this category goes for drink, which is sold on the fringes of the market and in the villages. Even this item is not really indigenous; distilling was traditionally a monopoly of the Kallar (distiller) caste, of higher ritual status than the Muria. Nowadays the Kallar are legally prohibited from plying their trade so the Muria have to make their own, which they claim to be inferior to the Kallar product. Liquor is an essential element in all aspects of social and ritual life; for the Muria, the very notion of sociability, of belonging to a social group and maintaining social relationships, is unthinkable without alcoholic accompaniments. The Muria passion for liquor, much remarked by outsiders, is by no means a symptom of anomie or despair, as alcoholism may well be in some tribal societies, but the outcome of the conformism, the paranoia about belonging, which marks all phases of Muria life.

In short, Muria consumption is bound up with the expression of collective identity and the need to assert commitment to the village as a political unit and to its institutions. Particular items are singled out from the range of Hindu prestige symbols and incorporated into a collective style, which all Muria try to approximate as best they can. Consumption is not associated with competition, but with the demonstration of adequacy, the ability to come up to the collective mark. The emphasis on the collective style, rather than on individual differences, explains the anachronistic nature of Muria tastes and their conservative approach to consumption. The Muria are dedicated followers of fashion, followers being the operative word. Their fashions are anachronistic because no one wants to defy the restraints of the collective style. Even now, when some young men are cutting their hair and dressing more like the local Hindus, their motive is not to look smarter than before, but to look less conspicuous in a world that is perceived as increasingly Hindu-dominated.

Recent economic changes

This collectivist consumption ethos has its roots in a phase of the tribe-caste conversion process in which interhousehold economic differences was minimal and inequalities in wealth between households would be at most temporary, owing to the absence of media of capital accumulation. Since this pattern was set, however, there have been crucial changes in the economic basis of Muria society. Around the turn of the century, the government imposed controls on access to forest land, controls that have been applied more and more stringently, so that the Bastar land frontier is now effectively closed. The government ban on the free exploitation of the forest was believed to have precipitated an uprising in the countryside in 1910, and between the two world wars Muria lands were subjected to survey and land titles were registered. Owing to the fear of renewed outbreaks of anti-government feeling, the amount of land ceded to the Muria was rather generous in relation to their numbers. At the time of the settlement the Muria must have appeared both poor and dependent on access to large areas of uncleared forest.

Today almost all the forest ceded to the Muria has been cleared and more has been encroached on, with the result that official census figures give the average land-holding per cultivating Muria family at more than ten acres. By now, thanks to the cumulative labor of generations, this land has been converted into leveled paddy fields, with water-retaining dikes, of considerable agricultural potential even without irrigation. It is common to find families holding 20, 30, or even more acres of paddy field, enormous acreages by Indian standards.

These fields can only be cultivated with animal-drawn plows, and many families cannot cultivate all the land they possess for lack of cattle or buffalo. But here again time is on their side: buffalo were rare in the area before the war, but now herds are gradually building up, as are cattle herds, enabling this initial shortage of agricultural capital to be overcome. New trade routes have opened up, bringing plow animals into the area. Land registered to adivasis cannot be sold to non-adivasis by government decree, so Muria land is no longer passing into the hands of Hindus. Moreover, the old easy come, easy go, attitude to land has vanished with the introduction of permanent fields whose construction and upkeep represent years and years of accumulated labor. The population has also increased, so that labor shortage, once the most important constraint on production, is becoming less of a problem and land can be fully and more intensively cultivated (two crops, one of rice and one a dry-season crop such as millet or oil-seeds, are the norm).

Muria family farms are much more productive now than they were in the past. Moreover, the Muria have access to wage labor at high rates of pay (eight rupees a day in 1982) in relation to their actual living costs. The government Public Works Department and the Forest Department are chronically short of labor, so that work is readily available during the agricultural slack season. Besides wage employment, Muria also employ one another as farm laborers for the standard rate of three kilos of unhusked rice per laborer per day.

In short, the local economy is in a flourishing condition, prosperous in good years and well able to withstand the rigors of bad ones. Despite being a notoriously "backward" area, supposedly occupied by miserable, poverty-stricken tribals, Bastar district exports rice year after year, and that, in India, is the bottom line.

Rich Muria families

It is against this background that I want to examine consumption in two "rich" Muria families, that is, families who in the general economic upsurge have done better than most. Rich men among the Muria are identified as *saukar* ("hundred-rupee men"), and they may be (and usually are) village elders (*siyan*, "wise men"). Wealth and influence in village politics usually go together, but the relationship between the two is ambiguous: wealth gives political standing because it is a tangible sign of intelligence and industry, not because the loyalty of the village can be bought. A rich man can finance the feast that a poor man gives the village when his son is married; but it is still the poor man's feast. The ethos of each family head's being equally and individually responsible for his duties and feast contributions vis-à-vis the village as a whole means that rich men cannot come to prominence by acts of outstanding public generosity. Everyone is required to make the standard contribution; the only difference is that it is easier to do this if one is rich. If a family loses its wealth, for whatever reason, it does not lose its prestige in the village arena, at least not immediately. And merely acquiring wealth, in the absence of a continuous demonstration of adherence to the traditional status quo in village politics does not confer siyan status. The first case I will discuss is of a man who has become wealthy in rather special circumstances. Usually wealth is associated with land, and land with membership in the dominant clan. This man is not particularly well off in land (with his parents and his brother he farms 13 acres), and he belongs to neither of the two important clans in his village. He is a recognized siyan, respected for his formidable intelligence, drive, and finesse in public speaking, but at the same time he is an outsider. But before discussing this man (Tiri) and his consumption problems, let me briefly indicate two ways in which rich Muria can develop two kinds of saukar identity, neither of which is appropriate in Tiri's case.

The archetypal saukar in the neighborhood of the village (Manjapur) where I mostly worked was called Dhol Saukar. Dhol had an enormous house and a great deal of land, as well as the cattle and labor to work it. He was always more or less drunk and was the fattest Muria I have encountered. He clearly ate a vast amount, even by the generous standards of the Muria. In public, he was invariably excessively affable, greeting everyone with prolonged embraces and slurred words of humble greetings. He knelt on our porch for about five minutes on one occasion, intoning again and again, "Great gods! Please don't be angry, don't be angry!" (*Mahaprabhu! hongaima, hongaima.*) He was locally well-known and well-respected, but his public demeanor was always ultra-disarming, so that his drunkenness seemed to be more a matter of self-defense than anything else. By becoming a living embodiment of the high value placed by Muria on copious eating and drinking, Dhol Saukar managed to be notoriously rich and at the same time completely inoffensive. Moreover, like most of the other rich Muria I will be discussing, he preserved an external appearance of relative poverty. His turbans were small and shabby, his loincloth was of the briefest and most traditional kind; only his gold necklace and earrings marked him out as having any wealth at all. Dhol Saukar, a relatively older man, is a rich Muria of the old school – a hard drinker, a lover of feasting and company; that is to say, he is like any other Muria, but more so. This persona, however, is unsuitable for ambitious men. Specializing in eating, drinking, and conviviality is implicitly a retreat from engagement in the struggle of recognition in the village arena. Old men behave this way once they have relinquished control to their sons, but the ambitious up-and-coming siyan cannot simply concentrate on drinking, even though this is an activity that the Muria regard as respectable in itself. The Muria also admire sobriety, intelligence, the power to exercise control over domestic and village affairs – all of which are inconsistent with permanent inebriation. It was said that affairs in Dhol's house were a shambles, despite his universal popularity outside it. This perhaps is the consequence of Dhol's attempt to combine richness and Murianess by simply stepping up traditional consumption.

Next, and in sharp contrast to Dhol, whose strategy was successful enough in its own terms, I want briefly to discuss a youth who has attempted to go to the opposite extreme, with notably little success so far. This youth, who was about 18 years old when I met him, had 40 acres of paddy land, and so was a saukar, but he was not a siyan and by the look of things never would be. He was drunk at our meeting (tending to truculence) and was surrounded by disreputable non-Muria hangers-on. Whereas Dhol's dress was modest, this youthful saukar wore a weird mixture of Muria and "modern" clothes. On his feet he wore army boots, many sizes too large, without socks; above these, baggy bottle-green shorts, a nylon string vest, dark glasses, and a towering but rather lopsided tussar silk turban. From the pocket of his vest protruded a leaking fountain pen, which had deposited irregular blue stains over his chest. (I was informed by disapproving Muria companions that he could neither read nor write.) I gathered that he was ill-regarded in his own village and spent his time away from it, in the society of low-grade officials, forest guards, and other marginal fellows. He had no prestige and was considered "mad" (*baihal*). Had he not suffered from the handicap of excessive wealth, this young man presumably would have been as well-adjusted and as well-liked as his poorer contemporaries. He can be considered an Awful Example, the opposite of Dhol Saukar, a man whose consumption behavior establishes an incoherent personality, leading to social rejection.

My two main examples are less extreme cases than these, and involve men I know better. By repute at least, Tiri is the richest man in Manjapur, and because we lived across his courtyard for a year we were in a good position to monitor his consumption. Tiri is rich not because he has a lot of land, but because he is a hard-working and exceptionally efficient farmer, a brilliant organizer, and a wheeler-dealer who works hand-in-glove with the Forest Department, local contractors, and the Public Works Department. He must have inherited his acumen from his equally redoubtable mother, another organizational genius. Together this pair have carried all before them, despite the fact that Tiri's mother and father arrived as penniless runaways from a distant village, and that Tiri's childhood was spent as a farm servant in the house of a rich man in the locality. Tiri's is the only hosehold of his clan in the village; he is a classic *nouveau riche*, an upstart, but he is also a siyan, an excellent public speaker, negotiator, and village politician.

Both Tiri and his mother were extraordinarily conservative in consumption matters. He wore only the traditional short loincloth, turban, and the blue shirt worn by all the men of his generation. He used *ganda* (handloomed) cloth rather than machine-made – more durable and therefore cheaper in the long run, but less sparklingly white. He told us that it was wrong for Muria to wear shoes, trousers, loincloths, and the like. He had neither a bicycle, a wristwatch, nor a wireless (his younger brother had acquired all three). It was not that he was trying to look poor; his actual riches, accumulating in the form of cattle and buffalo and various publicly known debts, could not be effectively concealed. It was rather that he was determined not to enter into kinds of consumption that would make him out to be a different kind of person than he regarded as morally appropriate, in the evaluations of both his society and himself. Unlike Dhol Saukar, he did not drink or eat more than the average Muria. When drinking was obligatory he drank, but between times he often became a conscientious abstainer for months at a time, believing that when he was drunk he was not fully in control. Tiri attempted, in other words, to consume exactly as if he were no richer than the average man. In his production activities and acquisition of money he assiduously sought mastery, but this same mastery when translated into consumption behavior became a consistent series of denials; if he were to spend as he gained, his behavior would cancel out the very achievement by which he set such store. It was only if he consumed as if he were not wealthy that he would remain so. In fact, despite the village consensus confirming his affluence, he often complained to us of financial insecurities, enormous losses impending, and the like. In a poetic moment, he made a comparison between riches and the moving shadow of a shade tree, now here but soon gone; on another occasion he described riches as being like the sand bars in a riverbed, seemingly solid but washed away in the wake of a rainstorm (S. Gell 1984).

Tiri's mother is equally puritanical, but as an old woman she can take nonconsumption to extreme lengths. Her saris are outrageously shabby. She buys the cheapest kind of machine cloth, the kind that falls to pieces in a fortnight, and wears it as long as decency permits. She has hardly any personal possessions besides a tobacco pouch and a silver neck torque (*suta*) of the kind worn by many Muria women. She had no blanket (she said, though I don't know whether to believe this) until we gave her one – a light shawl. She will spend money in the market only on food, vegetables, chilis, spices, dried fish, and an occasional fried delicacy. Like her son, she seems determined to protect her wealth by denying its consumption consequences.

Meanwhile there are certain objects in the Tiri household that receive special attention. Most conspicuous of these is the brass water-pot, which stands on a post facing Tiri's verandah and from which the members of the household take drinking and hand-washing water. All households have such a water-pot, but usually only an earthenware one. Tiri's mother is unusual in possessing such a fine specimen, which she keeps in spectacularly gleaming condition and prominently displayed. Inside the kitchen, hidden from view, she has a stack of four or five more brass pots. The family also possesses more than the usual number of smaller brass water pots and a beautiful set of heavy brass plates, which are used for company and for ritual meals.

Brassware of this kind is manufactured in Raipur and is normally unavailable in local markets. However, it had been traded in Bastar for a long time at the big annual fairs (*mardhai*), particularly the ones attended by Muria at Narayanpur and Kondagaon. Brassware is an important category of prestige goods, and like all such goods is associated with high-status Hindu manners. The local Hindus eat off brass plates all the time, whereas even rich Muria households like Tiri's eat off plates only exceptionally; usually they make do with plates and cups made from leaves, which are more efficient in that they involve no washing up and can be fed to domestic animals immediately after the meal. Tiri's set of plates is engraved with the family name (though none of the family can read), together with swastika emblems and other Hindu symbols. Brassware, like jewelry, has penetrated the Muria consumption system because it is associated with public consumption rather than private luxury. All the richer households of the village possess some brass plates and perhaps a water pot or two, but there is no outright competition. They are brought out to do honor to guests, or to do honor to the village and its gods on ritual occasions.

But it seems that Tiri's mother, in amassing such a large collection of water pots, and in displaying her best one so prominently, has gone further than other women in her village, none of whom have collected nearly as many pots. It would appear that she is unusually susceptible to brass water pots, since one pot costs about as much as four blankets, and she thinks she cannot afford a blanket. I believe that there is an element of fetishism here, but the object of Tiri's mother's fetishistic attitude is not one that takes her out of her quotidian world (like the fishermen and their television sets), but one that stands as a powerful symbol of traditional Muria feminine activities.

Tiri's mother told Simeran Gell that she was glad there was no well in the village, and that the part of the day she enjoyed most was the late afternoon, when she went off to the river (more than a mile away), together with her faithful pot, driving a herd of cows before her. There she would water the cows and vigorously scrub the pot with sand to make it shiny, before filling it and another pot of lesser value with water, bringing them back balanced on her head, so as to arrive, dripping but unbowed, surrounded by cows, in time to start organizing everyone for the evening meal.

The energy and skill that Tiri's mother puts into the performance of her domestic tasks is breathtaking to behold, and she herself is thoroughly conscious of it. I think her fierce pride in her performance of her role as Muria matriarch is projected onto her collection of brass pots, particularly the one that is displayed. Psychoanalytically, and also in certain systems of Indian symbolism, pots are female symbols; so there may be depth-psychological grounds for thinking that she identifies herself with the pot she cherishes so much. On the other hand, it is worth noting that the local Hindu castes use pots as symbolic bridegrooms: girls who reach puberty without finding a husband are married to pots (Dubey 1953). So it could also be that the pot is a male symbol. In any case it is likely that the symbolism involved is multivocal and overdetermined.

Depth psychology aside, it is notable that the brassware-collecting propensity of the Tiri household is one of the few ways their affluent status is overtly demonstrated. Because brassware was one of the first items of Hindu wealth to be traded in Bastar, it can be amassed without seeming to reject basic Muria identity. Probably, in years to come, Muria and tourists will be the only purchasers of traditional brassware, just as Muria and tourists are the main purchasers of traditional silver – most of the traders are moving with the times and going over to stainless steel, which is much more popular with modern-minded Hindus.

Curiously the Muria, a traditional people with no home-grown tradition of craft and prestige-good production, are actually much more similar to Westerners, seeking authenticity in the exotic, than they are to traditional craft-producer societies, the category to which they are erroneously believed to belong. Traditional craft producers, like the Turkmen whom Spooner discusses in Chapter 7, do not seem to care about authenticity, and, to the dismay of collectors, seem happy to prostitute stylistic purity to please the degraded taste of modernity. But the reasons for Muria conservatism are different from the reasons underlying Western purism in matters of craft. The Muria are conservative because they do not want to depart from the communally sanctioned consumption ethos, because they do not want to appear individualistic; Westerners on the other hand seek purity in order to demonstrate superior taste, to enhance, rather than conceal, their individuality.

Consumption in the Tiri household is centripetal, designed to bring everything within bounds that can be rigidly controlled. It is a cause of great satisfaction for Tiri's family that they eat only their own rice, and that the food introduced from outside is exclusively the produce of traditional suppliers, notably, Maraars, the local market-garden caste. This conservatism arises not from a variant of the Protestant ethic, but from the determination on the part of a house that is rich but (rationally or not) insecure, not to transgress, not to presume, not to behave as if circumstances had changed and more adventurous consumption were really possible, lest the whole fragile edifice crumble overnight. Meanwhile, they become richer and richer. Because their land is limited (thirteen acres), it would indeed be rational for them to accumulate wealth with which to buy more fields; but it is unlikely that fields will become available, and if they do, a powerful coalition of clan interests would be ranged against the isolated Tiri household. In any case, one does not get to buy fields by skimping on blankets. Tiri's puritanism, which is not really un-Muria since it is an attempt to preserve a Muria lifestyle in defiance of the economic facts, is still arguably rational and sensible in some long-term sense, and Tiri's son will no doubt benefit from the parsimony practiced by his father and grandmother. Tiri is clearly in control of his destiny and is pursuing a strategy that makes sense to him and to his village associates.

My last example is of an even richer household, in which consumption is tending toward a much more radical degree of incoherence.

During my most recent trip to Bastar, in 1983, I chose to work close to the burgeoning local administrative and commercial center, Narayanpur. I lodged in a house in Duganar village belonging to a Muria in his sixties, Ram. Ram Saukar has five excellent houses but he chooses to sleep – year in, year out, winter and summer – on an open threshing floor in the midst of his fields. He is, to all appearances, a man of the most abject poverty. He wears a cotton g-string and an old woolen pullover, filthy and full of holes. He is tall and skinny, with close-cropped silver hair and a bristling growth of beard (the one way I could do something for him that he seemed really to appreciate was to shave him for free).

At the outset I assumed that Ram was a typical Muria old man, that is, a nonentity in his own house. In traditional Muria villages (among which Duganar can no longer be counted), it is typical for men with adult sons to be forced to relinquish control of domestic and productive organization and devote their time to drinking with cronies of their own age. Tiri's father, for instance, whom I did not even bother to mention when I was describing his house, is such a bibulous old man, charming if occasionally tiresome, but treated with undisguised contempt by his wife and son. With Ram Saukar things were very different, as I soon discovered. He did no physical work, but he controlled and directed everything, the execution being in the hands of his two adult sons, their wives, his unmarried daughter, and two permanent farm servants. Ram Saukar was the senior member of the dominant clan in Duganar, the *sarpanch* of the village, literate in Hindi and fluent also in Halbi and Gondi. He owned 35 acres of land, absolutely prime paddyfields with a government irrigation channel running straight through them. He had so many buffalo that he had stopped counting them, merely remarking, when I asked, that he thought he had "enough." He even had a Tata lorry and a driver at his disposal, though I am sorry to report that he had achieved this by allowing his daughter to become the mistress of the Sikh lorry driver who actually owned the vehicle and who had become his permanent client. This arrangement suited Ram Saukar perfectly; his daughter remained at home, where her labor could be exploited, he had the use of the lorry whenever he wanted and none of the expense of maintaining it, and he made money by providing board and lodging for the lorry driver and his assistants.

The product of the 35 acres was considerably more than required to feed even Ram's large and motley household. However, I was puzzled to learn that nothing was ever taken to Narayanpur market, only a couple of miles distant, except pure cash crops (such as mustard seed). This unwillingness to sell rice, which I had encountered in the more "traditional" Muria village, I initially ascribed to respect for the rice itself (which is how Tiri had explained his own abstention from the sale of rice, which is too sacred to be commercialized). I discovered later, however, that the Ram household was in the rice-selling business, but that instead of selling rice to the cooperative in the local market at government rates, they waited until supplies became short and prices high, whereupon they sold rice privately in the village. They also collected and sold large quantities of mahua pods (the raw material for *darngo*, the local liquor), always waiting for the best moment to unload their supplies – just before the Narayanpur *mela* or the marriage season. Ram's house was stacked to the rafters with mahua pods, but never a drink was to be had there, unless one of the brothers or the lorry driver obtained a bottle in Narayanpur. Ram himself neither smoked nor drank. I once offered him a cookie. He accepted, ate half of it in tiny nibbles, and then put the uneaten half aside "for the children."

Given that Ram Saukar had a large income by peasant standards, and never spent, or had anyone spend on his behalf, a single *paisa*, what on earth did he do with his profits, apart from putting them in the bank?

The only way in which the Ram Saukar family conspicuously spent more money than other, poorer households in Duganar was in the construction of new houses. The old main house comprised three houses built around a courtyard, with the fourth side of the square being occupied by stalls for livestock. In one house lived his wife, in one his elder son, in the other his younger son. He himself, as I said, lived out in the fields. On the main road leading into Narayanpur, he had built a kind of condominium consisting of three attached two-story houses of elaborate construction. This *burha lon* (great house) was intended for letting to migrant families working in Narayanpur. It had been standing two years and was beginning to show signs of decrepitude. Only one house was occupied, and that by the assistant of the Sikh lorry driver, who was not paying much rent. The whole thing looked like a dead loss commercially, but everyone in the family was extremely proud of having created such an imposing edifice, and they spent a lot of time there, chatting to the wife of the lorry driver's assistant. Next to the much-admired burha lon was a building that was not admired at all, one that was frankly admitted to be the old man's folly. Ram had decided to construct a house of stone, eliminating at a stroke the maintenance problem that besets mud-walled houses. He had hired stonemasons to chip the local granite into quadrangular blocks, but at this point his architectural inspiration had run out, or his nerve, and the house had been built as a single small room, no more than about twelve feet square, without windows. It was in fact a stone replica of a little hut that a very poor man might put up for himself. It was plain that this stone hovel was useless for any purpose, and it had never been roofed. The stones and cement were expensive and well joined, but this house, like the burha lon, was pointless as an investment of time and money. Nonetheless, despite their already having two surplus houses, at the time of my stay Ram Saukar's family were constructing no fewer than three more houses for themselves. These houses were to be for Ram's two sons and, following some shady deal, for the lorry driver. This latest round of construction had been stimulated by the government's offer of 5,000 rupees for building materials, plus title to house lots along the Narayanpur road, to "homeless" tribals. Without this incentive perhaps these houses would have been built elsewhere and not in such quick succession, but both brothers were enthusiastic at the prospect of having houses of their own, even though they were away from their own land and the family's main house, and would be squeezed in between the *ganda* (weaver) settlement and the main road, surrounded by strangers from other castes.

The Ram Sauker family could put money into buildings they did not need because building a house was sufficiently like a traditional, "practical" use of resources, so as not to be obviously, even to them, a way of playing with money. But playthings, or objects of aesthetic enjoyment, are what the excess houses, particularly the burha lon, had become. The old man's stone hut was obviously some kind of personal statement, expressive of his stony nature, of his desire for permanence, perhaps also of his antagonism toward his sons since he had insisted on building it despite their protests. This object may also represent a tomb; the only stone structures ordinarily built by Muria are funerary monuments. But it is characteristic that the symbolic statements incorporated in the family's excess houses viewed as objects of consumption are disguised by the fact that the houses are not represented as objects of consumption at all, but as investments, albeit with some kind of ulterior purpose.

The old man, as has been described, consumed only the bare minimum needed for physical survival. Yet in many ways he was no skinflint. His sons were allotted fields from which they derived good incomes of their own, and both undertook contracts from the government from which they could derive more money. Both had long since acquired the trinity of status symbols beyond which Muria peasants, even educated ones like these, do not aspire (radio, bicycle, wristwatch). In their dress they were modest in the extreme. Neither wore long trousers, only shorts, when they went to town. Normally they wore cheap, knee-length cloths and tattered t-shirts, though each had a few better shirts for wear on formal occasions. Neither wore shoes or sandals, except to town. They had cut their hair and did not wear turbans. In fact, they appeared to have spent less on clothes than a young man in a traditional village would spend on clothes and adornment, quite irrespective of whether he came from a rich family or a poor one. They drank far less and ate no better than the average "poor" Muria in a traditional village. They wore no jewelry. To be sure, the women of the house were quite well-dressed when they wanted to be. The younger brother's wife said that her husband gave her saris when he could, but he was inhibited by the attitude of his elder brother's wife , who objected to the squandering of family money on her sister-in-law, whom she considered an interloper. This led to quarrels between the brothers, episodes the younger woman greatly feared.

The Ram family was inhibited about spending money because any consumption initiative was seen as a threat to power. The old man, I think, avoided spending money in order to keep his iron grip on the organization of the household as a productive unit. If he had started drinking and enjoying life like an ordinary old man, he would have lost his power, like ordinary old men do. The brothers did not spend money because each was determined not to give the other an excuse to level accusations of spendthrift behavior, accusations that would have threatened the other's position as claimant to the eventual inheritance. But behind these intrafamilial conflicts there remains the general fact that neither brother really fantasized about consumption beyond a very basic level. I held lengthy discussions with the Sikh lorry driver concerning the price of tape recorders in Delhi as opposed to Raipur, Jagdalpur, Narayanpur, and so on (he wanted one for the cab of his lorry). Both brothers participated eagerly in these conversations, but it was quite clear that neither of them regarded a cheap tape recorder as an object they could conceivably buy. The stores in Narayanpur and Kondagaon, with which they were very familiar, were stuffed with modern goods, usually sold to salaried employees of the government and other aspiring urbanites, which they never expressed the slightest wish to buy.

But the most striking instance of the brothers' attitude toward consumption concerns not modern goods but supposedly traditional ones, to whose consumption possibilities the Ram family, imprisoned in its wealth, was entirely blind until those possibilities were pointed out by me.

Among the items of tribal art for which Bastar is famous, the most prominent are the gunmetal figurines made by the lost-wax process. Like all Muria material culture with "tribal" associations, these sculptures are not actually made by tribals at all, but by the local bronze-working caste (*Ghassiya*). These objects are placed in temples, and they are also avidly collected by tourists. They can be bought in quantity at any large fair in Bastar, or directly from the manufacturers, who are settled in villages throughout the district. While I was in Bastar researching markets, I visited a center of metal-casting at Kondagaon and acquired, for my own touristic purposes, a little collection of the smaller bell-metal figurines to decorate a mantelpiece at home. I bought a horse, a cow, a deer, a tiger, a scorpion, and so on, making as nearly as possible a matched set of all the animals offered. When I got back to the Ram household (where I was staying) after my trip to Kondagaon, I produced my set of little animals and arranged them on the floor, thinking they might amuse the children for a while. The effect was electric. Not only were the children absolutely entranced, but a large and enthusiastic group of adults, including both brothers, gathered around as well. The animals were picked up, minutely examined, placed in various arrangements, and admired from every angle. I was complimented on my ingenuity in finding these objects and acquiring them, and when the session was over they were lovingly packed up for me and placed in my suitcase. Yet the entire set did not cost more than 100 rupees (eleven dollars) in all (tourist prices), and all of them were available to my admiring audience at any local fair for much less than I had paid for them. But it was apparent that it had never occurred to any member of the household to buy such objects, even though they are supposedly redolent of Muria culture. Of the culture, perhaps; of the consumption system, not at all. Only by being a tourist – by buying these animals as a set and displaying them in a particular context – did I make it apparent to Muria themselves that they had something there to consume. Clearly, it will be a long time before the Muria embark on consumerism in its modern forms with the panache of even the most diffident tourist. But perhaps I made a start with the Ram family on that occasion.

Conclusion

The foregoing account of the Muria consumption system and its ambiguous future in the context of current economic changes has been fragmentary in many respects. But I hope it suffices to indicate the complex interaction between aspects of peasant societies that are not usually considered conjointly: the economic transformation brought about by technological change on the one hand, and on the other the symbolic order that conventional economics assigns to the category of tastes. The study of taste has recently become an important preoccupation of Marxist sociology (Bourdieu 1979), and quite rightly, because nothing so acutely expresses social class, and the educational system that reinforces and perpetuates classes in modern society, as consumer preferences in the cultural domain – music, films, furnishings, pictures, and so on. In the study of aesthetic production, attention has shifted from the creative activity of the lone artist or craftsman to the social conditions that are reproduced in art and craft production, and that foster this kind of productive activity. Here too, I think, there is a lesson to be drawn for the study of "primitive" art, where the "lone genius/enlightened public" schema of conventional art theory is even less applicable than it is in its original bourgeois context.

The Muria, as I have suggested, have created nothing in the material sense, except a landscape and a market, a market supplied by other groups – cloth weavers and dealers, Marwari silversmiths in far-off Rajasthan, Ghassiya workers in bronze, potters and smiths, and so on. These material elements have been selected and integrated into an immaterial cultural matrix, a collective style tightly integrated with the processes of Muria social reproduction (village political institutions, the ghotul system, the cult of the clan gods and earth goddess, the marriage alliance system, and so on). It is this collective style, this productive consumption, which is the creation of the Muria in the sphere of art and which has given rise to the illusion that the Muria are (like other tribals in India) innately artistic. Their artistry, insofar as it exists at all, is confined to the nonmaterial sphere of singing, dancing, and story-telling. But if one studies the ethnographies describing the Muria during their period of efflorescence (notably Elwin's work of the 1940's), it is impossible not to concur with the view that the Muria contrived, in their collective consumption practice, to create an astonishing synthesis, one that lingers even as the Muria are being absorbed into the mainstream of Indian rural society. This display of market-bought finery transcends the limits of mere borrowing and becomes a form of art in itself.

But this collective style depends on specific sociological conditions, ones that are increasingly unfulfilled as Muria society becomes more internally differentiated. In this paper I have outlined both the traditional consumption ethos and the pressures to which it is now subject, particularly where rich Muria are concerned. As time goes by, the Muria will eventually cease to dress as Muria, but will *dress up* as Muria when making explicit their ethnicity, heretofore implicit. Already, to a limited extent, they have become producers of "traditional" artifacts. The Kondagaon lost-wax sculpture establishment, where I obtained my set of animals, produces mainly for tourists. Significantly, the leading craftsman is an educated adivasi, not a member of the low-ranking (Hindu) Ghassiya caste traditionally occupied with this work. He has traveled to Delhi and even London, exhibiting his "tribal" craft. Just as the items traditionally imported by the Muria, through fairs and markets, underwent a sea change while being incorporated into the Muria consumption system, so now they are undergoing a further revaluation as they are reflected back into the great world, hungry for authenticity and for this reason the worst possible judge of it. We enter a hall of mirrors, with images endlessly reflected and re-reflected, much as Lévi-Strauss says of myths. And we can conclude with a suitably modified Lévi-Straussian aphorism: The World of Goods is round.

Notes

The research reported on here was supported by the ESRC Social Affairs committee, to whom I express my gratitude. Additional research support was provided by the International Centre for Economics and Related Disciplines (ICERD) at the LSE.

References

Bourdieu, P. 1977. *Outline of a theory of practice*. Cambridge: Cambridge University Press.

1979. *La distinction: Critique social du jugement*. Paris: Editions de minuit.

Brown, P. 1978. *Highland peoples of New Guinea*. Cambridge: Cambridge University Press.

Douglas, M., & B. Isherwood. 1980. *The World of Goods*. Harmondsworth, Eng.: Penguin Books.

Dubey, S. 1953. Token pre-puberty marriage in Middle India. *MAN* (o.s.) 53:21.

Elwin, V. 1943. *Maria murder and suicide*. Bombay: Oxford University Press.

1947. *The Muria and their ghotul*. Bombay: Oxford University Press.

Freeman, D. 1970. *Report on the Iban*. London: Athlone.

Fürer-Haimendorf, C. von. 1982. *The tribes of India: The struggle for survival*. Berkeley: University of California Press.

Gell, A. 1982. The market wheel: Symbolic aspects of an Indian tribal market. *MAN* (n.s.) 17:470–91.

Gell, S. 1984. The ghotul in Muria Society. Ph.D. thesis submitted to the Australian National University, Canberra.

Grigson, W. 1938. *The Maria Gonds of Bastar*. London: Oxford University Press.

Hill, Polly. 1983. *Dry grain farming families*. Cambridge: Cambridge University Press.

Jaspers, K. 1971. *Philosophy*. Chicago: University of Chicago Press.

Leach, J. W., & E. R. Leach, eds., 1984. *The Kula: New perspectives on Massim exchange.* Cambridge: Cambridge University Press.

Malinowski, B. 1922. *Argonauts of the Western Pacific.* London: Routledge.

Sartre, J-P. 1976. *Critique of dialectical reason.* London: Routledge.

Sinha, S. 1962. State formation and Rajput myth in tribal Central India. *Man in India* XLII/1:35–80.

Stirratt, J. (to appear). Attitudes to money among Catholic fishing communities in Sri Lanka. Paper read at seminar on "The anthropology of money" held in 1982 at the London School of Economics and Political Science, to be published under the editorship of M. Bloch and J. Parry.

PART III

Prestige, commemoration, and value

CHAPTER 5

Varna and the emergence of wealth in prehistoric Europe

COLIN RENFREW

A contrast is often drawn between societies with relatively undifferentiated and unspecialized economic systems on the one hand, and those where craft-specialist production and large-scale exchange of commodities take a significant role on the other. In the former, sometimes described as operating under a "domestic mode of production," activities yielding food for local consumption occupy most participants for most of their working time, and the exchange of goods takes place mainly in order to obtain necessary or desirable items from neighboring territories. In the latter, commercial activities play a significant role, and production and exchange for gain occupy a substantial proportion of the population.

This distinction was emphasized by the "substantivists" among economic anthropologists, notably Polanyi (1957), who stressed the "embeddedness" of the economy within a wider social matrix in most early societies. They criticized the tendency of the "formalists" among their colleagues to apply the analytic techniques of the modern economist, developed primarily for the description of modern industrial economies, to the very much simpler societies under consideration. The substantivists argued that the economic man of the modern economist could not be assumed to have operated in the societies in question. Clearly there is much justice in that critique, but Adams (1974) has pointed out that the market mentality, the desire to make a profit, is certainly not restricted to the modern world or to that of classical antiquity. To claim that the market was an innovation of ancient Greece, as Polanyi effectively did, may have been to oversimplify.

While it is no doubt the case that the distinction between "simple" and "complex" economies has been unduly exaggerated in the past, and such polarizing categories are perhaps best avoided, there are nonetheless valid differences and contrasts underlying these debates. The archeologist cannot fail to be aware that in most hunter-gatherer economies, and in the early days of farming in any area, the emphasis seems to have been primarily upon subsistence and there is thus some equivalence with the first of the two polar categories. Likewise in early

141

state societies, and especially in the early empires, there was often an emphasis upon the intensification of production, with the concentration of several products within the hands of an élite, thus making comparison with the second category appropriate.

The interesting question is how, in what circumstances, and by what processes, did the latter situation come about? How did these more complex economies emerge? To ask this question, let me stress, is not to adopt a prepared theoretical standpoint: it does not, for instance, assume an "evolutionary" or "neo-evolutionary" perspective. It does, however, imply a development through time of the societies in question, and hence a diachronic perspective. This is something that only the archeologist can provide, since almost without exception societies in the first category had not developed their own writing systems, and without written records the techniques of the historian are not appropriate. Nor has the transition to a developed economy, in the absence of significant external factors of acculturation, been studied, so far as I am aware, by any anthropologists over the past century or so. For almost by definition, the presence of anthropologists bespeaks the beginning of the process of absorption of the economy under study into what neo-Marxist writers would term a world system.

The investigation of such processes of economic development is thus in most places a task for the prehistoric archeologist. But the interest of the study goes beyond archeology, for the significant innovations are of several kinds. In the first place, the processes of intensification of production that are involved generally imply technological developments. Some of these lie in the sphere of subsistence production – development of improved crop species or animal breeds, the use of the plow and other features of what Sherratt (1981) has termed "the secondary products revolution," and perhaps irrigation in some cases. Some technological innovations are of another kind, resulting in the development of new products and sometimes of new materials, such as pottery or metal, often as a result of developments in pyrotechnology. Such developments do not work in the technological sphere alone. They imply, and sometimes arise from, developing social systems. New products, new commodities (such as pottery, or bronze) do not come into the world simply as a direct and inevitable result of their own physical properties. They may, indeed, in some cases be the result of some fortunate invention, but, as I have argued elsewhere (Renfrew 1978), it is the widespread *adoption* of the new activity or product, not simply the discovery of a new technical process, that constitutes the true innovation. This means, then, and no economist has ever denied this – not even a formalist one – that we cannot discuss commodities or the development of the economy without considering such embedded social concepts as value and demand.

Now the notion of value is not an easy one to analyze, even in a society where rates of exchange can be directly observed. I should at once add here that I see some force in the arguments of Binford (1969, 163) that "psychological preferences" in archeology, using explanations based upon assumed states of mind of prehistoric people for which there is no direct evidence, are best avoided. Binford, I rather think, regards a concept like value as belonging to what Pike (as quoted by Harris 1968, 571) would term an "emic" category: something existing primarily in the thoughts and minds of individual members of a given community. But value can also be an "etic" category: something that acts upon the material world in a manner that can be observed and evaluated cross-culturally, for which the modern observer can therefore gather relevant material evidence.[1]

Some years ago, in considering the growth of complex society in the prehistoric Aegean and the development of a trade in metal goods, I suggested that a crucial equation was "a symbolic equivalence of social and material values":

The essential kernel of many of the interactions between activities and between subsystems, interactions which are the mainspring for economic growth, develops from the human inclination to give a social and symbolic significance to material goods. For in this way a whole complex of activities in the material world satisfies aspirations, ambitions, and needs which are, at first sight, entirely without adaptive significance in facilitating the continued existence of the individual of the species (Renfrew 1972, 497).

This observation was made primarily in relation to a single specific instance of the emergence of a state society. But there is no doubt that it can be applied in several other areas. In prehistoric Britain, for instance, around 2000 B.C. we see for the first time the use of various materials, including gold, amber, and bronze, in contexts indicating that they were associated with high prestige. Indeed, what we see emerging is not simply certain new commodities, but in a sense, a new *kind* of prestige. Or at least an altogether new way of expressing prestige. To assert this, of course, opens up exciting new possibilities in the development of social archeology. For it is generally accepted that high status, associated with prestige, was in general not a feature of small and early human societies, in particular hunter-gatherer societies. Ranking and stratification, in whatever area of the world we may have under study, seem in general to have appeared later. That is, of course, a very broad generalization, but it rests only partly on the archeological evidence. Its main validation comes from the observation of living hunter-gatherer societies by anthropologists.

This is an area ripe for analysis, for even though archeologists have often, quite reasonably, assumed certain assemblages of objects – for instance, rich gravegoods accompanying a burial – to be indicative of the high status of the individual, the precise grounds for such a view have never been analyzed in any very satisfactory manner.[2]

There is also a further interesting question, recently stressed by Hodder (1982b, 212) concerning the active role of material culture. As he argues, it does not follow that the prestigious objects that we see, whether in a burial or elsewhere, associated with a notable individual, are simply the *reflection* of his or her high status. That is a reflectionist mode of thought into which many archeologists have too easily fallen (Hodder 1982a, 4). On the contrary, these aspects of material culture may themselves have been responsible in large measure for bringing about that high status, a point very much in harmony with the thinking, years ago, of Veblen (1899) on conspicuous consumption and display. High status can actually be achieved by the manipulation of material goods and by displays of wealth, as many analyses of big man systems have indicated. In studying commodities of high value we may, therefore, be doing more than monitoring the assertion of high status; we may be investigating what brought it about. What is evidently needed here is a framework of inference that allows these issues to be handled lucidly.

In several areas of the world it has been noted, in the case of metallurgical innovation in particular, that the development of bronze and other metals as *useful* commodities was a much later phenomenon than their first utilization as new and attractive materials, employed in contexts of display, when they were clearly associated with high prestige and evidently regarded as of high value. In the sections that follow I first develop some of these ideas in relation to interesting finds from Varna cemetery in Bulgaria. That gold at Varna was a commodity of high value is argued, not taken as given. The significance of changing notions of value for the development of an economy with more intensive production and more widespread distribution of products is discussed in the final section of this essay.

Varna and early copper metallurgy

Commodity and innovation

The development of metallurgy is one of the clearest cases in which essentially the *same* innovations were made repeatedly and independently, in different parts of the world at different times. For though it can be argued, for instance, that the domestication of maize is not at all the same thing as the domestication of wheat, and that the notion of the development of food production is thus very much the construct of the archeologist, the domestication of each species being in reality a very different happening, the same can hardly be said for metal working. The smelting of ores to produce copper, or the alloying of copper with tin to produce bronze, are in most cases ultimately the same from the technical point of view wherever they are carried out.

For this reason, perhaps, there have been frequent suggestions that there was only one invention of metallurgy. This view was well expressed and well argued by the late Theodore Wertime (1964) twenty years ago: "One must doubt that the tangled web of discovery, comprehending the art of reducing oxide and sulfide ores, the recognition of silver, lead, iron, tin, and possibly arsenic and antimony, as distinctive new metallic substances, and the technique of alloying tin with bronze, could have been spun twice in human history." However, this is an argument that need not be replayed here. It has effectively been demonstrated that metallurgy in the New World had separate origins and developments from those in the Old World. It is even likely that metallurgy in China developed independently of that in Western Asia. It has been argued on several occasions that there is a good case for the independent origin of copper metallurgy in southeast Europe. The same is true for Iberia. What interests us here is to understand more clearly how these independent innovations of a new commodity may have occurred.

There are two other old misconceptions that need to be clarified. The first, which goes back to the original Three Age System, and more particularly to Gordon Childe's Marxist elaboration of "Archaeological Ages as Technological Stages" (Childe 1944), was to regard the inception of copper/bronze metallurgy, and later of iron working, as technologically and productively significant events in their own right. In most cases, however, as noted earlier it was many centuries after the basic techniques were explored and understood that they became of economic and productive significance.[3] The same observations hold for iron working. Iron was known and valued in the Near East for centuries before the iron age began. Similarly, there are not-infrequent finds in Mycenaean Greece at least two centuries before iron weapons begin to be seen in appreciable numbers. One might predict that similar circumstances would apply in most areas where there was an indigenous development of metal technology, although clearly the impact of an imported technology upon a less developed native one can be decisive (as was the case, for instance, with the demand for iron nails in eighteenth-century Polynesia). It should be stressed, then, that it is not the new technology itself that is decisive, but the use to which it is put.

The second and related point that deserves emphasis is the misconception that the key to the adoption of important innovations is the diffusion of the essential new knowledge that underlies most of them. This view underlies the work of many geographers, who speak of "the diffusion of innovations" as if they were dealing with the propagation of some new virus, or the dissemination of a gene through successive generations of a population. Such models may be appropriate when there really are major demographic shifts, as in the case of the spread of farming, but what Hägerstand (1967) calls innovation diffusion as a spatial process is only one approach to the subject. Another is to stress factors endogenous to the society in question. In many cases the technology has been readily available for a considerable period of time before it comes into widespread use in a manner that is so productive as to promote efficiency in a way that is adaptively advantageous.

The social context

It is my argument, then, that the decisive innovation in the development of a new commodity is generally social rather than technical. Often the technology is already there.

This point is, I believe, well exemplified by the case of metallurgical development in southeast Europe in the so-called chalcolithic period. Indeed, the explanatory problem there, as perhaps in most cases of early metallurgical development, is not to explain why people did not at once use this great technology. It is, on the contrary, to understand why they bothered at all. For until the technology develops a great deal further, as it can only do through intensive use, early copper metallurgy does not produce anything decisively useful at all. The artifacts that can be produced from native copper by an annealing process have very few properties to recommend them in comparison to well-chosen stones, and many that are lacking.

In most cases early metallurgy appears to have been practiced primarily because the products had novel properties that made them attractive to use as symbols and as personal adornments and ornaments, in a manner that, by focusing attention, could attract or enhance prestige. It is striking that copper had such a key place in the prestige systems of North America, for instance. In the same way in China, evidence for a copper age or for the very early development of bronze metallurgy may largely be lacking precisely because metal was used primarily for the production of prestige objects, notably bronze vessels, and stray finds of inconsequential objects are very rare. In the same way in the Old World we find iron in the early phases always as a material of great worth, whose context in rich burials and in other finds indicates a prestigious status. Only much later was it used to make productive tools, and at the same time it became commonplace.

The case of Varna

Let us now turn to the case of the Varna cemetery. The discovery there, some ten years ago, of a series of burials with rich gravegoods including many objects of gold, aroused great interest when their very early context was appreciated. Although copper metallurgy can be documented earlier in the Near East, the goldwork of Varna is the earliest significant (that is, substantial) occurrence of the use of gold anywhere in the world (Renfrew 1978a). (It should be noted that in addition to the main cemetery near Varna, sometimes termed Varna I, a second cemetery has been found in the area, designated Varna II. It is earlier, and the gravegoods are much less rich. When no distinction is made, the main cemetery – Varna I – is meant.)

But Varna had a second significance for southeast Europe. Hitherto the chalcolithic cultures of the Balkans have always appeared within an economy in most respects egalitarian. The villages so far discovered have houses of about the same size, and the one larger building some- times observed has quite reasonably been regarded as a communal structure analogous to the "men's house" in some societies. Special finds such as the earlier figurines of Nea Nikomedeia or the gold amulets from Chotnitsa have given rise to the suggestion that there may have been village shrines. Hitherto neither the village plans nor the artifacts found have suggested any very salient social ranking in the Balkan chalcolithic.

Very few cemeteries have been well documented from this area and period. But what we have known of them has not conflicted with the impression given by the contemporary cemeteries of Hungary. There are disparities in the gravegoods, perhaps comparable to those doc- umented for a slightly later period at Branč in Czechoslovakia by Susan Shennan (1975). She was able to show distinctions between the sexes and some indications of hereditary status, but no very salient ranking.

Varna gives a very different impression. The quantity of the grave-goods in some of the graves is in itself very striking. Moreover, there are special artifacts in some of the rich graves that are likely to be in themselves indicative of very special status. The finds at the cemetery have not yet been published in full, but there is a good preliminary publication by Ivanov (1978), and the same author (Ivanov 1982) has detailed many grave groups in the catalog of the 1982 exhibition of the Isetan Museum of Art. It is not yet feasible to give any quantitative analysis, but some important points of qualitative analysis can be faced. By 1982, 204 graves had been found. Among these are 35 containing no skeletons. These are classed by the excavators as "symbolic graves" (cenotaphs) in the context in question (although the possibility of bone decay must be seriously considered). The "symbolic graves" are sub-divided into rich graves (three in number, with numerous gravegoods: Graves 1, 4, and 36); graves containing clay masks of human faces (three in number); simple symbolic graves (21 in number); and graves containing reburied parts of human skeletons (seven in number). The second major category is "graves with skeletons situated in a straight supine position," of which 59 are reported. The third category is "graves with skeletons placed on one side and flexed"; 41 are reported. These three main categories total 135; presumably some of the total of 204 have not yet been excavated or assigned a category. Five major issues present themselves.

1. *Relative value of materials.* It cannot be assumed that materials that we esteem highly, such as gold, were necessarily of high value in the context in question. For instance, four of the richest graves contain a total of 2,200 gold objects weighing, 4,921 grams, and it could therefore be argued that gold was not so rare or valuable as other materials. But five arguments serve to stress its value: First, gold is used as a personal adornment in proximity to the body in two key positions that are recognized as particularly important in a cross-cultural perspective: the face (numerous adornments, in position, for instance, on the clay masks, as in Grave 2); and the genitals (gold penis cover, Grave 43). Second, gold is prominent in objects that from their position may be regarded as of prime symbolic value. These are the "maces" or "scepters," which the position in the grave indicates were buried in the hand of the deceased (Grave 43) or were otherwise prominent in the assemblage (Graves 1, 4, and 36). Third, gold is dissembled; that is to say, objects sometimes are made to look as if

they were made of gold when they are not. This is an important general principle, for in cases of deliberate deception it is axiomatic that the device has the purpose of making the object look more rather than less valuable. (A different principle might apply when taking valuables through a customs examination). This point is illustrated by the piece of gold leaf still adhering to the shaft-hole axe of stone that was carried on top of the golden scepter of Grave 4. Clearly the intention was to make the axe look as if it were made of gold.

Fourth, gold is used more economically (in terms of mass) than comparable materials such as copper. It is notable that there appear to be no gold items made by a casting process.[4] The melting points of gold and copper are approximately the same, and it would be interesting to learn if there are technical aspects, apart from the abundance or rarity of the material, that make the former more difficult to cast. The copper objects from Grave 4 are solid, and though their weights are not published, must together come close in weight to the five kilograms that the gold from the cemetery totals. The use of sheet gold in effect gives the maximum surface area of the material in terms of its weight: a good criterion of ascribed value. Fifth, gold is inherently attractive. This criterion is listed last because I have not yet presented arguments to make it other than subjective. Two objective points are relevant: it reflects light efficiently; that is, it is bright, indeed dazzling; moreover, it does not tarnish (oxidize); it is unchanging through time, incorruptible. This point is further discussed below.

These arguments warrant the inference, which is thus no longer an intuitive assumption, that gold was a high-value material at Varna. The arguments could be further developed to show that it was probably the highest-value material that is found in several graves.

2. *Inherited (ascribed) rather than achieved status.* Several children's or infants' graves in the cemetery are rich in their gravegoods, although none falls within the wealthiest class (Graves 17 and 110 fall into this class). It is suggested that these children had inherited status. However, the argument could be put that they are children of adults of high achieved status, and that the manner of interment reflects the status of the parents rather than that of the child.

3. *Salient ranking.* There are massive disparities in the cemetery in terms of (a) the number of gravegoods; (b) the quantity of high-status materials, mainly gold; (c) the presence of symbolic insignia, including gold headdresses, gold pectoral ornaments, and scepters; (d) the presence of unusual categories of artifacts, for instance, the pottery vases decorated with gold paint from Grave 4. Prominent status, reflected

in conspicuous burial, raises the possibility that the Varna society should be considered a chiefdom, in the sense employed by Service (1962) and by Sahlins (1972).

4. *Sex of high-status individuals.* Both women and men were buried with rich gravegoods. Unfortunately, three of the four richest graves, the only ones where gold scepters are buried, are cenotaphs, containing no skeletons. The fourth is Grave 43, where the deceased was male, aged 40 to 45 years. It is possible that the hypothetical office of "chief" was held exclusively by males, but there is no case at present for assuming that it was not held also by females.

5. *Symbolic distinctions between the sexes.* Full publication of the archeological findings will be necessary before the gender of the putative chiefs can be satisfactorily settled. It might be possible to determine the likely sex of the deceased honored in the three rich cenotaphs. A preliminary analysis suggests that two artifacts – the shaft-hole axe of stone or copper and the bone (or marble) "Idol" – are of considerable symbolic significance, since they are found singly, although with other objects in many graves. They are found with skeletons of both men and women, and the idol is found with children. The pattern of occurrence needs further study.

The wider social context

It is meaningless to talk of a "chiefdom" on the basis of a single place, especially a single cemetery. For the interest of such a term is that it relates to social organization, and the whole point of a chiefdom society is that the center has an organizing role beyond the domestic or village level. The concept thus has spatial implications. A question that needs to be answered for Varna, then, is what is the larger spatial significance of the Varna finds? Are we to expect other Varnas, other cemeteries with very pronounced disparities in status, consonant with chiefdom society?

Hitherto our picture of the Balkan chalcolithic has been one of a mosaic of essentially independent, autonomous villages – indeed, a segmentary society whose components are cellular and modular. Of course, these societies were linked by exchange networks and no doubt by many ties of kinship. The larger unities, reflected in the geographic distribution of pottery styles, were often considered tribal by earlier generations of scholars, who sought to see behind the Gumelnitsa culture or the Vinča culture or the Cucuteni culture corresponding "peoples." But these ethnic categories are now much less clear. We lack recent work that discusses in sufficient detail the evidence for social or political groups beyond the village level. The means of integration, other than kinship and exchange, are – if they existed – still obscure. We do not have in southeast Europe ceremonial centers of evidently public nature to compare with the Stonehenge monuments of Britain or the Hopewell ceremonial complexes in the United States.

What, then, was the regional organization, if any, during the chalcolithic? Ivanov (1978) has hinted that the different scale of the tell mounds in the chalcolithic may indicate some settlement hierarchy; this is an important issue not yet argued in detail. If we are to regard Varna as the seat of a chiefdom, as the cemetery finds certainly suggest it may have been, it should also be the center of an organizing hierarchy that can be interpreted in spatial terms.

One specific issue that may be helpful here, when more progress has been made, is the question of the source of the gold. Occasional gold finds are quite common in the chalcolithic, although the Chotnitsa find is the only other one that might be termed a treasure. There has already been speculation about far-flung trading links and remote sources for this gold. But I shall be astonished if the gold was procured outside the immediate territory of the Varna polity. Its radius of direct influence cannot have been, I would suggest, more than 100 kilometers at the outside, and that would make a very large territorial unit. The distance from center to periphery in an Early State module is rarely more than 70 kilometers (Renfrew 1975, 19), and chiefdom societies are often of comparable scale. I shall be very surprised if the source of the Varna gold were more than 50 kilometers from Varna itself.

This is not to deny the more extensive nature of the exchange networks then in existence, most graphically illustrated by the distribution of marine shell, much of it originating in the Mediterranean, rather than the Black Sea (as has been securely shown for *Spondylus gaederopus*). It is possible that the Varna *Spondylus* was carried thither by sea through the Dardanelles, and it is significant that the largest workshop for *Spondylus* yet known for the Balkan chalcolithic was at Hiršova, again on the Black Sea coast. But the efficiency of the land-based exchange routes operating up from Aegean coastal settlements and those of the immediate hinterland, such as Sitagroi, should not be underestimated.[5]

Metallurgy at Varna: the "chrysolithic"

In the foregoing section several problems were raised about the nature of chalcolithic society in the light of the Varna discoveries. It is clear that copper metallurgy developed in the Balkans long before it did in the Aegean, although there are stray finds in the Aegean that indicate, as suggested earlier, that the technology in its rudiments had been invented or acquired during the late neolithic. The essential difference is that in the Balkans the metallurgical products were integrated much more closely into contexts of social use within the contemporary material culture. This created demand or need, and from this demand came increased output, and a steady increase in technical accomplishment.

This stage is splendidly exemplified by the Varna finds, which are of course chrysolithic (that is, gold-stone) as much as they are chalcolithic (copper-stone). Indeed, it is gold that is used, and takes pride of place, for most purposes of display. Copper ornaments are in fact *less* common at Varna than in copper-age cemeteries farther north and west because they are largely displaced by gold.[6]

Comparison of the occurrences of gold and copper at the main Varna cemetery (Varna I) makes it clear that copper has already moved from the role of the merely decorative, which it seems to have had in the earlier Varna II cemetery, to the productively useful. The main copper forms found in Varna I are the pin, the flat chisel, the narrow chisel or wedge, the long, narrow chisel, sometimes with curved end, and a range of forms of shaft-hole axes, ranging from the squarish Vidra type to the very elongated. It is, however, particularly interesting that there is still a comparable range of shaft-hole axes of stone – in this form we catch the evolution at the transition from stone to copper. The stone axes are found in some of the poorer graves (for example, Grave 7), but an elegant and slender one, sheathed in gold, was mounted on the scepter to form part of the rich assemblage of Grave 4, where it obviously had a ceremonial role. In Grave 1 the comparable position is taken by a copper axe.

We see here the replacement of stone by copper in what seems to have been initially a ceremonial or prestige role. This lends force to the suggestion that initially the material was appreciated as a new vehicle for display, and that its genuinely novel and productively useful mechanical qualities only later came to govern its use.

Value and commodity in wider perspective

Wessex and the Aegean bronze age

The case of the Varna cemetery suggests a number of interesting problems and questions that deserve further investigation. It raises the issue, seen also very clearly in the early bronze age of the Aegean and of northern Europe, of the relationship of the use of metal objects for display purposes to the development of personal ranking within the societies in question. The recognition by the archeologist of personal ranking within a prehistoric society depends in part on the recovery of artifacts associated with the person, generally accompanying burial of the body. In some cases the very artifacts that suggest early ranking in society simultaneously document the early use of metal. The association is thus not a coincidental one, and there is a risk of circularity in the argument here; but it can be overcome by careful analysis.

One of the most interesting features of the Varna cemetery, as noted above, is that it appears in a context that was previously regarded as more or less egalitarian – that is to say, where evidence for marked disparities in personal possessions was lacking, not only from the gravegoods of the known cemeteries, but also from finds in domestic contexts. There is, of course, again the risk of circularity, since without such archeologically notable indicators of possessions as metal objects, it is inherently more difficult to observe such disparities as may have existed. But our conclusion here does not depend exclusively upon the presence of metal objects. Other materials have a significant place among the gravegoods, which also include significant forms, such as the scepters, that could still be recognized if they were made, for instance, of stone.

In Varna, then, we see striking indications of high personal status occurring at approximately the same time as the development within the society of attractive commodities by which high status may be expressed. Yet it would have been possible for high status to be expressed, albeit less effectively, by the inclusion of very large quantities of high-value objects already in circulation (such as shell bracelets) without the presence of the new metal commodities. It is, moreover, possible that gold was available as a material at an earlier date but was simply not exploited until the Varna period. (This conclusion of course depends upon a local origin for the gold, proposed earlier.)

A similar conjunction between new commodities and the new kind of prestige that is seen in the personal possession of attractive objects is reflected in the Wessex culture of the British early bronze age and in the preceding Beaker period. Here, however, it is accompanied by another very interesting and suggestive feature: the widespread appearance of burial by individual inhumation, often under a prominent burial mound. Although there was a wide variety of burial practices in the preceding neolithic period in Britain, many of these were collective, and involved the placing of the remains (often after a process

of excarnation – that is, allowing the bones to become free of flesh)
within a collective burial place, sometimes of impressive, indeed monumental, scale. Cemeteries of individual inhumations are not found,
in contrast to the position in central Europe, where there are numerous cemeteries of the Linearbandkeramik culture, as well as in
some succeeding phases.

In the British case, a distinction was drawn some years ago between
the earlier societies, which practiced conspicuous collective burial,
entirely without notable gravegoods, and these later ones, where rich
gravegoods are found accompanying favored individuals. At one extreme lie societies where personal wealth in terms of valuable possessions is not impressively documented, but where the solidarity of
the social unit was expressed most effectively in communal or group
activities. At the other are societies where a marked disparity in personal possessions and in other material indications of prestige appears
to document a salient prestige ranking, often without evidence of
large communal meetings or activities (Renfrew 1974, 74).

The discussion has been taken much further in a number of recent
articles by S. J. Shennan (1982), Thorpe and Richards (1982), and
Braithwaite (1984). Shennan (1982, 157) draws upon work by Gilman
(1976) in southeast Spain, where it is argued that emerging hierarchies
need to be sanctioned by appropriate ideologies, and that the ritual
of collective burial was not appropriate to such ideologies. Instead
there emerged a new ideology, in which hierarchy was legitimated
through the consumption of prestige items by individuals. Shennan
accepts this perspective, but suggests that the increase in social differentiation had taken place in Britain earlier, during the neolithic,
and that we can see the early bronze age changes rather as the catching
up of conservative ritual with the social changes that had already
occurred. He makes the same point in relation to comparable changes
in Brittany: "The monumental nature of the late neolithic tombs, and
other megalithic phenomena of Brittany suggest again that here we
have a hierarchically differentiated society prior to the early bronze
age, and that the early bronze age sees a change in the form of its
ritual expression, with a move from collective monumentality to individual consumption of goods" (1982, 157). The important point
here is that "the rituals involved in this new ideology were based not
on the collective labor of the community but on the consumption in
burial of prestige items and symbols obtained by means of contact
with members of elites elsewhere and/or through the activities of
specialist craftsmen." This tendency toward the expression of male

prestige in burial can be traced back to the preceding Beaker period, but then in the context of only a very limited degree of hierarchical differentiation. And Shennan stresses, as others have noted from Childe onward, that over this period "it is difficult to avoid relating the increase in social differentiation in some way to the growth of the copper and bronze industry and the opportunities it offered for the generation and control of a surplus" (Shennan 1982, 159).

Braithwaite has again discussed this issue within a broader context of ritual discourse and conflicting ideologies, concluding that "there was a gradual move away from the genealogical basis of the earlier system of prestige and towards a system in which material symbols, such as metal artefacts, were used more directly to signify status and accrue prestige" (Braithwaite 1984, 106).

This case has many analogies with the position in the prehistoric Aegean. There we see the appearance around 3300 B.C. of the practice of inhumation in cemeteries in the Cycladic Islands, although in small family graves rather than as individual burials. At the same time, the gravegoods reflect increasing disparities in wealth and prestige. A similar process is seen in Crete (although the burials there in the round tombs remain collective ones, but they are accompanied by rich gravegoods), and it culminates there in the formation of Minoan palace society around 2100 B.C.

The aftermath was very different in each of the three cases under consideration. At Varna, the period of rich burial was followed by, and indeed may in part be contemporary with, the development of a full copper age, when copper axe-adzes were common, along with other useful tools. But this was a short-lived phase, followed by the effective collapse of this flourishing society of Old Europe, and by a period of decline, with reduced metal production and with none of the indicators of hierarchical organization that we glimpse at Varna, nor of the ritual sophistication that we infer from some of the domestic sites of the Varna period.

In the Aegean the early bronze age, which is the period when individual burial and differences in ranking first emerge, is followed by the Minoan and Mycenaean palace civilizations. But we should note that it is not until the later bronze age that bronze tools were of frequent and widespread occurrence, as evidenced by the tool hoards of the Mycenaean period. During the early bronze age, despite the finding of a few tool hoards, bronze was used mainly for objects of high prestige value, notably for weapons.

Likewise during the British later bronze age, metal objects no longer

accompany burials to the same extent, after the early phase of flo-
rescence, and individual burial with rich gravegoods is no longer seen.
This is not difficult to understand within the perspective advanced
by Shennan and Braithwaite, from which the rich burials of the early
bronze age are viewed as establishing or validating through ritual
practice a hierarchy based in part upon new acquisitive principles.
There is evidence that in the later bronze age, land tenure was an
increasingly important issue, and metal objects are then found in
hoards and sometimes in ritual deposits, but not in graves. This was
the period of the development of the flourishing bronze industry of
the developed European bronze age, as Sherratt (1976) has well described, with its extensive trade networks. In northern Europe by this
time bronze was no longer a novelty, nor any longer a commodity
prestigious in itself.

There are many differences between the trajectories of social development in the three areas here discussed. This is to be expected,
particularly in view of the differences in the sources of metal and in
the exchange systems by which metal and metal objects were distributed. It is, however, the similarities that are relevant here. I suggest
that there are real structural or processual similarities between the
use of prestige goods accompanying individual burials in the Aegean early bronze age, and their comparable use in the early bronze
age of Britain nearly a thousand years later. The Varna finds are
very different; it is not yet clear how typical the Varna cemetery in
fact was among its contemporaries in southeast Europe. But again
it raises, and perhaps helps to solve, some of the analytical problems
involved.

What we appear to be seeing in each case is the very early use of
metal in the area in question in contexts that at the same time are
documenting the emergence of personal ranking, reflected in what
may have been individually owned goods, buried with the deceased
in the grave. Copper and gold clearly afford in each case a new vehicle
for the expression of ranking, and thus in this sense a new channel
of communication. Indeed, it may be suggested that they are not
merely reflecting or documenting a degree of ranking in society that
would have existed in any case without them. On the contrary, the
ownership and display of these valuable objects may have constituted
an essential part of the prominence of their owner and have contributed significantly to his or her prestige. It may be permissible, then,
to see these materials as playing a more active role, and rather than
simply reflecting a social structure, as taking a significant role in its
very formation.

Aspects of value and prestige: the perspective of Marx

In view of the wide influence upon anthropologists of Marx's discussion of value and of commodities and of the useful categories that he established, it is convenient to relate his views to the cases just examined. As early as 1867 Marx usefully redefined the distinction between *use value*, "the utility of a thing" (Marx 1970, 44), and *exchange value*, "the proportion in which values in use of one sort are exchanged for those of another sort." He proceeded in his analysis to stress that what commodities have in common is that they are products of labor. "As values, all commodities are only definite masses of congealed labor time" (ibid., 47). In shorthand it may be convenient to think of this aspect in terms of *labor value*.

These terms were used lucidly by Marx in his analysis of capitalist economies, but they form part of what may be termed a formalist analysis. They are less satisfactory when applied to those classes of object that Dalton (1977) has described as "primitive valuables." These are the objects that are especially prized, and have symbolic significance, such as the *vaygu'a*, the valuable exchanged in the kula ring in the Trobriand Islands. These are to be contrasted with the mere *gimwali*, the everyday objects circulating in petty market exchange. Here it is possible, so Dalton asserts, to identify different spheres of exchange, and it is simply not appropriate to exchange valuables for common, everyday goods. These valuables, such as shell bracelets – or in the case of the British neolithic, perhaps, the jade axes that are handsome objects but unsuited for the productive functions of an axe – serve to call into question Marx's dictum (1970:48) that "nothing can have value without being an object of utility." But it should be noted here that Marx may not have intended his labor theory of value to apply to precapitalist situations.[7]

Here it is appropriate to turn to another famous passage from Marx, entitled "The fetishism of commodities and the secret thereof," in which he speaks, with justice, of "the mystical character of commodities": "A commodity appears at first sight, a very trivial thing, and easily understood. Its analysis shows that it is, in reality, a very queer thing, abounding in metaphysical subtleties and theological niceties" (Marx 1970, 76). It is worth quoting a further celebrated and suggestive passage, although it is one that leads to a conclusion seemingly not appropriate to the cases under consideration here, however relevant it may be to capitalist economics:

But it is different with commodities. There the existence of the things *qua* commodities, and the value relation between the products of labor which stamps them as commodities, have absolutely no connection with their physical properties and with the material relations arising therefrom. There is a definite social relation between men, that assumes, in their eyes, the fantastic form of a relation between things. In order, therefore, to find an analogy, we must have recourse to the mist-enveloped regions of the religious world. In that world the productions of the human brain appear as independent beings endowed with life, and entering into relations both with one another and the human race. So it is in the world of commodities with the products of men's hands. This I call the fetishism which attaches itself to the products of labor, so soon as they are produced as commodities, and which is therefore inseparable from the production of commodities.

This fetishism of commodities has its origin, as the foregoing analysis has already shown, in the peculiar social character of the labor that produces them (Marx 1970, 77). In the case of primitive valuables, or indeed of valuable materials in our own time, such as gold, this fetishism, as Marx aptly terms it, is easy to recognize. But it is not so easily analyzed in terms of labor value.[8]

Marx's useful discussion establishes a number of valid distinctions, but from the standpoint of precapitalist socieities, it is curious that he should attach the term "fetishism," in relation to commodities, "the products of labor," rather than to the much less rationally based and less functionally valid prestige value, which is commonly assigned in many societies to objects and commodities that have negligible use value, in a utilitarian or productive sense, and which sometimes represent minimal labor value. It may perhaps be useful to recapitulate, taking Marx's helpful distinctions as a starting point.

In general, value is a property that is assigned to an object in a manner that arises from the social context in question, and it is to some, usually significant, extent arbitrary. It is never a property inherent within an object or material in the manner of such physical and measurable properties as hardness, density, refractive index, and so on. It cannot be measured outside a social context. We speak of value as if it were inherent within the object or commodity, and in doing so we create a metaphor, or mask a reality. So Marx was right to speak of "the fetishism of commodities," although labor is not the only crucial consideration.

Value is something assigned by an individual or by a group. This value may be assigned because of the use potential of the commodity (use value) or because of the work involved in its production (labor value). (Exchange value is a different kind of category: it is a measure, a parameter of value, always expressed as a ratio between *two* materials. Unlike the preceding, it is not a primary quality.)

Often the term "sentimental value" is used to refer to the estimation that a specific person accords an object when the high estimation is not widely shared. It generally depends upon the specific history of that object in relation to the person in question – it may be grand-mother's brooch, or the photo of a close friend. The specific history of an individual object, which is of no particular interest because of its raw material or its workmanship, can also afford it a generally agreed value – for instance, a memento of Queen Elizabeth or of George Washington, or the Stone of Scone. The same is relevant to the reverence accorded objects of religious veneration, whether they be supposed relics of an actual person, or images that command re-spect, even when the constituent material is not prized – fetishism in the original sense. This may derive in part from the specific history of the object, and in part from an implied use-value, since the image may be believed to have active powers.

So far we have considered two aspects, labor value and use value, that may be considered functionally based. Exchange value is iden-tified as simply a measure, a ratio. Historic or association value (in-cluding sentimental value) depends solely upon the unique history or association of the specific object in question.

Turning now to prestige goods, we can see that they generally have value of another kind. Of course, some prestige goods do have unique status: "This was the sword that Prince X used to slay a hundred enemies." But most prestige goods also have a value that, within the given cultural context, is regarded as intrinsic. Following a suggestion of Arjun Appadurai, it may be useful to introduce the term prime value in relation to those materials that in a given culture are regarded as having intrinsic value. This allows us to avoid the use of the term intrinsic, which is desirable because, as noted earlier, no materials have a universal intrinsic value. Prime value is thus the equivalent of ascribed intrinsic value. It was earlier shown that objects of gold had a position in some of the graves at Varna that seems a particularly privileged one. Although each specific object may itself have had a special status through its history of associations, the fact that it was made of gold does seem (in terms of the pattern established) to have been relevant. In view of our own preconceptions about gold, that is not surprising to us. But these simple objects of gold have no special use value, in the utilitarian sense, and little labor value. The same observations can be made about amber in the Wessex graves, and about shell in many contexts.

It is, in fact, easy for us to compile a list of commodities that are of prime value in many cultural contexts (but not in all), and that tend to function in the exchange sphere. Gold and silver are among these, and with them crystal and jade and a series of other translucent stones, as well as objects of shell. Furs may be included and also various fabrics, but since these are manufactured products, their high value does often relate to a high labor value, as Marx suggested.

Having listed these valuable substances, we can go on to find more general underlying principles. We can seek to ask, in other words, what properties genuinely intrinsic to the materials in question may have led to their being regarded as of prime value in many (but not all) societies. These objects and materials are in general conspicuous: they operate upon the senses in an agreeable and attractive manner. They are also rare; only in special (generally ritual) circumstances can very common materials have a high value. Many of them share the property of durability. But others are consumables, such as perfumes or very fine wines. There is in fact a polarity among primitive valuables, between those that are suitable for conspicuous consumption (and that need to be consumed in order to be used at all), such as frankincense and myrrh, and those that have an enduring or even eternal quality, like gold and jade.

It is goods with this prime value that feature prominently in the Varna cemetery and in the two other cases considered. Many burials contain a few useful objects, such as pots or stone tools, and the remainder of the gravegoods are of shell or metal or of fine stone. There are very few objects that can be recognized as of symbolic value that are not also made of a material we can recognize as of prime value at that time. At Varna the bone figurines or idols are the most prominent objects clearly of symbolic value that are made of a material lacking in prime value.

These points take us beyond the categories established by Marx in his classification, and suggest that in many societies some commodities were accorded prime value, regarded by each society as an inherent, intrinsic value. This prime value we may regard as a symbolic construct, and like all symbolic value, it is ascribed, to some extent, in an arbitrary way.[9]

Commodity, value, and ranked societies

Halstead and O'Shea (1982) have discussed transactions in which food is exchanged for more durable items of value in terms of "social storage." They have rightly stressed that such valuable items form a suitable vehicle for the development of institutionalized inequality. Halstead (1981, 177) has countered the view that valuables could never be exchanged for food, whereas Gamble (1981) has recently emphasized the need to consider the system of production, especially of agricultural produce, with as much care as the distribution and circulation of goods.

These various studies, like that of Woodburn (1982), usefully introduce the dimension of time into the discussion, and this may prove crucial to our understanding of prestige expressed by, and achieved by, the ownership of goods, which in consequence have high prime value. Many of these goods, as noted above, are durables, indeed conspicuous durables: gold, like diamonds, is forever.

Analysis of gift exchange has always laid great stress upon the standing or prestige an exchange partner achieves in offering a splendid gift. The gesture is in itself a transitory action, but it sets up obligations for a reciprocal gesture of comparable dimensions in the future. But the acquisitive character of the three societies we have been examining suggests rather that the main emphasis may then have shifted to the ownership of prestige goods, as well, no doubt, as their conspicuous consumption in various ways, including burial. Ownership, carrying with it the direct association that can go with personal property, is a state rather than an action. The possession of rich objects carries with it more than the ability to exchange some of them in return for goods and services. By virtue of the prestige it confers, ownership offers access to social networks and to other resources that are closed to those lacking such prestige. In these two senses the ownership of rich objects reflecting and conferring prestige may be regarded as wealth, rather than as an implied obligation to generosity.

The question we are now approaching is at what point and by what means does the value set upon prestige commodities, such as jade axes or gold ornaments, change? How does the ceremonial nature of the primitive valuables of the simpler, egalitarian societies develop into the more active role of the prestige items in the acquisitive societies of the early bronze age Aegean or Wessex? That is to say, at what point does the ownership and display of important objects of desirable materials such as copper and gold play an important part in the achievement and maintenance of the high status of a high-ranking person? There is no doubt that in earlier times jade axes were valuables, appreciated for their constituent material. But with the inception of metallurgy the material itself – first copper, then bronze, and later iron – came to be used in a number of ways, some of them highly productive, and so took on a more economically significant role. Quite soon we see that the material in question had become a commodity, valued for itself and for the uses to which it could be put, rather than for the actual form it had taken in the specific artifact in question. So it is that we find ingot bars in the late bronze age Mediterranean, and ingot torques in the Central European bronze age, both forms indicating that the metal was valued now as a raw material and was no longer exchanged primarily in the shape of valuable objects reflecting and conferring prestige. By this stage we are talking of a commercial trade, sustained by well-organized production in mines; the process of commoditization is complete.

One aspect to consider here is the manner in which such wealth can be further accumulated. Are ten items ten times as valuable as one item, and one hundred of them ten times more valuable than ten? This rather obvious point does seem significant – the extent to which fungibles are additive in value. It has been usefully discussed by Kopytoff in Chapter 2; this additive quality is one of the attributes that distinguish commodities from "singular" things. In our first case, that of the egalitarian society, we can readily conceive that a person will gain in prestige by giving or by owning a very special axe. The language of prestige could be devalued slightly rather than enhanced, however, if he were to receive or to own ten identical axes. In the acquisitive society of the modern world, this restriction would seem not to hold: wealth here is cumulative, and goods are valued for their exchange potential as well as for their cumulative effects on prestige through display (see Douglas 1967, 126).

What I am grasping at here, of course, is the special factor that distinguishes the role of value and commodity in the simple and undifferentiated societies discussed earlier from their operation in the more complex, ranked ones. For as we saw in the Varna case, such social questions sometimes take precedence over technological ones, even when technological advance is the subject of consideration.

In some cases we seem to see two stages to the process. In the first, which we have looked at in the three cases discussed, high prestige is immediately reflected and perhaps constituted in the ownership of high prime value objects, in their display, and in their consumption.

The second phase, which is seen in the later bronze age of Europe, is accompanied by the production of useful objects in much greater quantities, sometimes with the richer, "primitive" valuables going out of use, or at least declining in significance. In this phase, rich burials may be less common than in the preceding one, and often quantities of mass-produced goods are now seen. The relative lack of exceptionally conspicuous prestige objects (except in a few favorable cases) can give the impression that society is now the poorer, or less prominently hierarchical in structure. But such inferences may be misleading. In the later British bronze age, for instance, there are other indicators of a highly organized, hierarchical society, including the emergence of hill forts, and of extensive territorial boundary systems that are generally interpreted as reflecting more emphasis upon the ownership and control of land. Rathje (1975, 415) has rightly pointed out that mass production does not mean impoverishment. Certainly Henry Ford accumulated more wealth than did competitors who manufactured more prestigious vehicles.

One may suggest that by the later bronze age, commodities were very freely exchanged across the countryside, with less prominent divisions separating the spheres of exchange. Such a situation implies a measure of specialist production, and perhaps the existence of well-defined units of exchange. Such units are generally seen represented by specific objects (such as currency bars in the later British iron age), which can therefore be termed money. As noted earlier, this would to some extent be true both for the aftermath of the early bronze age in northwest Europe and for the later bronze age Aegean.

It is interesting to note here the relationship among three important variables: a developing system of production and exchange; the circulation of goods of prime value (especially in the early stages); and the emergence of prominent social ranking.

The obvious inference is that the three can most readily develop together through a kind of multiplier effect, where each mutually enhances the others. The key in each case may lie in a measure of technical advance, large enough to maintain the novelty and attractiveness of new products. It is the absence of suitable products for this developing process that may explain why fully complex societies did not develop so markedly in some areas of the world (for instance, the Pacific) as in others. From this perspective there had to be a fairly rare commodity, accessible to the society in question but not too readily so, that could serve as a material of prime value. Ideally it should be a commodity whose nature admitted of gradual technological change, so that one year's manufacturing techniques did not provide quite so useful or high-grade a commodity as the following year's. Such a view would, of course, hold for many of the complex societies of the Old World, where developing technology, especially metal technology, had a major role to play. It might serve to explain why the processes of change in other areas rarely led to such sustained growth; the Hopewell complex in North America would be a case in point.

In expressing the beneficial role of a potential for technological growth, and in excluding thereby some areas of the world from such potential, one is not developing a determinist, nor even a strictly functionalist, argument. For the possibility of developing new commodities, within the framework of intensification of production, is certainly not a sufficient condition for the processes of change under discussion; and it may well not be a necessary one. Moreover, we have been insisting upon the importance of the concept of prime value for setting the process in motion and for sustaining its impetus. As discussed earlier, the ascription of high prestige or notional intrinsic value to commodities of low use value and sometimes of low labor value is to a large extent arbitrary and certainly nonfunctional. Yet in the societies under discussion, the practice of ascribing prime value seems to lie at the root of further growth in the economy.

Notes

I should like to acknowledge the useful comments made on the first draft of this paper by Arjun Appadurai and Robert C. Hunt, as well as by other members of the symposium.

1. In "exchange value," for instance, value is a descriptive term, specifying what has been observed to happen in certain exchange transactions. I would argue that the distinction between emic and etic, although useful in some ways, should not be allowed to dominate research. I am in broad agreement with Binford's view, which boils down to an assertion that what counts is what happens rather than what people think about what happens. Yet clearly the latter does and did influence the former. We use theoretical concepts in many areas of our discipline, and are not debarred from doing so in the field of cognition by any a priori principle. The real danger is, however, of circular reasoning, of the kind so often found to surround the use of such concepts as adaptation and contradiction.

2. The question of whether gravegoods accompanying a deceased person necessarily imply an association while that person was alive has indeed been discussed in recent years. The more interesting issue of the way such an association with special material goods during life may have been indicative of high status has not. If an adequate framework for analysis can be developed (and the contributions in this direction of Winters 1968, S. Shennan 1975, and O'Shea 1978 among others should be noted), then there are good prospects for learning much more of the social behavior of early societies.

3. This is certainly true of the long use of copper in the Aegean late neolithic, when it had a very minimal impact, and of its use, for instance in the Balkans, during the Vinča-Turdas period, when there are not infrequent finds of small objects but no explosive development until much later, during the Vinča-Pločnik phase.

4. The curious gold astragalus of Grave 36, weighing 33 grams, appears to be the heaviest single gold object in the cemetery, although it is only two centimeters long; I predict that metallographic examination will show it

to have been shaped from a nugget by hammering rather than by casting.

5. We must refer also to the marble objects at Varna. They include not only simple bowls (for example in Grave 36), known from other Balkan chalcolithic contexts, but a pointed vessel from Grave 41 that has points of resemblance with a find from the Kephala cemetery in the Cycladic Islands. These vessels have been used by some scholars to reopen the question of possible contacts between the chalcolithic Balkans and the Aegean bronze age. But the chronological question is now largely settled, and the only difficulty seems to be the reported presence of Early Helladic II pottery at the Thessalian site of Pevkakia in association with late neolithic/chalcolithic black-on-red painted ("Galepsos") ware. At Sitagroi such painted pottery was a frequent feature in phase III, and the Pevkakia material is closely similar. It is the status, or rather the stratigraphic context, of the Early Helladic II pottery at Pevkakia that must be questioned.

6. We should, however, note the copper bracelet from Grave 3 of the Varna II necropolis; significantly, this is earlier than the main cemetery, and, also from the Varna II cemetery, the copper needles from Graves 3, 5, 6, 11, 15, 17, 26, and others. In fact, analysis shows that the copper needle has a role comparable to that of the copper shaft-hole axe, as a frequent and useful object. Outside these classes, copper finds of small decorative items are not frequent: there is merely a bracelet and ring from Grave 51, three rings from Grave 60, and no doubt a few other examples from graves still unpublished.

7. Evidently the discussion here would center upon the notion of "utility." It can certainly be argued that the "usefulness" of such prestige objects is to excite admiration, to indicate prestige, and to function as valuables in prestige exchange. Such usefulness, however, would be difficult to measure or otherwise quantify.

8. In the treatment quoted, Marx (1970, 95) does not develop the distinction between labor value and exchange value. Of course the price of gold is determined not simply by "the labor time required for its production" (Marx 1970, 95), but by what people are prepared to pay for it; in favorable circumstances, gold nuggets could be found on the surface of the ground, and the labor value could be negligible. What interests us here is precisely why gold, rather than some other material, should be considered a commodity of especially high value. Marx was not primarily concerned with this point.

9. We should note that most societies operate with such notions. Certainly among the hunter-gatherer societies of Australia and the segmentary communities of New Guinea, axes of stone valued as prestige items were traded over long distances from the quarry itself, a practice that finds clear parallels in the British neolithic (Clark 1965). The exchange of exotic materials in such a way seems a near-universal of human existence (Mauss 1954). A number of writers, including Rappaport (1967, 106) and Wright and Zeder (1977) have suggested that these ceremonial exchanges of

prestigious objects may fulfill a utilitarian, material function. For by keeping alive gift partnerships and long-distance links even in times when little evident purpose is served by the exchange, societies preserve the opportunity to draw upon the obligations of goodwill and reciprocity, in the form of useful goods including foodstuffs, in times of shortage. The notion of this kind of effective time scheduling is an important one, and Woodburn (1982) has shown how the concept of immediate return versus delayed return is important in societies developing some of the facilities and approaches that are used also in farming societies. Prestige goods of high prime value become a kind of banking mechanism against food shortage, although it should be noted that in normal times ordinary foodstuffs are often considered unsuitable as an object of exchange against primitive valuables, which move in a different sphere of conveyance.

References

Adams, R. M. 1974. Anthropological perspectives on ancient trade. *Current Anthropology* 15, 239-58.

Binford, L. R. 1969. Comment. *Current Anthropology* 10, 162-3.

Braithwaite, M. 1984. Ritual and prestige in the prehistory of Wessex c. 2200-1400 B.C. In D. Miller and C. Tilly, eds., *Ideology, Power, and Prehistory*, 93-110. Cambridge: Cambridge University Press.

Childe, V. G. 1944. Archaeological ages as technological stages: Huxley Memorial Lecture 1944. *Journal of the Royal Anthropological Institute* 7, 7-24.

Clark, J. G. D. 1965. Traffic in stone axe and adze blades. *Economic History Review* 18, 1-28.

Dalton, G. 1977. Aboriginal economies in stateless societies. In T. K. Earle and J. E. Ericson, eds., *Exchange Systems in Prehistory*, 191-192. New York: Academic Press.

Douglas, M. 1967. Primitive rationing. In R. Firth, ed., *Themes in Economic Anthropology*, 119-47. London: Tavistock.

Frankenstein, S., and Rowlands, M. J. 1978. The internal structure and regional context of early iron age society in south-western Germany. *Bulletin of the Institute of Archaeology* 15, 73-112.

Gamble, C. 1981. Social control and the economy. In A. Sheridan and G. Bailey, eds., *Economic Archaeology* (B.A.R. International Series 96), 215-30. Oxford: British Archaeological Reports.

Gilman, A. 1976. The development of social stratification in bronze age Europe. *Current Anthropology* 22, 1-8.

Hägerstrand, T. 1967. *Innovation Diffusion as a Spatial Process*. Chicago: University of Chicago Press.

Halstead, P. 1981. From determinism to uncertainty: Social storage and the rise of the Minoan palaces. In A. Sheridan and G. Bailey, eds., *Economic Anthropology* (B.A.R. International Series 96), 187-214. Oxford: British Archaeological Reports.

Halstead, P., and J. O'Shea. 1982. A friend in need is a friend indeed: social storage and the origins of social ranking. In C. Renfrew and S. Shennan, ed., *Ranking, Resource and Exchange*, 92-9. Cambridge: Cambridge University Press.

Harris, M. 1968. *The Rise of Anthropological Theory*. London: Routledge.

Hodder, I. 1982a. Theoretical archaeology: A reactionary view. In I. Hodder, ed., *Symbolic and Structural Archaeology*, 1-15. Cambridge: Cambridge University Press.
1982b. *The Present Past*. London: Batsford.

Ivanov, I. S. 1975. Raskopki na Varnenskija eneoliten nekropol prez 1972 g., *Izvestija na Narodnija Muzeji Varna* (Bulletin du Musée National de Varna) 11, 1-16.
1978. *Sukrovishtata na Varnenskiya Chalkoliten Nekropol* (Treasures of the Varna chalcolithic necropolis). Sofia: "September." (Text in Bulgarian with translation into Russian, English, and German).
1982. The Varna chalcolithic necropolis. In *The First Civilization in Europe and the Oldest Gold in the World – Varna, Bulgaria*, 21-121 (exhibition catalog, Isetan Museum of Art, Tokyo). Tokyo: Nippon Television Network Cultural Society.

Marx, K. 1970. *Capital*, vol. I. London: Lawrence and Wishart (first German edition 1867).

Mauss, M. 1954. *The Gift*. London: Cohen and West.

O'Shea, J. 1981. Coping with scarcity: Exchange and social storage. In A. Sheridan and G. Bailey, eds., *Economic Archaeology*, 167-186 (B.A.R. International Series 96). Oxford: British Archaeological Reports.

Polanyi, K. 1957. The economy as instituted process. In K. Polanyi, A. M. Arensberg, and H. W. Pearson, eds., *Trade and Market in the Early Empires*, 243-69. New York: Free Press.

Rappaport, R. 1967. *Pigs for the Ancestors*. New Haven, Conn.: Yale University Press.

Rathje, W. L. 1975. The last tango in Mayapan: A tentative trajectory of production-distribution systems. In J. A. Sabloff and C. C. Lamberg-Karlovsky, eds., *Ancient Civilization and Trade*, 409-48. Albuquerque: University of New Mexico Press,

Renfrew, C. 1972. *The Emergence of Civilisation: The Cyclades and the Aegean in the Third Millennium B. C.* London: Methuen.
1975. Trade as action at a distance. In J. A. Sabloff and C. C. Lamberg-Karlovsky, eds., *Ancient Civilization and Trade*, 3-60. Albuquerque: University of New Mexico Press,
1978a. Varna and the social context of early metallurgy. *Antiquity* 52, 199-203.
1978b. The anatomy of innovation. In D. Green, C. Haselgrove, and M. Spriggs, eds., *Social Organisation and Settlement*, 89-117. Oxford: British Archaeological Reports.

Sahlins, M. 1972. *Stone Age Economics*. Chicago: Aldine.

Service, E. R. 1962. *Primitive Social Organization*. New York: Random House.

Shennan, S. E. 1975. The social organisation at Branc. *Antiquity* 49, 279-88.

Shennan, S. J. 1982. Ideology, change, and the European early bronze age. In I. Hodder, ed., *Symbolic and Structural Archaeology*, 155-61. Cambridge: Cambridge University Press.

Sherratt, A. 1976. Resources, technology and trade in early European metallurgy. In G. Sieveking, I. H. Longworth, and K. E. Wilson, eds., *Problems in Economic and Social Archaeology*, 557-82. London: Duckworth.
1981. Plough and pastoralism: Aspects of the secondary products revolution. In I. Hodder, G. Isaac, and N. Hammond eds., *Pattern of the past: Studies in honour of David Clarke*, 261-305. Cambridge: Cambridge University Press.

Thorpe, N., and C. Richards. 1982. The decline of ritual authority and the introduction of beakers into Britain. Paper read at the fourth meeting of the Theoretical Archaeology Group, Durham (England), Dec. 1982.

Veblen, T. 1899. *The Theory of the Leisure Class*. New York: Macmillan.

Wertime, T. 1964. Man's first encounters with metallurgy. *Science* 146, 1257.

Winters, H. D. 1968. Value systems and trade cycles of the Late Archaic in the Midwest. In L. R. and S. R. Binford, eds., *New Perspectives in Archaeology*, 175-222. Chicago: Aldine.

Woodburn, J. 1982. Egalitarian societies. *Man* 17, 431-51.

Wright, H., and M. Zeder. 1977. The simulation of a linear exchange system under equilibrium conditions. In T. K. Earle and J. E. Ericson, eds., *Exchange Systems in Prehistory*, 233-54. New York: Academic Press.

CHAPTER 6

Sacred commodities: the circulation of medieval relics

PATRICK GEARY

An examination of sacred relics as commodities in the Middle Ages may seem to be pushing the definition of commodities as "goods destined for circulation and exchange" to an extreme. Could one reasonably describe a human body or portions thereof as *destined* for circulation? Can we really compare the production and circulation of saints' remains to that of gold in prehistoric Europe, cloth in pre-Revolutionary France, or qat in northeastern Africa? The differences are of course great. Nevertheless, although relics were almost universally understood to be important sources of personal supernatural power and formed the primary focus of religious devotion throughout Europe from the eighth through the twelfth centuries, they were bought and sold, stolen or divided, much as any other commodity was. As a result the world of relics may prove an ideal if somewhat unusual microcosm in which to examine the creation, evaluation, and circulation of commodities in traditional Europe. Like slaves, relics belong to that category, unusual in Western society, of objects that are both persons and things (Kopytoff, Chapter 2). Reflecting on the production, exchange, sale, and even theft of sacred relics enables one better to understand the cultural parameters of commodity flow in medieval civilization.

"Medieval civilization" is an extremely imprecise designation, obscuring rather than defining a wide variety of distinct cultural and social traditions that appeared across Europe over a period of a thousand years. The specific period I shall discuss embraces the Carolingian and post-Carolingian eras, roughly 750–1150, and the region will be generally the Latin West, with an emphasis on those areas that had formed part of the Carolingian Empire.

The analysis of relics as commodities requires the investigation of two complexes of cultural activity. First, we must examine how commodities in general were produced and circulated within this society, and in particular the relative significance and values assigned to various modes of transfer: sale, exchange, gift, and theft. Second, we

169

must consider how relics fit within this transactional culture; that is, we must understand the cultural context within which they moved.

Commodities in medieval society

A century ago medievalists looked upon the emerging society of feudal Europe as one based on a "natural economy," in which barter and payments in kind were the normal means of exchange. According to this view, Western Europe gradually began to develop a money economy only with the growth of towns, increasing long-distance communication, and the development of first Italian and later northern European trade, phenomena that were largely credited to the Crusades, which began in 1095. This view of medieval commerce owed more to the ideologies of nineteenth-century colonialism than to the evidence of medieval economy and trade in the West, and by the end of the last century economic historians were emphasizing the very real evidence that pointed to the important roles of money, coinage, and commerce in the eighth through eleventh centuries.

At no time in the Middle Ages was the European economy strictly speaking a "natural economy," in which barter and self-sufficiency characterized the production, exchange, and consumption of commodities. Nor was it a "peasant economy" in the classical sense of the term. Peasants presumably use not capital but cash; profit and the accumulation of captial on an ever-increasing scale are not supposed to be a part of peasant strategies. In the West, even by the ninth century this image can be applied only with some difficulty. For over thirty years, scholars have been investigating the role of great monastic estates in the complex economy of Carolingian Europe. Most recently, J.-P. Devroey has examined the complex network by which food surpluses (principally grain and wine) from these estates were circulated in a flourishing local and regional trade (Devroey 1984). Although Devroey does not directly address the question of how much of this distribution was effected by barter as opposed to sale, the sources he examines clearly indicate the importance of both regional and international markets (Devroey 1984:581–4).

Nor did the transformation of the Carolingian Empire in the tenth century result in the creation or return of a "classic" peasant economy. One example of the complexity of medieval peasant society has been presented by Paul Bonnassie from Catalonia, a region particularly rich in documentation on peasant families (Bonnassie 1967). He describes the family of one Llorenç (died before 987) and his sons and grandsons. Llorenç was quite well off: he owned several houses, a free holding, livestock, military equipment, and a reserve of grain and wine produced from his fields. Bonnassie describes him as typical of a peasant élite that was "enterprising, free, and capable of self-defense when necessary" (Bonnassie 1967:104). Within 25 years, the more enterprising of Llorenç's sons, Vivas, entered into 45 land transactions, up to six a year. Land was no sooner bought than it was resold. Other types of property, too, were constantly sold: crops, horses, mules, armor. Vivas and his descendants improved their position in society considerably by the first half of the eleventh century. Their world included a fairly lively market and abundant specie as means of payment. These peasants were clearly moving up socially and economically, and they were using commodities produced from their increasingly specialized agricultural operations as the capital base of their move. Bonnassie considers this family "neither very typical nor very exceptional," and attributes its rise to the breakdown, already in the tenth century, of early medieval social relations, which he characterizes as "on the whole kindly, relatively undifferentiated as to status, still patriarchal in type." (Bonnassie (1967:116). To be sure, Barcelona is a unique place, but then so is every location. The forces at work in this region, which also appear in France and Germany in the twelfth century, may differ not so much in their nature as in their frequency, and these Catalan peasants may differ from those elsewhere in their success in achieving their goals more than in the goals themselves.

The evidence of peasant involvement in markets and what might anachronistically be described as capitalist strategies seems to be paralleled by the evidence of long-distance commerce. Not only do mentions of cash sums to be imposed as fines or forfeits abound in charters and laws, but archeologists discovered coin hoards spread across Europe that contain monies minted at places thousands of kilometers distant. Moreover, isolated but tantalizing references to merchants, to trading expeditions, to "eunuch factories," and the like seemed to suggest that even during the darkest of the dark ages, commerce continued to play an important role, at both the local level and the international level. A generation of historians began to revise the image of the commercial world of the early Middle Ages and to present a picture of a rudimentary but nonetheless important commercial structure tying together the lands between the Mediterranean and the North Sea that differed from later medieval trade more in organization than in volume or nature (Pirenne 1937; Dopsch 1930; Latouche 1956).

Yet even in the midst of this enthusiasm for commercial history,

England's leading medieval numismatist, Philip Grierson, sounded an important warning in a paper entitled "Commerce in the Dark Ages: A Critique of the Evidence" (1959). Grierson argued that the view of a largely monetized commercial economy was incorrect, and that it had resulted from the failure to distinguish between three sorts of evidence: evidence of persons making their living by commerce; evidence of the sale of specialized or surplus goods directly by producer to consumer; and evidence of the distribution of luxury goods and money by unspecified means (Grierson:124). Too often, he warned, historians suppose that the existence of trade means the existence of traders, whereas most buying and selling of agricultural products seems to have taken place without middlemen. Likewise, historians tend to suppose that luxury goods were normally distributed by commerce, and that specie was primarily a tool of commerce and its discovery *prima facie* evidence of commercial exchange. Grierson suggests, by contrast, that trade is by no means the only or even the usual means by which commodities change hands. Much of the exchange network connecting the monasteries of the ninth century probably operated by barter rather than sale (a view with which Devroey would no doubt agree). The Catalan example of Llorenç, Grierson probably would argue, might represent the future, but it would remain a marked exception in Western Europe well into the twelfth century. In the early Middle Ages, Grierson argued, gift and theft were more important than trade in distributing commodities. Under gifts, he included all transfers that take place with the consent of the donor not for material and tangible profit but for social prestige. Under theft he included "all unilateral transfers of property which take place involuntarily," including simple larceny but, more important, plundering in warfare (Grierson 1959:131). Of course, he pointed out, payments and exchanges such as ransoms and compensations might fall between the two.

Grierson strongly suggested, and Georges Duby later affirmed (Duby 1974:48–72), that gift-giving and theft were probably the most important means of property transfers among the elite. Plunder, extortions from neighboring peoples or kingdoms, and ransoms demanded for the return of enemies taken in war formed the major means by which both luxury goods and money circulated in the medieval world. Certainly the circulation of gold seems less connected with commerce than with the payment of tribute, and gold acquired through such payments was often put into circulation again through the conquest of one's neighbors.

Property exchanged through mutual consent was often less the material of trade than of gift and countergift (Mauss 1967). Ritual exchanges of goods and services formed the normal means of distributing wealth acquired either through plunder or from agriculture. The dynamics of gift-giving were quite different from those of commerce, even though both involved exchanges of material goods. The goal of gift-giving was not the acquisition of commodities but the establishment of bonds between giver and receiver, bonds that had to be reaffirmed at some point by a countergift. As Grierson (1959:137) puts it, "The 'profit' consists in placing other people morally in one's debt."

Not only were theft and gift more basic forms of property circulation than trade in the early Middle Ages, but they enjoyed higher prestige. Between equals or near-equals, cordial relationships were created and affirmed by the exchange of gifts. Between individuals or groups of differing status, the disparity of the exchanges both articulated and defined the direction and degree of subordination. Similarly, hostile relationships were characterized by violent seizures of property or persons under the control of an enemy. In both situations, the relationship of relative honor and status was at stake, and the property that changed hands functioned symbolically to affirm or deny that relationship. Commerce suggests neutrality, a relationship that, though not unknown, was the weakest of the three alternatives; between the status of *amicus* (friend) and that of *inimicus* (literally nonfriend, enemy), there was little middle ground. A stranger, someone not tied to the local community by a bond both formed and manifested in gift exchange, was dangerous and suspect. And conversely, he was himself in danger, since unless he could form such a bond with one of the powerful figures in the community, there was no one to guarantee his safety. From this perspective, it is little wonder that purchase was suspect: If one's goal was the realization of a profit, then such a transaction, if carried on with one's friends, was base, and if with one's enemies, cowardly. Only in the late twelfth century did the cultural perceptions of Europeans change sufficiently to allow for the possibility of a just price and the morality of mercantile activity (Baldwin 1959; Little 1978).

However, even while acknowledging the validity of this image of exchange in medieval society in general, the exceptions must also be considered. Although early medieval Europe was a traditional society, it was by no means either simple or homogeneous. Goods exchanged may have served to create bonds between giver and recipient, but they were also desired for themselves. They could be and at times were converted into cash or even capital, so that both a system of objectified, alienable commodity exchanges and a system of subjective, inalienable gift exchanges coexisted. Rather than positing a developmental model of transition from a gift-based economy to a commodity-based economy, one should examine the specific social and political circumstances that might favor circulation of goods by the one or the other means.

This general examination of the nature of early medieval commerce is necessary to an understanding of the specific structure within which one finds the production, sale, exchange, gift, and theft of sacred relics. The circulation of high-prestige articles in general, of which relics were but one sort (others were luxury imported cloth and illuminated manuscripts), did not occur primarily within a commercial structure. Moreover, even when a purchase lay at the heart of such exchanges, contemporaries were likely to look askance at such transactions or to understand them within the context of one or another of the two more significant forms of circulation of goods, theft and gift. Nevertheless, such purchases did take place, and at times a real production and marketing system did exist for the creation and distribution of prestigious commodities.

The social construction of relics' value

Relics of saints, whether particles of clothing or objects associated with them during their lives, particles of dust or vials of oil collected at the site of their tombs, or actual portions of their bodies, had no obvious value apart from a very specific set of shared beliefs. Such relics were of no practical use. Once removed from their elaborate reliquaries or containers, they were not even decorative. The most eagerly sought after relics of the medieval period – bodies or portions of bodies – were superficially similar to thousands of other corpses and skeletons universally available. Not only were they omnipresent and without intrinsic economic value, they were normally undesirable: an ordinary body was a source of contamination, and opening graves or handling remains of the dead was considered abhorrent. This was true even though the cult of the saints and the Christian belief in the resurrection of the dead had, by the eighth century, altered in some essentials the strict taboo of Roman society, which considered the dead a source of pollution and forbade burial within the confines of the city. Nor had the late medieval preoccupation with death and decay yet produced the image of the macabre that, in the fifteenth century, would permeate artistic and literary reflections on death. Nevertheless, remains of the ordinary dead were normally disposed of quickly and definitively through burial (Ariès 1981:110–39).

The value attached to the special corpses that would be venerated as relics required the communal acceptance of three interrelated beliefs: first, that an individual had been, during his life and more important after his death, a special friend of God, that is, a saint; second, that the remains of such a saint were to be prized and treated in a special way; and third, and for our purposes most important, that the particular corpse or portion thereof was indeed the remains of that particular saint.

The first aspect, that is, the belief that an individual enjoyed special favor with God, was based on a received tradition of Christian veneration that originated in the Judaic cult of martyrs in the Maccabean period (Rothkrug, in press). In Christian antiquity martyrs, through their passion and death, were seen to have a special relationship with Christ, and the celebration of their *memoria* came to involve not simply a remembrance of the dead, but the petitioning of these special dead to continue to intercede before God for their friends in this world.

With the toleration and support of Christianity in the Roman Empire that began in the early fourth century, the production of martyrs ended; henceforth, with rare exceptions, only opponents of Christianity died for their faith. Almost all the holy men of the following centuries were those who lived heroic lives as friends of God rather than those who died heroic deaths. These confessors became the objects of the devotions previously reserved for martyrs, and both during their lives and after their deaths Christians came to them for assistance of all sorts: cures, protection from oppression, help in finding lost objects, assistance in settling disputes, and the like. In return for this assistance, the faithful offered them veneration in the form of pilgrimages, vigils, prayers, and offerings – either symbolic (candles or votive offerings of wax or wood, for example) or material (property or money).

The determination of just who these friends of God were remained well into the twelfth century a largely spontaneous and pragmatic evaluation, based upon the efficacy of the individual holy man's miracles and the strength of his cult. Although it was the responsibility of local bishops and increasingly, from the twelfth century on, of the Pope to recognize the feast of an individual holy man and include it among the official feasts of the Church, the role of the ecclesiastical official was that of recognizing an already established cult, not of creating it. If a dead person worked miracles that attracted an enthusiastic following, then that person was a saint whether or not he had received formal recognition. Conversely, without a cult, without a following, an individual, regardless of the holiness of his or her life, would not be considered one of those special companions of God through whom he chose to act in the world.

In the West, the preferred medium through which God used his saints to act was their bodies. Their corpses were seen as the *pignora*, literally, the security deposits left by the saints upon their deaths as guarantees of their continuing interest in the earthly community. At the end of the world, the saint's body would rise and be glorified; in the meantime, the saint continued to live in and to work through it. This of course was the learned theory of educated churchmen. The perception of the operation of relics on the part of most people, lay and clerical, seems to have been much more immediate: relics *were* the saints, continuing to live among men. They were immediate sources of supernatural power for good or for ill, and close contact with them or possession of them was a means of participating in that power. To the communities fortunate enough to have a saint's remains in its church, the benefits in terms of revenue and status were enormous, and competition to acquire relics and to promote the local saint's virtues over those of neighboring communities was keen.

Relics, then, were highly desirable, even essential, since every church altar was supposed to contain the remains of a saint. Although the demand of relics cannot be quantified, one can in general identify two particularly critical periods of demand: the first was roughly from 750 to 850; it resulted both from an aggressive Carolingian expansion in northern and eastern Europe – an expansion in which conversion to Romano-Frankish Christianity and specifically the cult of Roman saints was an essential feature – and from the development of rural parishes with their churches throughout the Empire. The second period of high demand occurred in the eleventh century; it resulted in part from the growth of population across Western Europe with its concomitant need for new churches, and in part from the competition between cult centers for the enormously increasing pilgrimage traffic.

In general, the cultural assumptions about relics, about their value and utility, were broadly shared. The few dissenters, such as Claudius of Turin in the ninth century and Guilbert of Nogent in the twelfth, were the rare exceptions. From the twelfth century on, some heterodox groups denied the efficacy of relics, but often even these groups had their own versions of saints and even of relics. What was frequently at issue, however, was the specific identity of a corpse or grave with a saint: How could one be certain that a bone was not simply that of an ordinary sinner? Even for one who had no doubts about the efficacy and value of relics in general, great doubt could be entertained concerning the identity of any particular bones with those of a particular saint.

For remains to be valuable, they had to undergo a social and cultural transition from being perceived as ordinary human remains to being venerated as the remains of a saint. Thus one can well apply Kopytoff's suggestion that one examine the career or biography of objects as they pass from ordinary remains to treasured relics, and then perhaps back again (Kopytoff, Chapter 2; 1982).

With few exceptions, the career of relics was seldom one of unbroken veneration from the time of the saint's death through the Middle Ages. Some recently dead saints achieved such status. Indeed, the remains of Simeon Stylites and Francis of Assissi, for example, were eagerly sought after even before they were dead – the danger of someone murdering an aging holy man in order to acquire his relics, or at least stealing his remains as soon as he was dead was ever present. Much more common, whether for saints long dead (if indeed they had ever lived), or for more recently living persons, was the necessity of identifying a particular set of remains with a particular saint. This could be done through an examination of either extrinsic or intrinsic criteria. To the former category belong such formal processes as the examination of the tomb or reliquary and an examination of documents called *authenticae* found either in the tomb or reliquary itself, or in the descriptions of the burial of saints in hagiographical texts. These processes were usually carried out by the local bishop in public, solemn sessions attended by lay and clerical magnates. Following the positive recognition of the relics' authenticity was a public ritual known as the "elevation," in which the relics were formally offered to the public for veneration.

These external examinations, although quite common, did not constitute the only, or indeed the most important, aspect of the recognition of relics in any cases. The most telling evidence usually came from the supernatural intervention of the saint himself, who indicated where his remains were to be found. Then, during the process of determining the relics' authenticity, the saint often showed by miraculous intervention that they were indeed genuine. Thus the initial impetus for the consideration of a possible relic often came in the form of a vision in which the saint appeared to a holy person and revealed where his remains were to be found. Often this person was a revered member of the local religious community, a person who commanded respect and authority, by virtue of his office or of his own saintliness. When the vision came to a person of more humble status, its interpretation was often the responsibility of someone of superior status (Schreiner 1966).

The vision led to a search by the community at large, often an entire monastery or village, for the relics. When found, they exhibited their authenticity by working wonders. This need for relics to prove themselves efficacious was reinforced by the custom, in existence by the ninth century, of submitting relics to an ordeal by fire to determine if they were genuine.

These processes were essential in the creation of relics' value. The public, ritual discovery or invention (*inventio*) and examination of the relics publicized their existence and created or strengthened their cult. So important were these ceremonies that relics long recognized and venerated were periodically "lost" and "rediscovered." An excellent example is that of the remains of St. Mark, who had been a major patron of Venice since the ninth century. His remains were rediscovered in the eleventh century in the course of restoration of the Basilica of St. Mark – an orchestrated revitalization ritual that enhanced the value and importance of the saint in the community.

Thus corpses passed from the status of mere human remains to that of sacred relics through a public ritual emphasizing both the identity of the remains with those of a saint and the actual miraculous power exercised by that saint through those particular remains. This latter aspect was most important because different communities often disagreed, even violently, over which one possessed the genuine relics of a particular saint. The identification of false relics and the determination of genuine claims ultimately rested on very pragmatic, functional evidence: if the relics worked – that is, if they were channels for supernatural intervention – then they were genuine. If they did not, they were not authentic, regardless of the strength of external evidence. Once relics had achieved recognition – had come to be perceived as genuine and efficacious – their continuing significance and value depended on their continued performance of miracles and on their relative value compared with other relics and other sources of power. Studies of relics' value indicate considerable fluctuations in both the short and the long term.

The long-term, European-wide fluctuation is most obvious and easily documented. We have already seen that in antiquity, martyrs' remains were those most eagerly sought after. In time, the remains of hermits and bishops came to offer these earlier saints considerable competition. In the eighth and ninth centuries Roman saints were the most eagerly sought after, to the relative detriment of local saints

(Geary 1979). In the eleventh century, apostolic saints such as James, Mary Magdalene, Dionysius, Lazarus, and Marcial, who were reputed to have had direct connection with the West during their lifetimes, became more popular, eclipsing Roman saints who had lived and died in Italy. During the Crusades, biblical and Eastern relics became much sought after as booty carried back from Palestine and Constantinople.

Not only did the taste in specific relics change appreciably over the centuries, but relics' relative importance measured against that of other sorts of human and supernatural powers likewise changed. During periods of relatively weak central government, for example, in the later sixth and again in the eleventh century, relics were prized not simply for their thaumaturgic power, but also for their ability to substitute for public authority, protect and secure the community, determine the relative status of individuals and churches, and provide for the community's economic prosperity. When new political, social, religious, and economic systems began to develop in the twelfth century, the relative significance of relics in providing these services was weakened: churches attacked by local laymen could appeal to the king rather than to their saint for protection; a monastery able to rationalize its budget and exploit its agricultural holdings was less dependent on the income brought in by pilgrims (Geary 1978). Thus, although saints's relics continued to be valued as sources of supernatural power, particularly by pilgrims seeking miraculous cures, in other areas of life they were effectively supplanted by new and more effective forms of power and authority.

Even at the local, individual level, the saints' relative value underwent considerable change. The fluctuation seems directly related first to the impetus of the clerics responsible for promoting the cult – their efforts at elevations or translations (formal, liturgical processions in which remains of saints were officially recognized and transported from one place to another), the erection of new shrines, the celebration of feasts, and the like – and second to a rhythm of popular enthusiasm in which miracles seem to have led to more miracles, only to die out again in the course of the year. New efforts on the part of the clergy, or the celebration of the next feast, could begin them anew.

One of the most telling and detailed accounts of this process is the study by P. A. Sigal (1969) of the cult of St. Gibrian at Reims in the twelfth century. Gibrian was an obscure Irish hermit, long recognized but hardly venerated at Reims, until Abbot Odo of St. Remi in Reims decided to develop the cult, to the profit of the newly established monastery of Chartreux in Champagne. In 1145 the abbot commissioned a new reliquary shrine for the saint, and on April 16 the saint was solemnly translated into the new shrine in the presence of the Archbishop of Reims. A careful record of miracles was kept between that date and August 24 of the same year. Of a total of 102 miracles, only 20 occurred in isolation. Generally they occurred in groups of at least four on the same day; 39 took place on Sundays and feast days, for example, 24 on Monday, but only one on Tuesday. Moreover, the miracles, which began with one on April 6, gradually increased in frequency as the renown of the saint spread, until they reached a peak of ten on May 13, and thereafter gradually receded across the months of June, July, and August. Unfortunately the record breaks off in August, possibly because the miracles had by then become so infrequent. One hears little of Gibrian for almost two centuries, until 1325, when again his relics were placed in a more worthy and impressive reliquary, and once more his cult began to attract pilgrims (AAS Maii, VII, 651).

The career of Gibrian's relics is similar to that of many more famous saints' relics. Thomas Becket, for example, began to attract miracles at the time of his martyrdom, but these soon fell off; they started up again years later, after the erection of a new and impressive shrine (Ward, 1982; he does not note the pattern). In general, the career of a relic seems to begin with its elevation and continue with its exposure in a worthy and impressive shrine and with encouragement of the laity by the responsible clerics to make pilgrimages and seek cures (Geary 1977). When cures ensue, they develop their own momentum, only to gradually die out until the cult receives another impetus.

These fluctuations were also influenced by competition between cult centers for the devotion of the faithful. It was not sufficient that a relic be seen as efficacious – it had to be more attractive than that of other shrines to which someone might go for assistance. A graphic example of the dilemma posed by competing shrines was occasioned by pilgrimages to the body of St. Sebastian, brought from Rome to Soissons in the ninth century. Bishop Ostroldus of Laon, distressed at the loss of pilgrims to his church, is said to have exhorted his congregation with the words: "You have here the church of the venerable Mother of God; frequent it, in it swear your vows and make your contributions. You should not wander to other places to seek external help. All that you ask faithfully through her will be given by the Lord" (Geary 1979, 79). Competition between saints is seen most clearly in the devotional and propaganda literature that was produced at various shrines, in particular the books of miracles such as that of St. Gibrian, in many of which one reads that a cure took place only after the petitioner had tried and failed to find help from a long list of other saints. Sometimes these ineffectual saints themselves instructed the pilgrim to go to the saint who finally effected the cure.

This description of the process by which relics' values were constructed may seem to imply a certain cynicism on the part of the clerics responsible. Such was hardly the case. Clerics were among the most fervent pilgrims and often the recipients of miracles themselves; their desire to promote their cult over that of competing neighboring shrines in no way indicates cynicism toward the cult of saints in general. Categories such as "popular" and "elite" have little meaning in terms of relic cults. Moreover, the existence of purely popular cults, such as the cult of the dog venerated in southeastern France from the twelfth through the nineteenth century as St. Guinefort in the face of clerical and official condemnation, indicate the value attached by the laity to saints (Schmitt 1979). The clergy, in promoting particular saints, were simply attempting to win for their own patron a significant market share.

Circulation mechanisms

We have seen the social and cultural structures within which some privileged remains of the dead acquired value. Given this value and the need to have such objects in every church across Europe, some sort of ciruclation mechanism was necessary to provide churches far from the "production centers" (Rome, the Near East, the areas of Gaul and Spain that had formed part of the Roman Empire in late antiquity) to more recently converted areas of Christendom.

The circulation of relics, as we shall see, shared characteristics of the circulation of other valued commodities in the Latin West. Thus we shall begin by examining these mechanisms. However, the transfer of relics necessarily breached the cultural context that gave the relic its value. When a relic moved from one community to another, whether by gift, purchase, or theft, it was impossible to transfer simultaneously or reliably the function or meaning it had enjoyed in its old location. It had to undergo some sort of cultural transformation so that it could acquire status and meaning within its new context. The mere circulation of a relic was not enough – a newly acquired relic had to prove itself. Its authenticity, which the very fact that it had been transferred cast in doubt, had to be demonstrated. As we have seen, however, "authenticity" meant less identity with a particular saint's body than efficacy in terms of communal needs. Thus we must also consider the means by which the transferred relic acquired value within its new context.

Gift

Relics circulated as other valuble objects did – that is to say, by gift, by theft, and by sale. The normal means of acquiring relics was to receive them as gifts (Michalowski 1981:399–416). As Grierson pointed out, this is exactly how members of the elite went about acquiring other valuable objects in the early Middle Ages. He mentions, among others, the example of Servatus Lupus, who wrote to King Ethelulf of Wessex and to his agent to ask for lead for the roof of his church, promising prayers in return. The transaction would be accomplished entirely without recourse to merchants, since the lead would be collected at the mouth of the Canche by serfs of Servatus Lupus (Grierson 1959:129).

Exactly the same sort of request lay behind the acquisition of many relics. Alcuin of York (ca. 730–804), the head of Charlemagne's palace school and abbot of several important monasteries, was particularly eager to obtain relics, as his correspondence indicates. He requested gifts of relics from such persons as Paulinus, the Patriarch of Aquileia; Angilbertus, chancellor of King Pepin of Italy; Bishop Agino of Konstanz; and Abbot Angilbertus of Centula (*MGH Ep.* IV, to Angilbertus, no. 11, p. 37; to Paulinus, no. 28, p. 70; to Agino, no. 75, pp. 117–18; to Abbot Angilbertus, no. 97, pp. 141–2; to Volucrus and Vera, nobles of Aquileia, no. 146, pp. 235–6). Such requests differ not at all from requests for other precious objects, and occur in the same breath as a request for gifts of other "objects of ecclesiastical beauty" (no. 97). As in the case of Lupus, such transactions would normally take place without the assistance of merchants. The journey of Alcuin's messenger Angilbertus was the occasion for a request that Bishop Agino send Alcuin relics (no. 75). The trip of Angilbertus to Rome gave Alcuin the opportunity to ask him to acquire saintly relics there (no. 97). Again in the case of Lupus's request for roofing lead, the promised countergift was the daily prayers to be offered for the donor (no. 75).

The most important donor of relics was, of course, the Pope, who had at his disposal the vast treasury of the Roman catacombs, containing the remains of the early Roman martyrs. Prior to the mid-eighth century popes steadfastly refused to distribute these relics, preferring rather to distribute secondary relics or *brandia*, objects that had come into contact with the martyrs' tombs (McCulloh 1976). From the mid-eighth century on, however, the Roman pontiffs began to exploit their inexhaustible supply of relics in order to build closer relationships with the increasingly powerful Frankish church to the

north (Fichtenau 1952). The distribution of relics placed tangible
evidence of papal importance in every region that received these gifts,
either directly or through subsequent redivision of the relics. Moreover, as gifts, the relics were not alienated as they would have been
had they been sold or traded. They thus remained the Pope's, and
their recipients remained subordinate to the Pope by the ties created
in the distribution.

Others who possessed illustrious relics could use them to develop
similar patronage networks. Thus, for example, bishops distributed
portions of important saints to the churches in their dioceses and even
beyond. Rather than diffusing the importance of the central sanc-
tuary, these gifts increased both its prestige as the central location of
the cult now known more widely and the prestige of the ecclesiastic
who was able so to exercise his patronage. A prime example is the
case of the relics of St. Vanne, distributed throughout the diocese of
Verdun in the eleventh century (Geary 1978:84-5). Such parceling of
remains did not decrease their value but rather enhanced it, since the
value lay not in the bones themselves as alienable objects, but rather
in the relationships they could create as subjects.

An obvious and extremely significant aspect of the exchange of
relics by means of gift was the establishment of personal bonds between giver and receiver, the creation of "fraternal love" between the
two *amici*, as Roman Michalowski has emphasized (Michalowski
1981:404). Where such a bond did not exist, the parties were not *amici*
but rather *inimici*, and for the transferral of property to take place
either such a bond had to be formed, or if one of the parties, particularly the subordinate, did not wish to establish a relationship of
dependency, then the transferral had to take place by such mechanisms as purchase or theft.

Theft

Thefts of relics included the same wide spectrum of coerced transferrals as did other forms of theft discussed by Grierson: in the ninth
through eleventh centuries, the most frequent form was the isolated
theft of individual relics or the theft of the relics from an enemy's
church during a raid (Geary 1978). But theft can also include the
systematic extortion of Italian churches under the Ottonians (Dupré-
Theseider 1964), and the ultimate theft – the pillage of Constantinople's relic following the sack of the city by the wayward Fourth
Crusade in 1204 (Riant 1875; Constable 1966; Geary 1977).

The usual target of the isolated theft was a distant monastery or church visited by a cleric who, judging that the saints whose relics were there were not receiving proper veneration, entered the church at night, broke open the shrine, and fled with the remains. One example will suffice. In 1058 a monk of the monastery of Bergues-St.-Winnoc in Flanders was traveling to England in the company of merchants when the ship was blown off course and landed on the Sussex coast. The monk, Balgerus, explored the neighborhood and came upon a monastery in which were venerated the remains of St. Lewinna. Impressed by the account of her life and miracles he heard from the local monks, he decided to steal the relics. He entered the church at night and attempted to take the relics, but was first thwarted by the miraculous resistance of the saint. Finally, after much prayer and effort, the saint agreed to accompany him and he stole off to the ship with his prize (Geary 1978:76–8).

When, in the course of raids on neighboring nobles, an enemy's property was pillaged, relics were normally included in the spoils. Thus, for example, when Count Odo of Champagne in 1033 sacked and burned Commercy, amidst the booty was the arm of St. Pantalon (Geary 1978:83). Likewise, Count Arlulf the Old of Flanders (919-64) took the relics of Sts. Valerius and Richerius when he sacked the towns of St.-Valery and St.-Riquier (Herrmann-Mascard 1975, 380). Such appropriations of an enemy's sacred protectors to the benefit of the victor's community belong to an ancient tradition that could no doubt be traced to the tradition of appropriation of the city gods of enemies in antiquity. However, this sacred booty might be treated exactly like other spoils – the arm of Pantalon, for example, was subsequently sold to Abbot Richard of St. Vanne in Verdun for one silver mark.

The greatest theft of relics in the Middle Ages was the sack of Constantinople. Here the appropriation of saints was systematic and thorough, lasting several months. All relics were placed in the hands of Garnier de Trainel, Bishop of Troyes, who saw to their distribution: three-eighths each for the Venetians and the new Byzantine Emperor, the former Count Baldwin of Flanders, and two-eighths for the Westerners. The bishop and then after his death Nivelon de Cherizy saw to the distribution of relics that eventually found their way into churches across France and what is now Belgium (Herrmann-Mascard 1975:370).

Commerce

The third means by which relics circulated was by sale. Commerce in saints' remains took place not only simultaneously with the more regular systems of gift and theft, but even between the same groups. Here one finds professional merchants, price negotiation, efforts at quality control, and established patterns of transportation and marketing existing side by side with the other, presumably more archaic, systems of gift, countergift, and theft.

The best-documented regular trade in relics was that between Frankish churchmen and Italian merchants in the ninth century. The most famous merchant was one Deusdona, a Roman deacon who negotiated to provide a number of Alcuin's associates, among them Einhard, Abbot Hilduin of Soissons, and others, with the remains of Roman martyrs in the 820s and 830s (Geary 1978:51–9). Deusdona and his associates met their potential customers at the celebrations of important saints' feasts in the north and offered to obtain relics for them. During the winter months Deusdona and his associates systematically collected relics from one or another of the Roman cemeteries, concentrating on a different area of the city each year. In the spring their caravan crossed the Alps in time to deliver their wares at the celebrations of feasts; when they arrived at Mühlheim on June 2, 835, the feast of Sts. Marcellinus and Peter, the saints being honored were ones that Deusdona had himself supplied to the Franks.

Deusdona represents the most highly organized and independent sort of relic merchant. Others might be itinerant peddlers who traveled about obtaining relics at random as the opportunity presented itself and then hawking them in other dioceses. Still others, such as the Englishman Electus who operated along the Norman coast, sought primarily relics to sell to a particular patron, in his case King Athelstan (Geary 1978:60).

The official and quasi-official involvement of central authorities, ecclesiastical and royal, in the circulation of relics was part of a careful program of centralized control over the sacred. Carolingian control over the distribution of relics was in particular a means of orchestrating access to the sacred. Unlike living holy men in the Near East or the occasional Celtic pilgrim or local wonder worker who appeared on the Continent, dead saints could be controlled by the episcopal hierarchy. The churches in which they were to be found were supposed to have regular clergy attached to them; the decision to move them about was reserved to the local count and bishop; and Carolingian synods sought to limit the proliferation of shrines containing relics of saints not recognized by the Church (Geary 1972:40–50).

Similarly, one can see the frequently tolerated or even (as in the case of Athelstan) encouraged tradition of thefts as a deliberate attempt to acquire these important prestige objects in a way that would destroy the inalienable relationship between gift and gift-giver that characterized the regular distribution of relics by Popes and prelates. Carolingians needed important Roman relics for the control of their populations; however, the price for relics acquired by gift was subordination to the Pope. The theft or purchase of relics objectified these sacred objects; turned them, at least temporarily, into commodities; and allowed the new owner to escape being placed in the debt of the Roman Church. The same process might be seen in the means by which the Anglo-Saxon Athelstan sought relics from the Continent.

Reconstruction of value

However it happened, the very act of transferral removed the relic from the cultural structure in which it had originally acquired value. It thus arrived in the new community as an unproven object, the target of considerable skepticism. Was the object really an efficacious relic? If it had been acquired by gift, why would the donor have parted with it if it were really worth having? If acquired by purchase, how could one trust a merchant not to be a fraud selling the "pigges bones" of Chaucer's Pardoner? As in the case of oriental carpets entering the West discussed in the next chapter, newly acquired relics had to undergo a process of social negotiation within the new community (Spooner, Chapter 7). To allay suspicions, relics thus had to undergo once more the process of authentication described above. They had to be tested, and tested in such a way that the test itself would add to their fame. Thus transferrals of relics, referred to as "translations," were concluded with exactly the same rituals of authentication, both internal and external, associated with "inventions."

Moreover, the account of the relics' translation had to itself become part of the myth of production – the story of how they had come to their new community was itself part of the explanation of who they were and what their power was. In this context, accounts of thefts, as opposed to gifts or purchases, was particularly appropriate and satisfactory. A traditional literary subgenre of hagiography developed between the eighth and twelfth centuries in which translations were presented as thefts. The saints were clearly too precious to their communities to be parted with willingly. Thus they had to be stolen, or rather kidnapped. Moreover, the saints were too powerful to allow themselves to be taken unwillingly. A saint unable to prevent the sacking of his community or his own removal would hardly have been a desirable acquisition. Thus the thief had to have succeeded only by convincing the saint that he would receive more satisfactory veneration in his new location – a promise the flattered local community would have to keep.

A significant number of translations thus presented involve saints previously unknown. Whether this reflects missing documentation or saints who did not exist before someone took anonymous remains from a deserted churchyard is impossible to say. In either case, from the perspective of the community in which the remains came to be venerated, the construction of value and the mode of circulation reflected the same assumptions as the production context: acquiring the relic gave it value because it was worth acquiring, and this acquisition (often in the face of grave natural and supernatural dangers) was itself evidence that the relics were genuine. Circulation thus created the commodity being circulated, although to survive as a commodity it had to continue to meet the high expectations raised by the mode of its creation.

Conclusion

We have seen the creation and circulation of a particular type of sacred prestige commodity, saints' relics, within a complex traditional society. Although the existence and efficacy of such person-objects as relics was almost universally accepted, every individual case posed the problem of skepticism both because of the ubiquity of similar objects devoid of value (normal mortal remains), the recognition of widespread fraud, and the intense competition of different religious centers, each eager to discredit the main attractions of their neighbors. In addition we have seen that these commodities circulated in the broader context of an exchange system involving a variety of mechanisms, none of which were the exclusive domain of any social, economic, or educational group.

Within this context, human remains could go through a life-cycle closely related to the production-circulation context: a human bone, given by the Pope as a sacred relic, thereby became a sacred relic if the receiver were also willing to consider it as such. Likewise, a corpse once stolen (or said to have been stolen) was valuable because it had been worth stealing. Solemn recognition, by means of ritual authentication normally involving the miraculous intervention of the saint himself, provided assurance that the value assigned by the transfer was genuine. This value endured so long as the community responded by recognizing miraculous cures and wonders and ascribing them to the intervention of the saint. In general, however, enthusiasm tended to wane over time, and the value of the relic had to be renewed periodically through a repetition of transferral or discovery, which would then begin the cycle anew. So long as the relic continued to perform as a miracle worker, it maintained its value as a potential commodity and could be used to acquire status, force acknowledgment of dependency, and secure wealth through its whole or partial distribution.

These specific conclusions concerning relics as commodities suggest more general reflections on the theoretical problems of value and commodity exchange in medieval society. First, when discussing demand formed by need, taste, and fashion, the life history of relics suggests that one must be very careful to distinguish between demand in traditional societies and demand in industrialized (or industrializing) societies. Although the traffic in relics, like that of such commodities as textiles, pottery, and religious icons, was deeply affected by cultural values and collectively shared tastes (Schneider 1978), the needs generated by the political economy of the Carolingian Empire (and, at a later date, the Venetian Empire) are no less relevant.

Second, the transformations of relics from persons to commodities and in some cases back to persons through a process of social and cultural transition suggests that one should examine the biographies of other sorts of objects that may have been both persons and commodities. Along with slaves and relics, this might include sacred images, which in Byzantium and from the fourteenth century on in the West began to compete successfully with relics as sources of personal religious power; and other extremely important prestige objects such as royal and imperial regalia, art, and entailed estates. Under certain circumstances, all these might be the objects of commerce, but under other circumstances they more closely resemble persons. The boundaries between object and subject are culturally induced and semipermeable.

Third, as vital as cultural parameters are for the social construction of value, the problem of the authenticity of relics indicates that there need not be consensus within a society on the value, equivalence, or even identity of specific commodities. On the contrary, high-prestige objects such as relics can play an important role in deeply divided communities. Disagreements and conflicts within society may be expressed and even conducted through disputes over the identity and value of such objects (Brown 1982:222–50).

If the foregoing examination of these "personal commodities" has elucidated something of the complex values of medieval society, one is still left with intriguing and ultimately perhaps unanswerable questions, which, for want of sources, the paper has been unable to address.

First, one must wonder whether it is possible to speak of value equivalences of relics and other commodities, or whether one ought to talk of rank. Much theoretical literature would suggest that a conversion between relics and, say, livestock ought to be impossible to establish – that in gift exchange, the emphasis is on quality, subjects, and superiority, rather than on the quantity, objects, and equivalence emphasized in commodity exchange (Gregory 1983). And yet we know that relics were in fact dealt with both as gifts and as commodities, even though a price list could never be established. During the periods of their careers when relics were objectified, how was value equivalency determined? Did it cease to have any meaning once a relic had again become subjectified in a new social context?

Related to this first question is that of the relative value of different relics. Why was one relic more prized than another? In some instances – a local saint or a famous apostle – the answer is obvious. Usually, however, it is impossible to determine why, for example, Sts. Peter and Marcellinus would be sought by the Franks, or why one would steal the remains of St. Maianus or St. Fides rather than those of some other saint. Were these merely targets of opportunity, or was there a process of comparison and selection?

Third, one would like to be able to establish the relative importance of gift exchange as opposed to the theft or sale of relics. Here again we have no idea. In the cases discussed of Carolingian ecclesiastics who were active in stealing relics as well as in purchasing them and receiving others from the Pope, one sees all three mechanisms. We have suggested above that the mechanism selected depended on the type of relationship the recipient desired to establish with the previous owner. Perhaps here the concept of kin distance (in the sense of artificial kin groups within the Christian community) might be helpful in determining the parameters within which gift, sale, and theft were acceptable.

Fourth, one would like to know more about the acceptance of these objects as valuable within the broader, lay society of the regions into which they were introduced. We have seen that in the eighth and ninth centuries, much of the flow of relics was into the recently Christianized areas of northern Germany. Here they became the objects of officially sanctioned cults. However, in a controversial but fascinating study of pilgrimage sites in Germany in the later Middle Ages, Lionel Rothkrug has argued that pilgrimages to saints' shrines are almost totally nonexistent in such areas as Saxony, which had been the major focus of these translations (Rothkrug 1979; 1980). Could it be that despite the official propaganda attesting to the popularity of these relics, the native populations were never really drawn into the system of values within which they had meaning? Since Rothkrug shows, on both micro and macro levels, a startling coincidence between areas lacking pilgrimages and areas where the Reformation succeeded, it is tempting to argue that these regions never accepted the hagiocentric religion that was medieval Catholicism.

Finally, one would like more comparative studies and theoretical models of commodities that might elucidate some of the processes we have discussed. Most anthropologists tend to look either at industrialized societies in which the production and distribution of commodities operate in a very different context, or at traditional societies undergoing rapid transformation owing to colonization or at least increasing participation in alien markets and production systems. Neither model is appropriate for medieval Europe. Change was disjointed and internally generated, and was not directed toward a colonial, capitalist, or industrialized economy imposed from without. It is within this very different economy that sacred relics as commodities must be understood.

Note

This essay has benefited from the advice and criticisms provided by participants in the University of Pennsylvania Ethnohistory Seminar. The author wishes to thank particularly Arjun Appadurai, James Amelang, and Bertram Wyatt-Brown for their detailed suggestions for revisions.

References

Acta Sanctorum. 61 vols. (Antwerp, Paris:1643–1875).

Ariès, Philippe. 1981. *The Hour of Our Death*. New York.

Baldwin, John W. 1959. *The Medieval Theories of the Just Price*. Philadelphia.

Bonnassie, Pierre. 1967. "A Family of the Barcelona Countryside and Its Economic Activities Around the Year 1000." *Early Medieval Society*, ed. Sylvia L. Thrupp, 103–23. New York.

Brown, Peter. 1982. "Relics and Social Status in the Age of Gregory of Tours." *Society and the Holy in Late Antiquity*, 222–50. Berkeley, Calif.

Constable, Giles. 1966. "Troyes, Constantinople, and the Relics of St. Helen in the Thirteenth Century." *Mélanges offerts à René Crozet*, 2:1035–42. Paris.

Deveroy, J. -P. 1984. "Un monastère dans l'économie d'échanges: les services de transport à l'abbaye Saint-Germain-des-Prés au IXe siècle," *Annales E. S. C.*, 570–89.

Dopsch, Alfons. 1930. *Naturalwirtschaft und Geldwirtschaft in die Weltgeschichte*. Vienna.

Duby, Georges. 1974. *The Early Growth of the European Economy*. Ithaca, N.Y.

Dupré-Theseider, E. 1964. "La 'granda rapina dei corpi santi' dall' Italia al tempo di Ottone." *Festschrift Percy Ernst Schramm* I:420–32. Weisbaden.

Fichtenau, Heinrich. 1952. "Zum Reliquienwesen im früheren Mittelalter." *Mitteilungen des Instituts für österreichische Geschichtsforschung*, 60, 66–8.

Geary, Patrick. 1979. "The Ninth Century Relic Trade: A Response to Popular Piety?" *Religion and the People: 800–1700*, ed. James Obelkevich, 8–19. Chapel Hill, N.C.

1978. *Furta Sacra: Thefts of Relics in the Central Middle Ages*. Princeton, N.J.

1977. "Saint Helen of Athyra and the Cathedral of Troyes in the Thirteenth Century." *The Journal of Medieval and Renaissance Studies*, 7/1:149–68.

Gregory, Chris A. 1982. *Gifts and Commodities*. London.

Grierson, Philip. 1959. "Commerce in the Dark Ages: A Critique of the Evidence." *Transactions of the Royal Historical Society*, ser. 6, vol. 9, 123–40.

Hermann-Mascard, Nicole. 1975. *Les reliques des saints: Formation coutumière d'un droit.* Paris.

Kopytoff, Igor. 1982. "Slavery." *Annual Review of Anthropology*, 11:207–30.

Latouche, Robert. 1956. *Les origines de l'économie occidentale.* Paris.

Little, Lester K. 1978. *Religious Poverty and the Profit Economy in Medieval Europe.* Ithaca, N.Y.

Mauss, Marcel. 1967. *The Gift: Forms and Functions of Exchange in Archaic Societies*, tr. I. Cunnison. New York.

McCulloh, M. J. 1975. "The Cult of Relics in the Letters and Dialogues of Pope Gregory the Great: A Lexicographical Study." *Traditio*, 36:145–84.

Michalowski, Roman. 1981. "Le don d'amitié dans la société carolingienne et les 'translationes sanctorum,' " *Hagiographie: cultures et sociétés, IV-XIIe siècles*, 399–416. Paris.

Monumenta Germaniae Historica, Epistolarum Tomus IV, *Epistolae Karolini Aevi* Tomus II, ed. Ernest Dümmler (Berlin: 1895).

Pirenne, H. 1937. *Mahomet et Charlemagne.* Paris.

Riant, Paul Edouard Didier, Comte de. 1875. "Depouilles religieuses à Constantinople au XIIIe siècle. *Mémoires de la Société nationale des antiquaires de France.* 4ème series, 6:1–214.

Rothkrug, Lionel. In press. "The Cult of Relics in Antiquity." *World Spirituality: An Encyclopedic History of the Religious Quest.* Vol. I, *European Archaic Spirituality*, ed. Charles Long.

1979. "Popular Religion and Holy Shrines: Their Influence on the Origins of the German Reformation and Their Role in German Cultural Development." J. Obelkevich, ed., *Religion and the People.* Chapel Hill, N.C.

1980. *Religious Practices and Collective Perceptions: Hidden Homologies in the Renaissance and Reformation. Historical Reflections* 7:1.

Schmitt, J. C. 1979. *Le saint lévrier: Guinefort, guérisseur d'enfants depuis le XIIIe siècle.* Paris.

Schneider, J. 1978. "Peacocks and Penguins: The Political Economy of European Cloth and Colors," *American Ethnologist*, 5:413–47.

Schreiner, K. 1966. " 'Discrimen veri ac falsi' Ansätze und Formen der Kritik in der Heiligen-und Reliquieverehrung des Mittelalters." *Archiv für Kulturgeschichte* 48:1–53.

Sigal, P. A. 1969. "Maladie, pèlerinage et guérison au XIIe siècle: Les miracles de saint Gibrien à Reims." *Annales E. S. C.* 24:1522–39.

Ward, Benedicta. 1982. *Miracles and the Medieval Mind: Theory, Record, and Event, 1000–1215.* Philadelphia.

PART IV

Production regimes and the sociology of demand

CHAPTER 7

Weavers and dealers: the authenticity of an oriental carpet

BRIAN SPOONER

The Orient is an integral part of European *material* civilisation and culture.
Edward Said, *Orientalism*

Carpets, oriental

Oriental carpets have been recognized as prestigious furnishing in the West since the Middle Ages.[1] In many ways, they represent the epitome of Western concern with alien things – especially utilitarian alien things. Carpets entered the Western cultural arena as a rare alien item of interest and eventually became a commodity. But commoditization does not adequately explain their continuing success in the market or the special attention they receive from collectors.

Why should this Western concern with the Other be epitomized in the Oriental Carpet? More significantly why should oriental carpets still generate increasing demand, become ever more rather than less available, be stocked in a wider range of shops, and deployed in a steadily wider range of homes? The expansion apparently continues despite the changes in product and supply that result from accelerating social change and political disruption in the countries where they are produced. Oriental carpets are now bought and sold at a number of different levels of the market, from discount department stores to exclusive dealers available by appointment only. Objectively, they may be new or old (not "second-hand"), large or small. There is a wide range of price, durability, materials, designs, colors; the dyes may be natural or chemical. They may be purchased as floor covering, for decor, or as a collector's item. People who knew them only from books and museums now buy their own, join rug societies, become collectors. Like other objects of conspicuous consumption, carpets first became luxury furnishing for the elite, and have now gone the way of so many luxuries in recent times and become available throughout the middle class. But they have not lost their elitist appeal in the process.

Is the oriental carpet we buy today in fact, as we like to think, the same commodity that began to be traded in bulk in the last century – let alone the same as rarer examples that are displayed in museums, such as the Boston Hunting Carpet (*Boston Museum Bulletin* 1971) or documented in medieval paintings such as the fifteenth-century Memlings (see, for example, the "Madonna and Child Enthroned" in the Louvre)? The criterion of age tends (implicitly, at least) to be foremost in any evaluation. Even if it were possible to produce identical artifacts today, they would not compete on the market with antiques because of the value we attribute to relative age. But even though antique rugs still no doubt provide much of the basic inspiration and rationale for the market and for collecting, they supply only a very small and still declining proportion of it. Moreover, if we compare what was written about carpets around the turn of the century with what is being written now, it is clear that despite the quasigenetic relationship – the continuity of the craft – there is a difference between what the average buyer thought he was buying then, what it meant to him, and the equivalent today. The change can be seen in the value and the supply of antiques, in the logistics of production and the social context of consumption. In the straightforward material sense (which seems always to be uppermost in our consciousness), it is still possible to come by an antique – technically, that is to say, in the definition of U.S. Customs, assumed to have been produced before about 1880. But most of the examples we see at auctions, in dealers' showrooms, and in stores and homes, even in museums, however good, are not antiques in this sense. Why do we assess them differently?

Assessment in this context is related to demand. But the factors that come immediately to mind to explain assessment and demand – superlative craftsmanship, exotic design, snobbism, for example – are inadequate, if only because they apply also to other types of furnishing and utensil that have not generated demand so continuously and successfully. Why do people want carpets rather than other materials on their floors? Why do so many want oriental rather than other carpets? No sooner do tentative answers to these questions appear within reach than others, more difficult, arise. For instance, why and how do we distinguish, as we do, between different types of oriental carpet? The conventional answers to these questions – answers that focus on material factors in the carpet and on the carpet's place in the history of the craft – are unlikely to satisfy our curiosity.

For aspiring buyers there is much to know. Besides being able to recognize a carpet as oriental, they must be at least vaguely aware of a hierarchical taxonomy of types of oriental carpet, rationalized in terms of criteria such as age, provenience, materials, color, design, "handle" (that is, feel or pliability), condition, fineness, and evenness of weave. The existence (though not necessarily the details) of this taxonomic scheme is recognized in different degrees by a wide variety of consumers, from those just trading up from wall-to-wall at one end of the social scale to the most discerning collectors at the other end. Becoming an aficionado means entering the debate about the recognition and application of the criteria – criteria of authenticity.

The fact that these criteria of classification and appreciation are only imperfectly translatable into market prices alerts us immediately to a discontinuity between the criteria of commerce and those of connoisseurship. The dealer has his sources of supply and his costs. The average consumer has his budget and his social needs. The connoisseur and the collector have their exhibitions, public and private, and their literature. Each stands in a different position in relation to both the prices and the values and has a different understanding of them. Different carpets mean different things to different people.

Where there is so much to know, we expect the information to be accessible. Why should it not be as available as the carpets themselves? Superficially, it is. Carpet primers abound. Exhibitors vie with one another in the sumptuousness of their catalogues. Dealers have ready answers to questions. For those who wish to delve further, there is a literature of history, ethnography, travel, technology, and connoisseurship. But somehow, despite vast improvement over the last ten years, the now voluminous literature on oriental carpets is unsatisfying. Most of the perhaps fifty works devoted to the subject before 1900, and probably over a thousand that have appeared since, though they are addressed to various levels of the market, are concerned primarily with illustrating, classifying, and identifying the inventory of carpets in the West (cf. Enay and Azadi 1977). They are one-sided. However academic or scientific some of them may appear, they are with few exceptions consciously or unconsciously informed primarily by the lore of the dealer. This lore is generated by the history of the trade and of Western interest, rather than by the conditions of production. For example, a Bukhara was a carpet that entered the trade through Bukhara. The meaning naturally came to be extended to carpets of similar designs, wherever they came from. Most "Bukharas" now come from Pakistan. The term does not – whatever one may be led to expect – represent a homogeneous craft tradition from Bukhara. The dealer deals, naturally, not with the weaver, but (often through a chain of other dealers) with the producer or local merchant. The weaver is barely represented in this operation. The dealer's information is trade lore, generated in the process of negotiation entailed in commercial transaction. Works on carpets by collectors and art historians are also based largely on this lore. Very little other information has been available to them. They rarely have access to independent ethnographic data. Early travelers, however fascinating their descriptions in general, barely noticed the rugs they occasionally admitted sitting on. The weavers themselves were not literate, and the literary-minded of their culture and time, even up to the present, have shown little interest in work produced by the skills of the poor, even where it was financed by a royal court. It is not surprising, then, that the literature is often confusing, difficult to understand, even contradictory. For an amateur who is not easily satisfied, it can be exasperating. For the determined scholar it leads sooner or later to the realization that so long as the problem is defined as one of material culture, or even of the history of design in the narrow sense, there are limits to what can be known and the limits often seem not to be recognized by the experts.

The carpet business involves not just the supply of carpets, as in the case of other commodities, but also the supply of information about them. In fact, most of the available information about carpets has, at least until recently, come with them. But the journey from one cultural area to another affects the information differently from the carpets. The carpets arrive in Europe and America in basically the same condition as when they left their point of origin (though special techniques are sometimes used to age them or to change the colors according to particular conceptions of Western taste). The information, as any schoolboy learns to expect, suffers reinterpretation with each transaction. The dealer's interest is primarily economic. The lore he acquires with his wares is often purveyed incidentally. On the other hand, the connoisseur who is the public arbiter of authenticity scarcely controls the sources of the information on which he bases his judgment.

So there are questions both of economics and of values, and they are linked. The question of values is complicated by the fact that oriental carpets compete in the open market as floor covering, but with an unfair advantage: they are recognized most immediately by their designs, which over the centuries have become an integral part of our own cultural repertoire, but without losing their exotic appeal. We copy and imitate them so commonly, both in carpets and in other media, that we are scarcely aware of our cultural debt. The initial borrowing and imitation is buried in our history and almost completely assimilated in our cultural heritage. Our appreciation of the superficial factors that tend to dominate discussions of the technological, economic, and cultural history of the genre and the social history of the producers, the middlemen, and the consumers is conditioned by the fact that oriental carpets became culturally familiar to us by their basic designs long before the present generation. They surround us in Western products that imitate oriental originals. Now, every year more and more people become familiar with – and want – the real thing.

The real thing is not simply an artifact; it is made by particular individuals, from special handcrafted materials, in particular social, cultural, and environmental conditions, with motifs and designs learned from earlier generations. The original meanings of the decorative elements have been largely forgotten by the people who weave them (who probably anyway think about their work in terms that would not provide answers to Western queries about meaning) and must be reconstructed by Western specialists in order to rationalize their need for authenticity. The social conditions in which the carpets began their journey from weavers through the hands of dealers to consumers (including collectors) are known only imperfectly. We receive them divorced from their social context. Our desire for authenticity prompts us to reconstruct that context. We do it mainly by seizing on the information that comes incidentally with them, which it must be said does serve our immediate purpose. But at the same time such information enables us to deceive ourselves about what we are doing: because of the inherent distortion and paucity of the information, we are easily able to make it fit our needs, instead of being constrained to fit our ideas to the information.

Nevertheless, our interpretations are sophisticated. We discriminate among a seemingly infinite variety of traditions and subtraditions. We deal with questions of both authenticity and quality. Good is distinguished from bad, old from new, genuine from imitation. But the criteria of overall quality are vague, and tend to be complicated by questions of authenticity. Even in the case of the most lowly specimen, the determination of value invariably involves at least an implicit assessment of authenticity.

Analytically, however, authenticity must be distinguished at the outset not only from the question of quality, but also from the idea of a classic carpet. A classic carpet would be an example of the highest quality in its class, such as the famous sixteenth-century Persian Royal Hunting carpet that hangs splendidly 6.8 by 3.2 meters, in the Oesterreichische Museum für angewandte Kunst in Vienna. In most cases a classic carpet would also be authentic. But a carpet of very high quality could be a later imitation of a classic, in which case it would not be authentic. Authenticity cannot be determined simply by retailing the objective material attributes of the artifact. It has to do not only with genuineness and the reliability of face value, but with the interpretation of genuineness and our desire for it. The material attributes, however, are generally treated as though they were clues to the arch-criterion, the supposed origin of the piece and its place in the history of the craft. But since the history of the craft is poorly documented, it is open to continual revision (even more so than history generally). We must not be misled by the values ascribed to craftsmanship, for these values have also changed significantly over the past hundred years. They are based explicitly on the search for historical truth, but we are of course steadily moving further and further away in time from the sources on which the reconstruction of that historical truth depends.

Our interpretation and reinterpretation of the sources available to us may become ever more sophisticated and ingenious, but only in the service of our own needs. We are confronted, therefore, with (1) the material facts before us in existing carpets, (2) the history of the craft that produced them, reconstructed by us from poor and inadequate data, and (3) our concern for authenticity. We talk commonly as though our idea of authenticity depended on our reconstruction of the history of the craft, which in turn depended on a combination of the material facts before us in the carpets and in scanty textual and archeological sources. In this chapter this commonsense understanding is turned heuristically on its head: underlying the discussion is an interest in the possibility that the evolving constellation of social relations in our complex society generates a need for authenticity, which leads people to cast around for cultural material on which to work out the obsession for distinction. In some sectors of social life, oriental carpets serve this need. The service of this need conditions our reconstruction of the history of carpet weaving, and our reconstruction gives meaning to the material evidence before us.

Although carpets generally are commodities, oriental carpets are only imperfectly commoditized. They are part commodity, part symbol. It is in the nature of a symbol to bear more than one meaning, even in a particular social context. Carpets bear many different meanings for different types of people in different cultural contexts. They began as domestic products that acquired a symbolic dimension for the people who produced and lived with them, because of the cultural significance of what they did with them. The producers projected the meaning of what they did onto what they did it with. In anthropological terms, carpets became an object of cultural elaboration among the people who produced them. Over the history of the craft, over the past two and a half millenia at least, these symbolized artifacts have become first partly commoditized in the Orient and then wholly commoditized in international trade. In the history of the greatly increased interest in them in the West over the past one hundred years or so, they have become partly decommoditized, or (in the terms of Kopytoff's discussion in Chapter 2) resingularized. Certain attributes have reacquired special meaning through the reconstruction of the social and cultural provenience of the artifact. As a result, whichever way we turn in an attempt to explain our interest in oriental carpets, we run sooner or later into mystification. Since this is so obviously a problem that poses questions of both oriental and Western experience, careful investigation of it promises to be especially rewarding in our continuing struggle to understand better our relationship both with our own material world and with other cultures.

These questions require and would I think repay the attention of writers trained in any one of a number of academic disciplines, each of which would approach them from a particular point of view that might illuminate a new aspect of how the appreciation of oriental carpets among us today has developed. They concern the technology of weaving and how and why it has changed at different rates in different parts of the oriental-rug-producing region of the world; the social history of these areas; the international political economy as it affects the terms of trade, especially in certain raw materials such as wool and dyestuffs; and the history and evolution of design, style, and fashion, in both the Orient and the West. The field is difficult to define in intellectual terms. Although the oriental carpet may legitimately be a single topic in the history of technology, the technology is obviously diverse since it has been practiced over a vast area since before the Islamic era. It is not legitimate, for example, to address it as many have done as a genre of Islamic art. I discuss it here from the vantage point of a type of social anthropology that, because of the way it has developed over the past two decades, suggests a promising approach. If in the process I trespass on the preserves of other disciplines in which I claim no competence, I apologize; my defense lies in my claim to be pursuing a significant point in the dialectical process of modern life – between the social and the cultural, and between us and them.

Given the complexity of the subject, I have chosen to narrow the focus of discussion to the Turkmen pile carpet. Since all Turkmen pile carpets are woven by Turkmen in a particular part of southwestern central Asia, they constitute a category that is recognized both in the trade and in the craft, and they have a unitary geographical and cultural provenience. This focus also has the advantage of illustrating a number of misconceptions that pervade the literature. Turkmen carpets derive from an interesting cross-section of socially diverse but culturally similar communities in the areas now incorporated in Afghanistan, Iran, and Soviet Turkmenistan over a historical period that has included severe political and economic dislocation. Finally, Turkmen carpets are tribal (and so are woven largely by women who learn domestically from one another in small, cohesive communities, rather than by men or children working for wages under a foreman), without being rustic or unsophisticated. This last point may explain the place of Turkmen rugs as favorites among collectors – a place that has twice in the last five years been confirmed by the results of polls conducted by the "ruggist" magazine *Hali*[2] – suggesting that a tribal origin helps to satisfy the quest for authenticity.

This introduction must not be closed without notice of the fact that there are oriental carpets for which the question of authenticity, though not irrelevant, is less significant. The Persian carpets of the great urban traditions, such as Isfahan, Tabriz, and Nain, were always woven on vertical looms, mainly by children at the direction of a male *ustad* (master craftsman), and in largely figurative designs rather than mysterious symbols. In these conditions quality *is* the dominant criterion.

Finally, from the point of view developed in this chapter, the crux of the problem entailed in the growing popularity of this changing commodity among consumers, and in the related concern with authenticity, lies in the history of the relationship between the weaver and the dealer, as it relates both to the supply of carpets and to the flow of information about them. This relationship must be investigated with due regard to the changing status of each in his own society and the continuous negotiation of commercial terms between them, which has allowed the growth of a flourishing lore on both sides that can be understood only in its own social context. The weaver is embedded in a complex system of social relations. The dealer must cultivate the market. It is in the nature of the business of the Western dealer that he has built up a corpus of practical knowledge of the Other that goes back to the Middle Ages and possibly beyond. The weaver's knowledge of the market, on the other hand, is probably for the most part of relatively recent growth. Until the later nineteenth century, the proportion of total production that went for export (despite a thirteenth-century reference given below) beyond the boundary of the Islamic world was presumably small and involved a relatively small part of the productive community. Since then, the dialogue between weaver and dealer has become increasingly direct, especially in the last ten years or so, to the extent that direct negotiation can be recognized. The negotiation of authenticity of the rug derives at least to some extent from the indirect negotiation between weaver and dealer and the evolving bargaining power and social status of each. But the process of negotiation is complex.

In what follows I address three types of questions: (1) Of cultural values and practices – what is a carpet, and how did oriental carpets come to transcend for us in the West the purely utilitarian function they share historically with other textiles? (2) Of material and social facts – how has the technology (in the broadest sense) of carpet production changed over time, especially with regard to the changing availability of raw materials, labor and the organization of society in the East and in the West? And (3) of the intersection of facts and values – how and why do we negotiate standards of authenticity as distinct from quality, and what does the history of this particular intercultural problem reveal about the dynamics of modern society and social change? In the course of this argument I review a particular type of oriental carpet as material textile, as cultural furnishing, as social product, as commodity, as object of demand and of specialized knowledge, and finally as partially naturalized alien landmark in our shifting constellation of Western values. I have defined my topic and restricted my field in a way that obviates the need to review everything that has ever been written about oriental carpets, though I cannot of course avoid some discussion of the literature.

The remainder of the chapter falls into three sections. The first of these is a reconstruction of the traditional technologies and social contexts of carpet production and a critique of modern hypotheses concerning their symbolism; the second deals with the economic and cultural changes attendant upon the transformation of the carpet into an object of Western commercial interest. Finally, in the third section, the test of authenticity is reviewed in terms of the resingularization of commodities in Western society.

The manufacture and the symbolization of floor covering

The technology of weaving has a history of its own (see, for example, Ackerman 1938a, 1938b, Farnie 1958, Forbes 1964, Wulff 1966). A carpet is a particular type of woven fabric, which though now diffused over much of the world probably evolved from a particular tradition of weaving that began somewhere between southwest and central Asia. It is arguably the most sophisticated fabric ever invented.

Besides weaving skill, carpet production has a number of requirements: specifically, the ability to provide certain basic materials, such as wood and metal for the loom and weaving tools, different types of wool, and dyestuffs; the knowledge of certain skills and motifs; certain forms of cooperation; and certain amounts and types of financing. Each of these requirements allows room for innovation, as the last hundred years of Turkmen history shows – but not a great deal, unless the nature of the end product is to be changed. At the same time, these requirements condition the activities, the organization, and the expressive culture of everyone involved in carpet production. The dynamic of the technology is interdependent with the dynamic of social interaction, of ways of thinking, and of the natural processes that provide the raw materials. These technological, social, cultural, and natural constraints constitute a fourfold framework of production, in which the individual weavers express themselves by innovating within the limits imposed by their need to maintain their place in the society on which they depend for their material and emotional security. Any discussion of the significance of carpets in the society where they are produced must give weight to each of these factors.

The origin of carpet weaving lies beyond the middle of the first millennium B.C. The earliest extant fragment was found in a frozen barrow at Bash-Adar in the Altai area northeast of Turkestan and is dated to the sixth century B.C. An almost complete carpet was recovered from a similar site at Pazyryk in the same area, dated to the fourth century B.C. (see Rudenko 1968). These finds provide evidence of an already fully evolved tradition. The details of invention are of course unknown and unimportant – except to the extent that they may perhaps illuminate the evolution of the motifs and designs, and the history of the relationship between settled and nomadic populations. With some justification the carpet has been compared to a fleece. This comparison may be more than a felicitous insight, since it suggests a connection with pastoralism. It may, however, be misleading, because it does not necessarily argue for an origin among nomadic rather than settled populations. In fact, the sophistication of the technology – the combination of conceptualization and workmanship in color and design, and in fineness and evenness – warns us not to accept unquestioningly the common thesis that carpet weaving originated among nomadic populations. The early evidence is in fact ambiguous.

Like other fabrics, a carpet is woven on a loom of warp threads, the ends of which usually provide the fringe at either end of the finished product. The webbing at the beginning and end of the weaving may be simple weft on warp, but may be elaborated by one or other of a number of flat-weave techniques. The body of the carpet is produced by tying rows of knots (two basic types are used in the area; only one of them is a true knot), one- or two-ply, around pairs (or pairs of pairs) of warp threads. A good-quality carpet may have as many as 400 or even more of these knots per square inch, though an excellent carpet need not have more than 100. The ends of the knots are cut evenly to constitute the pile of the carpet. In a fine carpet they are usually cut very close to the base. The design of the pile is composed by the use of different-colored wools for the knots. Each row of knots is held in place by the insertion of one or more weft threads, before the next row is added. In order to achieve the desired degree of tightness and evenness of weave and density of knots, after every few rows of knots the weavers beat the weft threads, and the pile, back toward them with a comblike implement, the teeth of which fit over the warp threads. This action also has the effect of making the pile incline permanently in one direction, toward the end the weaver started from. For this reason throughout the life of the carpet, light strikes the ends of the knots at a different angle according to the position of the viewer, and in the case of some qualities of wool (and especially of silk) makes the colors appear different from different angles.

For the tribal weaver, apart from the wood for the loom, which was a simple horizontal affair, all the materials could be generated locally, for the most part within the household. It was feasible for each family to provide all of its production needs. The typical Turkmen carpet until recently was made entirely of wool, except perhaps for a little cotton or silk to provide a color, often white, that was rare or difficult to achieve with their own karakul breed of sheep. The fact that the weaver, typically a daughter or wife, was closely associated in everyday life with the flock manager, typically the household head, was important. A good carpet required wool spun differently for three different purposes (warp, weft, and pile). A good warp is so fine and strong that the unaccustomed observer sometimes fails to recognize it as wool. The secret lies in the choice of the longer fibers from the fleece, in the carding as well as the spinning. For each purpose the weaver selects wool sheared at a particular season, from a particular part of animals of a particular age.

There is much in the technology of carpet weaving that is easier to organize on the level of the household than on higher, more complex levels, and independent household production encourages a particular type of identification with the product and symbolization of it. For example, weaving on a wool warp is tricky. The wool snaps easily under the tension that is necessary to allow efficient and even weaving and knotting. If the household must buy wool on the market, the weaver loses control of both the quality and the differentiation of fibers. In these conditions cotton, which is significantly easier to work with but must always be obtained from the market, eventually replaces home-grown wool in the warp. Again, working in her own environment, for herself and her family, the weaver reproduces the technology and design of her senior female relatives, and with occasional personal innovative touches produces a special rug – special because of the meaning imbued by the labor and the domestic context and relations of production. But can the Western consumer, far removed both socially and culturally, recognize and appreciate those differences? Should we recognize them? How do they affect *our* appreciation of the rug?

Not all stages of the technology were necessarily conditioned in this intimate social context. The dyeing was probably in most cases done on a larger scale, since even though many of the dyestuffs were gathered locally, outside the settlements and around the camps, the techniques were complex, and in dyeing at least there must always have been some economic benefit in working on a larger scale (see Holmyard 1958, Schneider 1978, 419).

Reds generally predominated, and may have been easier to produce, but since they were all from mordant dyes there was a wide range of shades.[3] Madder (*Rubia tinctorum*), which was the most common and must have been the cheapest, seems to have provided the widest range of color, from rusty brown to red, though not so brilliant a red as some insect products. Of these, the local kermes (from the female *Kermes ilicis*), although it had provided the Persian language with a word for red (*qermez*), seems not to have been used in any extant carpets. We know that cochineal (from the female *Dactylopius coccus*) was introduced early in the sixteenth century and was important in the nineteenth century. The Indian lac (*Coccus lacca*) is also found, but seems to have been displaced by cochineal. They are both sometimes found mixed with madder. Scarcely any details of the traditional dye process are on record. (See Wulff 1966, 189–94 for more detail and the best discussion of dyeing and of the technology of weaving in Iranian civilization generally; see also Farnie 1958, Forbes 1964.)

The dyeing process was the first part of the technology to undergo change as a result of factors of the world economy. The first synthetic dyes reached Persia early in the second half of the nineteenth century, but seem not to have entered western Turkestan or to have been used in Turkmen carpets. They were generally inferior to the natural dyes they replaced. A second generation, known as azodyes, which arrived after 1880, gave better results (Whiting 1978a, 1978b, 1980, 1981; see also *Oriental Rug Review*, vol. 3, nos. 7–8, 1983). It was inevitable that the chemical dyes would take over because they were easier to use and less time-consuming. But their success must have been clinched by the fact that dyeing was already out of the control of the domestic unit. It took time for them to filter down to the household end of the production spectrum. When they did, at the end of the century, they were often combined with vegetable dyes. Unlike vegetable dyes, they did of course cost money, and were better suited to commercial production or to household production that was financed from a market center. Presumably their assimilation must have been associated with some increase in the commoditization of the product.

The logistics of dyeing suggest that it was the thin end of the wedge in the final commercialization of carpet weaving. On a regional level, within different parts of western Asia and the Middle East, it is likely that this commercialization began slowly quite early in the history of the craft, and proceeded in fits and starts up to the modern period, when it provided a point of entry into the commercial backwater of central Asia for some of the more drastic influences of the modern world economy, driven in this case by the consumer interest that began in the West on a commercial scale in the last century. If this view is correct – and it has the attraction of helping to explain some other problems we must attend to, such as the history of carpet design – traditional carpet production must always have been spread out over a social continuum (with repercussions for the cultural tradition) from the isolated, self-sufficient nomadic or village group through the urban hinterland to the city-controlled production. In this century the hither end of this continuum has been spliced to the world economy, and the influences of that splicing are still spreading through the continuum.

It would be helpful to know more about the way carpet production fitted into the lives of weavers and producers on the one hand and into the commercial system on the other, before any significant change took place in the relations of production. What did it take to weave a carpet in terms of labor and time? Which parties took which decisions? In one of the few informative accounts by nineteenth-century travelers, O'Donovan (1882, 2, 352) describes a situation that is probably closer to the more market-oriented end of the time:

The female members of the family are mainly occupied in household duties. They do all the cooking and fetching of water, and the daughters for whom there is no other occupation occupy themselves in the manufacture of embroidered skull-caps, carpets, shirts, saddle-bags, and socks of variegated tints for the better classes. The silk and cotton robes worn by the men and women are made by special persons. The women manufacture their own garments, the cloth being purchased from the merchants at the bazaar. When a Turcoman is blessed with a large number of daughters, he contrives to realize a considerable sum per annum by the felt and other carpets which they make. In this case, an *ev* is set apart as a workshop, and three or four girls are usually occupied upon each carpet, sometimes for a couple of months.

Each girl generally manufactures two extra fine carpets, to form part of her dowry when she marries. When this has been done, she devotes herself to producing goods for the markets at Meshed and Bokhara, where the Turcoman carpets fetch a much higher price than those manufactured in Khorassan or beyond the Oxus. Sometimes these carpets are made partly of silk, brought from Bokhara. They are generally twice the size of the ordinary ones, which are made from sheep's wool and camel hair mingled with a little cotton, and are almost entirely of silk. They fetch enormous prices. I have known as much as fifty pounds given for one measuring eight feet square.

In the modern period, Irons (1980, 36) who worked among Yomut Turkmen in northeast Iran between the late 1960's and the mid-1970's, calculated that "one woman could weave roughly one square foot in a day of heavy weaving, about twelve hours at the loom." We know almost nothing about the other end of the continuum.

It is worth noting first that the passage from O'Donovan places carpet production plainly in the context of textile production generally. For the producers, carpets are a special form of textile, special locally because of the way they combine labor value and symbolic value, and (as the trade developed) because of their exchange value. This reminds us that the differentiation between floor and other furnishing is a relatively recent Western development, though it has now spread to most of the world. It seems to be only since the eighteenth century that our words "carpet" and "rug" have become specialized in the meaning of floor covering. It is likely that all our carpeting is derivative of oriental carpets (even though neither word is of oriental origin), and that before oriental carpets were available for the rich in the Middle Ages, and began to be simulated (first in 1755 at Axminster, which became in England a branch name standing, like Hoover, for the product) for the not quite so rich in the eighteenth century (see Fowler and Cornforth 1978, 213), Western floors were not covered. Axminster was followed by Wilton and Kidderminster in England, by Brussels, and later by other names in the United States. (The American products were less successful because of higher labor costs

– a fact that reminds us how much the success of oriental carpets owes to the availability of cheap labor. Urban carpet weaving in Iran's oil economy priced itself out of the international market in the 1970's.) Mechanization did not begin until the middle of the nineteenth century. Oriental carpets, when they first began to take on, appear (from paintings) to have been used to cover and decorate any flat surface, especially tables. In the past, Turkmen rugs were made for a wide range of local uses. There is a long catalog of local names for different types and sizes of carpet, as well as traditions of weaving. Functional types, for example, include door hangings, bags, and cushions, besides those that are for sitting on or for floor covering, though it is not always easy to distinguish function from other criteria.

As long as carpet production was a household activity, it enhanced the standing of the craftsmen who were the producers. There was a link between the social value of the carpet (as a valued item of furnishing) and the social status of the weaver. The status of women generally was relatively high in Turkmen society. Irons (1980, 35) relates how one Turkmen woman in northeastern Iran told his wife that the "ability to weave a carpet was like literacy. It is a skill acquired over many years, one that beginners cannot hope to master in a short time. Our ability to scan a page covered with small letters and produce words and sentences seemed as amazing to a Turkmen woman as her ability to weave an intricate pattern from memory seemed to us." Apart from increasing the income of the household, the women produced artifacts that were both functionally and symbolically important. It is understandable, therefore, that the designs may have acquired the type of restricted social reference that we would interpret as heraldic (see Moshkova and Morozova 1970). Closely related weavers worked with closely related designs. The designs became associated with the identity of the producers, and that identity was conceived in tribal or genealogical terms. In fact, it is not clear how explicit this quasi-heraldic meaning was, and it appears to have been exaggerated by Moshkova and other Western commentators (see David 1980). However, although there was plenty of variation, a general association between form and identity seems to have been recognized, at least until tribal identities were disrupted in the wake of Russian encroachment toward the end of the last century.

Whatever the extent of commercialization, carpets continued to be produced for domestic and personal purposes, especially for dowries. They were eminently storable and were stored for long periods. In some cases they were brought out only in order to be converted into cash in time of crisis, such as the drought of the early 1970's, by which time they had changed hands by inheritance and marriage and come to embody the biographies of their succession of owners as well as that of their producer. They provided the personal intimate furnishing of the producers' and owners' family life. In the nomads' camp they domesticated the ground they were spread on, provided a surface for the family meal, which symbolized the unity and integrity of the family, and a surface to pray on. Turkmen carpets probably even more than other tribal carpets and unlike the more famous and spectacular carpets produced under the Safavids in the sixteenth and seventeenth centuries, were therefore fraught with implicit meanings for the people who produced and lived with them.

In our appreciation of these carpets, we have been quick to see symbolic values, but we have seen them in the motifs and designs rather than in the production and functions. It is difficult enough to find or gather information about the symbolic dimension of their use, since there are barely any historical records and the social context has changed. It is almost impossible to study the symbolism of their design either historically or ethnographically, because the tradition was fully formed when it came into historical view. Not surprisingly, however, there is a considerable literature on it. Insofar as it is systematic, this literature is based on the comparison of forms and motifs from different cultural traditions, with little or no reference to their social context. Although this method has been all-important in our understanding of the great artistic traditions of the world, it is sometimes difficult to follow the logic of those who would apply it to folk traditions. In the case of carpets the evidence suggests that we are dealing with a poorly differentiated variety of urban, village, and nomadic products. The greatest source of confusion in the interpretation of the symbolism of oriental carpets may derive from this peculiarity – that the craft extended socially from isolated nomadic camps to royal palaces, and the motifs moved back and forth along that continuum, meaning different things in different social situations.

Most commentators focus on the recurrent similarities in the design of all oriental carpets – repeating designs cut off by border frames, stylized flowers and animals. Much is made of the evidence of the design and craftsmanship of the Pazyryk carpet, of the well-known animal style of the prehistoric steppe, and of the appearance of certain elements reminiscent of Chinese imagery. The repeating geometric and other patterns are interpreted as giving the appearance of a section of a larger whole framed by the borders, symbolizing the limitlessness of paradise. The animal motifs are simply referred to as "the animal style of the steppe" (Rostovtsev 1929), which is read as representing nomadic vitality, though the conjunction of the two styles in one craft tradition is left unexplained. Finally, a common origin of all carpet design is suggested in central Asia, whence the style would have diffused westward with the movement of the Turkmen in the train of the Seljuqs in the eleventh and twelfth centuries A.D. (see, for example, Denny, 1978, 1982, Mackie and Thompson 1980, Schurmann, 1969, Thacher, 1940, and Wagner 1976).[4]

I have consciously oversimplified this type of interpretation, perhaps to the point of caricature, in order to show on the one hand that it makes excellent sense of the evidence, while adding a mystical touch by the introduction of a link to the limitlessness of paradise; and on the other that it gives no consideration to the problem of how symbolic forms are generated or how they change (except perhaps to imply that we are dealing with *Homo orientalis*, who is by nature mystical and concerned with great religious ideas), or generally to the social context of the craft. I shall suggest later that this type of interpretation owes its success to the fact that it overtly earns our praise by being scholastic in an exemplary way while covertly serving an important need in our society: it makes us feel we are making headway in our quest for authenticity. I do not argue that it is wrong – necessarily; only that it is inadequate.

Since there are so few data for either social or cultural reconstruction, we are debating a question of approach rather than documentation. It is worth seeing to what extent a change in approach can help to incorporate more of the available data and demystify the interpretation. It has been suggested that the carpets preserved from the middle of the first millennium B.C. in the Altai had been brought from Persia. A large alabaster slab from the entrance of the Ashurbanipal Palace at Nineveh (on display in the British Museum) is carved in patterns closely comparable to those of the Pazyryk carpet. Khlopin (1982) has suggested evidence for carpet weaving in settled communities from a thousand years earlier in the same general area. From what we know of the cultures of nomadic populations we should not expect them to develop more complex technologies than nearby settled populations, but we should expect them to be closely related economically and demographically to those populations and to copy and adapt the technologies of settled communities to their own purposes. There is ample evidence to suggest that nomadic pastoralism throughout the Mediterranean, Mesopotamia, and central Asia is culturally derivative of settled life, both in origins and in continued interaction. Since there is no essential difference in design between the carpet production of settled and nomadic Turkmen communities, we can say that they both worked the same symbols, possibly with minor variations in form and probably with larger variations in meaning, in the same economic and cultural system, but in different social conditions. Although the cultural differences between nomadic and settled populations have probably been exaggerated, there is no doubt that they do differ markedly in one respect, their perception of nature. There is ample evidence that although nomads share symbols with nearby settled populations, they differ in their understanding and use of them (Spooner 1973, 35–40).

In the Iranian tradition "paradise" and "garden" are not clearly differentiated. A "pardis" (from which "paradise" comes to us through Greek) was not originally a religious concept, but a type of royal park, a walled enclosure within which nature was to a certain extent brought under human control. The king, like royalty elsewhere and especially in Asia, wished to hunt. But he wanted the experience without too much trouble or discomfort. In the Iranian tradition generally there is a desire for intimacy with nature, fresh air, light, open spaces, but a distaste and apprehension for nature in the raw, without protection from the threat of the elements. In the wilderness, devoid of the comforts of settled life, where nature was uncontrolled, only nomads lived, and nomads symbolized insecurity, social disorder, and lack of political control – the absence of civilization (cf. Hanaway 1971, 1976).

Symbolic traditions are easy to recognize but notoriously difficult to interpret. The Sufi tradition (the mystical tradition in Islam) provides an excellent comparative example of the problem of interpreting imagery, because of the sexual and emotional ambiguity in its use of imagery for love and loving. Similar ambiguity has misled Western interpreters of carpet and design who are hungry for "pure" symbols and reluctant to see ordinary gardens reduced by the constraints of the medium to a rigorous overstylized simplicity. But there is a relationship in the symbolic dimension between different types of gardens and the idea of paradise. We know that at the Sassanian court (third to seventh centuries A.D.) there were large, spectacular carpets that represented gardens. We have noted that the word paradise derives from the pre-Islamic Persian for a special type of royal garden. Most of the individual motifs that appear in the carpets have a place in a Persian garden, because in Iranian civilization (which provided the great tradition for central Asia as well as the Iranian plateau and farther west) a garden (of which the ideal was a royal garden) was a place to live. A house should ideally be in a garden, and the ideal design for the furnishing of a house would be a garden design. The court carpets have magnificent figurative gardens.

Of course, not all carpet motifs even among the Turkmen are derived from concepts of gardens. Gardens appear to have been a particularly important source of design. But it is easy to see the influence of a number of other crafts and ornamentation from other media. The most noteworthy other crafts are jewelry and lanterns, and there are abundant examples of influence from the design traditions of tilework, pottery, and metalwork, and the decoration and form of the *mihrab* (prayer niche) of the mosque. The Turkmen had silversmiths, and the city of Bukhara, an important market center for them, had a major tile industry (Eiland 1980, Mackie and Thompson 1980, 21). Apart from the garden, which could have been a local folk interpretation of a royal tradition of design, women's jewelry seems understandably to have been the most fertile source of motifs in Turkmen tribal weaving. But in every case the motifs take on a life of their own. They generate their own dynamic and live independently of whatever originally inspired them. If the meaning of these symbols to the weavers who weave them in carpets today is inauthentic in any meaningful sense, the same was most likely true for all the best carpet weaving.

Central Asia was part of Iranian civilization throughout the medieval period. The cities of central Asia were basically Iranian cities. Turkmen society comprised nomadic pastoralists and settled cultivators as well as urban traders and merchants. It is not clear at any stage of the historical process what proportion of carpets were woven by nomads or what proportion were financed by merchants or political centers. Even the nomadic Turkmen were heavily Persianized. It is not surprising, therefore, that Turkmen carpets have simple stylized gardens with geometric motifs, which they call (generically) by the Persian word for flower. The only essential design difference between carpets of different functions is that, for example, prayer rugs and door hangings are unidirectional rather than symmetrical, but the underlying design still derives from the garden concept. In the great tradition of urban life the concept of paradise was always present. But the unlettered did not necessarily have such elaborate conceptions of paradise. They understood the stylization and simplification of nature in a Persian garden, and represented flowers more than anything else in their designs. Different tribal groups represented them differently, as they spoke with different dialects.

In Turkmen rug weaving, therefore, there seems to have been a social-technological continuum from the market center, through the village, to the nomad camp; and a cultural-symbolic continuum from the Iranian royal courts, through the agricultural to the nomadic world view. Wherever patronage was exerted, as it was in the major centers of central Asia, especially Bukhara, the designs became more elaborate, modified and rationalized by the lettered elite.[5] The almost figurative "flowers" of a type of Turkmen carpet known as Beshir (which, significantly, is a local rather than a tribal term) may be the result of greater patronage in more permanent communities (cf. König 1980, 201, Pinner 1981, Vasil'eva 1979, 560). But in the central Asian interior, the tribal ideology was always independent of the city, and even the most expansive urban patronage could not develop there the magnificence of the famous Persian royal carpets or expropriate the symbolism of the craft. When the tribal organization was disrupted by Russian encroachment and domination toward the end of the nineteenth century, the relationship between the carpets and their social context also broke down. The eclecticism of the forms that have developed since that time have obliged the critics, according to their own Western terms of reference, to withhold from them the insignia of authenticity.

The commoditization of carpets

Although oriental carpets became known in parts of Europe at least seven centuries ago, little was known about their production or the economics of their supply until much later. At this early stage of the trade they were seen as a special type of textile rather than a separate product. However, carpets were from the beginning something of an anomaly in the textile trade. For example, in the later medieval period a relatively close economic relationship grew up between Anatolia and Italy, which makes it often difficult to tell on which side of the politico-religious divide a particular textile was produced, but this problem never arose in the case of pile carpets. The carpet trade is in this sense reminiscent of the silk trade in the ancient world: probably no other exotic craft has been so successful for so long. The carpet trade has an added peculiarity: no other trade has been so marked by lack of communication between producer in one area and consumer elsewhere.

The modern trade took shape toward the end of the eighteenth century.[6] Carpets began to move in bulk along a chain of economic connections in which major focal points were Bukhara, Istanbul, and (later) London. Wholesalers began to classify the merchandise for their own purposes – which combined criteria of commercial provenience (where they entered the market, rather than where they were woven) and saleability. The development and application of these criteria generated a lore, which despite later accretions from art history (mainly Islamic, but also Chinese), the notes of travelers, and a very little professional ethnography, still informs the literature on carpets.

As the Western experience of carpets has evolved, the nature of the carpet itself, as well as of the trade, has steadily changed, and lately at an increasing rate. The relationship between weavers and dealers, and between producers and consumers, is now much closer, largely as a result of changes in the political economy at both ends. But this closeness has brought in train its own particular problems of understanding and communication. There is now a conscious effort on the part of the producer to cater to the Western market. This effort is only partly successful economically, and it might be argued that success is only complicating the communication problem. The reasons for this complication are, once again, social. They have to do both with social needs within each society and with perceived inferiority and superiority between societies, as these perceptions affect cultural borrowing and the communication and diffusion of ideas and symbols. They need to be addressed, therefore, against the background of our experience of chinoiserie, japonisme, and orientalism generally.

Our interest in oriental carpets and our imitation and assimilation of their designs is analogous to the process that produced chinoiserie, the imitation of Chinese designs in the eighteenth century (Jourdain and Jenyns 1950). As an economic process it is more specialized, because of the focus on one specific commodity, the carpet, which continued to be produced exclusively by Turkmen. But culturally it has supplied an infectious series of motifs that now pervades our lives. The analogy with chinoiserie, however, may help to explain the increasing Turkmen interest in adapting their product for the Western market, and the effect of their efforts on our attempts to satisfy our desire for authenticity.

Most of what we know about the Turkmen and their carpets dates from the point when Russian expansion began to interfere with their political independence, disrupting their tribal life.[7] Of the eight major tribes into which they were divided at the time, the Salor (who were generally recognized to be descended from the senior line and were major carpet producers) suffered a major defeat at the hands of the Qajar dynasty of Iran in 1831 at Sarakhs, which now lies at the northeast corner of Iran's border with Soviet Turkmenistan. The Yomut lost Khiva to the Russians in 1871. The Tekke lost their best territory (Akhal, well-known as the name of a type of Yomut carpet; see Koenig 1962) to the Russians in a series of battles culminating at Geok Tepe in 1881. Marw (now transliterated into English from the Russian as

"Mary"), their capital, from which the present Mauri designation of carpets derives, was lost in the same way in 1884. Since about 1870 the Turkmen have been negotiating, with only occasional respite, with the Russians on one side and the Afghans and Iranians on the other, while the Afghans and the Iranians responded in turn to pressures from both the Russians and British.

Unfortunately, so far as I can ascertain, neither the social history nor the carpet history of this period has been studied in any detail (even locally in Soviet Turkmenistan).[8] But certain important points seem clear. As a result of the upheaval and social disruption following on the Russian encroachment, large numbers of carpets found their way north into Russia. The Turkmen themselves became gradually more commercially oriented, but directed their attention southward. Most of the nomads gradually settled (which was not difficult because most of them had probably been nomadic mainly in order to avoid political domination, rather than in order to ensure access to the best grazing) (see Irons 1975). Settlement brought with it an increasing tendency to identify with a spatial community rather than the tribe, and tribal identities began to lose some of their significance. Later, in the 1920s, during the Sovietization of Soviet Turkmenistan, many Turkmen moved south across the border into northern Afghanistan, into country that had been depopulated by earlier hostilities (N. Tapper 1983, 233–4).

The impact of this century of political and social upheaval on the everyday life of the Turkmen, which involved for many people a long series of household and family dislocations, endangered the continuity of Turkmen carpet weaving. In most communities it appears to have ceased altogether by the end of the 1930's. It was only with the improvement of political and economic trends after the Second World War that the tradition was gradually rescued and revivified, especially in the 1960's – in government factories on the Soviet side, and in a few small villages on the Afghan side. The organization of production of Soviet factories emphasizes quantity rather than quality and compares only with the relatively cheap end of the scale of production across the border. A few Turkmen communities in northwestern Afghanistan have rebuilt their family traditions and developed a fine-quality cottage industry (which may, however, not survive the current renewed upheavals). Some of these have settled in the city of Herat and benefited from the existence of the established carpet industry, which belongs to the Persian urban tradition. Finally, possibly taking a cue from the Soviet factories, some wealthy Turkmen merchants began in the 1960s to establish small factories in northern Afghanistan that employed men and children to weave cheap carpets specifically for the Western market, seeking where possible direct contracts with Western dealers. The movement soon spread to the capital, Kabul. After what we know as the Sahelian drought, which although it did not make the news was equally devastating in west-central Afghanistan, enterprising Turkmen began to hire orphans and refugees and train them to weave. Whatever the political future of Afghanistan, it is likely that these factories will expand, because it is unlikely that present social trends toward modernization will be reversed. It is interesting that the drought had the effect not only of flushing out long-stored heirlooms, sold to help people through the crisis, but of increasing the production of poor-quality carpets.

This final establishment of an almost direct link between producer and consumer, though it is still insecure and at the lower end of the market, was the logical outcome of a process that had started centuries before. Traders had obviously penetrated Turkmen society early on. As early as the thirteenth century an Arab geographer, Ibn Sa'id, was able to write that Turkmen carpets were being exported to all countries (see Barthold 1962 [1929], 130, who considers that although the reference is to Turkmen in Asia Minor, they must have brought the craft with them from central Asia). This information suggests strongly that, although nothing can be dated earlier than the eighteenth century at the earliest with any certainty (Thompson 1980), Turkmen carpets derive from a tradition that goes back at least as far as the eleventh century, when they, along with the Turkmen, made their entry into Middle Eastern and Islamic history. We have already argued that the tradition is neither socially nor economically homogeneous, for it represents the products of nomadic camps, isolated settlements, villages closer to the market centers, and probably also of production units inside the cities. Each of these social types of production unit, although culturally closely related and accustomed to using the same motifs, was presumably infiltrated to a different extent by traders and merchants who would therefore be able to exert different degrees of influence on the nature and quality of the final product.

Exactly the same situation obtains today. But modern carpets, however fine the weaving, are immediately distinguishable from the antiques from, say, before the battle of Geok Tepe, because the designs and certain other features, though still recognizably Turkmen, have changed. Whatever the relationship between design and tribal identity then, today's weaver or designer is presumably no longer reworking the old motifs according to ideas of what they should look like based on an appreciation of old carpets produced in the same social group.

Rather, they are modifying the motifs they happen to know in ways they calculate will please people who are buying for foreign markets (cf. Silver 1981). This change of orientation has led to very obvious changes in modal size of rug, in size and combination of motifs, and in choice of colors. Today's total production may well include basically the same range of quality as always. The changes are in the distribution within that range and in the relationship between weaver and dealer. Many more medium- and low-quality carpets are being produced directly for the market, because not only has Turkmen society been entirely reorganized, but more significant, the pattern of patronage and financing of carpet production, which must always have affected the majority of the carpets that were exported, has been transformed as a function of the transformation of the world economic order from the rise of colonialism to the onset of modernization. The most obvious differences between old and new rugs lie in the loss of constraints from old tribal or local associations on innovation in design. It is this evolution that underlies the major question of authenticity, to which we shall return in the final sections of this chapter. For these and other reasons there have been complex changes in the terms of trade. These changes now involve competition between new carpets (which must be priced to pay for labor and materials) and old, and in the West between both and machine-made floor covering. This pricing problem has been complicated by the return to the use of silk (a more expensive material than wool but easier to use for the warp) and to factory production, which increases quantity over quality. However, these technical changes are not necessarily innovations, since some type of factory production of hand-woven carpets and greater use of silk appear to have been known in earlier periods.

These obviously social and economic changes can be reconstructed with relative certainty despite the lack of historical detail. But what about the changes in design? What was the relationship between the weaver and the motifs she (mainly at home) wove and he (in the factory) weaves? Has it changed? If so, is the change a function of the changes in social context? Did motifs generally have the same meaning for the weaver, the designer (who presumably could have been the weaver or somebody socially close or distant who financed the materials and perhaps also the labor), the consumer, and later critic? If the design was originally worked out on the philosophical level of, say, a conception of paradise in tune with symbols from either the Chinese or the Islamic tradition, or both, would the unlettered weaver have understood it as such? Assuming that different weavers wove at different removes (cultural as well as social) from any rationalized theology, what held the tradition together, facilitated its continued coherence and identity over so many centuries?

To recapitulate what we have argued so far in answer to these questions, Turkmen society has for the last thousand years included a socially diverse population from urban market to nomad camp: it was at once commercial, agricultural, and pastoral; tribal and peasant; nomadic and settled. Some parts of Turkmen society were even ethnically diverse (Irons 1975). In a single society, however ethnically diverse, all think in basically the same concepts, the same vocabulary of words and visual symbols. But social diversity meant that people interpreted these symbols differently, according to social and personal differences, *especially* – to give an extreme example – insofar as the nomads' distinctive conception of nature and space would lead them to put their thoughts together differently, and manipulate symbols differently from villagers or city-dwellers. These conditions produce a range of different uses of recognizably related symbols, which must have varied throughout the history of Turkmen weaving. But the evolving market integrated these symbols by collecting them together into a single market genre.

In the Western world ruggism seems to have been born in the same generation that produced the machine-made carpet. This development may not surprise us, but it suggests that until that time Western interest in the oriental carpet was primarily in the design, rather than the handicraft, and that this emphasis changed when native handicraft gave way to the industrial revolution. Once started it expanded fast, leading to the rise of the issue of authenticity. Mumford (1900) writes of thousands of rugs with Bukhara patterns being shipped to the United States each year. Although the handmade Axminsters and others had opened a market in the middle of the eighteenth century, presumably providing for the first time in the West a fabric especially designed for covering floors, it was only a century later (with the invention of the mechanical Jacquard loom) that carpets became a commodity on a scale available to all who could pay. The new market was soon stratified. The collectors stood at the top and, in complex combination with the dealers on whom they depended for their acquisitions, set the values that led the market. Illustration of their values may be seen in Bogolubow 1908-9, Martin 1908, Pope 1926, Sarre and Trenkwald 1926-9, and Society for Textile Art Research 1983. Those values have not been constant. The market is still hierarchical, led by antiques, among which antique Turkmens hold a high place. But the room at the top has continuously expanded, especially since the 1950's. The most recent additions to the respectable collector's repertoire are various types of tribal rug from Iran and Afghanistan, which received no attention twenty years ago. The Baluchis and the south Persian tribal rugs are two examples. The justification for including for the first time these exclusively rustic productions has to be quite different from that which applies to the classic Turkmens. Is it simply that since there is more room at the top of modern society, the hierarchy of goods had to be reorganized, in order to provide enough top *objets* for the top people?

The authentication of commodities

Having reviewed the evidence on the significance of carpets in Turkmen life generally and in selected sectors of Western society, we can return to the question of how we determine their authenticity. The discussion so far suggests that we are faced with not one but two related questions: (1) What in fact is authenticity? and (2) Why is it so important to some of us?

On the elusiveness of authenticity

Have our standards of authenticity changed? Why are we interested in a wider range of carpets now than before? Could it be simply that our knowledge has increased? Or do we perhaps not really know objectively what we are looking for?

Although it would seem that certain objective material attributes are involved in the definition of authenticity, authenticity cannot be explained by reference to them alone. It also involves subjective interpretations. But there are still more questions. How do we explain the choice of objective attributes (since they cannot be explained as criteria of quality)? And given that each person in search of authenticity does not make his or her determination in isolation from everyone else, what is the social mechanism by which the value of different interpretations of authenticity is negotiated and renegotiated over time? We now have four basic questions, which concern (1) the objective attributes of authenticity in oriental carpets; (2) our subjective assessment of those attributes; (3) the shared cultural choice of what to look for authenticity in (why, that is, do we care about carpets at all?); and (4) the social mechanism of the negotiation of authenticity, in which we all to some extent participate. The interrelation of the answers to these questions presents us with a Kantian dilemma: If the criteria, the choice, and the negotiation are genuinely independent, how do they coincide? This type of dilemma underlies all anthropology. As a step toward resolving it in this case, I shall try to illuminate each question in turn, taking what guidance I can from Kant and his commentators.

We can pick up here the argument that was introduced at the beginning of the second section of this chapter. The same fourfold framework of experience – natural, social, cultural, and technological – that conditions the production of the individual weavers also conditions the reception of their products. To begin with, the physical and material world provides the basis, the context, and the means of human experience, and we look for authenticity in material objects according to objective attributes. However, the material world does not have clearcut distinctions and definitions – these come from our conceptualization and ratiocination. Our application of the criteria of authenticity is therefore complex and depends on negotiation among ourselves. Since social situations are always to some extent in flux, this negotiation is unending. Furthermore, beyond their immediate physical needs, people generally decide what they want according to cultural (that is, shared) values, which are historically given but socially renegotiable. Where several values are relevant to a particular situation, it may be necessary to choose among them or to give precedence to one over others. Such choice or ordering is also subject to social negotiation. Both values and choices are affected by natural and economic factors of supply, and by the historical continuity of experience. But natural, economic, cultural, and social processes all unfold historically according to their own dynamic. The technology of weaving, as a tradition of praxis, also has its own dynamic. A satisfactory treatment of the question of authenticity must interrelate these various dynamics, in order to arrive at a definition that is not simply either a social or a cultural fiction, relative and unreal, but part of our continual process of compromise between the various dimensions – psychological, cultural, social, technological, and natural – of our experience.

The objective attributes: Let us begin with a review of the objective attributes. The idea that an authentic carpet is essentially one in which the weaver was living her symbols in her weaving will not stand the test of either historical or cultural analysis. We have no good reason to believe that there ever was a Golden Age when Turkmen culture was an integrated systemic whole, within which noble tribeswomen conscientiously worked out their religious problems in their daily craft. In the products available to us it is easy to show, for example, that neither age nor the number of knots per square inch is necessarily

consonant with quality or a reliable guide to authenticity; that vegetable dyes are often not distinguishable visually from chemical dyes,
and until recently were not even reliably distinguishable by chemical
analysis (Whiting 1978), nor are they faster; that the values we attribute to provenience have changed and are likely to change again.
Our interest in handicraft probably began at a certain stage of our
industrial revolution. Until the mechanization of carpet weaving in
the West in the mid-nineteenth century, oriental carpets seem to have
been important more as an exotic textile for which (until Axminster)
there was no Western equivalent, and (once they were culturally assimilated and recognized as exotic) valued for their design, rather
than for their utility. From that time on, however, the fact of their
being hand-made became a significant characteristic, and as the craft
was gradually drawn into the world economy the survival of traditional
relations of production became an additional factor – the rug was an
exotic product made in its own exotic production process for its own
exotic purpose. These two factors made the oriental carpet irreducibly
different from any Western product, and both began to be associated,
if not identified, with age as a tangible measure of authenticity. The
minimal criteria of authenticity are objective and reasonably explicit,
but we easily fall into a habit of reducing then glibly to something
less tangible, and relative. For example, we slip from age to relative
age. At the same time, we elaborate some criteria over others. For
example, age becomes antiquity and bestows an aura on the chosen
object (cf. Benjamin 1969, 221; Shils 1981, 75).

The subjective criteria: All these attributes have to do with distance,
especially the interpretation of cultural distance over space and time
from one social situation to another (see Benjamin 1969, 222). Any
reduction in that distance threatens authenticity. As early as 1908, in
a classic work on "Oriental Carpets before 1800," the Swedish scholar
F. R. Martin provides an interesting example. He wrote that Kirman
carpets

often accommodated to European taste. Anyone who has devoted some attention to carpets knows that the Kirman carpets are the most firmly knotted,
and in technique the very best now made in Persia. It is very unlikely that
the European demand has created this superior technique; in fact it has
existed from days of yore, and become so firmly grafted that not even the
Europeans have succeeded in destroying it, since its basis is the excellent wool
and the custom of the inhabitants, inherited from their ancestors, of producing good and lasting work. In these mountain regions they have not yet
learnt that 'Time is money!' (1908, 76.)

In fact, of course, if oriental carpets were out of tune with European taste, Europeans would not be so interested in them. What does it then mean that influential writers considered that by the beginning of this century (and even earlier) some producers were "accommodating to European taste?" Obviously, the writer is making a distinction between his own taste and the taste of others who are unfamiliar with traditional designs. As long as his claim to be a master of taste is accepted, he can use it to reinforce his social position (see Canclini 1979). But apart from its elitism, the statement implies that authenticity is considered (1) to be a measure of quality; (2) to require special knowledge to recognize; (3) to reside not in the carpet itself but in the relationship between carpet and weaver; and (4) likely to become rarer as time goes by. However, if authenticity lies in cultural distance, how is that distance determined, and why should the distance be as important as the objective attributes?

The cultural choice: Although there are objective criteria for authenticity, and a major mark of those criteria is cultural distance, nevertheless we look for authenticity according to *our* cultural concepts, not *theirs*. Authenticity is our cultural choice.

Western societies have a longstanding cultural interest in the Other. Something comparable may be common to all societies. Even in the West this interest takes many forms, our interest in carpets being one. The search for difference is a familiar feature of our intellectual and artistic traditions, dating from long before authenticity became the type of issue it is now. Both classicism and romanticism are characterized by rejection of the commonplace. Orientalizing, in one form or another, began in Greek pottery, continued in the Roman taste for textiles, and was renewed with the experience of the Crusades. Orientalist scholarship, the beginning of *academic* interest in the Other (of which the Orient was still almost our only example), was institutionalized in universities in the seventeenth century. However, something new happened when this same interest, through the stimulation afforded by economic expansion, give rise to the chinoiserie of the eighteenth century, and later (helped by the opening of Japan in 1860) to japonisme. Even before the effects of the industrial revolution began to be felt, the quantities of exotic decorative commodities had increased unprecedentedly (Honour 1961, Impey 1977, Wichman 1981).

Another change came with Western commercial expansion beyond Asia into Africa and the Pacific. New non-literate Others swarmed into our consciousness in the second half of the last century. Our responses included anthropology in academia and primitivism in art. Primitivism (Goldwater 1938) was yet another incarnation of romanticism, responding to a different Other because our relationship with the rest of the world had changed. Similarly, the differences between primitivism and romanticism in art are illuminated by consideration of the fact that in the meantime our society had changed.

Given the fact that the nature of our society, and of our ideas generally, changed radically over this period, it is noteworthy that our interest in difference was strangely consistent. Only the nature of this interest changed. A significant feature in that social change was the rise of the issue of authenticity. In the sixteenth century the word meant sincerity. By the end of the nineteenth century it had taken on its modern meaning, but had still not become the issue it is today (Trilling 1971). Toward the end of the nineteenth century, the academic discipline of anthropology became established in our universities, and along with psychoanalysis led the scientific search for authenticity, beyond our social boundaries and within ourselves (Foucault 1973, 373–85).

Along with these changes came the rise of commodities, and gradually the production of meaning in Western society became thoroughly bound up with commodity consumption (Brenkman 1979, 103). But because of their interest in cultural distance, anthropologists were slow to take an interest in the meaning of commodities. As a product of our own society, commodities were left to economists, who naturally took them simply at their exchangeable (supposedly) face value. It was of course not long before their social values were illuminated, beginning most significantly with the work of Marx. But it was left to the semioticians to reintroduce us to the grossly neglected symbolic values of commoditized products, and to show us how essential these values are. The position is particularly well stated by Rossi-Landi (1973, 626), who starting from Marx, shows how essentially resingularizable the average commodity is:

A commodity does not go to the market by itself; it needs somebody to sell it; and it is not sold until somebody buys it, that is, accepts it in exchange for money (or for other commodities in the case of barter). A product does not transform itself into a commodity like a caterpillar into a butterfly; it undergoes such a transformation because there are men who put it into significant relations. And when a commodity is used to satisfy a need, this means that its character as a commodity is, so to say, dropped, forgotten.

Carpets provide an excellent example of an alien utilitarian commodity that is simultaneously a complex message in the Western world. The authentic carpet combines within itself the properties of utility, commodity, and exotic meaning. How do we differentiate among such commodities? Obviously age, or at least continuity of the tradition of production, is an important factor. We differentiate according to values that we realize in the past, in this case the commodity's past, because we have a social need for order and we see more order in the past than in the present. It is easier for us to impose order on the past, though in fact that order has to be continually renegotiated among all who have an interest in it (Appadurai 1981).

The social mechanism: The process of differentiation, which is similarly never once-and-for-all, makes sense if we see it as a continuous process of negotiation in a social arena that is poorly defined, and for social objectives about which we are very vague. We use our own concepts to identify points of cultural interest in the Other society and then negotiate the extent of that interest according to our own social positions. In working out ways of distinguishing between different carpets and choosing some over others, we make social statements about how we see ourselves, and by implication how we see others who choose differently.

However, both our values and our choices are affected by the supply of carpets. Over the last hundred years the supply of rugs, the range of rugs traded, and the number of collectors has increased at an accelerating rate. As the material and social context of our interest changes we have to make choices continually in such a way that we maintain continuity of identity, or as Peckham calls it, "persona stability" (1979, 253–4).

Authenticity is a conceptualization of elusive, inadequately defined, other cultural, socially ordered genuineness. Because of our social expansion recently we have been needing more and more of it, and it has been necessary to alter our criteria in order to be able to continue to satisfy our needs. How does this come about? The problem is similar to that faced by those who would understand the processing of fads and fashions in what have come to be called the culture industries (for example, the book, record, and film industries). These studies use the concept of gatekeepers to describe the social concentration of decision making in relation to significant changes (see, for example, Hirsch 1972). Although much of this chapter has been devoted to showing how different the relationship between carpet producer and consumer is from the situation in such industries, nevertheless there is a comparable social concentration of dealers and collectors whose relatively heavy investment gives them the power and the will to lead opinion and manage the shifting secrets of authenticity for others.

The need for authenticity

If it is true that no combination of objective criteria can explain our concern with authenticity, we must look at ourselves and inquire why we need it anyway. It appears that the concept of authenticity belongs to industrial (even more to "postindustrial") society – not because of the direct social implications of industrial technology, but because of the concomitant social scale and the plethora of objects and categories of objects that it generates for our consumption, and, more significant, the cultural processes that those objects engender. If this interpretation is valid, then authenticity (as we understand it now) became an issue at a particular stage in our social evolution – when with the appearance of mechanically produced clone-commodities we began to distinguish between the social meaning of handicraft and that of mechanical production, as well as between uniqueness and easy replaceability. This process had been discussed from different points of view by Benjamin (1969), Berman (1970), MacCannell (1976), and, Trilling (1971), among others. As one aspect of this process authenticity became the watchword of Existentialism (Barrett 1958). Authenticity is a form of cultural discrimination projected onto objects. But it does not in fact inhere in the object but derives from our concern with it. In seeking authenticity people are able to use commodities to express themselves and fix points of security and order in an amorphous modern society. But the evolving relationship between the search for personal authenticity inside and the search for authenticity in carefully selected things outside has received relatively little attention. Perhaps, although we know all about fetishism, we are still inadequately aware of the range and variety and mechanics of many fetishistic processes in modern society (Douglas and Isherwood 1978).

Authenticity operates in an arena constituted by (1) supply, and (2) Western concepts concerning the Other – an arena constituted by the intersection of the social and cultural dimensions of our lives. It has become an issue more and more in modern life because of our social experience of ever-increasing complexity. Complexity lies in the numbers and types of interaction we have to enter into in a society that not only steadily grows in size but adds new media of interaction – face-to-face, bureaucratic, electronic. As complexity increases, the social order becomes less constraining. There is more need for choice, and the individual's need for self-expression is given full rein. But individuality is expressed through choice in the material world, but the use of objects to make personal statements, to say something about who one is in relation to others. Authenticity, though stated in terms of objects, bears implications about the person. Turkmen (and other oriental) carpets (among other things) are used to negotiate not just relative social status, but quality of personality, or how one should be understood and appreciated as an individual by others, and on a scale that has significance only for the individual's sense of social identity, not for the structure of the society as a whole.

Western society is the extreme example of a complex society, unique of its type. It is leading the information race and setting its cultural stamp on it, so that as more and more parts of the world are caught up in the information network of modern Western society, they become cultural appendages to it. Authenticity would be determined differently in a different culture, but we should expect it to become an issue of this type (as distinct from the type of issue it may be in a socially less complex society, such as the Turkmen) in any human situation that reached this stage of social complexity. We tend to forget that cultural evolution is an entirely different process from social evolution and is not directly linked to social complexity (Wallace 1961). Culture develops in traditions that can theoretically be unlimited in number, whereas forms of social life are directly related if not to numbers of people then to quantities of interactions and are based on a limited number of basic patterns of relations. In our attempts to understand human experience, therefore, we are confronted by a seemingly infinite cultural diversity and relatively much less, and limited, social diversity.

Our concept of authenticity facilitates our working out and working up our individualism in our everyday lives. It is integral to the cultural dimension of our multidimensional experience, of which natural resources, economic supply, numbers of people, and structures of social interaction are the most immediate other dimensions. But as Kant (once again) argued, our lives unfold as a continuous dialectic between our sociability and our selfishness, or the conflict between our need to belong and feel secure and our need to express our individuality. Society, operating within a particular cultural framework, provides the necessary order, but at the cost of inhibiting the self-expression. There is always some room for maneuver. The maneuvers generate a dialectical process between each individual's conflicting needs to belong to something securely ordered on the one hand and to be free to self-express on the other. Both these drives are evident in our concern for authenticity, though because of the complex and shifting forms of modern society, the latter drive is generally the more evident. The answer to the question of why we need authenticity, therefore, lies in our social evolution.

Compare us with the Turkmen, in relation to their carpets. An oriental carpet is something we not only use, but enjoy and take pride in. The same is true, of course, for the Turkmen. But the Turkmen are not concerned with authenticity in their carpets – primarily, because, I suggest, they are socially different from us. Although Turkmen society has diversified in the recent past, it is still nowhere near so diverse as Western society. What is true about carpets for Turkmen is true for all Turkmen. But what is true about carpets for us is true for only some of us, those of us who have chosen to take an interest in them. The reasons why some of us have taken this interest and not others are social rather than cultural. When Turkmen do things for social reasons they are concerned with playing out their identity within a particular subgrouping of Turkmen society. Because of the complexity of Western society our reasons have to do more with personal rather than group identity – more so now than a hundred or even fifty years ago. These reasons may still have to do to some extent with what group or (more likely) category of people we wish to be identified with in our society, but, more than that, they derive from our desire to express our individual selves distinctively in relation to the others among that group or category.

There is another side to this story. Authenticity is also needed by the Turkmen, but in different ways because of their different social condition (cf. Douglas 1978). At the same time they are affected by our search for authenticity in their production. It is noteworthy that we tend to search for authenticity in economically dependent societies. Is there a relationship between the processes of (a) cultural use of alien forms and (b) social dominance? Perhaps the greater the dependence of the other society, the more desperate our quest in it for authenticity. Authenticity is elusive because it is projected not only outside ourselves, but outside our social selves, outside our society, in the same way that the totemic tribal fixes his identity in the tribe by symbolic reference to something outside in nature. The concept is a product of interaction between us (dominant) and them (dependent) and becomes more important as the gap grows, partly because as the gap grows we appropriate more and more of the symbolic dimension of life in the other society, and inhibit the indigenous symbolization that would generate the authenticity we seek. It is in the nature of things, therefore, that our search for authenticity is continually frustrated by the people among whom we seek it. The more we reveal our need for authenticity to the Turkmen, the more they frustrate our search by adapting their wares in ways they imagine should please us.[9]

How did the changes in the importing society – the accelerating increase in social complexity in the West and the emergence of the concept of authenticity – affect the Turkmen? We have no means of knowing how early some Turkmen (financiers/producers at this stage, rather than household weavers) became conscious that more than a negligible amount of Turkmen carpet production was being syphoned off by the external economy, and consequently began to be interested in producing carpets for export. On a small scale it must have been much earlier than the last century. Since that time they must have begun to formulate ideas about the tastes of their potential customers and to modify their production accordingly.

How did the Turkmen weaver and carpet producer begin to conceive of those Others who were interested in their production? Unfortunately, we can only guess. But it is helpful to remember that there is a tendency for all people to conceive of Others – if only as part of a cognitive process of sharpening their conception of themselves – and to conceive of them as essentially and distinctively different from themselves, rather than trying to work out what they really are like as an internally coherent other way of life. We should expect that the Turkmen would grossly oversimplify in their efforts to conceive of us and our needs, as we do in relation to them (Ben-Amos 1976, Southall 1961, 29). We naturally form stereotypes of each other, and the Turkmen application of these stereotypes leads to discordances in carpet design that both frustrate and fuel our search for authenticity.

The Turkmen have quite naturally developed first an interest in our tastes, leading to an oversimplified conception of them: each element of their conception is constructed in distinction from elements in their own taste, rather than as a coherent whole. This type of process in the art of the Fourth World generally has been addressed by Graburn (1969, 1976, 1982) under the heading of tourist arts, and by Kubler (1961) for the fate of the native art forms of Mesoamerica. Most modern Turkmen carpets, certainly the best ones, do not in fact suffer from quite the same problems (in our Western view) of juxtaposition of inconsonant elements that are familiar to us under the heading of tourist art – perhaps because Turkmen society in Afghanistan (the basic source of Turkmen carpets since the 1950s) has not yet disintegrated socially to quite the extent of the people who produce "airport arts." But the same sort of thing is evident in Turkmen carpets, more than enough to justify our search for the real thing. Meanwhile, the Afghan teenager in the new urban middle class seeks authentic American jeans and alligator (Izod) polo shirts (Newcomer 1974). While we seek authenticity in their past (as well as in our own), they seek it in our present.

The Western interest in Turkmen carpets has had the effect of alienating the Turkmen from their own forms of artistic expression. Before, they worked with designs embodying symbols that were for them extensions of their own social identity. They did not understand these symbols or need to know their origins. Now, these symbols have become the property of others. To repossess them they must now find out from others what they mean. They are concerned only with how they will look to others. In the words of another branch of the literature, on nationalism, the Turkmen have chosen epochalism ("The Spirit of the Age") and lost essentialism ("The Indigenous Way of Life"; Geertz 1973, 240-52), or they have taken universalism and abandoned nationalism (Bahnassi 1979).

The process is the cultural dimension of the condition of dependency formulated by neo-Marxists to explain the economic state of the Fourth World. It demonstrates that we are not alone in our experience of the problem of authenticity. But whereas for us authenticity is something we search for as individuals, for the Turkmen it is a larger cultural process, in which the stakes are not personal identity but the identity and therefore the survival of Turkmen society. In the words of Uberoi (1978, 2) the Turkmen "have lost themselves." What they have left over, they market: they market their ethnicity, their culture, as a commodity. Our search for authenticity in their carpets will not help them find themselves again. It is part of the cause of their problem.

This consideration of the difference in the meaning of authenticity in Turkmen and Western society may help us to understand better the social dimension of the issue in Western society and to avoid a simplistic relativist solution. Many of the differences that anthropologists seek to explain between the various societies into which humankind is divided — which are commonly conceived to be cultural — are probably, although superficially cultural, basically social, especially in the case of the differences between societies at different stages of social (in the sense of demographic, economic, and technological) development.

Turkmen society differs from Western society both socially and culturally. The relationship between the social and cultural dimensions of modern change is too often overlooked. Dependency is an example of a type of unequal social relationship between societies that might repay comparison with various examples of unequal cultural relationships, such as primitivism and orientalism. Authenticity has become an issue for us only since the condition of dependency has developed in the Other.

The history of oriental carpets right up to the present can be understood in relation to the history of the particular societies that produced them. Our interest in them, and the history of it, must be understood in relation to our own history. In this sense, as Geertz (1976) has taught us, carpets are a text. Rather than being simply a reflection of something in society, they represent a tradition with its own independent dynamic. In their production over time we can read about the history of a relationship between East and West. Whether they are produced in our society or in another,[10] whether or not, as a consequence of processes of cultural underdevelopment or dependency, they have become "our art not theirs" (Graburn 1976), carpets are a primary document. They are like literature. They have their own dynamic and historical continuity, and their relationship with any other cultural or social form is likely to be dialectical rather than unidirectional (Cohen 1974, 58).

The definition of authenticity of a Turkmen rug is a product of choice and negotiation within our society, based on supply from theirs. But it is inspired by an interest in the Other and its products, and can only choose from what the Other provides. The Other must therefore be preserved in its pristine form. Meanwhile, our choice has become crucial to the economy of the Turkmen.

Notes

I acknowledge with gratitude the encouragement and assistance in work related to this essay that I received in the past from Mohammad-Ewaz and Bairam Badghisi (Kabul), Froelich Rainey and David Crownover (University Museum, University of Pennsylvania), Anthony N. Landreau (Textile Museum), and Mary Martin (University of Pennsylvania). In the writing I have benefited considerably from the critical comments of my colleagues, especially Arjun Appadurai, Leah Glickman, and Renata Holod, for which I thank them, though I have not known how to use all their suggestions.

1. "Carpet" and "rug," which are respectively of Romance and Germanic origin, have not been sufficiently distinguished in either meaning or usage to be worth discriminating here. I use them interchangeably for all forms of woolen knotted (pile) floor covering.
2. The appellation "ruggist," has recently appeared in magazines directed at aficionados.
3. A mordant, essential with most plant dyes, is a substance that fixes that dye, by combining with it chemically. Its choice and manner of application determine the shade of the final color. Alum was the most commonly used mordant.

4. The question of where the craft fits historically between Chinese east Asia and Iranian west Asia is not important for the present argument. It is worth noting, however, that the evidence as presented in Lauffer (1919: 492–98) points in the Iranian direction for the origin of the craft. With regard to design, the history of reciprocity in symbols between the Chinese and Iranian worlds is obviously intricate and complex. Given the prevalence of geometrical motifs, some of which are reminiscent of split representation, it is impossible to ignore the possible significance of the *t'ao t'ieh* tradition of decoration on Shang and early Chou bronzes in mid-second to early first millennium B.C. China (cf. Lévi-Strauss 1963). Our understanding of this connection suffers from the dearth of scholars who might be able, Janus-like, to look without logistical bias in both directions. The writings of Cammann (1958, 1978) are especially interesting in this regard; see also Mackie in Mackie and Thompson 1980, 20.

5. Thompson (1980, 181) makes a similar argument.

6. For a review of the early history of the trade, see Impey 1977, 68–9.

7. For a summary of the history of this period see Mackie in Mackie and Thompson 1980, who also review the relevant scanty information up to that time. For more detail see Agadzhanov (1969) and Barthold (1962).

8. This statement stands despite considerable publication on the Turkmen in Moscow and Ashkhabad (see Agadzhanov 1969 and Vasil'eva 1979.)

9. As an example, the University Museum (University of Pennsylvania) has been presented with a genuine Turkmen carpet woven in the design of the American flag!

10. For example, carpets are manufactured in New Jersey under the apparently meaningless but obviously orientalizing name "Couristan."

References

Ackerman, Phyllis. 1938a. Textiles through the Sasanian Period. In *A Survey of Persian Art*, ed. Arthur Upham Pope, 1:681–715. London: Oxford University Press.
　　1938b. The textile arts: History. In *A Survey of Persian Art*, edited by Arthur Upham Pope, 3:1995–2162, 2175–220. London: Oxford University Press.
Agadzhanov, S. G. 1969. *Ocherki istorii Oguzov i Turkmen Srednoy Azii ix–xiii vv.* Askhabad.
Appadurai, Arjun. 1981. The past as a scarce resource. *Man*, 16:201–19.
Azadi, Siawosch. 1975. *Turkoman carpets and the ethnographic significance of their ornaments*. Trans. Robert Pinner. Fishguard: Crosby Press.
Bacon, Elizabeth E. 1966. *Central Asians under Russian rule*. Ithaca, N.Y.: Cornell University Press.
Bahnassi, Afif. 1979. Authenticity in art: Exposition, definition, methodology. *Cultures*, 6:65–82.
Barrett, William. 1958. *Irrational man. A study in existential philosophy*. New York: Doubleday.
Barthold, V. V. 1962. A history of the Turkman people. In *Four Studies of the History of Central Asia*, vol. 3. Leiden: Brill.
Beattie, May H. 1976. The present position of carpet studies. *Apollo*, 103:292–5.
Ben-Amos, Paula. 1976. A la recherche du temps perdu: On being an ebony-carver in Benin. In *Ethnic and Tourist Arts*, ed. N. H. H. Graburn, 320–33.
Benjamin, Walter. [1936] 1969. The work of art in the age of mechanical reproduction. In *Illuminations*, by Walter Benjamin. New York: Schocken.

Berman, Marshall. 1970. *The politics of authenticity: Radical individualism and the emergence of modern society*. New York: Atheneum.

Bogolubow, A. 1908–9. Tapis de l'Asie Central, faisant partie de la collection réunie par A. Bogolubow. 2 vols. St. Petersburg: Manufacture des Papiers de l'Etat. Leipzig: Karl W. Hiersemann.

Boston Museum Bulletin. 1971. Special Issue. The Boston Hunting Carpet.

Brenkman, John. 1979. Mass media: From collective experience to the culture of privatization. *Social Text*, 1:94–109.

Brooklyn Botanical Garden. 1980. *Dye Plants and Dyeing: A Handbook*.

Cammann, Schuyler v. R. 1958. The animal style art of Eurasia. *Journal of Asian Studies*, 17:323–39.

1978. Meaning in oriental rugs. *Arts Exchange*, Jan.-Feb. 1978:31–6.

Canclini, Néstor García. 1979. Crafts and cultural identity. *Cultures*, 6:83–95.

Cohen, Abner. 1974. *Two-dimensional man: An essay on the anthropology of power and symbolism in complex society*. Berkeley: University of California Press.

David, Michael. 1980. The new Turkoman mythology. In *Tribal visions*, ed. Peter E. Saunders, 17–22. San Rafael, Calif.: Marin Cultural Center.

Davis, Ralph. 1970. English imports from the Middle East, 1580–1780. In *Studies in the Economic History of the Middle East*, ed. M. A. Cook. London: Oxford University Press.

Denny, Walter B. 1978. Turkmen rugs in historical perspective. *Yörük. The nomadic weaving of the Middle East*, ed. Anthony N. Landreau, 55–9. Pittsburgh: Museum of Art, Carnegie Institute.

1982. Turkmen rugs and early rug weaving in the western Islamic world. *Hali*, 4/4:329–37.

Douglas, Mary. 1978. Cultural bias. Royal Anthropological Institute Occasional Paper no. 35.

and Baron Isherwood. 1978. *The world of goods*. Harmondsworth: Penguin.

Enay, Marc-Edouard, and Siawosch Azadi. 1977. Einhundert Jahre Orientteppich-Literatur 1877–1977. *Bibliographie der Bücher und Kataloge*. Hanover: Verlag Kunst und Antiquitäten.

Eiland, Murray L. 1980. Speculations around the development of Turkoman rug designs. *Tribal Visions*, ed. Peter E. Saunders, 25–31. San Rafael, Calif.: Marin Cultural Center.

Erdmann, K. 1960. *Der orientalische Knüpfteppich*. Tübingen: Wasmuth Verlag.

Farnie, D. A. 1958. The textile industry: Woven fabrics. In *A History of Technology*, ed. Charles Singer et al., 5:569–94. Oxford: Clarendon Press.

Forbes, R. J. 1964. The fibres and fabrics of antiquity; dyes and dyeing; spinning; weaving and looms. In *Studies in Ancient Technology*. 4:1–81, 99–150, 151–74, 196–224. Leiden: Brill.

Foucault, Michel. [1966] 1973. *The order of things: An archaeology of the human sciences*. New York: Vintage.

Fowler, John, and John Cornforth. 1978, 2d ed. *English decoration in the 18th century*. London: Barrie and Jenkins.

Geertz, Clifford. 1976. Art as a cultural system. *Modern Language Notes*, 91:1473–99.

1973. *The interpretation of cultures*. New York: Basic Books.

Goldwater, Robert. 1938. *Primitivism in modern art*. New York: Vintage.

1973. Art history and anthropology: Some comparisons of methodology. In *Primitive Art and Society*, ed. Anthony Forge, 1–10. London: Oxford University Press.

Graburn, Nelson H. H. 1969. Art and acculturative processes. *International Social Science Journal*, 21:457–68.

1982. The dynamics of change in tourist arts. *Cultural Survival Quarterly*, 6/4:7–11.

ed. 1976. *Ethnic and tourist arts*. Berkeley: University California Press.

Hanaway, William, Jr. 1971. The concept of the hunt in Persian literature. *Boston Museum Bulletin*, 69:21–33.

1976. Paradise on earth: The terrestrial garden in Persian literature. In *Fourth Dumbarton Oaks Colloquium in the History of Landscape Architecture: The Islamic Garden*, 43–67.

Hirsch, Paul M. 1972. Processing fads and fashions: An organization-set analysis of cultural industry systems. *American Journal of Sociology*, 77:639–59.

Holmyard, E. J. 1958. Dyestuffs in the nineteenth century. In *A History of Technology*, ed. Charles Singer et al., 5:257–83. Oxford: Clarendon Press.

Honour, Hugh. 1961. *Chinoiserie: The vision of Cathay*. London: John Murray.

Impey, Oliver. 1977. *Chinoiserie: The impact of oriental styles on Western art and decoration*. New York: Scribner.

Irons, William. 1975. *The Yomut Turkmen: A study of kinship in a pastoral society*. Ann Arbor: University of Michigan Museum.

1980. The place of carpet weaving in Turkmen society. In Mackie and Thompson, 23–38.

Jourdain, Margaret, and S. Soame Jenyns. 1950. *Chinese export art in the eighteenth century*. Middlesex: Spring Books.

Kant, Immanuel. 1950 [1790]. *Critique of Judgment*. New York: Hafner Press.

Khlopin, I. N. 1982. The manufacture of pile carpets in bronze age central Asia. *Hali* 5/2:116–18.

König, Hans. 1980. Ersari carpets. In Mackie and Thompson, 190–202.

Koenig, Wolfgang. 1962. *Die Achal-Teke*. Berlin: Akademie-Verlag.

Kubler, George. 1961. On the colonial extinction of the motifs of pre-Columbian art. In Samuel K. Lothrop et al., *Essays in pre-Columbian art and archaeology*, 14–34. Cambridge, Mass.: Harvard University Press.

Laufer, Berthold. 1919. *Sino-Iranica*. Chicago: Field Museum of Natural History, Publication no. 201. Anthropological Series. Vo. XV, No. 3.

Lévi-Strauss, Claude. 1963. Split representation in the art of Asia and America. In *Structural Anthropology*, 239–263. Garden City, N.Y.: Doubleday.

MacCannell, Dean. 1976. *The tourist: A new theory of the leisure class*. New York: Schocken.

Mackie, Louise W., and Jon Thompson, eds. 1980. *Turkmen: Tribal carpets and traditions*. Washington, D.C.: Textile Museum.

Martin, F. R. 1908. *A history of oriental carpets before 1800*. 2 vols. Vienna.

Mills, John. 1983. The coming of the carpet to the West. In *The Eastern carpet in the Western world from the 15th to the 17th century*, 11–23. London: Arts Council.

Moshkova, V. G., and A. S. Morozova. 1970. *Kovry Narodov Sredney Azii ix-Nachala xx veka: Materialy ekspeditsii 1929–1945*. Tashkent.

Mumford, John Kimberley. 1900. *Oriental rugs*. New York: Scribner.

Newcomer, Peter Jay. 1974. The production of aesthetic values. In Justine M. Caldwell, ed., *The visual arts: plastic and graphic*. The Hague: Mouton.

O'Donovan, Edmond. 1882. *The Merv Oasis*. London: Smith, Elder.

Peckham, Morse. 1979. *Explanation and power: The control of human behavior*. New York: Seabury.

Pinner, Robert. 1981. The Beshir carpets of the Bukhara emirate: A review. *Hali* 3/4:294–304.

Pope, Arthur Upham. 1926. *Catalogue of a loan exhibition of early oriental carpets from Persia, Asia Minor, the Caucasus, Egypt and Spain*. Chicago: Art Club of Chicago.

1938. Carpets: History. In *A survey of Persian art*, ed. Arthur Upham Pope, 3:2257–430.

Rossi-Landi, Ferruccio. 1973. Commodities as messages. In *Recherches sur les systèmes significants*, ed. J. Ray-Debove. Warsaw symposium, 1968. The Hague: Mouton.

Rostovtsev, M. I. 1929. *The animal style in south Russia and China*. Princeton, N.J.: Princeton University Press.

Rudenko, S. I. 1968. *Drevneishnie v mire khudozhestvennye kovry i tkani*. Moscow.

Said, Edward W. 1978. *Orientalism*. New York: Vintage.

Sarre, F. and H. Trenkwald. 1926–1929. *Old oriental carpets*. Trans. A. J. Kendrick. 2 vols. Vienna.

Schneider, Jane. 1978. Peacocks and penguins: The political economy of European cloth and colors. *American Ethnologist*, 5/3:413–47.

Schurmann, Ulrich. 1969. *Central Asian rugs*. London: Allen and Unwin.

Shils, Edward. 1981. *Tradition*. Chicago: University of Chicago Press.

Silver, Harry R. 1981. Calculating risks. The socioeconomic foundations of aesthetic motivation. *Ethnology*, 20:101–14.

Society for Textile Art Research, Vienna. 1983. *Antike Anatolische Teppiche aus Osterreichischem Besitz*. Vienna: Society for Textile Art Research.

Southhall, Aidan. 1961. *Social change in modern Africa*. London: Oxford University Press.

Spooner, Brian. 1973a. *The cultural ecology of pastoral nomads*. Reading, Mass.: Addison-Wesley.

Tapper, Nancy. 1983. Abd al-Rahman's northwest frontier: The Pashtun colonisation of Afghan Turkistan. In *The conflict of tribe and state in Iran and Afghanistan*, ed. Richard Tapper, 233–61. London: Croom Helm.

Thacher, Amos Bateman. 1940. *Turkoman rugs*. New York: Weyhe.

Thompson, Jon. 1980. Turkmen carpet weavings. In Mackie and Thompson 1980, 60–189.

Trilling, Lionel. 1971. *Sincerity and authenticity*. Cambridge, Mass.: Harvard University Press.

Uberoi, J. P. S. 1978. *Science and culture*. Delhi: Oxford University Press.

Vasil'eva, E. P. 1979. Folk decorative and applied arts as a source for the study of ethnogenisis: A case study of the Turkmenians. In J. M. Cordwell, ed., *The visual arts: Plastic and graphic*, 553–66. The Hague: Mouton.

Wagner, Walter. 1976. Gestaltende Kräfte der turkmenischen Knüpfkunst. *Ethnologische Zeitschrift Zürich*, 1:29–49.

Wallace, Anthony F. C. On being just complicated enough. *Proceedings of the National Academy of Sciences*, 47:458–64.

Whiting, Mark 1978a. Dye analysis in carpet studies. *Hali*, 1/1:39–43.

1978b. The dyes of Turkmen rugs. *Hali*, 1/3:281–3.

1980. The dyes in Turkmen carpets. In Mackie and Thompson 1980, 217–24.

1981. The red dyes of some east Mediterranean carpets. *Hali*, 4:55–60.

Wichmann, Siegfried. 1981. *Japonisme: The Japanese influence on Western art in the 19th and 20th centuries*. New York: Harmony.

Wulff, Hans E. 1966. *The traditional crafts of Persia: Their development, technology, and influence on Eastern and Western civilizations*. Cambridge, Mass.: MIT Press.

CHAPTER 8

Qat: changes in the production and consumption of a quasilegal commodity in northeast Africa

LEE V. CASSANELLI

This essay examines the circulation and consumption of qat in the changing society and political economy of northeast Africa over the past half century.[1] Qat (*gat* or *khat* in Arabic, *chat* in Amharic) is a small tree or shrub, whose young leaves, stem tips, and tender bark are chewed for their stimulating effect.[2] Qat (*Catha edulis*) was known and used for medicinal purposes in the medieval Islamic world and in traditional China. It has long been chewed in Yemen, where it may have originated, and more recently has become the chief source of entertainment and group recreation in the towns of Somalia. Fresh-cut leaves and branches are transported daily by road and air across deserts and international frontiers in marketing networks of remarkable scale and complexity. These networks link the hillside farmers of highland Kenya and Ethiopia with the nomadic pastoralists of the Somali plains and with merchants and street vendors in the coastal towns of Somalia and Jibuti (former French Somaliland). The attitudes of government authorities toward qat use have varied from awkward tolerance to outright opposition. Since 1921, bans on qat have been imposed by area governments at least half a dozen times, with little permanent effect. During this period, the economic value and cultural significance of qat have changed. The nature of these changes and the reasons for them provide the central focus for my analysis. I take as a starting point the participants' own ideas about qat and its qualities, and then move to a discussion of the roles of each of three groups that make up the qat network: cultivators, commercial dealers, and consumers. I conclude by examining the politics of qat and their implications for the legal status of the commodity.

Popular ideas about qat

Those who chew qat attribute to it a variety of beneficial effects. Practicing Muslims say that chewing it in the evening enables them to work and pray without becoming drowsy, particularly during the

236

Northeastern Africa

month of Ramadan, when Muslims are obligated to fast from sunrise to sundown. Farmers assert that it "keeps their bodies cool" while working in the fields, even during the hottest days. Other Somalis have told me that chewing qat helps them feel "relaxed but mentally alert"; they can concentrate on whatever they are doing much better. "Qat allows you to have strange and wonderful ideas," said one. "It helps you to express your thoughts to your friends." A team of doctors in Jibuti reported in a 1957 survey how day laborers felt as they gathered after work to chew:

A feeling of mental alertness comes over them, they become talkative and understand things which they did not understand before. They become imaginative, discuss matters and respond quickly; other things are forgotten; then their eyes are wide open and their sight slightly blurred, as if they had a veil before their eyes.

The whole process is in the mind; there is a pleasant sensation of things going round quickly in the head, which is so full of thoughts that it feels as if it may almost burst....The khat user can go on thinking all night without feeling sleepy; sleep seems totally unnecessary....There is a feeling of strength, heavy weights can be easily lifted; movements are effortless and the whole body experiences a sensation of well being (Guedel et al. 1957:34).

Those who chew late into the night may have difficulty sleeping. In the morning, they sometimes feel tired or slightly depressed; they cannot bear to talk. Within a day or two, however, they are ready for more. Most qat consumption takes place within small groups of friends; whenever a chewing session is planned, the air is filled with nervous anticipation as people await the arrival of trucks or airplanes carrying fresh supplies of the substance.

Given qat's stimulating effects, it is not surprising to find that a wide variety of people use it: laborers such as stone-cutters and dock and construction workers, who claim that it energizes them for their exhausting tasks; rural farmers in Ethiopia, who must daily climb and maintain their hillside terraces; Quranic readers and reciters, who lead long liturgical celebrations; students studying for exams; long-distance truck drivers and cabbies; animal hunters, couriers, and guides; night watchmen and (presumably) night burglars. Clan elders frequently chew qat before discussing important local issues or resolving disputes; Muslim judges chew to remain alert when hearing witnesses in lengthy court proceedings.

Popular lore suggests that qat has important medicinal properties as well. It is widely believed, for example, that qat affords protection against malaria; helps remedy coughs, asthma, and other chest ailments; cures stomach problems and rheumatism. The Maasai pastoralists of Kenya say it helps "chase hunger." In Somalia, qat is used to stimulate urination and to help cure genital and urinary infections. In Ethiopia, qat is believed to cure 501 different kinds of disease. Most regular users seem to think that it increases sexual desire but frequently inhibits sexual performance.

Most users of qat in northeast Africa are aware that the substance has a long history in the area, and that for much of that history it has been closely associated with religion. The inhabitants of Harar, an old Muslim city and major center of qat cultivation in the eastern highlands of Ethiopia, tell a story to the effect that qat's special properties were first revealed by an angel to two saints who appealed to Allah for something to help keep them awake during long nights of prayer (Hill 1965:14). The name of Shaykh Ibrahim Abu Zarbay is commonly cited in popular tradition as having carried the plant from Harar to Yemen in the fifteenth century, although some historians are persuaded that the diffusion occurred in the opposite direction (Distefano 1983:2). Qat is still commonly called "the meal of the holy man,"and believers assert that a proper moral and spiritual disposition should accompany its consumption.

In the districts around Harar, people say that farmers used to bathe before harvesting qat, and that they wrapped the fresh-cut shoots in a clean cloth (Getahun and Krikorian 1973:356). I have also heard it said in Somalia that people were forbidden to beat an animal or strike another person with a qat branch. The quasi-sacred properties attributed to the plant may also explain the popular belief that even smugglers refrain from contaminating their payloads of qat by mixing in branches from other plants.

Qat's religious importance can also be seen in the many ritual occasions with which it is associated in the region. Islamic celebrations surrounding births, circumcisions, marriages, and pilgrimages to the tombs of saints often include great public chewings. Qat has been used for grave offerings in northern Kenya, and offered as a gift to those entering into initiation ceremonies in the south Kenya district of Meru. The Oromo (Galla) of southern Ethiopia chew qat on the occasion of the Wedaja festival, which includes a nightlong ritual of communal praying (Distefano 1983:5; Getahun and Krikorian 1973:370-1; Margetts 1967:359).

Alongside the stories and customary practices that point to qat's sacred and spiritual properties, there exists a parallel "secular" tradition of its social origins. In this tradition the discovery of qat is attributed to a Yemeni goat herder, Awzulkernayien, who noticed the stimulating effects of some wild leaves on his goats, tried them himself, and experienced enhanced strength and wakefulness. Harari townsmen still invoke the name of Awzulkernayien in prayers that precede the start of qat-chewing sessions in Harar (Getahun and Krikorian 1973:353–5).

The existence of these variant traditions of qat's origins probably reflects wide variety of contexts, both religious and secular, in which the leaf nowadays is consumed. Any group of users can find in folk tradition a number of precedents that impart the authenticity of custom to their practice. What is more, a version of the Awzulkernayien story is often cited by Ethiopians to explain the discovery of coffee. As we shall see, the histories of qat and coffee are connected in an important way.

In fact, most users of qat are not really concerned to justify or legitimate their consumption of the substance by reference to historical precedent. Qat consumption is its own reward. This can readily be seen in a number of popular explanations offered by Somalis for the recent growing acceptance of its use among segments of the population that previously did not use qat. Among these are the longtime inhabitants of the southern Somali coastal towns of Muqdisho (now the capital), Marka, and Baraawe, and the sedentary farmers who live along the rivers of southern Somalia. The southerners had previously viewed qat chewing as the somewhat eccentric and amusing habit of northern nomads and traders. During a cholera outbreak in Muqdisho in 1969–70, however, southerners noticed that in those quarters of town where northerners had settled and where qat was regularly chewed, there were fewer reported cases of cholera. It was soon widely believed that qat consumption made for greater resistance to the disease. Such beliefs were reinforced by the subsequent experience of refugees who fled in large numbers into Somalia from the Ogaden region of Ethiopia following the Somali-Ethiopian war of 1977–8. In the hastily organized and overcrowded relief camps set up by the government of Somalia with international assistance, those resettled refugees who managed to obtain qat seemed less prone to dysentery. No hard evidence is available to corroborate such claims. Nonetheless, the beliefs were widespread and almost certainly contributed to the growing demand for qat throughout southern Somalia.

This is not the place to appraise the clinical and pharmacological evidence, nor the chemical and medicinal properties of qat. The literature is large and frequently contradictory in its conclusions. There is something of a consensus, however, on a few of the more general physiological effects (Halbach 1972; Luqman and Danowski 1976; Trellu 1959). To summarize, recent studies have identified cathine and cathinone as the major active ingredients in qat. These compounds have similarities to both d-norpseudoephedrine and d-amphetamine and like them appear to act on both the central and the peripheral nervous systems. Like the amphetamines, cathinone produces behavioral effects described as mood elevation; increased heart rate, locomotor activity, and oxygen consumption; and mild hallucinations or "bizarre" thinking. Large doses of these compounds can also induce the following physical symptoms: dilated pupils, reduced tearing and salivation, increased respiration, inhibited enzyme secretion in the digestive system, inhibited peristalsis of the colon, and constriction of the blood vessels near the surface of the skin.

These clinical symptoms clearly bear out the observations of ordinary qat users and help explain some of the popular beliefs that were outlined earlier. The slowing of digestive processes may explain why regular qat users frequently experience a decrease in appetite; the constipating effects, which several researchers attribute to the tannins in qat, may explain the lower incidence of observed symptoms of dysentery among qat consumers. Studies have also shown that fresh qat leaves contain significant amounts of Vitamin C (150–300 mg/100g), which may contribute to the user's ability to resist disease.

Medical opinion regarding the benefits of qat has, it seems, always been divided. Najeeb ad-Din of Samarkand (Soviet Central Asia) prescribed it in a thirteenth-century manuscript on compound drugs for the relief of melancholia and depression (Abdullahi Elmi 1983); it was prohibited in Yemen in the later eighteenth century because of its presumed deleterious effects on the brain (Distefano 1983:7,11). Twentieth-century researchers have equally varied opinions. Some have stressed qat's negative side effects: constipation, gastritis, insomnia, and anorexia leading to malnutrition. Others have stressed its benefits as an analgesic and euphoriant. Despite periodic attempts by medical or political authorities to label qat use a form of addiction, there is little evidence of true physical dependence even among heavy users. The World Health Organization considers qat a non-narcotic substance; most reports speak of user "habituation" or "psychological dependence" rather than "addiction," though the terminology used is not always consistent (Guedel et al., 1957; Halbach 1979; Kennedy et al. 1980; Luqman and Danowski 1976).

While the medical aspects of qat consumption are a challenging subject for research, it is the social and economic dimensions of the plant's use that will occupy us in the remainder of the essay. As I have suggested, qat was traditionally associated with public and ritual occasions: religious celebrations, *rites de passage*, judicial proceedings, and the like. What strikes one most about the contemporary situation is the remarkable growth of qat chewing as a popular form of recreation. Most chewers remark that qat enhances sociability. It helps promote feelings of generosity, hospitality, and good humor. "It is not a good thing for the solitary person," one Somali said; "rather it encourages you to share your ideas, to talk about anything and everything."

Qat sessions among groups of friends – usually males, but increasingly in the urban centers of northeast Africa, in mixed groups as well – typically last three hours or more. Steady chewing accompanies conversation, and the participants usually consume large quantities of water, tea, coca-cola, and cigarettes. While some of the conversation is trivial, most qat sessions are noteworthy for the participants' high degree of mental concentration on a single topic of political, legal, or theological import, sometimes for more than an hour. As I will suggest, it is the enhanced sociability and solidarity within the consuming group that, in certain contexts, is construed by outsiders to be antisocial in a larger sense. In this way, qat consumers share some characteristics of other communities of drug users. A bond is created among those who chew together on a regular basis, and they come to be perceived by the larger society – and by government authorities in particular – as a potentially subversive countercultural community.

Before elaborating on the changing cultural meanings that qat use may have acquired, we shall examine the ecology and economy of qat production, including the extensive commercial networks that have sprung up since the advent of modern road and air transportation.

The production of qat

The qat plant thrives best on moist, mountainous slopes of 5,000–8,000-foot elevation with good drainage. The major centers of qat production have thus always been highland areas: the ranges of eastern and northern Ethiopia, the hills northeast of Mount Kenya, and the mountains of Yemen. Leaving aside the last, the highland areas that produce qat in northeast Africa have historically been inhabited by non-Muslims. The consumers, predominantly (though never exclusively) Muslims, lived and live chiefly in the semi-arid lowlands. This means that qat historically has been exchanged across ecological frontiers that have also been cultural frontiers.

A second interesting feature of the qat ecology is that the areas best suited to its cultivation are also the areas where coffee grows best. Coffee, unlike qat, enjoys a world market and has been an important source of foreign exchange for Kenya, Ethiopia, and Yemen. As a result, the governments of these countries have preferred to encourage their citizens to grow coffee. From the viewpoint of the local farmers, however, qat is also a cash crop, and economies of scale and returns on investment seem clearly to have favored qat over the past two decades. With the rapid growth of local demand for the leaf and the ability to reach new markets by road and air, highland farmers have been turning to qat production on a large scale. The pattern was discernible in Yemen by the mid-1960's. When the Yemeni revolution of 1962 and the subsequent civil war disrupted coffee exports, most coffee farmers began to replant their fields with qat, which could be marketed locally. The return of peace in 1968 and subsequent attempts by Yemen's government to encourage the resumption of coffee cultivation did not succeed in reversing the trend. Coffee exports, which had earned $6 million the year before the war, earned only $1 million in 1971. While qat exports earned only $.5 million, qat's impact on the local economy was staggering. In 1978, it was estimated that $300 million worth of qat was consumed annually within Yemen. Ninety percent of the men and nearly 50 percent of the women in Yemen were said to be habitual users (Distefano 1983: 22–4).

In Ethiopia, the story was much the same. Between 1954 and 1961, the acreage devoted to qat production more than doubled, from 7,400 to 17,300 acres; and these figures presumably do not include those farms where there was limited intercropping of qat with other staples (Getahun and Krikorian 1973:357, 370). Qat has since become Ethiopia's second-largest export in terms of earnings, even though much of the trade across the strife-torn border with Somalia goes unrecorded.

It is not difficult to see why qat is winning the competition with coffee for scarce agricultural land. Qat trees start producing marketable shoots three to four years after planting, while new coffee trees do not begin yielding for six years. Qat leaves can be harvested almost continuously; less labor is required than for coffee (although owners frequently have to guard the qat plants at night to prevent thefts); and the qat plantations last for a generation or more once they are established. For all these reasons, as well as the greater responsiveness of qat marketing networks to short-term fluctuations of supply and demand, the farmers' choice of qat over coffee in many districts is an economically sound one.

Profits made by qat farmers are not nearly as astounding as those of the traders, but they are nonetheless striking. One study in Ethiopia showed that qat accounted for 30–50 percent of the total cash income per year per family in a district where qat trees occupied only 13 percent of the cultivated land (Getahun and Krikorian 1973:357, 366–7). In the Meru district of Kenya, various estimates have put the return per cultivated acre of qat anywhere from 30 to 300 percent higher than for coffee (Hjort 1974:31). Economically, then, qat production has increased both in absolute terms and in relation to other potential highland cash crops.

The scattered literature on qat cultivation offers some tantalizing hints on one particular cultural pattern that may be changing in the qat growing areas. In time past, when the uses of qat were more limited (and confined, perhaps, to ritual and religious occasions), the dissemination of qat plants appears to have been restricted. In Ethiopia, for example, tradition says that Adari merchants who owned qat plantations on the outskirts of Harar town jealously guarded their trees and imposed severe punishment on anyone who gave a qat plant to the despised Kotu (Oromo-speaking farmers who tilled the land beyond the town's suburbs). However, the story continues, following the famous battle of Chellenko in 1887, in which many Adaris lost their lives to the soldiers of the Emperor Menilek, the qat plantations were in danger of abandonment. The Adari widows, unable to keep the plantations up, took in the lowly Kotu as tenants. The latter thus obtained access to the fabled "tree of paradise" and contributed to its subsequent diffusion throughout eastern and northern Ethiopia (Getahun and Krikorian 1973:356). Trellu (1959) noted that in Harar, women were once said to be in charge of the qat farms; yet by the 1960's, anyone who could obtain a cutting and access to land could raise qat.

Kenya provides a parallel. The Meru used to restrict the cultivation of qat to those farmers whose forebears had owned trees; new trees could be planted only as replacements. Breaking the rule called down a curse on the offender. Nowadays, however, the area is known as the "Green Triangle," and virtually every Meru farmer has a few qat trees to provide added income (Distefano 1983:20; Griffin 1983; Hjort 1974).

What the foregoing two examples suggest is a change away from a pattern where the cultivation of qat was a culturally restricted enterprise, reserved to a special segment of the community, to one where qat has become an extensively planted crop with no apparent cultural constraints on its production. As we shall see, this broadening of the social base at the producing end finds a parallel in the growth of qat's use as a consumer good, and also reveals the extent to which the process of commoditization of qat has proceeded.

The distribution of qat

It is the marketing and trading of qat that links cultivators and consumers. In this context, the physical properties of the commodity carry more weight than the cultural ones. That is, qat is highly perishable.

Its potency degenerates quickly once the twigs and leaves are cut, and most users prefer qat that has been harvested within the previous forty-eight hours. For this reason, before the advent of trucking, the consumption of fresh qat was limited to areas near the sources of production. (It appears that dry leaves, ground into powder, have long been a well-known if less-favored substitute; religious pilgrims making the *hajj* to Mecca and Medina frequently carried dry qat with them.)

Nowadays, the cut qat is wrapped on the farm in green banana leaves or plastic bags and taken to the nearest large market town. Kenya's Meru suppliers go to Isiolo; Ethiopians of the eastern highlands go to Harar, Jijiga, or Diredawa. Somali dealers then truck the qat across the desert overnight to Somalia. Since the late 1960s, qat has also been transported by air. It was not unusual several years ago to see four or five rows of seats in the rear of a regularly scheduled Somali Airlines flight from Nairobi to Muqdisho piled high with bundles of fresh qat twigs wrapped in plastic. By 1980, charter flights given over entirely to qat had become commonplace.

The trade between the Meru district of Kenya and the markets of southern Somalia has been the best-documented qat route, and a description of its operation in the 1970s highlights the choices and risks involved (Abdullahi Elmi 1983; Ghari 1978; Hjort 1974). In the Meru hills, the production of qat was constant and high from October to June, and the prices were then at their lowest. The cut branches were sorted according to quality and tied in small bundles called in Somali *marduuf* (a large handful). Ten marduuf were put together and wrapped in banana leaves to keep them fresh. Meru buyers at the point of production payed 10 KSh (Kenya shillings, 10 = $1) per marduuf for the highest quality and 2 KSh for the poorest. At Isiolo, Somali dealers purchased the goods at approximately double the original price and loaded the bundles onto land rovers or Toyota trucks; they then headed out across the arid plains of northern Kenya toward Wajir or Mandera, near the Somali border. The cost of transporting the qat to the border and across it into Somalia has been estimated at 10,000–12,000 KSh. After paying customs duties at the border (and usually depositing a bundle of qat with the border guards), the drivers pushed on to Muqdisho. The entire journey could take up to thirty hours, and by the early 1980's several dozen trucks were making the trip daily.

Once in Muqdisho, the dealers had to go to the municipal office and pay a local tax of 15 SoSh on each marduuf (SoSh = Somali shilling, then officially the equivalent of its Kenyan counterpart). Each dealer then contacted his "agent" (*dilaal*) in the qat market, and the agent distributed the bundles to local vendors, who set the price according to the supply and demand. The street value of a marduuf of qat ranged from 100 to 240 SoSh when supplies were abundant, and as high as 700-1000 SoSh when they were particularly scarce. At the very least, then, the final selling price represented a tenfold increase over the price the grower received. Usually the vendors paid the agents only after the qat had been sold, which suggests both that personal trust and credit were important, and that vendors were probably the poorest segment of the qat distribution chain.

Clearly huge profits could be made by the dealers; but the risks were high. Apart from the continual threat from bandits in Kenya's northern province (many armed with automatic weapons as a consequence of the border war between Kenya's northern neighbors), there were accidents and vehicle breakdowns to contend with. Moreover, since the Kenyan suppliers usually accepted only Kenya shillings or U.S. dollars for their qat, and these were not legally obtainable in Somalia, the drivers frequently risked smuggling such items as traditional Somali dresses, watches, tape recorders, and transistors from Somalia, where they were cheaper, into Kenya, where they could be sold for the necessary currency. Direct currency exchanges on the black market were also a possibility, but they could put the dealers in jeopardy from government authorities.

But with the risks came substantial rewards. Two successful runs from Meru to Muqdisho, I was told, could pay for a Toyota truck. And one charter flight (cost: $3,000) from Meru to Mandera could net a qat dealer a $7,000 profit. This was big business, to be sure; and the Kenya trade, conservatively estimated at 1,000 metric tons of qat per year, represented only about 25 percent of the qat imported into Somalia in 1979. Most of the remainder came from Ethiopia (SDR 1983:14).

To service this long-distance, exacting trade, trucks had to be maintained in peak operating condition. Most vehicles used in the qat trade were rebuilt to carry heavy loads over rough terrain. They were outfitted with extra gas tanks, special shock absorbers, reinforced bodies, and roll bars. Highly trained mechanics were recruited into the operation, and relief drivers were usually ready to set out from the Somali side of the border in the event the initial carrier was late arriving at a transfer point.

In the absence of any detailed research on the subject, we don't know where the initial capital for this remarkable trading operation came from. It must be borne in mind that Somalis are first and foremost producers and (since the 1950's) large-scale exporters of livestock – camels, cattle, sheep and goats. Income from meat sales to the Middle East, for which Somalia was the major supplier until the early 1980's, presumably provided part of the investment capital for the expanded qat trade. Another source of income was the money remitted by the estimated 250,000 Somali migrant laborers who worked in the oilfields of the Middle East by the mid-1970's. Given the tendencies of Somali extended families to invest in a variety of economic enterprises – a way of spreading risk and providing multiple sources of income in an unpredictable physical and political environment – it would not be surprising if earnings from qat traders, livestock dealers, and overseas workers were constantly being recirculated in a region-wide "second economy" of tremendous complexity (see, for example, Miller 1981). Until more work is done on the patterns of private investment in contemporary Somalia, however, we can only suggest that the growth of the qat industry was in all likelihood tied to developments in the livestock and oil industries of the larger region.

Two final points about the commerce in qat. First, because qat is a perishable commodity whose marketing requires considerable commercial and political acumen, those who hoped to enter the trade had first to acquire the necessary expertise. Hjort (1974) has shown that qat dealers in Meru went through a period of apprenticeship under established traders before setting out on their own. Investigation into the Somali end of the trade may reveal similar mechanisms for bringing kinsmen or clients into the business. As yet there is no evidence that the qat trade is controlled by a narrow circle of powerful dealers; rather, it seems to be a business that is open to enterprising men and women from any number of kin groups and occupational backgrounds.

The second point is that along with a number of wealthy entrepreneurs, the qat trade has also provided income to many other segments of the population: farmers, drivers, mechanics, vendors. In Hargeisa and Muqdisho most of the retail trade in qat is in the hands of women. And in Kenya, while the long-distance operations are managed by men, many women in the small towns and hamlets along the truck routes help support their families by selling small bundles of qat in local teashops and marketplaces. In a part of the world where pastoral nomadism, labor migration, and sporadic warfare frequently remove men from the household, qat sales help provide women with the means to survive independently.

Qat and the culture of consumerism

If improved transport and commercial expertise have made it possible to supply qat on an unprecedented scale over the past 25 years, how does one account for the ever-increasing demand? The sociological literature of the past three decades offers many theories but little convincing evidence. Explanations for the steady rise in qat consumption range from boredom to escapism to the search for self-esteem in the group interaction of the qat session (Getahun and Krikorian 1973:374; Kennedy et al. 1980:331–41; U.N., *Bulletin on Narcotics* 1956:12. The growth of urban populations with more leisure and few leisure-time activities is another popular explanation.

One clue to the increased demand for qat may lie in the characteristics of habitual users, that is, people who chew it two or three times a week. Statistics are hard to come by, but recently the Pharmacological Section of the Faculty of Medicine at the Somali National University completed a four-year study on qat use based on interviews with 7,485 Somalis (Abdullahi Elmi 1983; SDR 1983). Because the findings were released in conjunction with the Somali government's March 1983 decision to ban qat (about which more below), the survey might be construed as part of the prohibition campaign. However, the data cited in Dr. Elmi's report seem straightforward; and the observations, if not the implications he draws from them, conform rather well to the impressionistic reports of Somali and foreign observers over the past decade.

The survey involved 4,136 inhabitants of Muqdisho and its environs and 3,349 inhabitants of Hargeisa and its suburbs. Eighty-four percent of the Hargeisa sample and 39 percent of the Muqdisho sample claimed to have tried qat. Habitual users (those chewing qat two or more times per week) were 55 percent of those surveyed in Hargeisa, 18 percent in Muqdisho. Elmi attributed these differences to the relatively recent introduction of qat in southern Somalia.

As might be expected, men were found to be the major consumers of qat; about three-quarters of the chewers in both samples were men, whereas 50 percent of the Hargeisa women and 80 percent of the Muqdisho women interviewed said they had never used qat. Dr. Elmi noted that "nice" women traditionally did not chew, but that this attitude was changing.

Most revealing for our purposes was Elmi's conclusion that "unlike Hargeisa, where qat is chewed among all professions, Muqdisho's chewers seem to be found most commonly among businessmen and the unemployed. The popularity of qat among businessmen may be attributed to its highly sociable association which makes it conducive to business transactions. Among the jobless, qat serves as a relief to frustration." The official booklet issued by the Somali government to explain its decision to ban qat (which drew heavily on the survey's findings) added that most qat consumers in Muqdisho were between the ages of twenty and forty, while in the northern region all age groups were represented in the habitual user category (SDR 1983:49). Finally, university-educated students and those without formal education were identified as important groups of qat consumers.

These findings suggest that although qat was used by virtually all segments of the Somali population, its consumption was growing most rapidly among students, town dwellers, and the under- and unemployed (many of them ex-Saudi workers). What these groups shared, it seems to me, was an increasingly "cosmopolitan" outlook and a recent exposure to the consumer culture of the towns of Somalia and the Middle East. They hoped to attain (or in the case of returned migrant laborers, temporarily had attained) a level of income that was high by Somali standards, one that made possible small home appliances, tape decks, new clothes, and further overseas travel. The influence of overseas workers was particularly important in shaping these attitudes. One estimate put the number of Somalis working in Arabia and the Persian Gulf in the peak years of oil property at a quarter of a million (Miller 1981:4), or approximately 5 percent of the Somali population. Given that these workers earned salaries eight to ten times higher than their counterparts at home, one can readily understand the economic and cultural pressures that stimulated the new consumerism.

At the same time, these very men who had been exposed to the capitalist consumer world of the oil boom years shared the condition of many recently traveled, recently urbanized, citizens of the Third World: once they returned home, they were underemployed, culturally deracinated, and politically impotent. In Somalia, they found a political regime espousing socialist austerity and dispensing political favors to a small circle of supporters united by traditional clan allegiances. Many disenchanted members of the new consumer-conscious culture turned to chewing qat. It helped pass the time in a society with few alternative leisure-time activities. And because qat was also chewed by the religiously respectable, the commercially successful, and the politically powerful, chewing could be regarded as an attempt to emulate the life style of the well-to-do. Qat consumption in this context thus expressed both aspirations for the "good life" and, for many Somalis, frustrations with their inability to attain it.

One sign of the emerging new culture was the proliferation in most large Somali towns of private houses that catered exclusively to qat users. These *majlis* (literally "gathering places") were privately owned or rented buildings with several comfortably furnished rooms set side for groups of chewers. They were frequently managed by divorced or widowed women or by women whose husbands were working overseas. For a fee, visitors were provided with taped music, food, and drink to accompany the qat they brought with them. In some majlis, the hostesses could also provide male patrons with female companions. The initial capital for house and furnishings almost certainly came from earnings by relatives in the qat trade, the livestock export business, or the oilfields of the Middle East. The majlis hostesses thus represent a new kind of "specialist" in the culture of qat consumption, just as the long-distance truck drivers are in the commercial sector.

Through the institution of the majlis, what once had been an activity confined to ritual occasions and informal gatherings of friends or kinsmen now became a business. Some Somalis have told me that certain majlis in the larger towns cater to particular occupational groups – teachers, truck drivers, civil servants, shaykhs. This specialization along occupational lines is a phenomenon that has been reported among qat chewing groups in Yemen as well (Kennedy et al. 1980:319). For Somalia, it represents a departure from the deeply rooted Somali pattern of association along clan or family lines. Can we say that qat has begun to erode traditional loyalties? No, but it probably is fair to say that the increasing opportunities for qat consumption have not only served to reinforce old loyalties (friends, kinsmen, business associates), but also to permit the expression of new ones. Groups of women who now occasionally meet to chew qat together in the majlis represent a case in point.

Qat and the politics of prohibition

On March 19, 1983, the government of Somalia issued a decree banning the cultivation, trade, and consumption of qat throughout the country. Qat plantations had to be destroyed within a year; Somalis caught dealing in qat were liable to fines up to 50,000 SoSh ($5,000) or to prison sentences of two to five years. In a lengthy pamphlet explaining the reasons for the ban (SDR 1983), the government put forward economic, social, medical, and religious arguments.[3] Yearly expenditures for the importation of the substance had cost Somalia $57 million in foreign exchange and boosted black market currency transactions to an unprecedented level. When the 1977 war with Ethiopia curtailed imports of qat from that country, Somali farmers in the northern mountains began to grow the plant, and local grain production was being abandoned. The report estimated that 200,000 Somali citizens were involved in some way in the production and exchange of qat and were therefore diverting their energies from other, more essential, economic activities. The widespread consumption of qat during working hours was damaging the overall efficiency and productivity of both government and manufacturing sectors. Family incomes were being dissipated on qat; men were frequently away from home at chewing sessions, and the moral and material needs of children were being neglected.

The government pamphlet then turned to the moral argument, perhaps best expressed in the section "Kat and Somali Culture." After noting that qat had been praised by religious figures, poets, and clan leaders through much of Somali history, the anonymous author wrote:

later [qat] spread to all stages of the society; it entered to the second phase of entertainment where it got its own social protocol. . . .
As history tells, previously Kat was a tree whose usage was intended for a special service, but at present the case is different and kat is chewed as entertainment and hobby. Everything in return gives problems when it passes its limit (SDR 1983:28, 30).

On the surface, the government's case was simply a restatement of old arguments about the economic, social, and medical hazards of excessive dependence on qat. But there seems to be another point: namely, an expression of the sense that qat use was creating a subculture of its own, one that was challenging the foundations of Somali society. As the pamphlet noted, "kat introduced to the country a way of thinking which is alien to our culture, religion, tradition, and values. It was the major cause behind this complete social change which gave priority to personal interest rather than the general public interest" (SDR 1983:35). Here we see an acknowledgment of the effects of the self-indulgent, consumer-oriented lifestyle characteristic of the 1970's and early 1980's. (For other Somali expressions of this view, see (Abdirahman D. Baileh 1982/83; Abdullahi Elmi 1983; Baiman 1983).

At the time of the ban, a few skeptical observers claimed the authorities simply wanted to suppress the existing traffic in qat in order to gain control of the trade for themselves and their political cronies. There may be more to this than characteristic Somali cynicism. Most knowledgeable observers were persuaded that Somalia's "secondary economy," which included qat, livestock, and currency exchanges across the country's poorly monitored borders, was outperforming the official economy based on meat and banana exports (Hoben et al. 1983:21–31; Miller 1981). Vast numbers of producers, shippers, and exporters were operating totally outside state-regulated channels, and some of these people were suspected, with some justice, of financing Somali opposition movements based outside Somalia. Widespread disaffection with the regime had led many Somalis (both educated and uneducated) to flee the country; those who could not find ways to leave had simply dropped out of the system. Qat use seemed to be prevalent among these disaffected elements. The sense that qat was contributing to the undermining of the economy and, by extension, of the regime, may have been a major factor in the decision to ban it.

In fact, the potential threat to political order posed by the use of qat was an issue that had troubled the colonial governments of Kenya and the Somalilands throughout the twentieth century. In 1921, the government of the British Somaliland Protectorate severely restricted the importation of qat from neighboring Ethiopia by refusing import licenses to all but four Somali dealers. The idea was to force up the price of the commodity until it was beyond the reach of ordinary Somalis (Distefano 1983:13). Political circumstances in the Protectorate at the time suggest one possible motive for the timing of the restrictive legislation. A movement of militant Somali opposition to British colonial rule that went back to the turn of the century had just collapsed, following the death of its leader, Shaykh Muhammad Abdille Hasan, in December 1920. The threat of a renewed Islamic *jihad* (holy war) remained, however, and Protectorate authorities were suspicious of qat's use in connection with the liturgical practices of a Sufi brotherhood that had been an important source of support for Shaykh Muhammad's resistance.

The 1921 ordinance was ineffective, apparently because the Protectorate police force was inadequate to monitor the many desert border crossings from Ethiopia, and also because some of the officers responsible thought it inappropriate to use an allegedly harmful substance as a source of government revenue (Distefano 1983:13). In 1939, however, the Protectorate government reimposed the right of search and seizure and penalties of imprisonment and fines for anyone found planting or cultivating qat. Here again the political context is revealing. The Italian invasion of Ethiopia in 1935 had provided Somalis with new opportunities for trans-frontier trade with newly occupied districts of the Ogaden region. The Fascist regime resurfaced roads and introduced trucks to help integrate their new Italian East African empire, and in 1937 concluded an agreement with the British Protectorate in Somalia that facilitated trade between Italian- and British-occupied territories. Among other things, the improved transportation network stimulated the growth of new markets for qat. (It also facilitated the short-lived Italian occupation of British Som- liland in August 1940.)

During the 1940's, young townsmen in northern Somalia began to express new political aspirations. Charles Geshekter (1983) has doc- umented the beginnings of social clubs and welfare societies that even- tually grew into the first political associations demanding Somali self- government. Chewing qat became popular at these gatherings; one can imagine the organizers offering a few sprigs as an inducement to attend a reading by the always popular Somali poets, whose compo- sitions tended increasingly to political commentary. By the late 1940's, according to the informants interviewed by Geshekter, chewing qat had come to symbolize refusal to accept colonial authority.

The connection between qat and politics can also be seen in the history of prohibition legislation in British colonial Kenya. During the 1940's, authorities in Kenya forbade military personnel to use qat; at the time, military operations were concentrated in the sensitive North- ern Frontier District, which bordered Italian East Africa. Security concerns in that predominantly Somali district continued to preoc- cupy the Kenyan authorities in the late 1940's, and several attempts to ban the qat trade through the district were attempted, again with little success. The ban of 1945 was preceded by a series of articles and an editorial in the *East African Medical Journal*, a publication widely read in British colonial circles. Whether or not the articles were "com- missioned" by the government, their tone and their titles reveal the same sort of admonitory rhetoric that preceded the 1983 ban in So- malia (Carothers 1945; East African Medical Journal 1945).

The use of "scientific" research to justify politically motivated action against qat is also illustrated with a final example from Jibuti, then French Somaliland. In 1957, an article by a French official appeared in the United Nations' *Bulletin on Narcotics* which, though presenting evidence that qat consumption produced neither physical addiction nor violent behavior, still concluded "it is obviously necessary to take energetic steps to combat this social evil without delay." Qat's effects on nutritional health, family stability, and paternal authority were weighed and judged to be negative. The article ended by declaring qat a narcotic drug and outlining the prohibitionary legislation. Im- portation, exportation, production, possession, trade in, and use of qat and all preparations made from qat were declared illegal (Guedel et al. 1957).

These prohibitions were intended to apply to all French overseas territories, but they were never promulgated in French Somaliland, even though the article's damning evidence had come from that territory. The governor of French Somaliland apparently deemed it prudent that the decree be ignored in the interest of maintaining good relations with neighboring Ethiopia, whose exports sustained the economy of the port of Jibuti (Distefano 1983:18). Here we see one of the dilemmas that confronted the region's governments in their periodic efforts to restrict the qat trade. Qat-importing territories (British, French, and Italian Somaliland) were often disposed to impose restrictive legislation because of the presumed effects of qat consumption on their citizens' health and incomes. The governments of qat-exporting territories, by contrast, have always been more ambivalent with regard to prohibition. While Kenyan and Ethiopian authorities occasionally expressed concern that expanding qat plantations took land that could otherwise grow food crops, they also recognized that production of qat for export meant added economic security for many of their citizen farmers and a substantial source of foreign exchange and tax revenue for themselves. Consequently, while governments at the consuming end of the qat network have quite regularly responded to the rising curve of qat use with prohibitionist legislation, authorities at the production end have tended, on the whole, to look the other way.

The context within which the politics of qat have operated is a fluid one. It is clear that the society at large has reached no consensus on whether qat is ultimately good or bad for its citizens. But precisely because of this lack of consensus, and because the balance between social acceptance and social condemnation of qat is a precarious one, the qat issue is always susceptible to manipulation for political ends. Governments, drawing on the advice of "experts," can make equally strong cases for banning qat and for restoring its legality. Qat has always hovered on that indistinct boundary between legality and illegality, and its official status at any one moment is the product more of political and economic calculations than of strictly medical or public health considerations.

It is the ambiguous legal status of qat that has made it more than a commodity; it is a political symbol as well. As the economic (or commodity) value of qat has grown in importance over the past half century, its role as a symbol has moved closer to the center of northeast Africa's political discourse. Just as qat the commodity responds to the laws of supply and demand in the economic sphere, so too does qat as symbol fluctuate in significance in response to social and political pressures. This dual reality makes qat an ideal subject for ethnohistorical inquiry: for to study the changing economy of qat production, trade and consumption is also to study the entire process of cultural transformation as it unfolds in contemporary northeast Africa, from a commodity perspective.

The expansion of qat production, trade, and consumption in recent times has encouraged homogenization within both the qat-producing and the qat-consuming communities. By the 1980s, qat was being grown by more people and used by more people than ever before, and all the evidence suggests that those people came from all religious groups, socioeconomic classes, and occupations, and from both sexes. New specializations, to be sure, have grown up around qat in its modern setting, among them the long-distance drivers and majlis hostesses. But these new specialists were helping to make the commodity more accessible, not less so. Over the course of fifty years, qat escaped its previous cultural constraints; it has come to represent and reflect an emerging new culture, a more cosmopolitan social and economic order.

As the scale of production and consumption has grown, more areas of life have been affected, and the lack of consensus over qat's relative costs and benefits, which always existed, has simply been extended into new sphere, of activity. It is too simple to say that qat consumption in Somalia today represents a new, self-indulgent life style, one that is challenging older ideas of moderation and responsibility to kin and clan. This is only part of the story, for the young urban consumers of qat can also be seen as emulating a way of life that wealthy and respected Somali shaykhs and businessmen had traditionally enjoyed. Nor does the fact that qat has from time to time been associated with groups regarded as potentially subversive mean that the commodity carries only an anti-authoritarian meaning. The opposition to qat does not come only from governments, even though the periodic bans, regularly circumvented, may make it seem so. There are many merchants, mechanics, and Somali war widows whose livelihoods depend on the continuation of the qat trade; but there are also those office managers, abandoned wives, and neglected children who see the culture of qat consumption destroying the fabric of work and family life.

Qat, then, provides us with one window on the cultural changes and social tensions that exist in northeast Africa today. Not only is it a subject in the ongoing debate about the changing values of society; it is also a source of change in the agricultural, commercial, and family spheres. We might say that qat is to the society of northeast Africa what it is to the discourse of the chewing sessions themselves: a sign and a facilitator of new modes of interaction. As a widely desired commodity, qat has enabled many Somalis to get rich, others to make a living, and still others simply to survive. As a symbol, qat has been one vehicle through which individuals and governments have periodically expressed their dissatisfaction with the direction their society seems to be taking.

Notes

I would like especially to thank Muhammad Haji Muktar, Endre Nyerges, and Susan Gunn for their thoughtful comments and suggestions on an earlier version of this chapter. Much of the information on popular ideas about qat and on the operation of the qat trade outside the borders of Somalia is based on informal conversations with Somali and Kenyan friends and participants over a period of several years. As will become apparent, it is frequently difficult to "document" many aspects of the qat network in northeast Africa.

For this paper, Somali place and personal names have been written in their anglicized forms rather than in the official Somali orthography. Somali authors cited in the references are alphabetized by first names, the standard practice in scholarship on the region.

1. For purposes of this paper, northeast Africa includes Ethiopia, Somalia, Kenya, and Jibuti (formerly French Somaliland).
2. Throughout Kenya, qat is known as *miraa* or *merow* after the Meru district, where it is cultivated.
3. I managed to obtain an English-language version of this important document. Like many official publications in Somalia, the pamphlet probably also appeared in Arabic and Italian versions, as well as in a Somali-language one.

References

Abdirahman Dualeh Beileh. 1982–3. Kat elimination in Somalia. *Horn of Africa*, 5/4:56–8.

Abdullahi S. Elmi. 1983. Khat (*Catha edulis Forsk*): History, spreading, and problems in Somalia. In paper presented at the Second International Congress of Somali Studies, University of Hamburg, Aug. 1–6.

Baiman, Jerome Giora. 1983. How the Tree of Paradise is used to undermine the Somali economy. Paper presented at the Second International Congress of Somali Studies.

Carothers, J. C. 1945. Miraa as a cause of insanity. *East African Medical Journal* 22/1: 4–6.

Distefano, John A. 1983. The history of Qat use in East Africa and Arabia. Paper presented to the Second International Congress of Somali Studies.

East African Medical Journal. 1945. Poisoning by khat or miraa: The need for control of khat. (editorial). 22/1: 1–2, 9–10.

Geshekter, Charles. 1983. Anti-colonialism and class formation: The Eastern Horn of Africa, 1920–1950. Paper delivered to a seminar of the Program in Atlantic History, Culture, and Society, Johns Hopkins University, March 29.

Getahun, Amare, and A. D. Krikorian. 1973. Chat: Coffee's rival from Harar, Ethiopia: I. Botany, Cultivation and Use. *Economic Botany* 27: 353–77.

Ghari, Capis. 1978. Miraa *Umma* (Nairobi), Jan.

Griffin, Michael. 1983. Qat ban hits Kenyan farmers. *New African* (May).

Guedel, L., et al. 1957. The medical and social problems of khat in Djibouti. *Bulletin on Narcotics* 9/4(Oct.-Dec.): 34–6.

Halbach, H. 1972. Medical aspects of chewing khat leaves. *World Health Organization Bulletin* 47: 21–9.

——— 1979. Khat: The problem today. In L. Harris, ed., *Problems of Drug Dependence 1979*. Washington, D.C.: NIDA Research Monograph 27.

Hill, Bob G. 1965. Cat (*Catha edulis Forsk*). *Journal of Ethiopian Studies* 3/2: 13–23.

Hjort, Anders. 1974. Trading Miraa: From school-leaver to shop-owner in Kenya. *Ethnos* 39: 27–43.

Hoben, Allan, et al. 1983. *Somalia: A Social and Institutional Profile*. Working Papers No. SP-1. African Studies Center, Boston University.

Kennedy, John G., J. Teague, and L. Fairbanks. 1980. Qat use in North Yemen and the problem of addiction: A study in medical anthropology. *Culture, Medicine and Psychiatry* 4: 311–44.

Kervingant, Dr. 1959. The consumption of khat in French Somaliland. *Bulletin on Narcotics* 11.2(April-June): 42.

Luqman, Wijdan, and T. S. Danowski. 1976. The use of khat (*Catha edulis*) in Yemen: Social and medical observations. *Annals of Internal Medicine* 85: 246–49.

Margetts, Edward L. 1967. Miraa and myrrh in East Africa: clinical notes about *Catha edulis. Economic Botany* 21.4: 358–62.

Miller, Norman N. 1981. *The Other Somalia. Part I: Illicit Trade and the Hidden Economy.* Hanover, N.H.: American University Field Staff Reports, Africa, No. 29.

SDR (Somali Democratic Republic). 1983. *Why kat was prohibited in Somalia.* Muqdisho, Ministry of Information and National Guidance.

Trellu, Michel. 1959. The pharmacodynamics of khat. *Bulletin on Narcotics* 11/2(April-June: 43–4.

U.N. (United Nations). 1956. Khat. *Bulletin on Narcotics* 8/4 (Oct.-Dec.): 6–13.

PART V

Historical transformations and commodity codes

The structure of a cultural crisis: thinking about cloth in France before and after the Revolution

WILLIAM M. REDDY

The great French Revolution of 1789–99 brought a general change in the way French people thought about commodities. This change occurred within a society that had centuries of experience with money-based exchange behind it, and one that, although undergoing rapid commercial expansion in the eighteenth century, saw no significant change in the predominant modes of production either before, during, or after the crisis. Industrial capitalism was all but nonexistent in France in 1789 and still quite exceptional in 1815. Yet millions of French people in the interim adopted what could only be called a capitalist mode of evaluating commodities. It is the object of this essay to show that this involved a change in the generally accepted notions of what a commodity was. This is a properly modest goal, made more modest by the concentration on a single kind of commodity, albeit an essential one, cloth. But even in pursuing this modest goal, one is forced to recognize that political institutions, the social hierarchy, the day-to-day relationships between persons at street level, and the far-flung workings of ideological control and commercial dependence all had to undergo significant reconstruction in conjunction with this shift in thought about commodities. (No suggestion about priority is implied here.)

At the same time it will become apparent that thought about commodities, like thought about persons and institutions, is necessarily encyclopedic in scope. That is, to act coherently, persons must organize vast numbers of detail according to simple, overarching categories and principles. This limitation of the human mind (if such it is), every bit as material in its own way as wool or stone, introduces limits to the kind of change that can occur, to the scope and character of such change. Along the way, then, this description of a shift in thought will attempt to provide glimpses, at least of how such limits – call them mental, cultural, or cerebral – may have influenced the unfolding of the *ancien régime*'s political crisis. To give more than glimpses of this aspect of the crisis would require the completion of

261

extensive research projects. For the time being it is enough to identify new problems worthy of inquiry, because current research efforts have brought understanding of the French Revolution to a kind of impasse.

The conflicts of the revolutionary period can no longer be seen as pitting one social class against another; this much is clear. That is, no one-to-one correspondence can be found between parties and classes. The revolutionary bourgeoisie once believed responsible for guiding the patriot and Jacobin parties has proved to be a phantom. Some have suggested rejecting class entirely as an irrelevant category. But even those who insist on seeing class antagonisms as the Revolutions' ultimate origin recognize that those antagonisms were expressed indirectly, translated into a language that could not distinguish classes as such. Thus all historians now agree that extremely painstaking interpretive work on revolutionary and prerevolutionary language is a prerequisite to adequate explanation.[1] Recent attempts to explain the rebellion of the Third Estate in 1788-89 have increasingly sought to discern a cultural crisis of some kind behind the Revolution.[2]

Documenting the existence of such a crisis is not difficult. It is easy enough to identify a host of institutions and practices of the old regime that had lost their legitimacy in the eyes of an increasingly self-conscious public as the eighteenth century drew to a close. The absolute power of the monarch had been repeatedly challenged in the press and in the royal courts with great popular success. The old restrictions on trade in grain and manufactured goods embodied in the guilds and the official marketplaces of the towns had been reformed, repealed, and partially resuscitated by 1780. No one really believed they could survive in their current form, if only because thousands of merchants and peddlers had been flouting these restrictions for decades. The privileges of Church and nobility were under attack by the crown itself as obstacles to a revitalized tax base after 1786. Privileges and pensions of all kinds had in any case been transformed into marketable properties; titles of nobility, high government offices, *seigneuries* (the French equivalents of manors), fiefs, church benefices, even bishoprics, were up for sale to the highest bidder, so long as that bidder had the right connections.[3] The old ways were still practiced, all the old forms of the feudal monarchy were still floating about detached and transmogrified, infused with unexpected meanings and put haphazardly to new uses. How could these forms be expected to retain the allegiances they once commanded? So much had been brought into question by the 1780's – from the old Christian cosmology to the equally old three-field system of peasant agriculture –

that it is surely not enough to see the Revolution as merely a governmental crisis.[4] The government, in any case, had its finger in every pie in the old regime; changing the government meant altering the center of gravity of millions of individual lives. This was a cultural crisis of the first order, of that there can be no doubt.

This is not to say that there was not also a political and economic crisis, nor that the old debate over the existence and aims of a revolutionary bourgeoisie has been definitively set aside. The notion of cultural crisis simply forces all consideration of the Revolution's outbreak onto a new terrain, requiring that conflict and faction be analyzed in the first instance in terms of the meaning and structure of political discourse. Whatever new economic or social configurations one may see behind the revolutionary crisis, it is certain that these configurations could not express themselves through the old cultural forms, and that the Enlightenment offered no new forms, providing at best only a few hints as to how to proceed. Normal guidelines used up to the 1780's to resolve political conflicts and shape day-to-day trade (as well as trade policy) were themselves brought into question and slated for reformulation. Party, interest, and opinion could not coalesce and be played out in the routine way (neither in Versailles nor in a provincial marketplace) because the routines themselves had lost credibility. For some period before 1789 it must be supposed that many old practices were followed with declining conviction (especially in certain branches of government), and also that many old principles were no longer adhered to in practice (especially in certain realms of trade). In just this sense the economic and political crisis was cultural in nature. In 1789 the French, or a large number of them, refused to continue down this path. An array of old institutions and practices were seized on and destroyed with an alacrity that still leaves historians breathless. The privileges of Church and nobility, the sovereignty of the crown, the corporate structure of urban government and of the royal judiciary – all were reduced to an ash heap in a matter of months. Provincial boundaries were swept away, venal offices abolished, feudal and seigneurial land tenure slated for oblivion. This zest for destruction suggests one should look for signs of half-hearted compliance and growing doubt in the immediately preceding period. But how is one to investigate rigorously such intangibles as doubt or half-heartedness? What kind of evidence can be used to uncover them? That is the real challenge that any new approach to the Revolution as a cultural crisis must meet.

As it is usually practiced, ethnographic method, the accepted means of determining the structure of a culture, deals exclusively in surfaces.

One might interpret at length the ritual forms, dress, and utterances of the first session of the Estates General in May 1789, however, without finding any evidence of the impending Revolution. This paper attempts to find traces of the crisis by looking at a single dimension of French culture over time – a very minor dimension at that. Because the crisis was really general, it is possible to find traces of it even in so small a domain as the way merchants and others in the textile trade talked about cloth. An important feature of these traces turns out to be an odd combination of rigidity and flexibility; that is, there are signs of the blockage of change accompanied by sweeping, improvisational policy shifts from the government. Consideration of these traces will enable us to formulate preliminary hypotheses about why people continued to cling to linguistic and institutional structures as the eighteenth century wore on that were increasingly out of touch with their deepest convictions on the one hand and with many facets of their everyday practice on the other.

Of course no records of casual talk about cloth have survived from the eighteenth century, and casual talk would be the ideal object for investigation. But there is a fascinating reference work that bears on the question, Savary des Bruslons's *Dictionnaire universel du commerce*, first published between 1723 and 1730 and reissued, pirated, and translated at least six more times between 1741 and 1784.[5] A general work on commerce, Savary's dictionary nonetheless had a great deal to say about cloth and other textile goods, which were a principal ingredient in the trade of this preindustrial era. The frequency with which the work was reissued, and hawked about Europe, not just France, usually with numerous superficial alterations intended to "update" it, suggests that it was used in a way that the luxurious coffee-table *Encyclopédie* of Diderot and d'Alembert was not; that is, that it was used by real merchants in their day-to-day dealings.

Savary was well placed to gather the kind of information that practical operators would have wanted. He was a royal customs official based in Paris in the closing decades of Louis XIV's reign. In his daily work, he needed to have knowledge of the complex production regulations of guilds from towns that shipped goods to Paris. France in the eighteenth century was riddled with internal customs barriers, and dotted with towns whose guilds were carefully controlled and scrutinized by the royal government; any manufactured article entering Paris legally could be expected to have, besides the shipper's bill of lading, proper wrapping, proper manufacturer identification, seals of inspection from guilds and local market inspectors, and certificates showing what duties had been paid at various points along the article's path to the city. Savary's familiarity with these details gave him the expertise necessary to take on the heavy task of preparing the first-ever dictionary of commerce. During the years of research he and his brother put into the project, Savary's experience of trade told him whom to turn to in the government and in merchant communities throughout France for accurate information. His access to royal files on guilds and guild law was indispensable, as was his concrete knowledge of the look and feel of the products that constantly flooded into Paris.

Savary's father, a merchant and ministry official of the late seventeenth century, had set an example for his son to emulate; he was the author of the famous *Parfait negotiant*, a guide to commerce that remained extremely popular in its own right well into the eighteenth century.[6] But the scope of this work was dwarfed by that of the *Dictionnaire universel du commerce*. The appearance of handbooks and reference works on many subjects in this period was an important facet of the emergence of a public sphere in Western Europe, itself a necessary but hardly a sufficient condition for political revolution. The ready availability of voluminous, accurate information on practical matters – commerce, law, music, architecture – came to be viewed in the eighteenth century as a goal worthy of heroic effort.[7] Savary was a pioneer in this respect. His was a first attempt to systematize the everyday knowledge and beliefs of merchants, producers, government officials, and consumers about commerce. As such, it is possible to glean from Savary something of the mental landscape of the textile trade at the beginning of the eighteenth century. The organization of articles and the discrimination of relevant details reflect an industrial and commercial Weltanschauung that has long since disappeared.

The article on *toile* (plain linen cloth), for example, includes a list of seven points to check when buying a piece of *toile*. This list places great emphasis on the purchaser's ability to judge by eye. One must make sure, the article recommends, that the weave is tight and the weft threads evenly closed up with one another. The threads themselves must be of uniform twist, as tightly spun on the edge of the cloth as they are in the middle. No part of warp or weft should be stretched or shifted out of alignment with the rest. The cloth must be of the same tightness and fineness at both ends as it is in the middle. The cloth should have as little finishing on it as possible; that is, there should not be so much gum, starch, or chalk applied to it as to conceal irregularities in color, weave, or twist. In addition, the cloth should have as many threads in the warp and weft as general royal regulations and local statutes require. One can imagine the sort of inspection procedure such recommendations would entail. The whole piece, all twenty to thirty yards, would have to be unrolled, different sections folded over each other for close comparison of thread and weave, and various parts carefully rubbed between thumb and fingers to check for tightness and for the presence of undue finishing. A lead seal affixed to one end of the cloth would certify that it had passed inspection at point of origin and therefore had the proper number of threads in warp and weft for that variety of cloth. Since the 1660s, final decisions even on such minor matters as dimensions of cloth and numbers of threads were made in Versailles, although usually the local guilds' recommendations were accepted without question. The royal government's interest lay in ensuring that high quality standards were maintained; by Colbert's mercantilist doctrine, quality was the key to prosperity.

In a number of places in Savary's dictionary, lead seals of inspection are described in detail. The Beauvais woolen guild, the Sergetterie de Beauvais, for example, specified a new design for their seal in 1666, when under the tutelage of Colbert they had revised and elaborated their production regulations. On one side of the seal a legend was to read "Louis XIV, restaurateur des arts et manufactures." On the other appeared the arms of the town and the words "fabrique de Beauvais." Cambrai linen held a seal with a spread eagle and the word "Cambray." Valenciennes used a lion rampant and the words "commerce de Valenciennes." Saint-Quentin used a bust of their patron saint; Armentières, on the Lys River, used a shield with fleur de lys and the town name.[8] These seals were important not just for the purchaser, but also for customs officers, who assessed different duties according to grade of cloth and place of manufacture. (Linen cloth entering the *cinq grosses fermes*, a customs zone in northern France, for example, had to pay a high duty unless the cloth could be shown to be the product of French provinces outside the *grosses fermes*.) Besides showing seals, French producers were to weave or sew their name and the name of their town into the end of the cloth.

These and hundreds of other details provided by the dictionary remind one that evaluating cloth in the eighteenth century required the skills of a connoisseur rather than those of a technician. Every bit of thread and of cloth was the product of handwork whose quality was dependent on the ability of the worker at each moment, as well as on the discernment and experience of those merchant manufacturers who bought thread and warped it and put it out to weavers.

At each moment personal attention was required. The fact that one end of a piece of cloth looked excellent was no proof that the other end was also good. One had to know what kinds of flaws to look for; one had to be familiar with techniques of production and finishing; one had to know the seals of the various towns and the regulations that lay behind them. The surest way to tell a *serge drapée* from genuine *drap*, the dictionary warns in its article on *serge*, is that genuine *drap* (high-quality open-weave woolen fabric) will have five blue stripes and seven white stripes on its border, while *serge drapée* produced in Berry (a coarser, inferior woolen fabric, given a similar finish) had only three or four blue stripes and as many white ones. To the knowledgeable dealer even minor details of a cloth's appearance could identify its geographical origin, quality, and value.

The geography of textile production was complex. The typical article in the dictionary on a cloth term like *serge* or *camelot* begins with a description of the type of cloth in question, followed immediately by the names of those towns which produced it. There might be some discussion – varying greatly in length – of the special varieties produced in each location, along with observations on the reputation of each. Valenciennes produced the highest quality *bouracan*, for example (a heavy woolen fabric used for coats and rain gear). Lille *bouracans* were also all wool and quite good, but inferior to Valenciennes'. Abbeville weavers made a *bouracan* they called *façon de Valenciennes*, but it was really neither as fine nor as good as genuine Valenciennes. Lille *camelots* (another variety of heavy, open-weave woolen fabric), were known for their luster, which was due to the hot pressing they received in the last stage of finishing. *Camelots* from Arras were, however, "very coarse, with a very rough texture, more like a *bouracan*." A fine white linen called *cambrésine*, although no longer produced in the Cambrésis but instead at Peronne, was much better than the equivalent article from Brittany. The Rouen area was known for the "quantity and variety" of coarse linens it produced; the article on *toile* politely refrains from saying anything about their quality, however, which was widely known to be of the lowest. A good number of *basins* (a pattern-weave cotton cloth) were imported from Holland, although not because they were any better than French-produced *basins*. They sold well only because of the consumer passion for foreign goods.

Having reviewed the places of production, the dictionary then lists the guild-mandated cloth dimensions and the numbers of thread in warp and weft used for each variety in each town, apparently because these were important items of information, ones that dealers expected to find in a reference work and needed for their purchasing. At the end of each article is a detailed listing of import and export duties for the cloth in question, both between France and other countries and within France's own customs zones. Such listings could run to two pages or more for common cloth varieties.

The rapid development of the rural putting-out industry in France in the late seventeenth and eighteenth centuries can only be guessed at from the dictionary. Reference is occasionally made to rural production, but in general the names of provinces and of the towns that were their commercial centers are used interchangeably, or the names of towns are used implicitly to stand for the rural regions that produced for them and traded through them.[9] The new, unregulated varieties of cloth associated with rural production are dealt with in a cursory fashion if at all – as if, because guild practices and regulations do not exist for them, there is really nothing to say about them. The dictionary says nothing of the growing contraband in French-produced *indiennes* – printed calicoes that were excellent imitations of the Bengali original. The nature of the cotton-linen blend called *siamoise* is only briefly described. The origin of the name is mentioned: a cotton-and-silk blend first worn in France by an ambassador from Siam in Louis XIV's day. But nothing is said of the extent of unregulated *siamoise* production in the Normandy countryside.

The focus of the dictionary is resolutely on the guilds; on the older varieties of woolen, linen, and silk cloth they traditionally produced; and on their government regulatory apparatus as reformed and centralized under Colbert late in the seventeenth century. The knowledge that is imparted aims at familiarizing the reader with guild regulations and with the complex geography and lore of cloth production. Some of the commentary, in fact, reads almost like the reports of a folklorist, as in the following passage from the article on *camelot*:

A prodigious quantity of little *camelotins*, very narrow, very light, are still manufactured in Lille and several other places in French Flanders. Most of them are shipped to Spain. The Flemish give them various quite odd names. The principal ones are: *l'amparillas* or *nompareille*; *polimitte, polemit*, or *polomitte*; *picotte* or *gueuse*; *quinette* or *guinette*; and *changeant*.

Hemp cloth made in Brittany for use in ships' sails came in five varieties, known by their village of origin: *noyalle, perte, locrenan, polledavy*, and *petite olone*. The four varieties of linen made around Morlaix were known as *crés larges de trois quarts, crés communes, crés graciennes*, and *crés rosconnes*. Each of these varieties is carefully distinguished in the article on *toile*. The fine loose-weave *étamines* used in sieves and sifters made in Reims were known as *bluteaux* or *bouillons* (*bluter* means to sift). These terms distinguished them for those varieties of *étamines* used in nuns' veils and other ecclesiastical garb, as well as from a large array of other gauzy, bright *étamines* varieties. The word *étamines* itself is related to the word *tamis* (sifter); but over the centuries, with the proliferation of varieties and uses, the word had completely lost its original associations so that real *étamines* for sifting had to be called something else.

Any wholesale dealer of the eighteenth century who had been long in the trade must have been full of this kind of knowledge, or must at least have been well-versed in those facets of it that touched on the products he regularly dealt in. At the same time, the vast amount of such information in the dictionary, which took the Savary brothers well over ten years to compile, was doubtless available to no one before the dictionary's publication. Producing the dictionary represented an effort, in effect, to turn lore into knowledge; but precisely because this was the earliest such effort in France, its value to the historian is that it opens a window onto the folklore of textile production before it had felt the influence of such systematizing projects as dictionaries, and at the very moment when the trade was beginning that last great boom that preceded mechanization.

It is characteristic of the outlook represented in the dictionary that interest in production is always secondary. Methods of production must be mentioned because they affect the appearance, wear, and value of cloth; because local quirks give certain cloths distinctive qualities; because guild regulations limit them. But production is seldom described; it is assumed that the reader has no direct involvement in production. This is quite true to the actual organization of the trade in Savary's day. Spinners and weavers worked on their own, applying their traditional skills to the making of legally defined varieties of cloth. Merchants put out fiber or yarn to them through commissioners, never laying eyes on the people who worked for them, buying the finished product back from the commissioner only after careful scrutiny to determine its value. Control of production by owners of capital was nonexistent. Except for certain finishing processes, the choice of production method was the guilds' or the rural weavers' to make.[10] Savary's attitude toward this fact is decidedly complacent. He accepts the whole complex status quo without question, from the capricious names that Flemish weavers gave their linens to the voluminous customs regulations issued in Versailles. Why should he have done otherwise? The bulk of his expertise lay precisely in his extensive knowledge of all these quirks and details.

It takes only a very cursory look at Savary's dictionary to recognize how intricately interlaced the textile trade was with the shape of old regime institutions. Merely to put a correct price on a bolt of linen it was necessary to be thoroughly familiar with the methods of operation of the government in Versailles, with the regulations and habits of the privileged corps of urban weavers and merchants, with the customs of the uncharted hinterlands of working peasants, and with the tastes in dress of a highly stratified corporate society. Knowledge of this kind was a daily source of profit to thousands of merchants and a livelihood to hundreds of government officials and lawyers.

But how was such knowledge affected by the crisis of the 1780's? At first glance, the only answer the dictionary offers is a negative one. Savary's work was, after all, republished yet again as part of Panckoucke's grandiose *Encyclopédie méthodique* in 1784. The changes made by Panckoucke's editors were minor ones. It would appear that the kind of expertise that Savary had systematized remained useful even at that late date, or at least the savvy Panckoucke thought it sufficiently useful to risk republishing the dictionary yet again.[11]

A closer look, however, reveals that the republication of Savary's work at so late a date in the life of the *ancien régime* may itself be a symptom of the depth of the unfolding crisis. The story behind Savary's continued success may suggest why it is sometimes necessary to continue doing things even after one no longer believes in them. It is odd, after all, that Savary's dictionary had not been replaced by a newer one by the 1780's, given the vogue for reference works following the success of the great *Encyclopédie*, and given the high status that commerce enjoyed in the eyes of the philosophes. In fact, someone had tried to replace Savary, but failed. In their Introduction to the 1784 edition, the editors apologize for having no newer work to offer the public. They lament the fact that the project of a certain Abbé Morellet to produce a new dictionary of commerce remained incomplete, and that Savary is therefore the only available alternative.[12]

Morellet, a school chum of Turgot and a protégé of Trudaine de Montigny, a powerful figure in government finance, had announced his intention to produce a new dictionary of commerce fifteen years earlier, in 1769. He had been asked by a publisher at that time to help update Savary for republication, but found the old dictionary sorely lacking. The customs official's outlook was not to his taste. Morellet was an avid supporter of the physiocrats, a champion of free trade and of the absolute right of property. His 1769 prospectus proposed an entirely new dictionary, in three parts: a geographical section covering towns, provinces, and countries, and their production and trade practices; a section on natural substances and the products made from them; and a third section covering the terms and principles of the theory of wealth.[13] Here was a systematic conception in tune with the new currents of thought of the Enlightenment. In his memoirs, written much later, Morellet explained why he never finished the project even though it absorbed his energies for twenty years.[14] When he originally proposed it, he was being considered for a post in the Bureau of Commerce, a perfect vantage point from which to gather information, giving access to all the resources and expertise of the Bureau's nationwide staff of salaried inspectors. Trudaine de Montigny, an *intendant de finance*, had promised the position to Morellet, but for some reason was unable to deliver. A rival patronage network had won out. This was just a small episode in a decades-long effort by Trudaine and his father before him to restaff the Bureau entirely with officials of physiocratic outlook. They were never completely successful; the personnel of the Bureau and its inspection system continued to harbor many pro-regulation officials alongside the new free trade advocates. Morellet's disappointment was one among many setbacks over the years. The Bureau's policies never became unequivocally free trade in orientation.[15]

As compensation for the lost position, Morellet received a government pension of 4,000 livres a year to continue his work on the new dictionary. He used it to hire assistants and to send out hundreds of questionnaires, but as he complained in his memoirs, his lack of authority as a private citizen handicapped his information-gathering efforts. Further, he says, as a government pensioner he could not afford to refuse requests from his protectors in the ministries to defend their policies with his pen. In the 1770's he spent a great deal of time writing tracts in favor of the free trade doctrines of royal officials. When his old friend Turgot was made Controller General in 1774, Morellet's office became overnight the destination of a stream of petitioners and influence seekers. At Turgot's request he wrote several lengthy tracts defending Turgot's policies in the pamphlet war his reforms had provoked.[16] The dictionary was neglected. After Turgot's fall, Morellet continued tracking current affairs. In the early 1780's, his acquaintance with the British Prime Minister Shelburne allowed him to help out in the British-French negotiations following the end of the American Revolutionary War. When Calonne called for the creation of an Assembly of Notables to approve new taxes and extensive reforms in 1786, Morellet's talents as a publicist were again called on, and soon he was drawn into the whirlwind of Revolutionary politics. In sum, in his own defense, Morellet insists that the job of

writing a dictionary of commerce was too big, that he did not have
sufficient resources, and that political debts absorbed too many of his
energies.

But each of these arguments really points to the same underlying
circumstance, that is, to the developing cultural crisis that culminated
in revolution. Political debts absorbed his energies because Enlightenment reformers climbing to high office in the 1770's and 1780's
faced great difficulty winning public acceptance of their policies. Their
opponents were learning to speak the same language, and could deftly
parry Quesnay with Montesquieu, or counter Turgot's reforming zeal
with calls for philosophic moderation.[17] Public debate over fundamental issues preoccupied an increasing number of people in the
literate strata. Likewise, Morellet was denied the resources of the
Bureau of Commerce because infighting over lower-echelon positions
and patronage went hand-in-hand with this larger public debate. Finally, the writing of a new dictionary of commerce became too large
a task for Morellet partly because of his patrons' own limited successes.
Guild monopolies were weakened in 1762, free trade in grain was
allowed for a time in the 1760's, then repealed, then reinstituted in
1775–6. On the last occasion Turgot tried to abolish the whole guild
system and all royal regulatory control over manufacturing with a
single edict, but fell from grace before he could fully implement the
new law. His successor restored the guilds on a slightly altered basis.
Necker in 1779–81 instituted another major reform of the guilds and
the government regulatory apparatus, establishing his so-called intermediate system.[18] Further changes in the grain trade followed in
the 1780's. And the new free trade treaty with Great Britain, signed
in 1786, promised to have incalculable effects on commerce in France.
Each one of these reforms would have required Morellet to go back
and revise tens, even hundreds, of pages of copy for his dictionary.
It is easy to imagine that, apart from his other distractions, Morellet
may have begun by 1780 or so to feel a real sense of futility about his
project. Why try to write a reference work before the situation had
settled down a bit? But it never did settle down.

One can get a sense of the problems Morellet faced from a dictionary
of commerce that was published later, in 1799, by one of Morellet's
former assistants, J. Peuchet.[19] That Peuchet drew on the work he
had done for Morellet seems likely. His 1799 dictionary is modeled
on one of the three sections that Morellet had proposed to write, the
geographical one. Peuchet's is a commercial dictionary of place names
only, in five volumes. The typical entry on a French town or province
gives only sketchy details on the current state of trade. These brief

remarks are then followed by extensive information on the state of things before the Revolution. Often there are long citations of the guild regulations that were enforced up to 1781, followed by vehement denunciations of the injustices of the pre-Revolutionary guild system. In other cases there are voluminous demographic and industrial statistics, drawn from publications of the 1770's or 1780's. In effect, Peuchet knew almost nothing about commerce in the 1790's – a common condition, since even the government faced grave difficulties gathering information during the revolutionary decade. And all that Peuchet did know no longer applied. This was a reference work of retrospection. This work, too, remained incomplete, confined to geographical terms only, doubtless because Peuchet saw the futility of going any further. When change reaches a certain pace, reference works become impossible. Savary was republished again in 1784 because his steady certainties, product of a more secure era, could not be duplicated. All the intellectual ingredients were there for a new kind of work. But the Enlightenment attitudes that had inspired Morellet's original plan were having such an unsteadying effect on the social reality around him that he could not hope to complete his dictionary on the new model. The old model, brought into doubt, remained unreplaced.

In the 1784 edition of Savary, its editors patched together a few alterations in a halfhearted effort to bring it into line with the present. In none of the hundreds of articles that cite guild production controls is there any whisper that these controls are now optional. Only if one looks up *jurandes* (guilds) can one find a discussion of Turgot's and Necker's reforms. Savary's extensive information on internal customs is all put within quotation marks, to what purpose is not entirely clear. Savary's pro-regulation remarks are countered with free trade propaganda that is simply inserted alongside from time to time. The whole effect is altogether haphazard and unsatisfactory. The fate of Savary's vast expertise was that it was brought into question, globally, by people who were unable to challenge or replace it in detail. But is this not, after all, one symptom of a cultural crisis? When the cumulative common sense of the past faces a fundamental challenge, the edifice embodying the former is bound to survive in a kind of limbo; it cannot be replaced in a day.

If this was the fate of Savary's work, then what was happening to the working expertise of textile merchants and guild officials across France as the uncertain prospect of extensive reforms loomed ahead? That their knowledge suffered a parallel fate emerges clearly from reflection on the circumstances surrounding Necker's formulation of his "intermediate system" for the textile trade in 1779–81. This system was full of incongruities. It left all the guilds and all the official marketplaces with their royal inspectors in place, operating exactly as before. But it made use of these institutions optional, at the choice of the merchant or producer. Anyone who did not wish to submit to guild restrictions or royal production regulations merely had to bring his cloth into the market and have it stamped with a special seal bearing the word *libre* (free). Necker envisioned this "intermediate system" as a compromise between the free trade and pro-regulation factions. But the very essence of guild control is that it is mandatory. If guilds did not have at least local monopolies in their trades, then they could not possibly function. Their very raison d'être was to ensure the livelihood of local producers by muting competition between them. How could they accomplish this task if they themselves had to compete on equal terms with nonguild producers?

But it appears that Necker was not concerned with the survival of guilds as institutions; he was concerned with the survival of something else, of a way of knowing – about goods, about society. The two kinds of knowledge were, as we have seen, intimately related.

The opinions expressed by a large number of merchants and others in letters and petitions sent to Necker while he was preparing his reform proposal show an overwhelming preoccupation with the danger of fraud. If the guilds were abolished, they argued, widespread fraud would turn consumers away from French products and lead inevitably to the withering away of commerce. Fraud would be easy without the guilds. Consumers lacked the necessary skill to tell if flashy finishing techniques had been used to cover up disproportions and flaws in spinning or weaving. They could not easily discern whether the wool was Spanish or French, whether linen had been mixed with hemp, whether the piece was a few feet shorter than standard length, whether the number of threads in the warp had been reduced by a small fraction to save money. Faced with such uncertainties, they would simply turn to Dutch or English products and avoid French goods.[20] This was not the favorite argument of conservatives. The Paris Parlement, when it denounced Turgot's edict dissolving the guilds in 1776, saw the threat of fraud as only of secondary importance; instead the Magistrates, in their Remonstrance to the King, emphasized the general breakdown in order, subordination, and discipline that would ensue if the guilds disappeared.[21] Those directly involved in commerce who argued in favor of guilds in memoirs to Necker's office in 1779, however, concentrated on the danger of fraud, the threat of fraud to French prosperity, and the function of the guilds in preventing fraud. This was the argument that Necker's compromise was aimed at answering. Under Necker's system, anyone concerned with fraud could still find the cloth he was accustomed to buying, still produced, inspected, and marked in the usual way. All others were free to follow the system of *caveat emptor*. The vast accumulation of expertise about guild regulations – about the appearance of guild seals, the border markings on *serge drapée*, the superior luster of Lille *camelots*, and so on – would not be rendered obsolete overnight.

Operators in the textile trade did not argue for the guilds in 1779 entirely out of fraternal concern for the fate of guild masters; instead, many recognized that their own livelihood was based in large part on detailed knowledge of the wide array of practices that guilds and government enforced. Whether or not they believed in the efficacy of the guild system, they remained attached to it simply because, as a cognitive device for making sense of the world, as an instrument of connoisseurship, it remained irreplaceable. Just as Savary's editors in 1783–4 scattered challenges and doubts through the pages of his dictionary without greatly altering its substance, so Necker's intermediate system suspended the mechanism of control without abolishing it. Had Necker followed Turgot's example and sought to abolish the guilds, no one would have dreamed of republishing Savary in 1784; the dictionary would have been reduced to the status of a historical curiosity. But Necker's compromise recognized what Savary's editors knew too well, that there was nothing yet available to replace Savary's kind of knowledge. The new policy was thus a marvelous combination of rigidity and improvisation.

We know today that massive fraud is not a necessary result of free trade. But in 1780 it was possible to believe in this danger because it was impossible to envision the knowledge that would develop along with free trade. In the French textile industry, as it turned out, the kind of knowledge that free trade engendered was starkly different from that of the eighteenth-century connoisseur. Connoisseurship was replaced by entrepreneurship. Concern for the appearance of finished cloth was replaced by a preoccupation with processes of production. In practice the activity of examining and setting a price on a piece of cloth might have looked much the same, but the thinking behind such activities was entirely reformulated on new principles. Establishing such habits of thought throughout the industry – getting the new principles clear and understanding their application to every variety of cloth that the industry produced – was a monumental task. A hint of its magnitude can be gathered from examination of yet another dictionary of commerce, put out by the Guillaumin publishing house in 1839, the *Dictionnaire du commerce et des marchandises*.[22] This dictionary was written not by one person but by a committee of forty-three professors, merchants, and bankers. By pooling their knowledge of special fields and by drawing on a large stock of new thinking about goods that had been painfully elaborated over fifty years of experience of free trade, these experts produced a reference work every bit as mature and consistent in its approach as Savary and far more detailed. By 1839 such a feat was possible.

In its overall format, the 1839 dictionary looks like a realization of Morellet's original proposal of 1769. It has geographical entries, entries on natural substances and their products, and entries on the theory of political economy. The major difference is that these entries do not appear in separate sections of the book, but are presented intermingled in alphabetical order. The role of entries on theory seems much reduced from what Morellet had envisioned as well; they take up hardly 5 percent of the 2,252 pages. The doctrines of political economy dominate the theoretical entries for *price (prix)*, *wages (salaire)*, *commerce*, and *capital*: but the authors are not afraid to differ from official doctrine when they feel so inclined. There are no entries at all for *commodity*, *raw material*, or *production*. The articles for *interest* and *market* are full of practical details but devoid of theoretical discussion. No attempt is made to cover the whole theory of political economy. In other words, theory was no longer a battleground by the time this dictionary was written. A new theoretical language was in place and accepted without question; disagreements expressed through its terms incited no passions.

But if explicit theory is muted in the 1839 dictionary, the implicit application of new principles to the organization of facts is everywhere in evidence. The appearance of the typical article is starkly different from Savary. The entry for *draperie*, for example, is anchored directly in the production process. An effort is made to emphasize those elements of the process which distinguish *drap* from other varieties of cloth:

Cloth *drapée*, properly speaking, is woven of cardedwool, fulled, brushed with teasels, stretched, cropped, and put through a press. One of its most distinctive features is to have an extremely loose weave on the loom, easily penetrated by light, of a width usually twice as great as it will have after all the finishing processes are complete. It is by the operation of fulling that this cloth is reduced to its normal width and acquires that thickness and feel characteristic of *drapée*.

Savary, by comparison, is vague in the extreme:

Drap is properly a cloth made of doubled threads interlaced, of which one group, called the warp, stretches lengthwise from one end to the other, and the others, called the weft, are disposed across the width of the cloth. *Draps* are made on looms, just like linen, *droguets, étamines, camelots*, and other similar varieties of cloth, which do not have patterns.

Savary provides a list of twelve things to look for when evaluating a piece of drap. It is crucial, Savary asserts, to see that the drap has been properly teaseled, so that all the loose fibers have been pulled out, and to see that these fibers have been closely and evenly cropped. Only here, as characteristics the connoisseur must evaluate, are the special production methods for drap finally mentioned. Savary describes these methods, but his description takes the form of a recipe for producing fine drap. In other words, he is concerned with production only insofar as it makes possible a high-quality outcome. (One must be sure, Savary warns, that the spinners make the warp thread one-third less thick than the weft thread and with much higher twist. Another typical recommendation: the cloth must be kept damp throughout the cropping process; this is done by occasionally sprinkling water over the surface. In the Guillaumin dictionary of 1839, by contrast, two pages of description of the production process appear in due course, replete with references to technical progress made in the previous fifty years, and the savings on labor costs these have made possible. The article explains how decisions made on raw material or on the thread used affect the quality and appearance of the outcome – without prescribing, as Savary does, that only the best methods be used. The advent of mechanical spinning is discussed, as well as the recent invention of an ingenious new machine for cropping (which worked exactly the way old hand-pushed lawn mowers do).

Savary's article concludes with a page and a half of internal customs duties applied on draps from various towns. The Guillaumin article concludes with a four-page, region-by-region breakdown of drap production, mentioning local varieties, output quantities and prices, and shifts in local fortunes as a result of competition in recent decades. The outlook of the quality-conscious, trade-oriented connoisseur has been replaced by that of the cost-conscious, production-oriented entrepreneur. But in making this change, it was necessary to completely rethink hundreds of familiar everyday details about drap production, reorganizing them to fit into a new set of general principles. For Savary, drap – like any other cloth term – was a word defined by guild regulation for a cloth produced in a number of towns where these regulations had been elaborated and imposed. He had no need to define the term carefully in terms of methods of weaving and finishing. His aim was to be able to distinguish quality correctly, just as maintenance of quality was the end of regulation. For the compilers of the Guillaumin dictionary, regulation is not an issue. Nothing stands between the producer and the purchaser; the production process itself is therefore the only possible source of distinctions for determining what a cloth is.

The differences in approach evident in the articles on drap show up consistently throughout the two dictionaries. In the article on *camelot*, for example, Savary again provides an extremely general definition:

CAMELOT. A plain-weave cloth composed of a warp and a weft, produced with a shuttle on a loom of two peddles, just like line or *étamine*.

Camelots are of different widths and lengths depending on variety and quality and on the place of manufacture. They are made in all kinds of colors, some of goat's hair in both warp and weft, some with goat's hair weft and warp of half goat's-hair, half silk thread, others with both warp and weft of wool, and still others with wool weft and linen warp.

Guillaumin, on the other hand, explains that camelots originated in Turkey, where they were made originally of Angora goat's hair, and spread from there to Europe:

It has been in vain that the various European producers have tried to imitate the camelots of Angora; it became necessary to combine other fibers such as silk, [European] goat's hair, cotton, flax — mixed by various methods. From this, diverse sorts of cloth have resulted, with various names under which they are traded.

Again, the distinctive feature of the cloth called camelot is located in the production process, in this case, in an exotic raw material that has proved difficult to imitate. The diverse kinds of camelot made in Europe are treated in Guillaumin as arising from a series of more or less failed experiments. For Savary the issue of imitation does not even come up.

In general Guillaumin has less to say about specific varieties of cloth than Savary, much more to say about large categories (like drap). Close inspection of articles on specific varieties shows why they are deemed less important: fashion has picked up its pace. *Napolitaine*, for example, a woolen fabric invented in the 1820's, is briefly discussed. It was first marketed as an imitation merino (another new variety) by merchants who had an overstock of combed-wool cloth that had not been fulled. Dyed bright colors, it looked something like merino, but sold for much less. *Napolitaines* soon found favor with a large number of consumers but were later challenged by newer varieties of cheap woolens. (The names of these challengers are mentioned but they do not merit articles of their own.) In such articles the new pace of change in fashion can itself be seen to be linked to constant alterations in production methods.

A consistent preoccupation with production shows up also in the wholly new categories of entry in the Guillaumin work. Geographical entries provide information almost exclusively on the kinds of things produced in the places in question; the Dictionary's attention is fixed on unique features of the local industries, their history, their size, their output and its value. In addition there are extensive articles on raw materials that dwarf anything Savary had to offer. The article on *iron* (*fer*) is fifteen pages long, that on *coal* (*houille*) twenty-three. *Cotton* (*coton*) is subjected to exhaustive treatment. There are thirty pages on the raw material itself, covering the plant, the fiber, and its chemical and mechanical properties, and the stages of its transformation into thread. A history of the cotton industry is provided, with special attention to the English case ("the most extraordinary phenomenon in the history of industry"). A comparison is made of the costs of production of cotton thread in England and France including extensive tables on harvests, prices, and consumption over the previous century. A separate four-page article appears elsewhere on *cotton cloth* (*tissus de coton*), dealing with the weaving process, prices, and the uses to which cotton cloth is put by consumers.

These differences do not reflect merely economic change; they cannot be explained as simply the result of technical advances encouraged by open competition. The very notion of what a commodity is had changed, and every specific commodity dealt in by European society had to be reconceived as a result of this shift. Such revolutions in thought are not accomplished quickly. Of course, the immense task of rethinking represented by the Guillaumin dictionary of 1839 was inseparable from equally large changes in practice. But it is important to recognize that changes in thought and practice did not perfectly mirror each other. To oversimplify a bit, a producer of drap might accomplish the work in much the same fashion in 1839 as his 1730 counterpart, whereas his conception of what he was doing would have changed drastically, making him, for example, prepared to accept at once the introduction of a new shearing machine when it came. In the meantime only those engaged in developing the new machine were altering their practice as well as their thought.

The period between the appearance of Savary's dictionary and the publication of Guillaumin's, then, may be seen as having been marked by a series of disjunctures between thought and practice that constituted one facet of the cultural crisis of the old regime. In the eighteenth century, until about 1760, certain features of practice – notably the extra-guild putting-out system in the countryside – broke dramatically with reigning principle. About that time certain thinkers (the physiocrats) sought to draw the necessary conclusions from these new practices and impose reforms from above on the basis of those conclusions (Laverdy's edicts of 1763–5 freeing the countryside to produce goods; Turgot's attempt to abolish guilds in 1776). But these measures met widespread resistance because most thought and some practice were threatened with legal disruption by these changes. Necker's intermediate system of 1779–81 did not aim at saving the guilds so much as preserving a guild-based way of thinking about textile goods that represented a kind of social capital, something so large and so necessary to day-to-day intercourse that it could not be dropped without throwing commerce into confusion. Those who predicted widespread fraud if guild monopolies were abolished, were, in fact, perfectly correct in their own way. Until knowledge was rebuilt on the firm foundation of the notion of a production process, it would be extremely difficult to categorize and evaluate goods in the absence of the old regulatory structure.

In 1789, however, perhaps partly as a result of the accidents of timing and institutional infighting (of the fact, for example, that a fiscal crisis coincided with a disastrous harvest), halfway measures of the kind represented by Necker's reform were abandoned. Savary's brand of connoisseurship was just one small faggot on the great funeral pyre that was set aflame in France between May and August of that year. A series of bold new general principles were enunciated (embodied in the Declaration of Rights of Man and Citizen) – principles so general that their practical application to everyday life was anything but clear at first. Thought leapt ahead of practice, but at considerable cost in the clarity and mutual ease of day-to-day interaction. Uncertainty and mistrust became widespread. Even if the new general principles had commanded unswerving universal respect (which they did not), even if there had been no animosities separating rich and poor (which there were), applying the new principles would have been a difficult task. As it was, over twenty-five years of turmoil passed in which several quite different modes of application were tried before a stable new world began to come into focus.

These reflections on the nature of the cultural crisis of the pre-Revolutionary decades in France may suggest a way to give prevailing theories of culture a badly needed historical dimension. The situation that reached an extreme in the 1780's may be a more or less permanent feature of all cultures at all times in their histories. French society at that juncture had a centuries-old, slowly evolved set of practices and institutions that had been brought into question in the most fundamental way. Both new modes of thought (only partially worked out) and new modes of production (only locally followed) that were now in existence did not mesh with these older structures and urged the wisdom of transforming them as soon as possible. The problem was that there was no way to replace them without a long and painful work of rethinking, yet no society could exist for long without some well-elaborated set of practices based on publicly recognized general principles. Hence the agony of indecision over reform measures and the shock of revolution, which, like an earthquake, knocked every habit of mind free from its accustomed place.

Surely every society to one extent or another is living in a similar state of tension, in which the inertia of habit based on old, well-established principles is under attack from the free play of speculative thought, which is constantly formulating new, potentially rival general principles, or else from unexpected technical, commercial, or military developments that demand new forms of thinking in response. Thought can never work through new principles in sufficient detail to put them at once into operation throughout a whole society. People stick with the known, without reference to its intellectual validity, because they value the detailed prescriptions for daily interaction that long years of effort have elaborated. If this is an acceptable inference, it would mean that a traditional notion of reform going back to the Enlightenment in the West is profoundly misconceived.

Enlightenment reformers like Turgot or Condorcet viewed society as fully receptive to instantaneous change on the basis of rational principles. It was simply a question of getting people to recognize the persuasive power of a new idea; practice would follow automatically. Hence the revolutionaries of 1789 realized neither how great a work of destruction they had achieved nor how difficult it would be to replace what they had torn down. This same notion – that practical change follows directly from intellectual persuasion – still informs most of our political life today, from demonstrations against racial prejudice or nuclear weapons to the routine rhetoric of political campaigns, press conferences, and reforming legislation. But it may be that people resist reform for reasons that have nothing to do with its intellectual merit, and that by the same token, their commitment to the present arises from no deep conservatism. Like the petitioners who appealed for a retention of the guilds in 1779, people may simply balk at the vacuum that results when a thousand familiar practices are abolished and replaced with abstractions.

Of course looking at commodities through the lens of reference works has many limitations as an approach to the problem of cultural crisis. If the advantage of this approach lies in the revelation of the profound structure of social thinking that stands behind the use and exchange of any commodity, the disadvantage lies in the fact that reference works full of descriptions of things and processes can depict only a steady state. It is impossible to gain access to living human relationships and the constantly changing terms of agreement and conflict that determine their shape. But students of society need such tools just as much as social actors do. Only with a solid understanding of a particular stasis (however abstract) is it possible to appreciate the implications of conflict and of aspirations for sweeping change.[23]

Finally, it is worth noting that close examination of the humble commodities of day-to-day commerce not only draws attention to the encyclopedic array of knowledge that persons must be able to command in order to maintain a social routine, but also reveals again the necessary intimacy that always subsists between social relationships and things.

Notes

1. See the excellent review of recent research, William Doyle, *Origins of the French Revolution* (Oxford, 1980); for a sophisticated defense of the class-conflict approach, see Michel Vovelle, *La chute de la monarchie 1787–1792* (Paris, 1972).
2. For example, François Furet, *Penser la Révolution française* (Paris, 1978); English trans., *Interpreting the French Revolution* (Cambridge, 1981). Another example: William H. Sewell, *Work and Revolution in France: The Language of Labor from the Old Regime to 1848* (Cambridge, 1980).
3. On these developments, see Steven L. Kaplan, *Bread, Police, and Political Economy in the Reign of Louis XV*, 2 vols. (The Hague, 1976); Eugène Tarlé, *L'Industrie dans les campagnes en France à la fin de l'ancien régime* (Paris, 1910); Alfred Cobban, *The Social Interpretation of the French Revolution* (Cambridge, 1964); Jean Queniart, *Les Hommes, l'église, et dieu dans la France du XVIIIe siècle* (Paris, 1978).
4. Theda Skocpol argues for an institutional rather than a social or cultural crisis in *States and Social Revolutions: A Comparative Analysis of France, Russia, and China* (Cambridge, 1979). On the impossibility of separating government from society in the old regime, see David D. Bien, "The Secrétaires du Roi: Absolutism, Corps, and Privilege under the Ancien Régime," in Ernst Hinrichs, Eberhard Schmitt, and Rudolf Vierhaus, eds., *Vom Ancien Régime zur französische Revolution: Forschungen und Perspektiven* (Göttingen, 1978), 154–68.
5. Jacques Savary des Bruslons, *Dictionnaire universel du commerce*, 2 vols. (Paris, 1723), was published posthumously under the direction of Jacques's brother and a collaborator, Philemon-Louis Savary. Philemon-Louis pub-

lished a supplementary volume in 1730, which was integrated into the first two in a second edition of 1741. A four-volume version was printed in Geneva in 1744. A revised edition published in Paris and then Geneva in 1750 included an additional volume of supplementary articles. Other editions with a greater or lesser number of "improvements" were published in London (in translation) in 1751–5, and in Copenhagen in 1759–65. The title page of the 1784 edition does not mention Savary, but reads *Encyclopédie méthodique ou par ordre de matières. Commerce.* For this study, both the 1750 Paris-Geneva edition and the 1784 edition were consulted. All references to the dictionary will be made by entry rather than by page number, so that any edition may be consulted. For a complete discussion of the dictionary's history, see J.-C. Perrot, "Les dictionnaires de commerce au XVIIIe siècle," *Revue d'histoire moderne et contemporaine,* 28 (1981): 36–67.

6. Perrot, "Les dictionnaires."
7. For a review of recent discussions, see Doyle, *Origins,* 66–95; see also Robert Darnton, *The Business of Enlightenment: A Publishing History of the Encyclopédie, 1775–1800* (Cambridge, Mass., 1979), 509–19.
8. For descriptions of these seals, see the articles *toile* (subsection "Marques des toiles blanches") and *sergetterie.*
9. For a good example, see the article *batiste.*
10. For a full discussion, see William M. Reddy, *The Rise of Market Culture: The Textile Trade and French Society, 1750–1900* (Cambridge, 1984), 22–47.
11. Darnton, *The Business of Enlightenment,* 395–472.
12. See the Advertissement, Vol. I, p. 1. On the *Encyclopédie méthodique* and its publisher Panckoucke, see Darnton, *The Business of Enlightenment.*
13. Abbé André Morellet, *Prospectus d'un nouveau Dictionnaire de commerce, par M. l'abbé Morellet, en cinq volume in-fol., proposés par sousscription* (Paris, 1769).
14. Abbé André Morellet, *Mémoires,* 2 vol. (Paris, 1821); these were written about 1802. The author is especially indebted to Robert Darnton for signaling the existence of these memoires and their bearing on the subject at hand. See also Perrot, "Les dictionnaires," for a discussion of Morellet's career.
15. On the Bureau, see André Remond, *John Holker, manufacturier et grand fonctionnaire en France au XVIIIe siècle, 1719–1786* (Paris, 1946); Harold T. Parker, *The Bureau of Commerce in 1781 and Its Policies with Respect to French Industry* (Durham, N.C., 1979). Professor Parker is also preparing a study of the Bureau's activities in the 1780s and graciously allowed me to examine his preliminary draft.
16. See, for example, Abbé André Morellet, *Analyse de l'ouvrage intitulé: "De la législation et du commerce des grains,"* 2 vols. (Paris, 1775).
17. See, for example, the Paris Parlement's Remonstrance of 1776 in Jules Flammermont, ed., *Remonstrances du Parlement de Paris au XVIIIe siècle,* 3 vols. (Paris, 1888–9), III, 368–88; or Necker, *Sur la législation.* For further discussion, see Edgar Faure, *12 mai 1776, la disgrâce de Turgot* (Paris, 1961).
18. See Parker, *The Bureau of Commerce,* 31–7; Archives Nationales (hereafter AN) F^{12}654, F^{12}657.

19. J. Peuchet, *Dictionnaire universel de la géographie commerçante*, 5 vols. (Paris, 1799–1801).

20. See especially the summary of pro-guild opinion in AN F^{12}654, "Extrait des avis."

21. Flammermont, *Remonstrances*, III, 368–88.

22. 2 vols. (Paris, 1839). Citations to this work in the text are also by entry rather than by page number.

23. I have considered records of numerous episodes of conflict from the period in *The Rise of Market Culture*.

CHAPTER 10

The origins of swadeshi (home industry): cloth and Indian society, 1700–1930

C. A. BAYLY

After 1905, the import of British-made cloth into India and the ensuing destruction of Indian handicraft production became the key theme of Indian nationalism. In the hands first of Bengali leaders and later of Mahatma Gandhi and his supporters, the need to support *swadeshi* (home) industries and boycott foreign goods was woven through with notions of neighborliness, patriotism, purity, and sacrifice, all of which provided unifying ideologies more powerful than any single call for political representation or independence. The destruction of indigenous weaving and the influx of foreign cloth became visible, material symbols for nationalists, comparable to those represented in other societies by literary or legendary motifs: "loss of country" in Indochina and China, the coming of the Just King in Indonesia, or the notion of the ending of Babylonian Exile in Caribbean and African societies.[1]

That cloth could evoke such powerful symbols of community and right conduct was due to the important role cloth and clothes played in Indian society – not merely in fixing and symbolizing social and political statuses, but in transmitting holiness, purity, and pollution. This essay seeks first to elucidate these roles of cloth in precolonial society and then to show how they were transformed in the colonial period. In doing so, the essay uncovers some special features of the role and meaning of commodities in Indian society over the last three hundred years. Recent studies of the rise of capitalism through "commoditization" of produce and labor have tended to assume an evolutionary or even dialectical development through time.[2] Commodities invested with the "spirit" of gift exchange, products that "seem to embody the social milieu from which they came," are progressively divested of value to become impersonal things whose value is allocated only through the market. Divine power and the devil are both separated from daily life; relics and talismans lose their worth. The mental and moral conditions of capitalism are established alongside its material manifestations. What is striking about India over these centuries, however, is that development in the external forms of proto-capitalism (credit, capital, markets)[3] was not matched by an equivalent development of mentalities. The spirit of the gift, the perception of "evil" (here pollution), continued to adhere to products that were circulated within a fully developed market system. That this should have been so reflects the nature of the specific form of commercial-ization that occurred in the economy of precolonial India. The labile expansion of a cash economy tended to bring "shares" in the royal rights of great and little kingdoms into the cash nexus. It did not, however, even under nineteenth-century colonialism, dissolve the so-cial relations of dominance that arose from the interplay between the norms of caste and the structure of the petty local kingdoms.

What follows is an attempt at the collective biography of cloth in India over time. In the first section, the broad characteristics of the Indian view of cloth as a thing that can transmit spirit and substance is sketched out. The essay then goes on to show how the meaning and function of transactions in cloth changed in response to general political and economic trends. In the long view, this is a study of commoditization, but only of partial commoditization. For if slavery was an example of how persons could be made "things," the history of cloth in Indian also shows how things could retain the quality of the people who fashioned and exchanged them, even in a fully mon-etized economy.

Cloth in Indian society: an overview

Symbol, talisman, and pledge

Transactions in cloth and the donning of new cloth or clothes attended every major life cycle ritual in preindustrial Indian society. Cloth transactions also took place during worship and in the creation or confirmation of political alliances.[4] We can distinguish three basic uses of cloth in the social process, which often in practice overlap: *first*, its use in symbolizing status or in recording changes of status; *second*, its magical or "transformative" use, in which the moral and physical being of the wearer/recipient was perceived to be actually changed by the innate qualities of the cloth or the spirit and substance it conveyed; *third*, its use as a pledge of future protection. These various uses and the meanings attached to them affected not only the social and eco-nomic position of donor and recipient, but also the status of the various artisans and service communities that encountered the commodity cloth as it passed from production into social use.

The use of cloth and clothes to symbolize social status or to change it is, of course, common to all societies, though the complexity of the Indian social order imparts unusual variety to the symbolism of nakedness and dress. But beyond this, cloth as a transactional medium was conceived as a unique conveyor of spirit and substance, holy, strengthening, or polluting. Thus, cloth of different textures, colors, or origins could do more than simply impart information in society; it could change the moral and physical substance of the individual. Two ideas are relevant here. First, cloth was porous, dense, and intertwining, and could thus absorb and retain spirit/substance for many years. As an artifact, cloth of cotton, wool, or silk could not approach the especially powerful transformative capacity of food,[5] but, on the other hand, it lasted longer than food, could travel over longer distances, and was much less "hard" and neutral than wood or metals. Second, Indians seem widely to have regarded the individual person as a peculiarly volatile combination of "bio-moral" substances, as an amalgamation of colors, qualities, and textures that each have their own spirit. In Hindu chemistry and physiology, for instance, it seems that color was not merely an accident of matter as in the Aristotelian tradition, but an independent manifestation of the spirit that goes to make up, say, a red cloth.[6] Thus, the spirit of red cloth, or redness can combine with the moral substance of a particular person and transform it. For this reason, when a man in parts of central India smeared himself with ochre and donned red garments, he was something more than a man dressed in red; he was, in effect, a red man, that is, sorcerer.[7] His costume did not symbolize a status acquired by other means; it was an essential component of the very transformation itself. Similarly, ascetics who smeared their clothes with mud and ashes seem to have been perceived not simply as men symbolizing their social death, but actually as ash-men, as corpses. Since their bodies are therefore devoid of active biological substance, when their brains and hearts ceased to function, they were simply buried and not burned.

The qualities imputed to cloth can best be appreciated through some examples. Barren women in central India used to obtain part of the breast cloth of another, particularly fecund woman who was pregnant. The barren woman burnt it and ate the ashes, "thinking thereby to transfer the pregnant woman's quality of fertility to herself."[8] Again, when a Hindu widow remarried, a risky activity at the best of times, her old clothes and ornaments were often buried outside the boundary of her second husband's village.[9] She would also put on a new set of clothes. This is because part of the spirit of her dead husband was thought to be trapped in the fabric of her old clothes and might cause trouble as a jealous and malignant ghost.

Of course, these transformative qualities of cloth were not unique to Indian society. In Islamic societies, the turbans of great teachers could transmit spirit; in medieval Christendom, cloth relics such as the Shroud of Turin were particularly venerated, while even in today's agnostic Western societies, a dead man's clothes are often considered inauspicious. But in India, a person's holiness or pollution was perceived as peculiarly lambent and cloth as an especially sensitive medium. It would be hazardous to claim that all Indian societies were critically aware of the principles of purity and pollution, but even for those that were not, transactions in cloth widely implied a pledge of future protection. In many rural communities, for instance, the gift of a man to a woman of a piece of cloth did more than simply symbolize an act of marriage: it *was* the ritual of marriage itself. In parts of the north Indian hills where poor cultivators were unable to afford whole garments, small squares of cloth were passed as the marriage ritual, and their number was a pledge of the degree of reciprocal aid owed by the bride's family to the bridegroom's. This role of cloth had deep roots in Hindu tradition. In the *Mahabharata*, for instance, the mythic female Draupadhi, under attack by enemies, was endowed by the gods with a sari that had no end. The more cloth the enemies unwrapped, the more remained to protect her virtue. A similar theme pervaded Indo-Muslim culture. According to the flowery Persian metaphor for creation and protection, "God clothes the bosom of nature with the mantle of existence." As God's mantle protects the creatures living beneath it, so the king protects men. Cohn has recently noted that the gift of dress was the essential act of homage and rule within the Mughal system of kingship, effecting the incorporation of the subject into the ruler's body. Thus, in 1857, during the Great Rebellion, the poet Ghalib berated Indians for leaving the skirt (*daman*) of their "just" rulers, the British, and falling instead into the net (*dam*) of wickedness.[10]

Cloth and the social order

Here we consider the qualities of different types of cloth or clothes as they affect producers, donors, and wearers. First, it is interesting to note that different fabrics, weaves, and colors were considered to have distinct individual qualities.

A loose, coarse texture in cloth was often deemed to be the most porous to spirit and substance, whether holy or polluting. The looser and larger the knots, the more could be entrapped in them. One class of very loose-textured fabric was the *raksha*, used for fancy silk and braid armbands, neckties, and the like and worn on religious festivals. These fabrics were woven by a particular occupational group, the Patwas, who were deemed to be ritually superior to most other weaving castes. During the preparation of rakshas and other cloth talismans, a Brahmin was often employed to tie loose knots in the fabric. Chanting prayers all the while, the priest was able to fasten within the very knots themselves part of the spirit of various beneficent deities.[11] The loose texture of the "sacred thread" that the high castes wore had similar qualities – it was a trap for godliness, but at the same time it was quite vulnerable to accidental pollution. During meals, for instance, the thread was often tied around the head to avoid its pollution by contact with food. As we shall see, the porous quality of coarse homespun (*khadi*) became something to be prized during the nationalist movement: it seemed almost to be able to capture and retain the spirit of the land itself. But the danger was that coarse, hard-wearing fabrics of this sort could easily pick up impurities, or irritate and damage the skin; until Gandhi's time, homespun was regarded as boorish, perhaps even dirty.

For this reason, the tight, dense weave of quality fabrics was prized, not only for its aesthetic refinement and market value, but also because it rejected pollution more easily. Thus, silk was a peculiarly pure substance for Hindus. For most central Indian and southern Brahmins in the last century, silk was par excellence the dress for ritual and worship, and by extension it was used in other ritualized cultural performances (musicians, for instance, commonly wear silk upper garments). Silk was considered so much purer than cotton even of the best quality that it was not necessary to wash it before ceremonial use. According to the *Mitakshara* law, mere exposure was sufficient for silk was "washed by the air," itself a divine spirit.[12] But there was a certain ambiguity here, since the production of silk involved the killing of the silkworm, a potentially polluting act, and many castes were prohibited from participating in the preparation of silk thread.[13] In general, long exposure and the operations of the market were deemed to have removed the pollution of death before silk reached the final purchaser. It is intriguing to note, however, that some holy centers such as Benares did produce large quantities of a silk called *mukta*, which was made after the moth had pierced the cocoon and had escaped alive.[14] This was an inferior fabric so far as utilitarian and aesthetic value was concerned because the threads were broken, but it was much prized and commanded a high price. It was purchased by orthodox Vaishnavite Hindus and Jains (who both abhorred the taking of life) and was also considered appropriate for the ropes of sacred processional chariots and for the ritual swings used during the Krishna festival of Sawan.[15] Mukta kept many artisans and merchants in employment; it exemplifies with great clarity the danger of taking any commodity as a utilitarian given.

The conventions regarding the quality of cloth among Indian Muslims were deeply influenced by the Hindu environment, but did have different rationales, at least among the elites. Both religions had a notion of ritual purity. Ablution was an important precursor of both Muslim and Hindu worship, and garments such as socks, which retain pollution, were to be avoided, particularly at the mosque. But in theory at least, pollution had different connotations for the two religions. For Muslims, impurity was to be avoided, not so much because it endangered "bio-moral substance," but because (like woman's hair or narcotics) it distracted the worshiper from the free use of reason during prayer. Paradoxically, whereas Hindus were enjoined to use silk, Muslims were encouraged by the sayings of the Prophet to abjure it, on the ground that the luxurious preening of the individual to which it gave rise inhibited the worshiper from proper submission to God. The tensions between the use of silk as an adjunct to kingliness and the religious injunctions against it were quite severe in Indo-Muslim society. Firoz Shah Tughluq banned its use, but later sovereigns and learned men compromised.[16] So silk was forbidden at worship in the mosque but permissible outside it and even encouraged on the battlefield, where it was said to deflect sword cuts. Later, a cotton-silk mix called *mashru* (permitted silk) was made by weavers and spread all over India since it helped the less orthodox to look fine while conforming to the law.[17]

Color as much as texture was an essential feature of the quality of cloth and could also modify the moral and material status of the user. The mental or natural origins of color coding are of less importance to us here than the social categories with which it became associated. It is possible, as Pupul Jayakar suggests,[18] that the distribution of cloth colors across India represents an adjustment to the natural environment; colors were softer in the lush, subtropical regions, brighter and more varied in the harsh desert landscapes. The dominance of certain color schemes by region may reflect the ancient boundaries of the natural substances and plants from which the dyes were produced; and the reservation of white and yellow to Brahmins and high castes may echo interdicts on relations between them and the tribal peoples who collected and processed the dyes. Be that as it may, a cultural color code, which continues to influence village life, had already emerged by the time of the *Laws of Manu* before the beginning of the Christian era. White was associated with purity and was thus the proper color for Brahmins and widows. Red, which evokes blood and danger, was appropriate for enhancing the persona of soldiers and powerful female essences of any sort. Soldiers wore red turbans in battle, and women wore red clothes and reddened their hands and hair during marriages or fertility festivals. According to *Garga Smriti*, a Brahmin should wear white, Kshatriya (warrior) red, a Vaishya (mercantile person or cultivator) yellow (a color that implies an easy, natural fecundity), and a Shudra (menial) 'dark and dirty clothes.'[19] Insofar as it is possible to recapture the meaning of these injunctions, it seems that cloth of different colors was considered to have a magical and not merely a symbolic function; it enhanced or destroyed the innate qualities in individuals. Thus, a man receiving a wrong or inappropriate gift is "reduced to ashes like a piece of wood." "Evilly taken ... gold and food destroy his longevity, land and cow his body, a horse his eye (sight), *a garment his skin*, clarified butter his energy, sesamum grains his offspring."[20] Cloth, then, was almost literally as integral to the person as his skin.

Islamic color conventions generally overlapped or were penetrated by Hindu ones, but green, the Prophet's color, acquired particular sanctity. Green banners and green awnings for mosques and saints' tombs were common, but very devout Muslims adjured the use of green for loincloths and trousers to avoid insulting, or possibly polluting, the color. Muslims also elaborated the use of shot gold and silver fabrics in endowing or creating royalty. Gold and silver cloths for use as dowries were an obvious way of passing on stored value between generations, and symbolizing royal status for the bride and groom, who were regarded as royalty on their wedding day. But gold and silver were also credited with the power of transforming and enhancing human substance, as witness their use in various forms of traditional medicine. For Muslims, gold and silver also had a special value because of their capacity to absorb light. According to Indo-Persian philosophy, light (*nur*) was a divine quality, a visible manifestation of God's reason working in the world. Light was essential for the patterning of Islamic architecture, it preoccupied Islamic astronomy and astrology and it gave rise to an enormous taste for mirrors and shiny fabrics. "Light" and "mirror" became pervasive themes in Persian and Urdu literature. A king or noble who donned a cloth of gold or silver was, in effect, becoming a mirror of God, a direct transmitter of his divine light, as regal as the sun and stars, which were no more than other celestial transmitters. An early-nineteenth-century Arcot chronicler is going beyond mere flattery and hyperbole when he states: "The embroidered *khilat* [dress] of high value worn by the Nawwab [ruler] that day and also the ornaments set with jewels emitted such bright light that the world-illuminating sun felt depressed";[21] and, later, an English general at Trichinopoly was outshone like a "star by the sun." As at Versailles, in Indian royalty the Sun King is surrounded by his courtiers as stars. But the quality of the clothes is deemed to do more than represent the emanation of royalty. They are an aspect of it; they catch and reflect the rays of God's light.

Hitherto this section has considered some innate qualities of cloth. But even if the market were considered a neutral medium, it is important to note that the context of giving, receiving, and wearing could also influence the quality of the cloth and hence the moral quality of those who come into contact with it later. A suit of clothes "evilly taken" conveyed sin and destruction. In the same way, clothes received on particularly auspicious days or from holy hands can store their good qualities indefinitely. Village women reserved particularly auspicious saris and colors for important days, but the convention also reached the King himself. In the Emperor Akbar's court, there was a special department for receiving the shawls and dresses (*khelats*) given as tributes or pledges by different notables and regions.[22] The articles received here were graded according to their quality, the appropriateness and fineness of their colors, but also according to the time when they were received and worn. Goods received on the "first day of the month of Fawardin" or the King's birthday had a higher rank assigned to them than pieces arriving on other days. These acquired qualities resided in the cloth until it was given to another recipient in a ritual exchange at court.

A cloth could influence the substance and spirit of the wearer, but it could also acquire qualities from him. These qualities depended on the status of the individual, but also the honor and purity of the part of the body on which it had been worn. The feet and loins were the least honorable, the head the most honorable. This accounts for the importance of the turban in Indian dress conventions. Among Hindus the turban not only protected the head, seat of the brain and of a man's semen, but was also imbued with the power of these substances. Pulling off a man's turban was indeed the gravest insult, a challenge to his rank, his reason, even his virility. Islamic notions added another layer of meaning. The turban, of course, had become a symbol of spiritual succession in the Muslim countries of the Middle East at an early date. Gravestones of the classical and early Christian period had often featured representations of the human form, but since this was forbidden by Islam, Muslims began to use the turban and hairpiece as a gravestone symbol.[23] The turban itself therefore became associated with the teacher-pupil relationship in the Sufi mystical orders. A holy man's turban became a powerful carrier for his *barakat*, or spiritual charisma, in Indian Islam. So in 1857 the Lucknow rebels carried as their standard the turban of one of the city's foremost religious leaders. When the teacher Sayyid Aḥmed of Rai Bareilly visited Calcutta in the early years of the nineteenth century, so great was the throng of would-be disciples that, unable to lay hands on all of them, he unraveled his twenty-foot turban and allowed them to initiate themselves by touching part of its length.[24]

Cloth and its producers

The qualities with which cloth was seen to be imbued by Indians had implications not only for the status of those who used it, but also for those who produced and serviced it. This section is concerned with the social and moral status of spinners, weavers, dyers, and washermen as it affected, and was affected by the qualities of cloth.

In India as in many other societies, the distinction between spinning and weaving was theoretically central to the division of labor within the family. According to the Laws of Manu, unmarried girls were the spinners ("spinsters"), whereas after marriage they graduated to weaving (becoming "wives"). With the development of professional weaving castes, this distinction became less important, though among artisans themselves, it seems to have persisted until the nineteenth century, when imported thread began to make domestic spinning redundant.

More interesting is the deep ambiguity that attached to the status of the weaver himself in Indian society. Most weaving communities hovered uneasily on the line that separated pure castes (best defined in this context as those from whom Brahmins could take water) and impure ones.[25] Yet the cloth the weavers produced was generally considered neutral. According to the Shastras, 'The hand of the artisan is always pure.'[26] The low, sometimes impure status of many weaving communities seems best explained in terms of historical contingencies. First, weaving communities had often differentiated themselves only recently from pickers of wild cotton or producers of plaited leaf baskets, groups of tribal origin on the fringes of Hindu society. Second, manual work was widely regarded as degrading in the Hindu scheme of occupational precedence. Finally, lower village artisans, including poor weavers, were usually in a dependent position in relation to the agricultural castes in that they received grain payments from their hands as payment for work. Since taking gifts depressed status, weavers were ranked below the clean Shudra agriculturalists.[27] Some evidence for this last interpretation can be found in the fact that urban weavers and more specialized craftsmen in the village who were paid in money through the operation of the market were usually of much higher status.

At the same time, the act of weaving was itself an act of *creation*, almost an act of worship, and this brought about the ambiguity in the position of the weaver. The notion of creation is central to the caste foundation myths of weaving communities, which themselves embody a claim for high status. According to the legends of the Devangas of Mysore, for instance, in the beginning men went naked and Brahma created Manu to weave clothes for them and hide their shame.[28] When Manu achieved beatitude, he was reincarnated from the eye on Shiva's forehead in the form of Devala. Devala went to fetch the thread for weaving from the heart of the lotus stems that grew out of the navel of Vishnu, the protector. In a battle against demons, Devala invoked the aid of Shiva's consort who slew them. The blood of the demons was used as coloring matter for the cloth and produced the five elemental colors, black, white, red, green, and yellow. This and similar myths all evoke the notion of creation through images of the navel and the lotus; other weaving caste myths have Vishnu seated by the primeval ocean or relate weaving to images of churning or the movement of waves, which also refer back to basic Hindu creation stories. The weaver was thus a flawed creator, a status that bears comparison with the Greek notion that Hephaistos, patron of artisans, was a divine being, but lame.

Indian weavers could improve on their dubious status by creating finer and "purer" commodities. The social position of coarse cotton weavers was almost always low; that of fine muslin weavers higher, and silk weavers or groups that produced various gold and silver brocades, the highest of all. Not only were the specialist weavers associated with commodities of greater fineness and purity, but their assured market among aristocrats and temples removed them from dependence on ordinary agricultural patrons. In areas where precolonial rulers had been particular patrons of specialist weavers, as in Bengal or Mysore, this appears to have acted to raise the status of the groups as a whole. Weavers also sought to improve their status through the claims to equality or rank offered by non-Hindu religions or sects within Hinduism. In north India, many followed the saint-reformer Kabir, himself a weaver; in the south many were Lingayats. Most common of all was conversion to Islam. This is not to say that weavers were highly regarded among Muslims. On the contrary, they were stereotyped as idle, stupid, and quarrelsome: "a female weaver will even pull her father's beard," went the adage.[29] Yet weavers were noted for their piety in observing festivals: "What is Id [the major Muslim festival] without the weaver?" it was said. In particular, weavers taxed themselves heavily on a corporate basis in order to prepare ceremonial floats (*tazias*) for the Mohurrum festival.[30] Muslim reformers of the nineteenth century, such as Sayyid Ahmed Shahid in north India or the Faraizis of Bengal, also found a ready audience among weavers who were attracted to the cry for a purified Muslim religion. But within their profession, Muslim weavers like Hindus could always seek to move up, producing finer and purer commodities as a tactic for raising status. For instance, they sought to throw off the rather demeaning title *julaha* and become instead *nur-baft* or *momin*.[31] *Nurbaft* implies "capturer [or weaver] of light," so here again the Islamic theme of light impinges on the production of cloth. Dacca muslins of the seventeenth and eighteenth centuries were peculiarly prized for their whiteness, their lightness in weight and texture, and their capacity to pass through a ring.[32] Many fine fabrics had names that evoked moonlight or cobwebs, which caught light or the substance of dreams. Weavers who sought the highest status, like the silk-weavers of Madanpura in Benares, often dressed from head to foot in white themselves. The Lucknow historian Abdul Halim Sharar mentions a group of specially favored silk craftsmen dressed all in white, who once produced the fabric for the slippers of the high ladies of the court before its fall in 1856. So attached to their hard-won status were they that those who survived under British rule, "though frustrated and reduced to poverty, will not agree to produce modern slippers to improve their position."[33]

The potentially high status of the weaver as a creator or craftsman in light is brought out if we compare him to two other occupational groups that came into frequent contact with cloth as a commodity and as a possession: the tailor (*darzi*) and the washerman (*dhobi*). Unlike the carder, spinner, or weaver, who were seen by Hindus as creators, the tailor was a cutter, a destroyer. Thus, stitched garments that had previously been cut were regarded as impious among highly orthodox families because in some sense they had lost their integrity, besides being difficult to wash and so acting as traps for impurity. The occupational habits of tailors were also rumored to be impure because they were said to use spittle in the preparation of thread for sewing and then to wind it between their toes.[34] Finally, for some Brahmins, stitched clothes were associated with Islam, in which wholly different perceptions of stitched garments obtained. The Koranic injunction to Muslims to cover all parts of the body necessitated tailoring; unstitched garments were regarded as barbaric. Thus, whereas Hindu women regarded the sari as the highest form of female garment and the blouse (*choli*) as demeaning until well into the nineteenth century Abdul Halim Sharar, the Lucknow Muslim writer, declared "The sari is an untailored garment and a relic of primitive times." Moreover, "embellishment was a principle of civilisation, otherwise the simplest thing would be to remain in the nude."[35] The tailor was thus an outcast when he lived in proximity to Hindus; among Muslims he was less condemned, but his work was "women's work" and therefore degrading.

Finally, the washerman or dhobi intervened when cloth had already become a possession but temporarily became a commodity once again in order to be reprocessed. Here we are reminded of Igor Kopytoff's analysis in Chapter 2. Commodities, once they have passed through the market, become individualized or "singularized" into a particular domestic or ritual role. But their cultural lives may not stop here. In the case of cloth, the act of washing temporarily brought it into society once again as a kind of commodity. But this was not a neutral process; the very act of washing transferred the accumulated dirt and pollution of the individual cloth to the dhobi who cleansed it, with ambiguous consequences for his social standing.

As is well known, the ritual position of the dhobi in Hindu society was particularly low in that his trade required him to touch highly polluting substances such as feces and menstrual blood. Orthodox families generally refused to allow dhobis within their houses, and some Brahmins even ceremonially rewashed their clothes after receiving them back from the dhobi by sprinkling them with Ganges water. Here again one encounters the peculiar quality of cloth retaining and transferring not only dirt, but sin. The dhobi was an inauspicious figure, to be avoided when beginning a journey: he was said to know "the defects of the village"; more precisely and dangerously, he knew its defecations. James Tod, the British historian of Rajasthan, mentions a revealing oath taken over a well in Rajasthan: "If I do not perform so-and-so, may all the good deeds of my fathers fall into the washerman's well."[36] The washerman's well here is literally a kind of hell hole, in which the accumulated sin and filth of the village are so powerfully concentrated that they can cancel out the good acts of a family and condemn its ancestors to perdition. Like all malevolent influences, the dhobi was thought to be particularly tricky. One of his favorite games was to pollute a man's garments without the latter's knowledge, so "the king's headscarf becomes the washerman's loin cloth."[37]

But the apparent paradox was this: precisely because the washerman was known to absorb dirt and sin and dangerous substances generally, he was also capable of playing the role of a minor ritualist, a base priest. At a very lowly level, the washerman reproduced the ambiguous position of the Brahmin priest. Because the priest was in contact with sin and pollution, even his great ritual purity could not always prevail against it. For this reason, priests who officiated at temples were often considered to be of relatively low rank within the Brahmin class, and those who took part in cremation ceremonies and absorbed the sin of the dead were even regarded as inauspicious. In the same way, the Mysore washerman, the Agusa, occupied an important ritual position in village society. No worship of the village goddesses could take place without the help of the Agusa, who officiated as a *pujari* (low ritualist), especially when the goddess of small pox, cholera, and plague had to be propitiated at the outbreak of one of these epidemics.[38] The theme of washing was prominent in these rites. The washerman would take the idol of the goddess from the family or village shrine and make offerings to it and cleanse it at the place where he normally washed clothes. The malevolent, overheated female powers of the deity, which had caused the outbreak, were thus washed away in the same way that dangerous female pollutants attached to clothes were dispersed by ordinary washing.

Cloth and the kingdom

The transformative and symbolic qualities of cloth ensured that it retained a position in marking the enhancing relations within broader arenas of society and politics. Like ceremonial food offerings, donations of cloth to temple deities among Hindus or to saints' shrines among Muslims were appropriate because they could be redistributed after worship as sanctified substances. They could capture holiness and pass it on slowly, long after worship – like food, which has a more powerful but only transitory effect. Whole suits of clothing were offered to the gods as to kings. At the tombs of Muslim holy men, it was customary to present a plain white sheet (*chadar*, the same type of cloth used for the winding sheet of a corpse); these sheets could later be cut up and distributed among the worshipers.

The role of cloth transactions in both petty local arenas and the wider polity may become clearer if we return to some of the general themes of this book. The concepts of purity and pollution in Indian society provided an unusual pressure in the direction of the singularization of things. That is to say, things were not easily separated from persons; cloth, for instance, could pick up the substance of the people handling it during manufacture, sale, wearing, even washing. In this context, the anthropologist Célestin Bouglé remarked, in a little-known essay, that patterns of consumption in India were broken down into vast numbers of small circles. No dynamic general market could exist in India, he thought, because each caste had its own food, its own vessels, its own clothing, insignia, and so forth. So, "Where the caste system reigns, the empire of custom which forces us to imitate our ancestors, opposes the inroads of fashion which invites us to imitate strangers."[39]

However, there were equally powerful forces working in the direction of commoditization. Things had to acquire a neutral status within the village for transactions in food and essential goods to take place. In larger polities, exchange had to be general for kings to amass resources, especially revenue paid in silver rupees. Some cultural strategies mediating this conflict have been noted: the "hand of the artisan" was held to be pure; fine, pollution-resistant materials could be used; cloths could be washed or sprinkled with Ganges water. But the major institution that mediated between commoditization and singularization was the office of the king, whether this be construed as the dominant caste brotherhood within the village or the emperor of all India. The duty of the king was to consume the wares of his subjects and to make his court the great engine of redistribution. In this way, the needs of the particularistic local community producing a good could be balanced with the needs of the polity as a whole. The propagation of diversity in patterns of consumption – of cloths, fruits, spices, grains – was the physical manifestation of the King's classic role as arbiter between the castes. And it was changes in royal consumption, or the consumption of those aspiring to local political dominance, that provided the Indian economy with the dynamism Bouglé thought it lacked.

For these reasons gifts of cloth retained their place within the ranking and tribute systems of Indian states long after payments and presentations in kind had been replaced by coin and the outward signs of a fully commercialized economy. But the relationship between flows of cloth and flows of money within early modern Indian kingdoms was extremely complex, for questions of value were intimately

bound up with matters of political economy. The use of cloth as a
medium for integrating the kingdom might precede, supplement, or
even outlast the operation of tributary flows of money, and at no point
did cloth become "merely" a commodity, whose production and distribution was solely determined by market forces. The close and ambiguous relationship between coin and cloth is seen at the very heart
of Mughal court ritual, for instance, the presentation of *nazar* or coins
in exchange for a suit of clothes or valued cloths (the *khelat*).[40] In this
transaction, the king was pledging protection and incorporating the
subject into his royal body through the action of the royal charisma
that was immanent in the cloth. The donation of cloth in effect prolonged the "sight" (*darshan*) of royalty for the subject, who was thought
to benefit morally and materially from his contact with kingship. But
since the subject could not himself confer benefit on the king (unless
he was an equal or near-equal) by a gift of cloth or food, the neutral
medium of money was used.

Cloth transactions continued to underpin the commercial structure
of the Mughal empire. In areas where gold and silver were scarce,
payment was often made in cloth. Thus a large part of the tribute of
Kashmir was paid in the fine woolen shawls that were its most prized
product. An important section of the royal household at Delhi was
devoted to the reception, grading, and storage of shawls and other
cloths remitted from the outer empire. Later, after the incorporation
into the empire of the rich province of Bengal, a new administrative
arm, the *malmul khas* (muslin house) was established to oversee the
provision of Bengal muslins and silks for the courts at Delhi and
Agra.[41] Heavy consumption of Bengal muslins (as of Gujarat silks)
was an act of patronage designed to tie the new provinces into the
empire and to legitimate the tribute taken from them. The Emperor
Jahangir himself set the pattern for wearing light muslins and pearls
at court, and the style rapidly diffused through the aristocracy and
administration. But the greatest source of demand was the women's
quarters of the north Indian courts. European visitors remarked that
in the early seventeenth century, the Delhi court alone housed 2,000
women, the vast majority of whom were aristocratic ladies obliged by
convention to replace every 24 hours their dresses, which comprised
two or three pieces of Bengal muslin each.[42] This demand alone
accounted for about one million pieces per annum, at an estimated
50-100 rupees each. The value of the *malmul khas* therefore equaled
a substantial proportion of the land tax that Bengal paid in coin to
the center, so that dress conventions established by court ritual exercised a formative influence on the whole structure of north Indian

trade. A later observer, William Hamilton, remarked that until about 1730, the tribute of Bengal had been remitted to the center by bankers' bills, "for the payment of which sufficient funds were at Delhi and Lahore supplied in the sale and consumption of the rich manufactures of Bengal. In fact, if it had not been so, no tribute could ever have been remitted."[43] When Persian invasions and internal turbulence impoverished the nobility of the empire's heartland, no more tribute was in fact paid "as it was utterly impossible that the same or indeed any considerable sum could have been transferred from a country of which gold and silver form no part of the natural products."

It can be seen, then, that the consumption preferences of the court played an important part in integrating the money economy of the Mughal Empire. These patterns of consumption, at the heart of which lay the "administered trade" in Kashmir shawls or Bengal and Gujarat clothes, had grown out of systems of ritual presentation. Transactions in goods continued to represent more than simple commodity flows. The Mughal emperor received cloth and other precious things from his domains because a great king was a great consumer and was honored in accord with the variety of fine products displayed at his court. The concept of variety is important here; all the chroniclers harp on it. Whereas "uniform" – a uniformity of clothes – has often symbolized and enhanced the unity of modern states, a *controlled diversity of styles* signified the greatness of the Mughal and other oriental monarchs. Like God's, the king's house must contain many mansions. Courtiers and officials from different regions developed stylized forms of the dress of their different regions and took care to display their particular cloth styles within the broad limits laid down by the prevailing court conventions. The variety of turban, cloak, and mantle represented, but also in a sense fixed, the styles of artisan production appropriate to the different homelands and divisions of the state.

This pattern was common to less exalted dominances also. Much has been written of the remittance of land revenue from peasant to official, landlord, or king. But the opposite flow, representing the duty of the notable to consume the natural and human produce of his territories, has been neglected. For instance, the rapid expansion and growing eminence throughout the subcontinent of the cotton products of the district of Azamgarh after 1650 appears to have been connected with the fact that this district was made over as a land revenue assignment to the daughter of the Emperor Shahjahan. By offering continuous patronage and a ready market, the royal lady's household ensured the development there of a new cloth industry.[44]

The importance of the role of presentations in cloth for the structure of Indo-Muslim kingdoms is emphasised by the persistence of these transactions even after the market or administration of the empire or kingdom had declined. At Delhi in the 1780s, observers noted the presence of the distinctive striped cloth of the small province of Kara.[45] Kara was almost the last significant political division outside the environs of the capital to be directly ruled by the Mughal emperor, and it was his place of exile during the late 1760's and early 1770's. The Muslim kingdom of Arcot in south India provides another example. After 1800 its erstwhile ruler was reduced to the position of a pensioner of the British. His agents had been replaced everywhere by British appointees, and he subsisted on a relatively small allowance. Yet a chronicle of about 1820 records a journey through "his" territory by the ruler with a retinue supposedly numbering 20,000 men, during which the Nawab visited the holy places and reaffirmed his sovereignty over all the petty kings and officials of the realm as it stood about 1760. At every point in this progress the chronicler noted in stunning detail the color, texture, style, and place of origin of the cloth and clothes that passed between the ruler and "his" subjects. Thus, a subordinate official was given a red shawl, a more important one a blue and gold turban manufactured at the reputed center of "Madhra."[46] The guardian of a saint's tomb received a pure white shawl, and in return a holy man gave the Nawab a dress of pure white,[47] which symbolized his own role as a guardian of the holy places of south India, Mecca, and Medina. Again, the particular colors and dresses of the Nawab were noted in great detail because each symbolized – but also enhanced – an aspect of his royalty. He rode at one stage in an "emerald-colored" coach and reclined on a cushion of red English hide for "these two colors betoken the prosperity and contentment of the Nawab."[48] In his aspect of royal sun, he wore a robe of gold thread, but when emphasizing his family and religious status, he rode in a "Wallajahi-green coach,"[49] Wallajahi being the family name and green the Prophet's color. It seems that each gift and each piece of cloth worn conveyed a precise status on the recipient or wearer, though the meanings of these gradations are often difficult to recover.

In the late seventeenth century, India was one of the greatest producers and certainly the greatest exporter of cloth in the world. Even in a society where state revenue was paid in cash and a sophisticated market system existed, direct transactions of gifted commodities – notably food and cloth – bonded a vast number of social relationships. A mid-nineteenth-century source reckoned, for example, that only

20 percent of the subcontinent's raw cotton production was sold as such in internal or external markets. The vast bulk was made up into cloth and used in local transactions, given as offerings by weavers to superiors, by villagers to Brahmins and temples, or by agricultural magnates to their dependents as patronage. Transactions in cloth or grain could transfer value and honor (though also pollution and dishonor) in a way money could not. Cloth, in comparison with grain or cooked food, was a safer medium of transaction since it stored "biomoral energy" longer, though it was unable to create the same immediate transfer of brotherhood (or pollution) as feast, for instance.

Even within the market, the supply, nature, and distribution of cloth was influenced, though more distantly, by cultural preferences and expectations. Kings and other great men were expected to patronize producers and markets without close reference to questions of price or immediate need. This explains the custom by which a royal cavalcade, entering or leaving the market area of a city, was expected to pause and purchase directly in the bazaars, stepping outside the royal provisioning system for a time. This helped to emphasize the king's immediate concern for the welfare of his producers. In fact, the totality of such transactions within and outside the market can be regarded as something like a political discourse upholding the legitimacy of the ruler and pledging the attachment of subjects. Indian society spoke partly in the idiom of cloth, though idiom is really too weak a word since cloth could actually transfer power and transform relationships. The penetration of European goods during the nineteenth century and the end of royal patronage for India's weavers and spinners represented, therefore, something more than a crisis in economic history. It actually came to be a crisis of legitimacy for the new colonial rulers. Following Habermas, we are used to thinking of crises of legitimacy in modern Western societies as the product of a breakdown in the discourse regarding duties and obligations linking state and society. In preindustrial agrarian kingdoms, however, transactions in goods representing the labor and integrity of communities, castes, or families were themselves elevated to the status of discourse. The failure of the king to consume, the artisan to produce, or the merchant to market was tantamount to a denial of political obligation.

The origins of swadeshi

The remainder of this paper concerns the disruption of India's internal transactions in cloth as a result of the import of European machine-made goods, and the attempt to reconstitute the basis of home consumption through the swadeshi movement of the late nineteenth and early twentieth centuries. These topics have received considerable attention from economic historians, from analysts concerned with the political history of the Indian National Congress and from nationalist writers themselves. The concern here, however, is first the perception of these events by Indians, and second, the elaboration in the modern period of attitudes to cloth, weavers, and weaving that informed the cultural ordering of cloth consumption before colonial rule. Historians have generally addressed the issue of colonial penetration in terms of the practical reason of the marketplace. Indians bought British textiles, it is asserted, because they were cheaper by 30-50 percent than the indigenous ones and of finer quality. Even if this were granted, some consideration is required of the impact of this utilitarian deluge on the customs, assumptions, and relationships that were built around the exchange of cloth.

In fact, though, the spread of British products in India was a reflection of changing culture and political economy and not merely a response to better prices. Similarly, the later rejection of European styles and British goods, partial as it was, transcended purely practical politics and touched on issues of national identity, which temporarily resurrected the transformative value of cloth. In fact, even those Europeans who sold cloth to Indians were aware that simple economizing was not the only issue: taste had to be considered and cultural preferences accommodated. As Sir George Watt put it about 1900:

Throughout India, certain localities are famed for the qualities, design, etc., of their goods. The merchant must ascertain the exact size and shape, the particular quality and colour in demand in each locality. The mere fact of offering a superior quality of goods is no inducement to trade. Few countries in the world are more conservative regarding their garments than the various races and castes of India.[50]

How, then, do culturally determined patterns of consumption change to accommodate alien manufactures in a society in which the market itself is not powerful enough to create taste? Here it is important that the first English broadcloths and cotton goods were beginning to be imported into India during the final metamorphosis of the Mughal political system after 1740, when new regional consumer aristocracies were establishing themselves, notably in Lucknow, Bengal, and Hyderabad. The elaborate patterns of consumption that emerged in these sub-Mughal courts proved to be an excellent medium through which European cloths and clothes could become valued articles.

Late Mughal kingship and consumption

The consumption patterns of the Mughal successor states of the eighteenth century, whether in food, cloth, or architectural style, were becoming more involute, varied, and elaborate. In part, this reflected political instability and the desire of new dynasties and their servants to validate themselves by use of the material symbols of as many earlier or contemporary rulers as possible. The very instability of office, particularly in a situation where short-lived arriviste dynasties were served by eunuchs and an increasingly professionalized administration severed from direct control of the land, encouraged competitive consumption. When the great Lucknow eunuch-administrator Jawahir Ali Khan paraded his contingent of soldiers and servants "*Sabit-khanis* [household troops] in mango green livery, irregulars in black, Mewatis [a Muslim convert group] in white," this display made other rich men of the city "burn with envy" according to the chronicler Faiz Baksh.[51] It is significant that this parading of military power by rulers and aristocrats provided the first important avenue through which English textiles achieved value in society and began to balance the English East India Company's exports in the manner previously reserved for silver. As European military advisers and armaments became more common in eighteenth-century India, rulers sought to enhance the prowess of their own armies by dressing them in scarlet English broadcloth. Thick dyed red cloth and red harness were peculiarly appropriate to the traditional color-coding of the Indian warrior classes; and the use of red serge spread from the Nawab of Awadh's 60,000-man army to those of his competitors and by degrees to a whole range of irregulars, guards, and doormen. The potency of the image of the "red coat" is evident throughout nineteenth-century India and persists even today. Red sepoys guard the doors of Rajput palaces as murals; redcoats march in marriage processions; and the red sepoy even became the symbol on the banner of the priest-genealogists who await pilgrims at the great Hindu river festivals.

The association of English broadcloth with military prowess was matched by the incentive to use imported styles and fabrics in what might be called political display. Factions in the Mughal court had often marked themselves off by particular dress and preferences for certain types of cloth. Sharar mentions, for instance, the example of the "Kandahari pyjama,"[52] which became fashionable at court when nobles wished to associate themselves with the valor of the soldiers from that town. Akbar's search for a syncretic Hindu-Muslim faith for his reconstituted empire was marked by a greater use of silk and the renaming of articles of Muslim dress with Sanskrit terms.[53]

Turbans became smaller at this time, to accommodate Muslim head-gear to Hindu style. Similarly, in the later eighteenth and early nineteenth centuries, court factions trying to establish alliances with the British community adopted some European styles and products. The rise of the "General's *topi*" (hat) and the European-buttoned frock coat (*sherwani*) at Lucknow in the 1820's[54] paralleled the court's shift from Mughal tributary to a growing dependence on the British. (It is splendid irony that the present-day rulers of Pakistan, embarrassed by the un-Islamic Saville Row suits that their founder, Mohammed Ali Jinnah, habitually wore in contemporary photographs, have re-touched him back into the *sherwani*, a garment that actually marked a much more critical shift toward Western dress.)

Another avenue of consumption preference by which European goods first breached oriental patterns of consumption was the insatiable desire of India's rulers for novelties. Trade routes and commercial connections established for the sale of clocks, china menageries, mirrors, and elaborate embroidery were later adapted to supply aristocratic taste in cloth, and finally helped create a mass demand for imported textiles. European writers tended to see the demand for novelties as a childish desire for trinkets. Actually, the profusion of novelties in a court was considered another mark of great kingship. It bespoke vast and varied realms, connections with far-off kings; as God the ruler of the universe had created all manner of beasts and objects, so his earthly shadow must rule over a profusion of creations. Commercial agents up-country remarked how much easier it was at first to find a market for novelties than for standard manufactures. Cloths from England with different colors on each side were favored at the Hardwar Fair.[55] Lucknow supported a huge demand for anything made with glass. Huge quantities of sheet glass from England were used in the creation of the great prayer halls (the Chhota and Bara Imambaras),[56] and looking glasses, spyglasses, and sequined cloth found a ready market.

Courts also borrowed and learned from one another, and though knowledge of the aristocratic style of Europe was minimal in India before the mid-nineteenth century, contact with other Asian courts was more frequent. The "Sultan of Rum" – the Ottoman Emperor – was an important model here because most Indian monarchs venerated him as Protector of the Holy Places and retained embassies at Istanbul. Ottoman style had already abandoned its classic Islamic line and color. During the eighteenth century, closer incorporation of Turkey into the concert of Europe had signaled the appearance of Louis Quinze furniture, Meissen porcelain, English velvet, and gloves. Then, after 1780, a wholesale Westernization of court dress occurred as pressure for military reforms grew within the empire.[57] What was happening in Istanbul, as in contemporary Indian courts, was a substantial shift in material culture, as the object and furniture replaced the classic line of formal Islamic art as the pattern for living space. The embellishment of the inside of buildings with a profusion of objects, pictures, tapestries, and furniture became the order of the day in India, reaching its apogee in the cluttered Malik Palace of Calcutta, with its crowd of Carrara marble statues, and the Salar Jang Palace in Hyderabad, where grandfather clocks jostled with huge French chaises longues. It was through this shift in aristocratic taste that English fabrics and English clothing styles first gained a foothold in the Indian market.

Two underlying principles were at work here. First, it is probable that, as with the sepoys' redcoats, a strong magical influence was operating in regard to European fabrics and styles. Hamilton Buchanan noted in 1812 in the up-country Bengal district of Dinajpur that articles used by European gentlemen who were returning home sold in the local market for considerably more than their Calcutta market price and costs of transport.[58] It was as if people wanted these objects as tokens of superior European power. Second, it is important that this first stage in the colonization of Indian taste occurred at a time when Indo-Muslim style was itself becoming more varied, embellished, and involute, thus facilitating the incorporation of foreign novelties in its principles of design. It may be that an aesthetic shift was taking place that was largely autonomous of changes in the political economy.[59]

A transition from pure, classical forms on the one hand to elaborate, "baroque" styles on the other has taken place from time to time within the great artistic traditions, and it is often both difficult and suspect to reduce these transformations to matters of social change or political economy. The mind of the artist, trameled by convention, may seek to break free, first by a dense repetition of themes, later by ornamentation. But if this period of change coincides with intense political competition or the inroads of foreign influences, as it did in eighteenth-century India, variety and complexity might be redoubled.

Cultural factors in the growth of mass imports

If changes in royal and aristocratic taste provide an opportunity for the entry of British commodities into India, what was the social context within which this market penetration dramatically broadened? By the 1870's, Britain was supplying 25-30 percent of eastern India's total demand for cloth. First, of course, the growing reputation of European dress styles in India greatly stimulated the market for textiles themselves. Dress, always a marker of identities, became an explosive issue in the early nineteenth century as an obvious marker of cultural change. Sharar's account of Lucknow in the 1860's and '70's illustrates how complex the process had become. Rival schools of theologians adopted different styles of headgear.[60] Modernizing Sunni Muslims like Sir Sayyid Ahmed adopted European clothes and a Turkish head-piece; modernizing Shia Muslims took European clothes and the four-pointed hat associated with Persian reformers. Loose-fitting pajamas were appropriate to the more orthodox among rebellious youth, while alcohol drinkers and meat eaters took to tight English trousers. The emergence of English-style professions after 1850, with their emphasis on occupational rituals and conformity, also tended to break down resistance to European clothing and hence to English fabrics. Class formation and access to the resources of the colonial power both demanded an accommodation with Europe, at least in the public arena. Hindus who had worn Mughal court dress with Hindu *dhotis* in private now exchanged the Muslim style for frock coat and trousers. European clothes and styles had a differential effect on various occupational groups. Professional men and government servants were the most Westernized, landowners in contact with magistrates and collectors the next so, whereas mercantile people and Brahmins generally retained their traditional loose white garments. In the countryside, there was no appreciable shift toward European *styles* of clothing. But by 1870, English textiles that could be made up into Indian styles were in widespread use.

The economic facts are well enough known.[61] The rapid improvement of internal and external transport after 1850 greatly reduced the costs that the Lancashire mill owners and exporters incurred in selling their goods in India. Railways and better roads opened up villages in the interior, so that by 1880, up to 30 percent of eastern India's demand for cloth was met by foreign imports. Two other factors were at work. First, the expansion of the silver money supply after 1857, combined with the faster pace of economic and demographic growth, pushed Indian prices higher. This tended to increase the labor cost of the indigenous artisan, who had to pay more for his food and essential supplies. The price differential between European industrial products and local, hand-woven cloth grew greater. Second, Lancashire's greater competitiveness coincided with a surge in Indian rural consumer spending as agricultural prices went up and the relative weight of state demand for land revenue came down throughout India. Only in the 1890's did the Indian mills in Bombay and Ahmedabad begin to take back these lost markets.

Although observers such as Watt and Watson emphasised the imperative need for exporters to pay attention to style, color, and use, preference for homespun cloth as such had generally broken down. C. A. Silberrad wrote of the United Provinces, "There is hardly a trace of preference for hand-woven over machine-woven articles on caste or sentimental grounds."[62] He did mention that a number of "old-fashioned landowners" in Bara Banki district patronized indigenous weavers, and other sources indicate that substantial numbers of artisans were still producing fabrics for specialist religious functions, a market completely closed to imported textiles. Superior color and fine texture, always valued in indigenous cloth production, gave English fabrics the advantage. Only where especially durable or very cheap cloth was required did hand-woven textiles hold out in the face of direct foreign competition. In the medium- and high-quality ranges, Lancashire was one-third cheaper at least and was making rapid inroads into the market until India's own factories moved into mass production in the 1880's.

However, explanations of the British penetration of the Indian market in these terms seem inadequate in that they seem to suggest that purely economizing and utilitarian consumption preferences had taken over in an area that had previously been influenced by ritual, notions of kingship, and questions of community. This was not so. In the initial phase of mass sales, English cloth succeeded because it was compatible with the cultural preferences of local consumers. In parts of the world where it was not compatible – the Far East, for instance – no such headway was made despite equivalent price advantages and better transport. The fact was the English cloth fitted into the area of consumption preferences once occupied by very fine, close-woven cottons and indigenous silks. Interestingly, a wide range of English-made cloths were designated *nankeen*, a word taken over from the high-quality, fine-textured Chinese cloths that the East India Company had once imported from the China coast. English nankeen looked good, was easily washed, and was more comfortable to wear than Indian cloth. It was beginning to acquire a cachet: the peasantry considered it "a mark of being well-off to be able to dress their wives and children in English manufactured cloth."[63] A reputation for fineness of weave and "cleanness" contrasted with the still lowly reputation of homespun. Foreign cloth avoided the many dangers and uncertainties associated with artisan products, which still retained the ghost of their transformative essences. Only the impact of nationalism began to shift these preferences.

Swadeshi and home industry

The swadeshi movement, which in its radical form was complemented by a boycott of English goods, bears comparison with other nativistic upsurges in Asia and Africa that rejected European products or refused to produce European crops as symbols of local or national oppression. The interest of these campaigns for this essay is how in their course, Indian nationalist leaders transformed and used the themes of protection, legitimacy, shame, and magic that were associated with cloth and dress in popular mentalities. In particular, Gandhi himself went beyond the use of homespun as a mere symbol to penetrate to even deeper levels of meaning about the nature of weaving as a creative act, about the dhobi's cleansing as a token of redemption, and about the capacity of cloth to retain the luminosity of place and people.

Before the 1880's, resistance to the colonialization of taste and the import of European goods was at best sporadic. The Madras army mutinied at Vellore in 1806, when British regulations seemed to threaten the customary style of turbans, and hence the virility of the sepoys. Muslim jurists at first allowed the use of European clothes, provided that indigenous dress (associated with the Prophet himself) was used at mosques. Later, some learned men issued injunctions against European dress and English cloth on the grounds that they damaged the livelihood of weavers who were the ballast of the Muslim community. But the most widespread ventilation of the plight of weavers, outside British papers, was seen during the north Indian Rebellion of 1857 against colonial rule. Many rebel proclamations referred specifically to the ill done by British imports. The Azamgarh population, for instance, noted how weavers, cotton dressers, carpenters, blacksmiths, and others had been reduced to penury. "But under the Badshahi government [restored Mughal rule] the Indian artisans will be employed exclusively in the services of the kings, the rajas, and the rich, and this will no doubt ensure their prosperity."[64] Artisans were urged to join the rebellion, and a substantial number of them did so in the small towns of the Ganges valley. It does seem that the failure of British government to purchase artisan wares – its failure to engage in reciprocal transactions in return for tribute or to provide service – amounted to a crisis of legitimacy for it. British officials in the early nineteenth century frequently encountered complaints that the East India Company had forgone its duty to consume and build, constructing instead merely "jails and courthouses." If in a literate society, a legitimacy crisis is manifested in the collapse of public discourse about the obligations of society to government, in a preliterate society, the failure of government to transact in an accepted medium of exchange, whether it be cloth, or cattle, or bird-of-paradise feathers, might have the same implication.

Articulate and sustained opposition to British imports, however, only took fire in the later nineteenth century, as a precursor to the nationalist movement. Its first peak was the swadeshi campaign in Bengal from 1905 to 1910, which was a concerted effort to boost home industry through a boycott of British goods. The spark that ignited swadeshi was political, the decision by the government of Lord Curzon to partition the province of Bengal and dampen radical nationalism in the process. But the ideas of the movement had been propagated for several decades by Indian businessmen and mill owners to promote their own products in a difficult commercial environment.[65] Swadeshi was also heir to a movement of artistic revival, which sought to protect the values of indigenous craft traditions against the impersonality of all mill production and the drab uniformity of chemical dyes. British officials such as E. B. Havell, long-time proponent of Indian crafts and champion of the fly shuttle, had been stimulating interest in handloom weaving since the 1880s.[66] Havell and others like him saw a growing market for Indian hand-made exotica in an England where urbanization and industrialization had brought about an "arcadian reaction" associated with the work of artists such as William Morris. Havell's ideas, however, were not purely practical. They reflected the stirrings of an idealist philosophy of social progress, conservative in nature, which stressed the integrity of the community and the idea of self-help. Havell warned artisans against taking help from the government, "all that is worth having you must and can do for yourselves."[67] This theme was taken up with passion by the first generation of Indian art critics. Ananda Coomoraswami, for instance, wrote of "the regeneration of India through art and not by economics and politics alone." The "vulgarization of modern India with its caricature of European dress," along with "cut glass and china dogs," was damning proof of "some mighty evil in our souls." Swadeshi therefore should be "a religious and artistic ideal."[68]

In practical terms the swadeshi movement was a limited success. A boycott of British manufactures that lasted more than a few months was usually effective only where powerful landowners took a leading part. Though the decline in the number of rural weavers in Bengal and eastern India seems to have slowed during the two decades between 1890 and 1910, swadeshi could have been only one of the factors involved. But regardless of this, handloom weaving had already been transformed from an endangered rural craft to a powerful symbol of the moral and spiritual regeneration of India. A variety of new themes had emerged. The boycott of British goods was part of a wider aim to "sever all connections with the colonial ruling classes." In the words of S. N. Bannerjea, *swaraj* (freedom) and swadeshi were linked: "We must be swadeshi in all things, swadeshi in our thoughts, and in our educational methods and development."[69] Freedom was more than just a European notion, it was "a return of the satyayuga [age of truth] of national greatness." Indians who sold British goods were also to be boycotted in what was a modern attempt to define the boundaries of community and polity in terms of the production and consumption of cloth. Frequent references were made to the prosperity of Bengal in the time when the Mughal emperors had patronized the weavers of Dacca and Murshidabad through the *malmul khas*. Indeed, the modern historiography of Mughal India started from this very point and is still infused with themes of swadeshi.

These themes were popularly enacted at the great mass protests against the partition of Bengal, when persons taking a vow to the nation ceremonially cleansed themselves with a dip in the Ganges, then emerged to dress in Indian cloth and tied on one another's arms the yellow and vermilion braids or bangles called *rakhis*.[70] Previously used to symbolize ties between brother and sister within the family, these bands, which were always locally woven, became symbols of a wider national brotherhood. Because the use of home-produced cloth often involved a financial loss of income, it being more expensive than imported cloth, some popular leaders developed the theme of sacrifice in their pronouncements on swadeshi. Sri Aurobindo, for instance, stressed that the discarding of foreign goods was an act of sacrifice that had to precede personal and national regeneration. "We must abandon the life of the individual and lead the life of the nation." British textiles were the poison, he said, which fosters the antidote, a new religious fervor and self-abandonment before the "glorified Mother," the goddess Durga, protector of Bengal.[71]

Not only the context of consumption and the soul of the consumer but the quality of country cloth itself attracted attention during these years. The cheaper country cloths had been regarded as rough, homely, perhaps even slightly dirty, whereas British cloths had a reputation for fineness and purity. Popular singers, actors, and preachers made strenuous efforts to reverse these stereotypes, directing their message to women in particular. Some rumors circulated to the effect that British cloth, which had been dyed with unknown chemicals was actually unclean, (imported sugar was rumored to be impregnated with cow fat).[72] At the same time, the very homeliness and loose, thick weave of village cloth were lauded for their naturalness, purity, and lack of sophistication, which here became a term of opprobrium. Village songs of the 1905-10 period associated country cloth with images of motherhood, with thick white rice and curd, and with the good things of the unpolluted countryside.[73]

This redefinition of purity and its association with the quality of cloth was, of course, taken to its most elaborate conclusion by Mahatma Gandhi himself. Whereas the Bengali swadeshi leaders of 1905-10 had in general used homespun as a political symbol, Gandhi emphasized its nature as a talisman and pronounced the creation of cloth through spinning to be a prayer. The production of cloth in villages by spinning and weaving was to transform the moral fiber of the nation in a quite literal sense. The themes of the artisan as a pure creator and the exchange of cloth as embodying an augmentation of moral status were, as we have seen, implicit in many popular notions of the quality of cloth. It was Gandhi's genius that notwithstanding the incoherence of his formal economic and political thought, he was able to enlist around a single issue a huge range of beliefs, aspirations, and popular symbols. Cloth stood alongside the symbols of mother cow and freely prepared salt at the heart of the national movement of the 1920's and '30's.

If we look at the voluminous works of Gandhi and his disciples on the issue of homespun (khadi), several subplots emerge. First there is the reappearance of the notion of protection as an important element of transactions in cloth and clothes. By a symbolic paradox, the consumption of millions of rupees worth of foreign goods leaves Indian men and women poor and naked (the image of female nakedness and shame was a particularly powerful one for Gandhi). Hence, patriotic Indians should spin their own yarn and commission country weavers to make it up into homespun. It was a moral and religious duty to make it possible to return to those prosperous days when "thousands of women of high birth spun their own yarn and got it woven by professional weavers."[74] Women should be brought once again into the labor process and augment India's productive power, but at the same time the ancient status of women would be reaffirmed: Manu says that the duty of a wife is to weave and of an unmarried woman to spin. On the consumer's side, total abstinence from machine-made goods was enjoined. Even Bombay-manufactured cloths must be abandoned as part of the elementary religious duty of being "kind and attentive to one's neighbors," which was also the basis of good polity. Speaking at the town of Godhra in 1919 Gandhi said:

So long as the Godhra farmers and weavers could supply the wants of the Godhra citizens, the latter had no right to go outside Godhra and support even (say) the Bombay farmers and weavers. He could not starve his neighbor and claim to save his distant cousin on the North Pole.[75]

The government, moreover, had forfeited its right to rule by failing to acknowledge the basic duty of the raja – to succor its clients and people through the encouragement of their arts and the consumption of their goods.

These arguments were an elaboration of the swadeshi ideology of 1905-10. But where Gandhi was an innovator was in his reaffirmation of the religious and magical aspects of cloth boycott and burning, of spinning and wearing homespun. Rabindranath Tagore perceived this easily and condemned its implications. Neatly turning the metaphor, he wrote: "Consider the burning of cloth heaped up before the very eyes of our Motherland, shivering and ashamed in her nakedness. What is the nature of the call to do this, is it not another instance of the magical formula?"[76] Gandhi replied that to him it was "sinful" for a man to wear the "latest finery of Regent Street when his neighbors the spinners and weavers starve. . . . The knowledge of sin bursts upon me; I must consign foreign garments to the fire and thus purify myself and thenceforth rest content with the khadi homespun made by my neighbors."[77] Later, during the 1920s, Gandhi further elaborated the theme that spinning was an act of prayer (a mantra), both a purgation of individual sin and a creation of new life in the spinner and in the community. Against considerable opposition, the spinning of certain quantities of yarn was temporarily adopted as a condition of admission to certain offices within the Indian National Congress. White homespun became and remained the uniform of its party workers and officials. If involute distinctions of dress had been a mark of caste society, the widespread adoption of khadi would create a uniformity of appearance in which good acts alone would distinguish superior castes. Gandhi sought in fact to resolve the ambiguity we noted between the pure and godly action that was embodied in the artisan's craft and the low, even outcaste status that characterized the country spinner and weaver himself. All Indians were to become spinners, weavers, and washermen, just as they were to become the lowest of all, the sweepers who cleaned lavatories. Finally, Gandhi sought to ritualize once again the very tools of the trade and the "commodity" itself. His own search for the appropriate spinning wheel was infused with the notion of spiritual quest, and at the same time harkened back to anthropomorphic ideas common among spinners and weavers, who held the wheel to be an actual member of the family. At the same time he constantly emphasized the purity and godliness imparted to its wearers by the homespun. Khadi in his hands regained its transformative and magical qualities, while the spinning wheel took its place on the Congress flag.

This article has suggested that the ideas and assumptions associated with cloth in Indian society can be analyzed at more than one level. In the villages and in the Hindu or Indo-Muslim state, the notion that cloth was a thing that could retain qualities imparted to it by individuals or groups who fashioned or came into contact with it stood in opposition to the need to make cloth a neutral commodity in order to facilitate a general exchange of food, silver, and essential goods. The role of the dominant village elite or of the King was to mediate between these processes of "singularization" and "commoditization." Ideas about the transformation role of cloth therefore continued to perform a functional role in the integration of Indian states and of caste society through the office of the king.

In the modern period, too, Gandhi's ideology of cloth making and cloth use fulfilled more than one function in the political economy. Gandhi and his closest supporters opposed Indian manufactured cloth as vehemently as foreign products. But industrialists, and politicians such as Jawaharal Nehru who advocated technological progress for India, adopted an ambiguous position on the issue. Consciously or not, they enlisted the moral and political capital generated by the Mahatma's campaign for village weaving in support of their own push for Indian freedom and industrialization. Bombay's mills, for instance, produced careful, machine-made copies of different sorts of homespun fabrics for distribution in the interior.[78] Industrialists such as the Birlas and Tatas gave money to Gandhi's swadeshi campaigns out of piety even while they implicitly opposed the anti-industrial tenor of his wider message. In turn, the Republic of India has spent large sums on the propagation of homespun through institutions such as the chain of Khadi Bhawans (homespun retail stores), which often function at a loss despite the government's strong commitment to competitive industry. Government must still be seen to protect local employment, community, and skills; it cannot promote commoditization through industrialization too rapidly; it must be seen to mediate between the singular and the commodity.

Conclusion

According to several recent formulations, the Indian economy in the immediate precolonial period was "proto-capitalist" and colonial India an example of "arrested capitalist development." These influential notions must presumably be taken to imply more than the existence of sophisticated markets and the longstanding payment of land revenue in cash. They must surely also mean that some degree of transformation had taken place in the values and assumptions that linked individuals to one another and to the market. Only in this way could the market itself have begun to allocate value and could a notion of impersonal capital have emerged. Whichever theorists or definitions of capitalism are employed, changes in ideology and social organization are now considered to have been causes and not merely consequences of the transition to early capitalism. Marx himself presupposed the creation of a stable state structure and concepts of property within which new modes of capitalist production could crystallize; many recent Marxist theorists have gone further, illustrating how the ideological and political "superstructure" intervenes as an autonomous force in the very process of production. Weber, of course, argued that the existence of an expansive capitalistic ethic was a precondition for economic transition. Sombart linked changes in family relationships and the "secularization of love" to the growth of a capitalist market through an increased demand for luxury commodities. It is this last angle of approach to the relationship between values and markets that has been least exploited by historians, who have characteristically examined the mentalities of entrepreneurs to the exclusion of any consideration of the relationship between people and commodities. One general test of the emergence of capitalist values seems to be the disappearance from everyday life of a widely accepted working definition of the concepts of "good" and "evil," of the "auspicious" and "inauspicious." Relations to people and things mediated through the market leave little room for such judgments of value. This is because it is imperative that individuals be severed from their preexisting statuses and allocated new, universally comparable ones in a capitalistic labor market. In the same way, it is essential that goods be shorn of the luminosity of place and the spirit of reciprocity in a full-fledged commodity market. Thus, the "evil eye" and the "devil" (characteristic incubuses of the peasant economy) had been eliminated from everyday discourse in that classic proto-capitalistic society, sixteenth- and seventeenth-century England, according to Alan Macfarlane.[79] The sense of sin and of the inauspicious had been displaced from ordinary parlance and ordinary things to the realm of theological controversy. Only on the fringes of capitalist development, as in tribal Latin America, did the devil retain a place in the village, as a representation of the gathering deluge of a capitalist labor market and capitalist commodities.[80] The village and the modern economy were marked off from each other by sin and the devil.

In India, such stark transitions have not been seen over the last three hundred years. What is striking here is the way in which the formal apparatus of markets and a monetized economy molded themselves to and were accommodated by mentalities that still viewed the relationships between men, commodities, and other men in terms of good (pure) and evil (polluting). For one thing, goods were only marketed commodities for a short span of their lives in society. As artifacts in the process of production, they carried the spirit of the maker and in turn influenced his ranking; as gifts they acted in complex ways to modify the nature of the donor and the recipient; as possessions, goods could retain and store good and evil. The life of a commodity in the impersonal market was a short one. But even here, market value did not wholly obliterate human value. Buyers and sellers were constrained by obligations that required that they purchase certain things at certain times, in certain markets. The widespread existence of markets, moneylenders, and double-entry account books was not incompatible with the persistence of precapitalist mentalities in material culture. In fact, material culture was never simply material, and it certainly cannot be simply opposed to capitalism or even luxury; money of itself could not transform relationships – an obvious point, but one that needs stating in the face of much contemporary Indian economic history. Even the eruption into India of British textiles occurred in the context of systems of redistribution and ideologies of taste that could promote or retard the development of a utilitarian perception of commodities in the market. Again Gandhi's movement, although as leftists continually assert, fully committed to the notion of private property, was decidedly anti-capitalist as far as relations between people and things, people and producers, were concerned. Obviously, questions of value and community have never been wholly banished from the market even in capitalist societies; witness recent

"Buy British" and "Buy American" campaigns. But the intricacy of relations reflected by the transactional role of commodities in rural India was of a different order. And if many of the attitudes demonstrated in this paper have begun to disappear, it is the very recent mechanization of production through factories, rather than pre-colonial merchants or the colonial state, that has effected the transformation.

Notes

This paper benefited greatly from the general seminar discussion in Philadelphia but particularly from the comments of Arjun Appadurai, David Ludden, Gyan Prakash, and Igor Kopytoff. In addition, I am grateful to Chris Gregory, Susan Bayly, Sugata Bose, Richard Waller, and Raj Chandavarkar. In the Netherlands, I was helped by the comments of members of the Kern Oriental Institute and the Centre for the Expansion of Europe in the University of Leiden. The ideas of Frank Perlin, Jonathan Parry, Tony King, and Bernard Cohn have also proved enlightening in a more indirect fashion.

1. See R. B. Smith, *Vietnam and the West* (London, 1968); David Marr, *Vietnamese Anti-Colonialism* (Princeton, N.J. 1973); Peter Carey, "The origin of the Java War, 1825–30," *English Historical Review*, i, xci, 1976; F. Fanon, *A Dying Colonialism* (London, 1970).
2. For example, Keith Hart, "On commoditization," in E. N. Goody, ed., *From Craft to Industry: The Ethnology of Proto-Industrial Cloth Production.* (Cambridge, 1982).
3. F. Perlin, "Proto-industrialisation and pre-colonial South Asia,' *Past and Present*, 98, 1983; see also my *Rulers, Townsmen, and Bazaars* (Cambridge, 1983).
4. When I wrote this paper, I had not yet seen Bernard S. Cohn's paper "Cloth, clothes, and colonialism: India in the nineteenth century," prepared for the symposium on Cloth and the Organization of Human Experience, New York, October 1983. It is hoped that the papers are complementary.
5. A. Appadurai, "Gastro-politics in Hindu South Asia," *American Ethnologist*, viii, 3, 1981, 494–512. M. Marriott and R. Inden, "Caste systems," *Encyclopedia Britannica*, iii (1974), 982–91; D. McGilvray, ed., *Caste Ideology and Interaction* (Cambridge, 1982), introduction.
6. See B. Seal, *The Positive Sciences of the Ancient Hindus* (Varanasi, 1958).
7. L. Ananthakrishna Iyer et al., *Mysore Tribes and Castes*, i, (Madras, 1935), 435.
8. R. Russell and Hira Lal, *Tribes and Castes of the Central Provinces of India* (1916, repr. Ossterhout, 1969), i, 123.
9. *Ibid.*, i, 123–5; G. A. Herklots, *Islam in India by Jafar Shah* (London, 1921), pp. 228, 269, 272.
10. Ghalib, *Dastunbuy*, trans. K. A. Faruqi (London, 1978), p. 28.
11. Russell and Hira Lal, *Tribes and Castes*, iv, 367.
12. A. Yusuf Ali, *A Monograph on Silk Fabrics Produced in the North Western Provinces and Dudh* (Allahabad, 1900), p. 120; see also S. N. Dhar, *Costumes of India and Pakistan* (Varanasi, 1969).

13. Sir G. Watt, *The Commercial Products of India* (London, 1908), pp. 1,011, 1,121.
14. Yusuf Ali, p. 75.   **15.** *Ibid.*, p. 67.
16. *Ibid.*, p. 121.   **17.** Watt, p. 1125.
18. Pupul Jayakar, "India fabrics in Indian life," in *Textiles and Ornaments of the Museum of Modern Art, New York* (New York, 1956).
19. P. Kane, *History of Dharmasastra* (Poona, 1963), ii, 670–2.
20. *The Laws of Manu*, iv, 189; trans. G. Bühler (Oxford, 1886), p. 158.
21. Ghulam Abdul Qadir, "Bahar-i-Azamjahi," *Sources of the History of the Nawabs of the Carnatic*, no. 11, trans. Nainar (Madras, 1950), p. 50.
22. Abul Fazl, *"Ain-i-Akbari,"* trans. H. Blochman, i (Calcutta, 1893), 91.
23. Council of Europe exhibition on "Anatolian Civilizations," Aya Sofya Museum, Istanbul, 1983.
24. S. Rizvi, *Shah Abd-al Aziz* (Canberra, 1982), p. 483.
25. See, for example, Russell and Hira Lal, ii, 144 (Julaha), iv, 144 (Muher), 385–6 (Patwa); ii, 581 (Kashti).
26. Manu, ed. Bühler, v, 129, p. 191; see also iv, 219, p. 163.
27. Russell and Hira Lal, i, 50.
28. Ananthakrishna Iyer et al., iii, 18–19.
29. G. Pandey, "The bigoted julaha," *Economic and Political Weekly* (Calcutta), Jan. 1983.
30. E. Blunt, *The Caste System of Northern India* (1931; repr. Delhi, 1969), p. 244.
31. Pandey, "Bigoted julaha."
32. For Dacca muslins, see J. Taylor, *Topography and Statistics of the City of Dacca* (Calcutta, 1840).
33. A. Sharar, *The Last Phase of an Oriental Civilisation*, trans. E. Harcourt and F. Hussain (London, 1969), p. 180.
34. Yusuf Ali, p. 70.
35. Sharar, 131.
36. Cited Russell and Hira Lal, ii, 523.
37. *Ibid.*, 526.
38. Ananthakrishna Iyer et al., ii, 21.
39. C. Bouglé in D. F. Pocock, ed., *Essays on the Caste System by Célestin Bouglé* (Cambridge, 1971), p. 153.
40. See Cohn, "Cloth, Clothes, and Colonialism."
41. Taylor, *Dacca*, p. 64.
42. N. Manucci, M. Edwardes (ed.), *Memoirs of the Mogul Court* (London, 1964), 73.
43. W. Hamilton, *An Historical Relation of . . . the Rohilla Afghans* (London, 1787), p. 169.
44. Yusuf Ali, p. 91.
45. Pollier to Ironside, May 22, 1776, *Asiatic Annual Register*, ii, 1800, 29.
46. "Bahair-i-Azamjahi," tr. Nainar, p. 92.   **47.** *Ibid.*, p. 82.
48. *Ibid.*, p. 77.   **49.** *Ibid.*, p. 50.
50. Watt, p. 618; see also Watson, *The Textile Manufactures and the Costumes of the People of India* (London, 1868), i, 5.
51. Munshi Faiz Baksh, "Tarikh-i-Farah Baksh," trans. W. Hoey, *Memoirs of Delhi and Fyzabad* (Allahabad, 1889), ii, 97.

52. Sharar, p. 177.
53. '*Ain*,' trans. Blochman, i, 92.
54. Sharar, p. 173.
55. Commercial resident Bareilly to Governor General, 13 January 1803, Board's Collections, 2947–53, India Office Library and Records.
56. Vazir Ali's marriage, 1795, *Asiatic Annual Register*, misc. tracts, 9, pp. 11–12.
57. See Topkapi Sarai Museum, collection of sultans' ceremonial dresses, 1770–1820.
58. Hamilton Buchanan, in Montgomery Martin, ed., *History, Antiquities, Topography of Eastern India* (London, 1838), ii, 999.
59. See, for example, M. Shapiro, "Style," in A. Kroeber, ed., *Anthropology Today*, (Chicago, 1953), and H. Wölfflin, *Principles of Art History* (London, 1963).
60. Sharar, 173*ff*.; for the relation between material culture and social organization, see I. Hodder, *Symbols in Action: The Ethnoarchaeological Study of Material Culture* (Cambridge, 1982); see also R. Tagore on "Coat or Chapkan," *Rabindra Rachanavali*, xii, (Calcutta, 1960), 223–9.
61. For the impact of British imports, see, for example, D. Kumar, ed., *The Cambridge Economic History of India*, ii, (Cambridge, 1983), 668–73, 842–3; J. Borpujari, "Indian cottons and the cotton famine of 1865," *Indian and Social History Review*, 10 (1973).
62. C. Silberrad, *Monograph on Cotton Fabric Production in the North Western Provinces and Oudh* (Allahabad, 1898), p. 46.
63. *Ibid.*
64. Azamgarh Proclamation, Aug. 25, 1857, reprod. R. Mukherjee, "The Azimgarh Proclamation," in B. De, ed., *Essays Presented to S. C. Sarkar* (Calcutta, 1976), pp. 497–8.
65. S. Sarkar, *The Swadeshi Movement in Bengal, 1903–8* (Delhi, 1973), pp. 20–30.
66. *Ibid.*, p. 120.
67. A. Coomaraswami, *Art and Swadeshi* (Madras, n.d.), p. 3.
68. *Ibid.*
69. H. and U. Mukherjee, ed., *India's Fight for Freedom or the Swadeshi Movement, 1905–6* (Calcutta, 1908), p. 203.
70. *Amrita Bazaar Patrika*, Oct. 16–17, 1905.
71. *Bande Mataram*, Oct. 10, 1907.
72. *Amrita Bazaar Patrika* Aug. 10, 1905; *Abhyudaya* (Allahabad), March 19, April 2, 1906.
73. Dr. S. Bose, of Tufts University, has kindly sent me the following note on the "Mota Kapar" ethic in Bengal at the turn of the Century:
   At the turn of this century, with the rise of swadeshi, we find a deliberate effort to propagate the virtues of *mota kapar* – the thick, unrefined, homespun cloth – as part of a philosophy of simple living ensuring loyalty to the mother country. This obviously had as its background the damage done to the indigenous refined cloth industry in the nineteenth century and the invasion of the home market by foreign milled cloth. The psychological attachment to the older light and sophisticated varieties, notably silks, with their connotations of ritual purity, as well as the new attraction to the glitter of manufactured commodities, had to be broken.

A number of rustic composers and singers and also a few more sophisticated poets tried to preach the new message. Most of their songs were written between 1903 and 1908. The best-known of the rustic singers is Charankabi Mukundadas.

Mota literally means thick or rough, but *mota kapar* had a wider range of connotations – it was thick and unrefined but also simple and homely cloth. In fact, *mota chal, mota kapar* (coarse, simple rice and thick, homely cloth) and *mota khabo, mota porbo* (we will eat mota and wear mota) went together. One of the best-known swadeshi couplets on cloth goes:

Ma-er deya mota kapar, mathay tule ne re bhai,
Ma je amar deen-daridra, er beshi aaj sadhya nai.
The Mother has given us this simple cloth, wear it with pride,
She is poor and destitute today and can afford no more.

The following is a free translation of a song that amounts to a simple but comprehensive summary of the *mota khabo, mota porbo*, attitude. It is by Rajanikanto Sen, quite well-known as a composer of swadeshi and devotional songs.

We may be poor, we may be small,
But we are a nation of seven crores [seventy million]; brothers, wake
   up.
Defend your homes, protect your shops,
Don't let the grain from our barns be looted abroad.
We will eat our own coarse grain and wear the rough, home-spun
   cloth,
What do we care for lavender and imported trinkets.
Foreigners drain away our Mother's milk,
Will we simply stand and watch?
Don't lose this opportunity, brothers,
Come and congregate at the feet of the Mother.
Giving away from our own homes and begging from foreigners.
We will not buy the fragile glass, it breaks so easily,
We will rather be poor and live our simple lives,
No one can then rob us of our self-respect.
Don't lose this opportunity, brothers,
Come and congregate at the feet of the Mother.

In another very famous song, Charankabi Mukundadas exhorts the women of Bengal to throw away their silk and glass bangles. He asks them not to be deceived by the false glitter of imported goods and not to wear *kalanka* (shame) instead of *shankha* (the white *chank* bangle, symbol of chastity). That they don't have real gold bangles is hardly a cause for mourning, he tells them. The daughters of Bengal must see to it that the Mother's wealth is not drained away any further.

74. M. K. Gandhi, *Collected Works* (Delhi, 1962–73), xv, 485.
75. *Ibid.*, xvi, 30.
76. Quoted by S. Sinha, *The Social Thinking of Rabindranath Tagore* (Calcutta, 1965), p. 48.
77. *Ibid.*, p. 49.
78. Personal communication, Rajnarayan Chandavarkar. See also his Cambridge Ph.D. dissertation (1983), "Labour and society in Bombay, 1918–1940."

79. Alan Macfarlane, "The root of all evil," in D. Parkin, ed., *The Anthropology of Evil* (Oxford, 1985).
80. Michael T. Taussig, *The Devil and Commodity Fetishism in South America* (Chapel Hill, N.C., 1980).

Index